ORIGIN

ORIGIN

**BILL JEMAS, JOE QUESADA
AND PAUL JENKINS**
Plot

PAUL JENKINS
Script

ANDY KUBERT
Pencils

RICHARD ISANOVE
Digital Painting

JOE QUESADA AND RICHARD ISANOVE
Covers

**JOHN ROSHELL & COMICRAFT'S WES ABBOTT,
OSCAR GONGORRA AND SAIDA TEMOFONTE**
Lettering

MIKE RAICHT
Assistant Editor

MIKE MARTS
Editor

JEFF YOUNGQUIST
Collections Editor

JENNIFER GRÜNWALD
Assistant Editor

MATTY RYAN
Book Designer

JOE QUESADA
Editor in Chief

DAN BUCKLEY
Publisher

INTRODUCTION

"**W**hat do you think of the idea of a limited series telling Wolverine's origin?" Two words immediately popped into my head ... bad idea. That was how my first lunch with Joe Quesada began back in September of 2000. I had just spent the past four years of my life working to bring X-Men to life on the big screen and Wolverine was a big part of me. X-Men was the movie I wanted to make since I was twelve years old and I had assumed the role as the protector of the mythology on the film. But now it wasn't the studio system that was going to screw Logan up but Marvel itself. Nightmare visions of the Spider-Man "Clone Saga" danced through my head.

For the rest of the lunch Joe and I went back and forth debating the pros and cons of finally revealing the greatest mystery of comicdom — the history of Wolverine. I used all the arguments. That it would ruin the mystique of the character, that Logan wouldn't be as tragic a hero if we knew his past, even stooping to 'you should let the reader flesh out that mystery in their own head'. None of it worked. For as passionate as I was Joe was equally as passionate; and I could see in his eyes that he had already made up his mind, he was going to tell the origin of Logan. At that point I asked him "Why? Why take the chance of damaging the character?" Joe looked me dead in the eye and said, " If anyone is going to tell the origin of Logan, Marvel should do it first, not the movie." You know what? I agreed with him.

At that moment all of my fanboy trepidation turned into excitement, now I wanted to read it. Over eighteen months have passed since that lunch and I've been patiently waiting for all of the issues to come out so I could read ORIGIN at one sitting. I resisted the urge to read it every time a new issue came out, although I broke down and peeked at the artwork and was blown away by the lushness and sweep of the visuals, which owed more to Mark Twain than spandex-clad four color heroes. But I was going to wait. Two days ago I got a call saying that Bill Jemas and Joe Quesada wanted to know if I would write the foreward to the ORIGIN hardcover. Needless to say I feigned indifference and immediately asked if I could get copies of all the issues published and unpublished sent to me overnight. Of course FedEx was a day late. Well, having just finished reading ORIGIN, I think back on Joe's original question, "What do you think of the idea of a limited series telling Wolverine's origin?" and now what pops into my head is ... damn, I wish I had thought of that.

A True Believer Always,

Tom DeSanto

TOM DeSANTO
Executive Producer/Co-writer,
X-Men: The Movie

P.S. — To Messrs. Jenkins, Kubert, Isanove, Jemas, and Quesada: Success belongs to those who take the risk; thanks for taking the risk. But an even bigger thanks for succeeding.

PART I
THE HILL

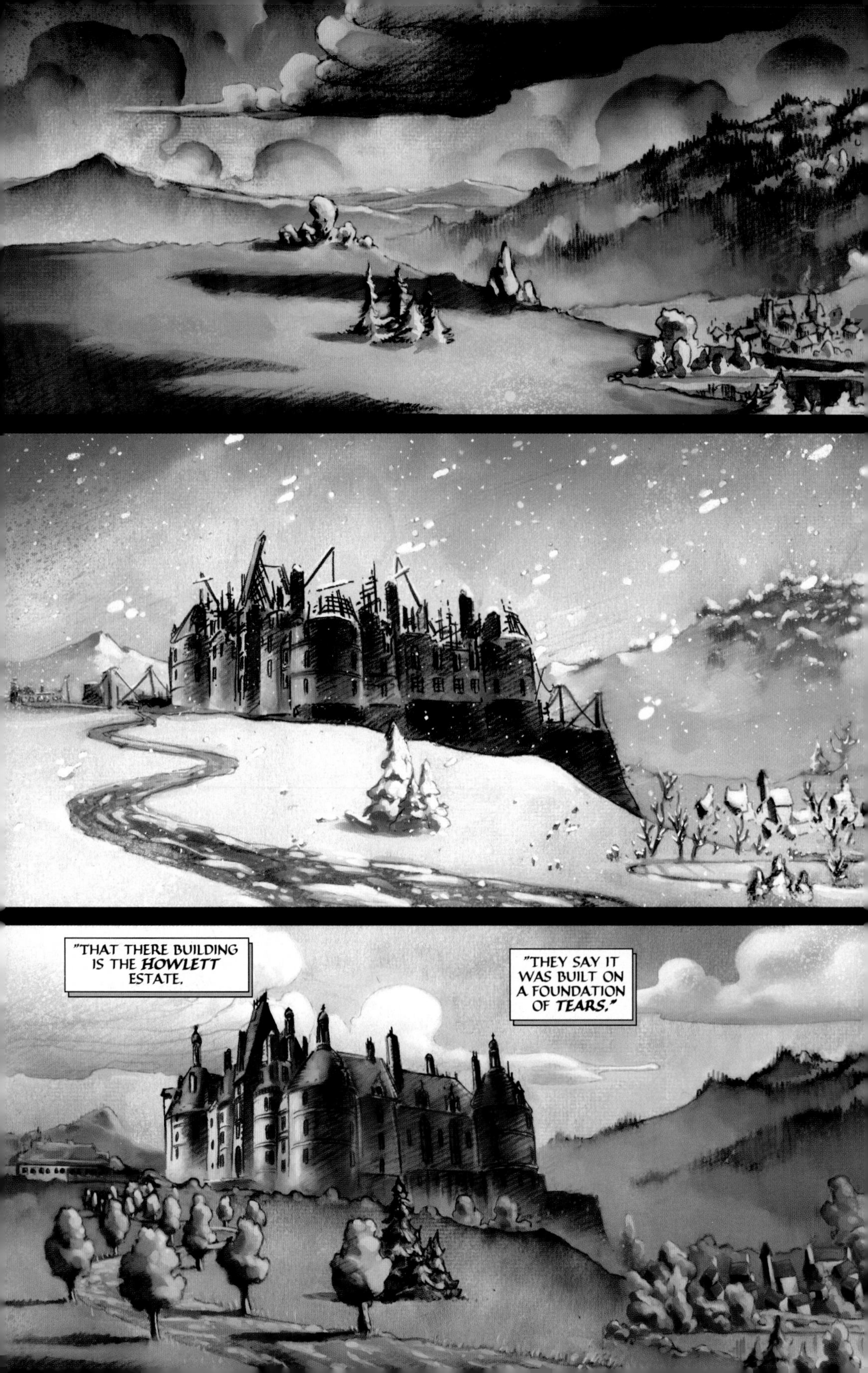
"THAT THERE BUILDING IS THE HOWLETT ESTATE.
"THEY SAY IT WAS BUILT ON A FOUNDATION OF TEARS."

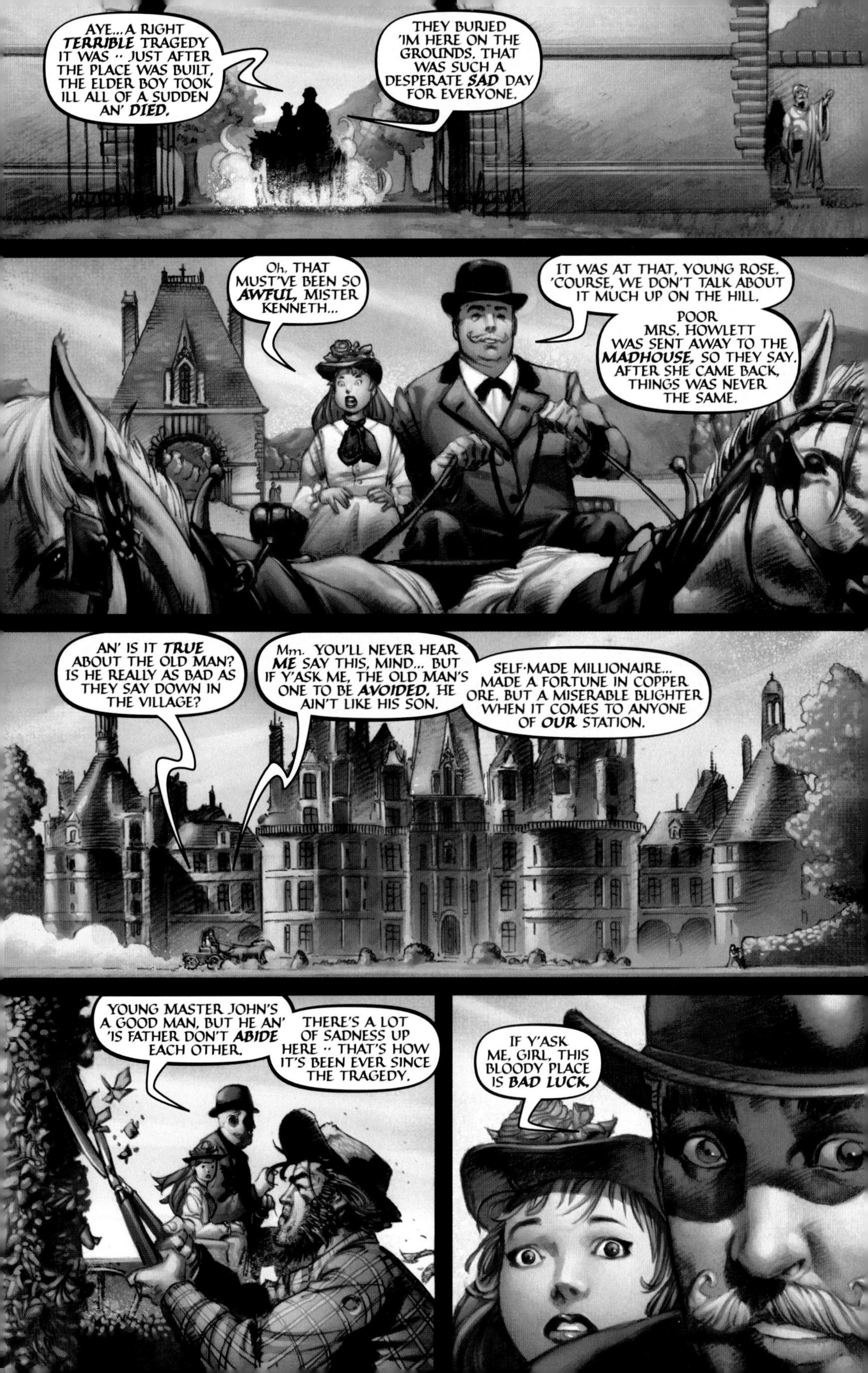
AYE... A RIGHT TERRIBLE TRAGEDY IT WAS -- JUST AFTER THE PLACE WAS BUILT, THE ELDER BOY TOOK ILL ALL OF A SUDDEN AN' DIED.
THEY BURIED 'IM HERE ON THE GROUNDS. THAT WAS SUCH A DESPERATE SAD DAY FOR EVERYONE.
Oh, THAT MUST'VE BEEN SO AWFUL, MISTER KENNETH...
IT WAS AT THAT, YOUNG ROSE. 'COURSE, WE DON'T TALK ABOUT IT MUCH UP ON THE HILL.
POOR MRS. HOWLETT WAS SENT AWAY TO THE MADHOUSE, SO THEY SAY. AFTER SHE CAME BACK, THINGS WAS NEVER THE SAME.
AN' IS IT TRUE ABOUT THE OLD MAN? IS HE REALLY AS BAD AS THEY SAY DOWN IN THE VILLAGE?
Mm. YOU'LL NEVER HEAR ME SAY THIS, MIND... BUT IF Y'ASK ME, THE OLD MAN'S ONE TO BE AVOIDED. HE AIN'T LIKE HIS SON.
SELF-MADE MILLIONAIRE... MADE A FORTUNE IN COPPER ORE. BUT A MISERABLE BLIGHTER WHEN IT COMES TO ANYONE OF OUR STATION.
YOUNG MASTER JOHN'S A GOOD MAN, BUT HE AN' 'IS FATHER DON'T ABIDE EACH OTHER.
THERE'S A LOT OF SADNESS UP HERE -- THAT'S HOW IT'S BEEN EVER SINCE THE TRAGEDY.
IF Y'ASK ME, GIRL, THIS BLOODY PLACE IS BAD LUCK.

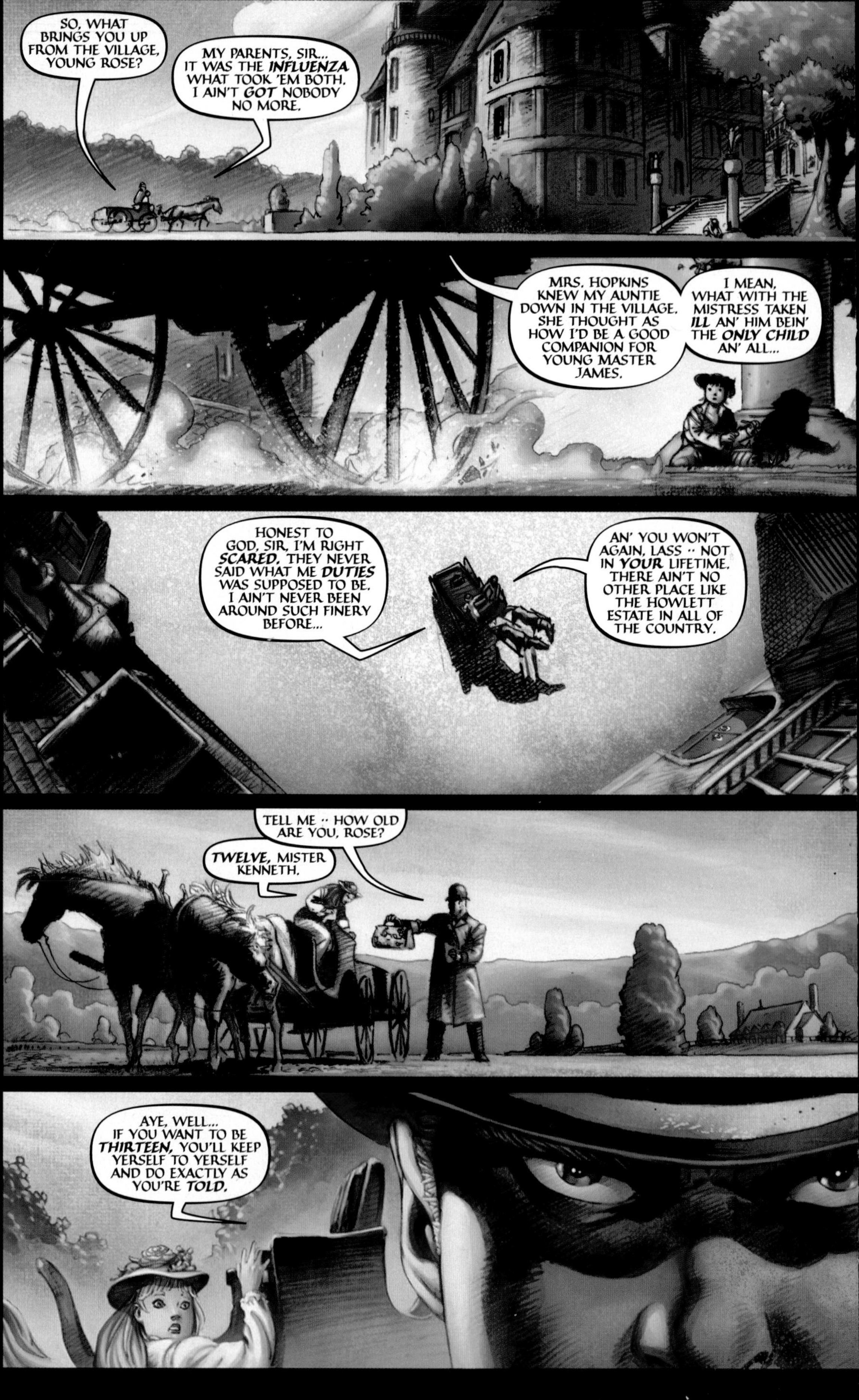
SO, WHAT BRINGS YOU UP FROM THE VILLAGE, YOUNG ROSE?
MY PARENTS, SIR... IT WAS THE INFLUENZA WHAT TOOK 'EM BOTH. I AIN'T GOT NOBODY NO MORE.
MRS. HOPKINS KNEW MY AUNTIE DOWN IN THE VILLAGE. SHE THOUGHT AS HOW I'D BE A GOOD COMPANION FOR YOUNG MASTER JAMES.
I MEAN, WHAT WITH THE MISTRESS TAKEN ILL AN' HIM BEIN' THE ONLY CHILD AN' ALL...
HONEST TO GOD, SIR, I'M RIGHT SCARED. THEY NEVER SAID WHAT ME DUTIES WAS SUPPOSED TO BE. I AIN'T NEVER BEEN AROUND SUCH FINERY BEFORE...
AN' YOU WON'T AGAIN, LASS -- NOT IN YOUR LIFETIME. THERE AIN'T NO OTHER PLACE LIKE THE HOWLETT ESTATE IN ALL OF THE COUNTRY.
TELL ME -- HOW OLD ARE YOU, ROSE?
TWELVE, MISTER KENNETH.
AYE, WELL... IF YOU WANT TO BE THIRTEEN, YOU'LL KEEP YERSELF TO YERSELF AND DO EXACTLY AS YOU'RE TOLD.

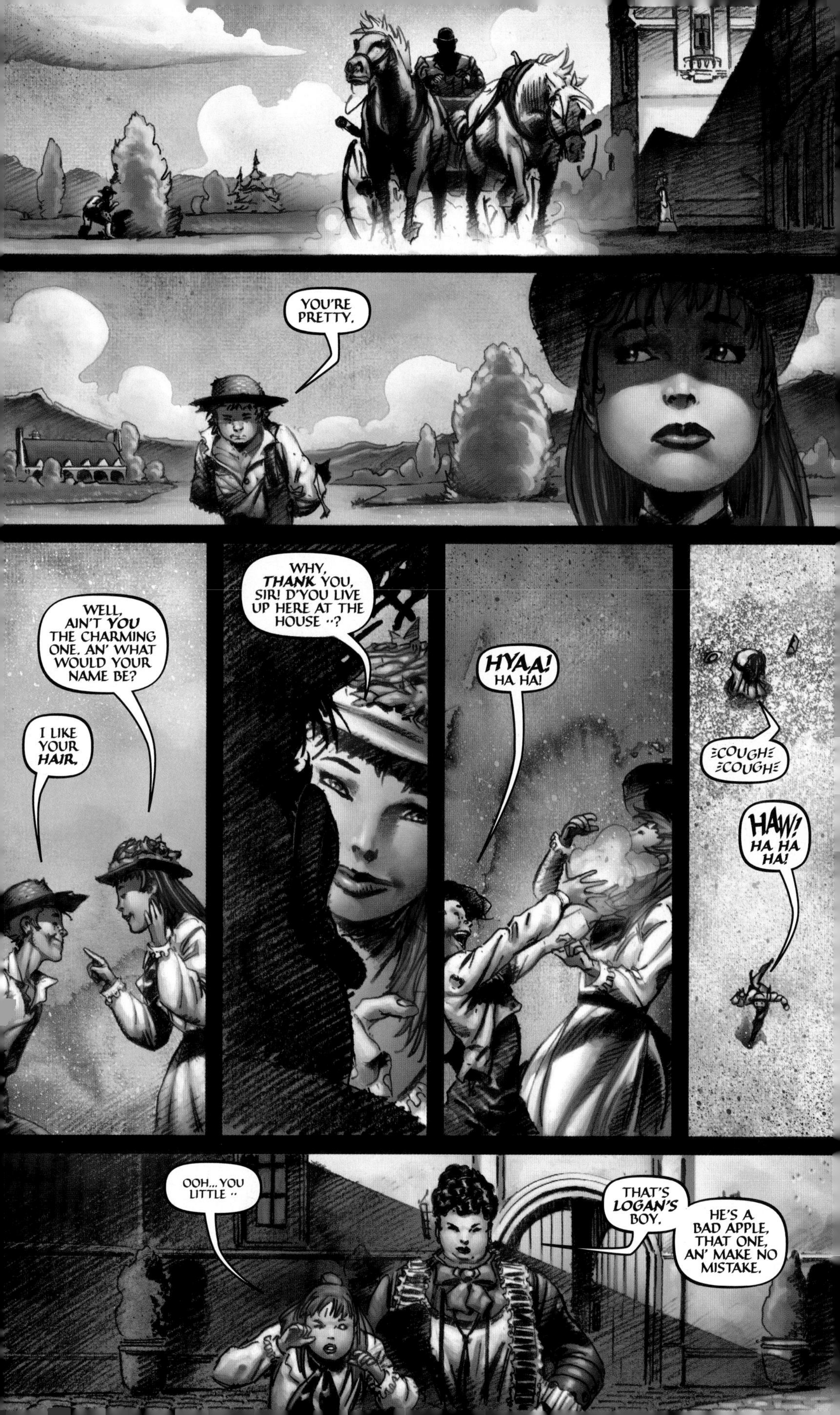
YOU'RE PRETTY.
WELL, AIN'T YOU THE CHARMING ONE. AN' WHAT WOULD YOUR NAME BE?
I LIKE YOUR HAIR.
WHY, THANK YOU, SIR! D'YOU LIVE UP HERE AT THE HOUSE ..?
HYAA! HA HA!
COUGH COUGH
HAW! HA HA HA!
OOH... YOU LITTLE ..
THAT'S LOGAN'S BOY.
HE'S A BAD APPLE, THAT ONE, AN' MAKE NO MISTAKE.

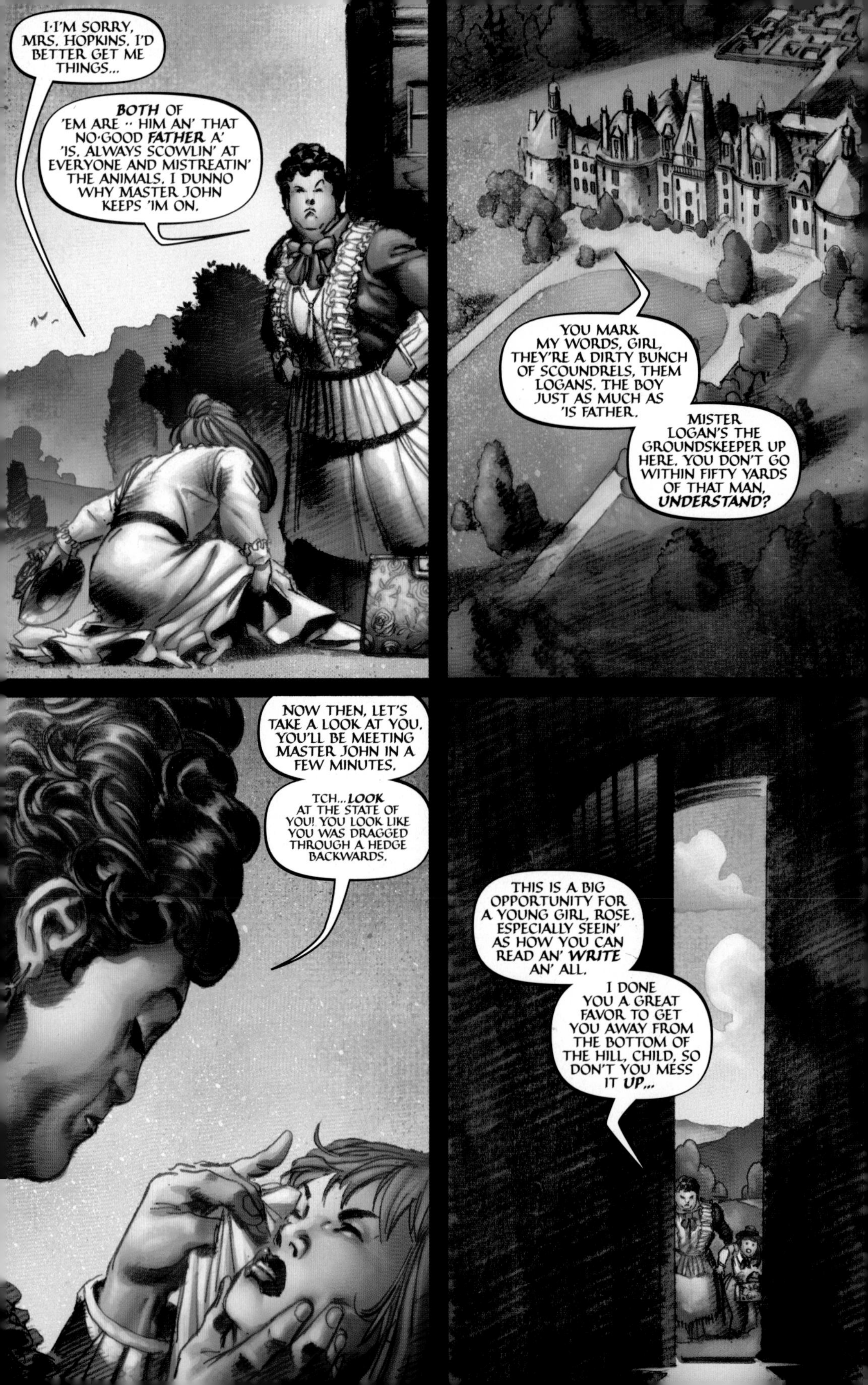
I-I'M SORRY, MRS. HOPKINS, I'D BETTER GET ME THINGS...
BOTH OF 'EM ARE -- HIM AN' THAT NO-GOOD FATHER A' 'IS. ALWAYS SCOWLIN' AT EVERYONE AND MISTREATIN' THE ANIMALS. I DUNNO WHY MASTER JOHN KEEPS 'IM ON.
YOU MARK MY WORDS, GIRL, THEY'RE A DIRTY BUNCH OF SCOUNDRELS, THEM LOGANS. THE BOY JUST AS MUCH AS 'IS FATHER.
MISTER LOGAN'S THE GROUNDSKEEPER UP HERE. YOU DON'T GO WITHIN FIFTY YARDS OF THAT MAN, UNDERSTAND?
NOW THEN, LET'S TAKE A LOOK AT YOU. YOU'LL BE MEETING MASTER JOHN IN A FEW MINUTES.
TCH...LOOK AT THE STATE OF YOU! YOU LOOK LIKE YOU WAS DRAGGED THROUGH A HEDGE BACKWARDS.
THIS IS A BIG OPPORTUNITY FOR A YOUNG GIRL, ROSE. ESPECIALLY SEEIN' AS HOW YOU CAN READ AN' WRITE AN' ALL.
I DONE YOU A GREAT FAVOR TO GET YOU AWAY FROM THE BOTTOM OF THE HILL, CHILD, SO DON'T YOU MESS IT UP...

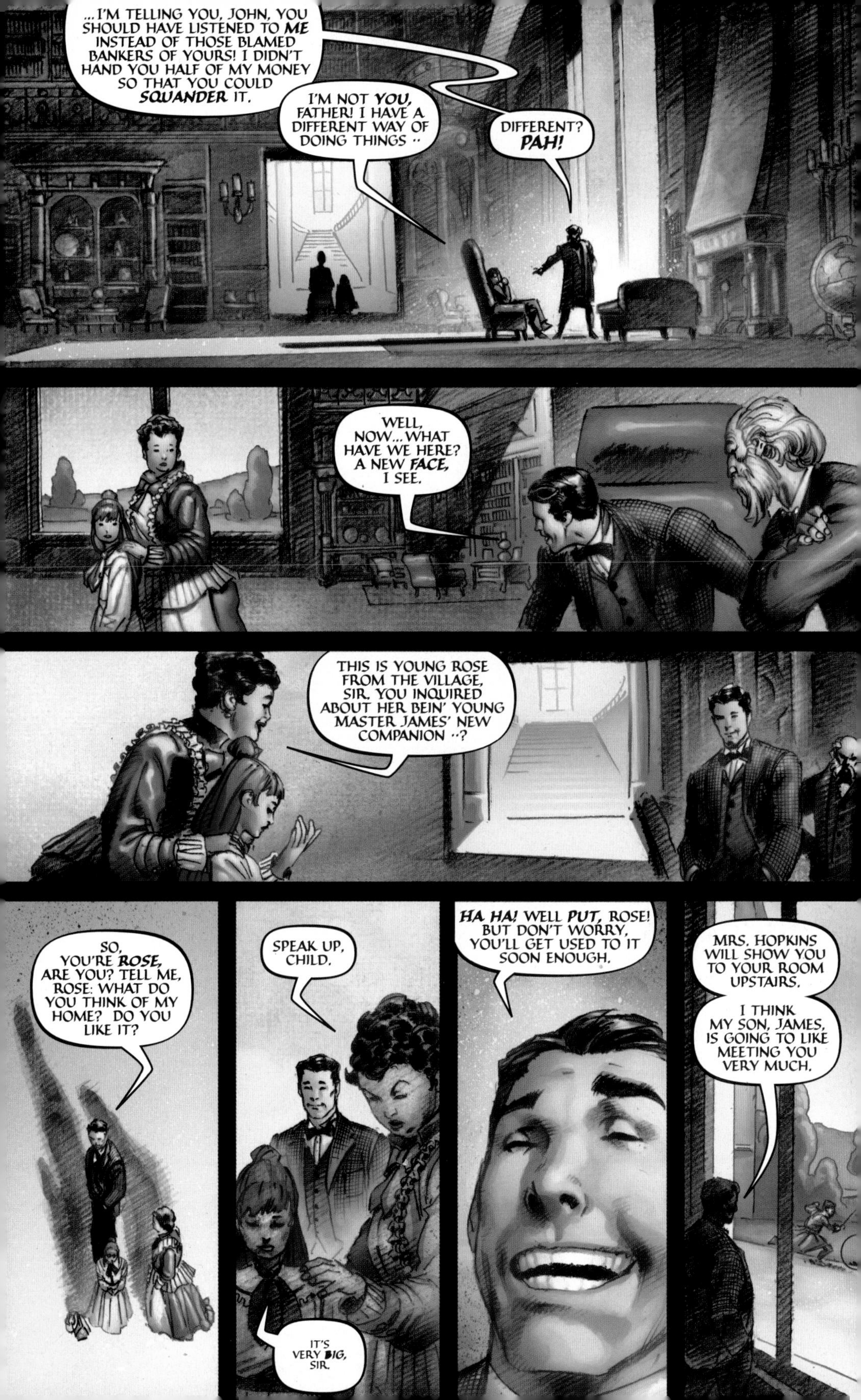
...I'M TELLING YOU, JOHN, YOU SHOULD HAVE LISTENED TO ME INSTEAD OF THOSE BLAMED BANKERS OF YOURS! I DIDN'T HAND YOU HALF OF MY MONEY SO THAT YOU COULD SQUANDER IT.
I'M NOT YOU, FATHER! I HAVE A DIFFERENT WAY OF DOING THINGS ..
DIFFERENT? PAH!
WELL, NOW...WHAT HAVE WE HERE? A NEW FACE, I SEE.
THIS IS YOUNG ROSE FROM THE VILLAGE, SIR. YOU INQUIRED ABOUT HER BEIN' YOUNG MASTER JAMES' NEW COMPANION ..?
SO, YOU'RE ROSE, ARE YOU? TELL ME, ROSE: WHAT DO YOU THINK OF MY HOME? DO YOU LIKE IT?
SPEAK UP, CHILD.
IT'S VERY BIG, SIR.
HA HA! WELL PUT, ROSE! BUT DON'T WORRY, YOU'LL GET USED TO IT SOON ENOUGH.
MRS. HOPKINS WILL SHOW YOU TO YOUR ROOM UPSTAIRS.
I THINK MY SON, JAMES, IS GOING TO LIKE MEETING YOU VERY MUCH.

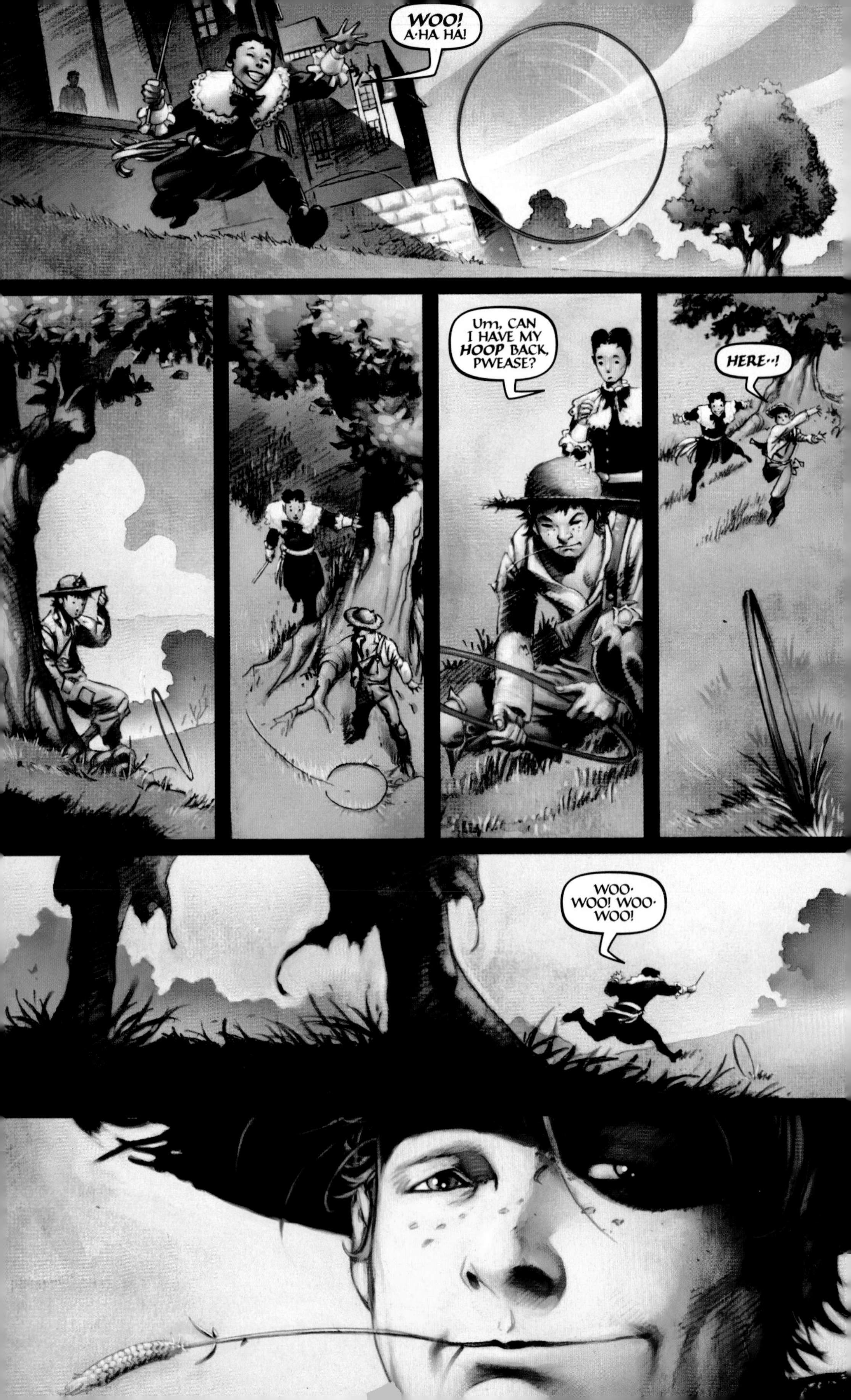
WOO! A-HA HÁ!
Um, CAN I HAVE MY HOOP BACK, PWEASE?
HERE--!
WOO-WOO! WOO-WOO!

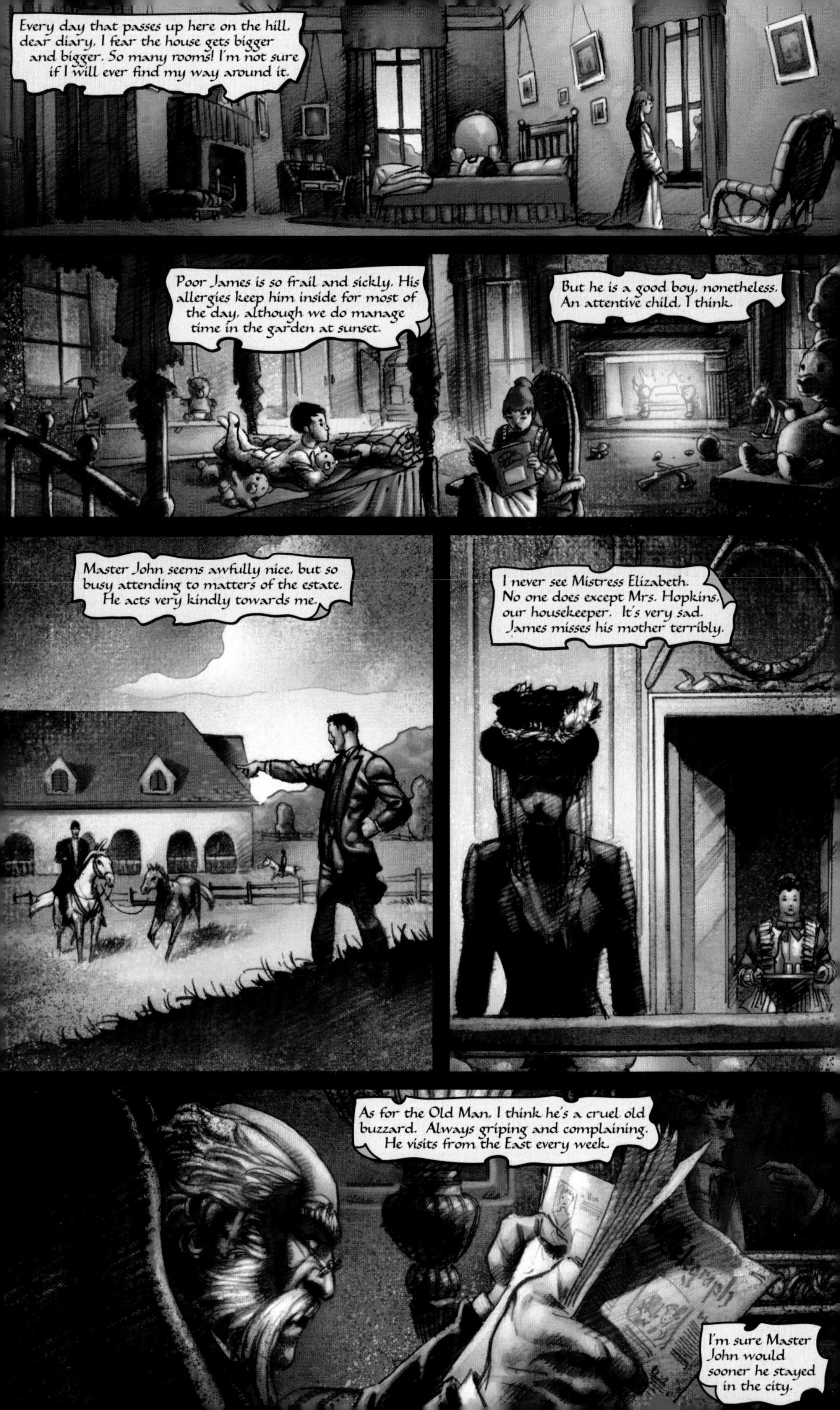
Every day that passes up here on the hill, dear diary, I fear the house gets bigger and bigger. So many rooms! I'm not sure if I will ever find my way around it.
Poor James is so frail and sickly. His allergies keep him inside for most of the day, although we do manage time in the garden at sunset.
But he is a good boy, nonetheless. An attentive child, I think.
Master John seems awfully nice, but so busy attending to matters of the estate. He acts very kindly towards me.
I never see Mistress Elizabeth. No one does except Mrs. Hopkins, our housekeeper. It's very sad. James misses his mother terribly.
As for the Old Man, I think he's a cruel old buzzard. Always griping and complaining. He visits from the East every week.
I'm sure Master John would sooner he stayed in the city.

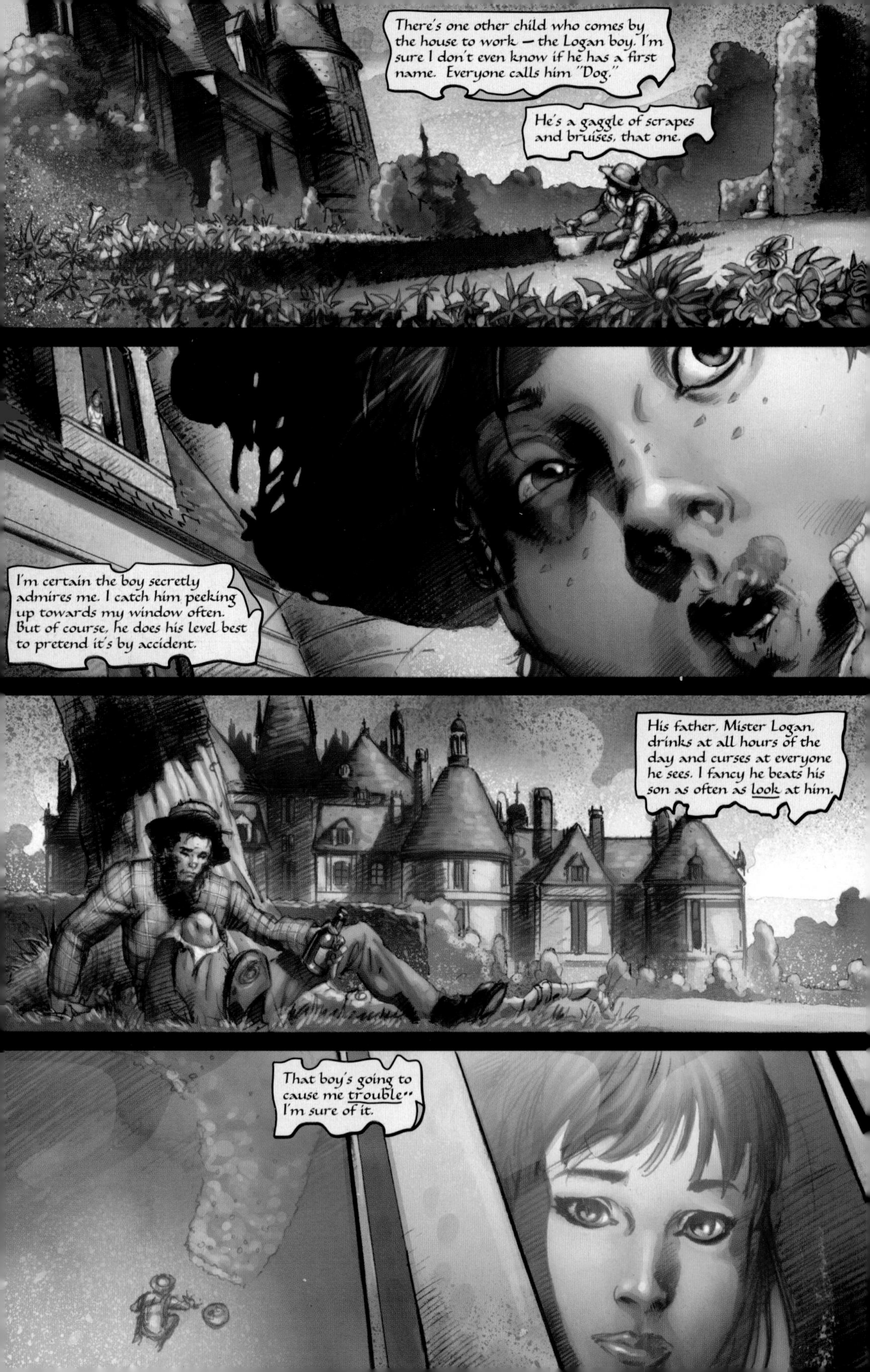
There's one other child who comes by the house to work — the Logan boy. I'm sure I don't even know if he has a first name. Everyone calls him "Dog."
He's a gaggle of scrapes and bruises, that one.
I'm certain the boy secretly admires me. I catch him peeking up towards my window often. But of course, he does his level best to pretend it's by accident.
His father, Mister Logan, drinks at all hours of the day and curses at everyone he sees. I fancy he beats his son as often as look at him.
That boy's going to cause me trouble... I'm sure of it.

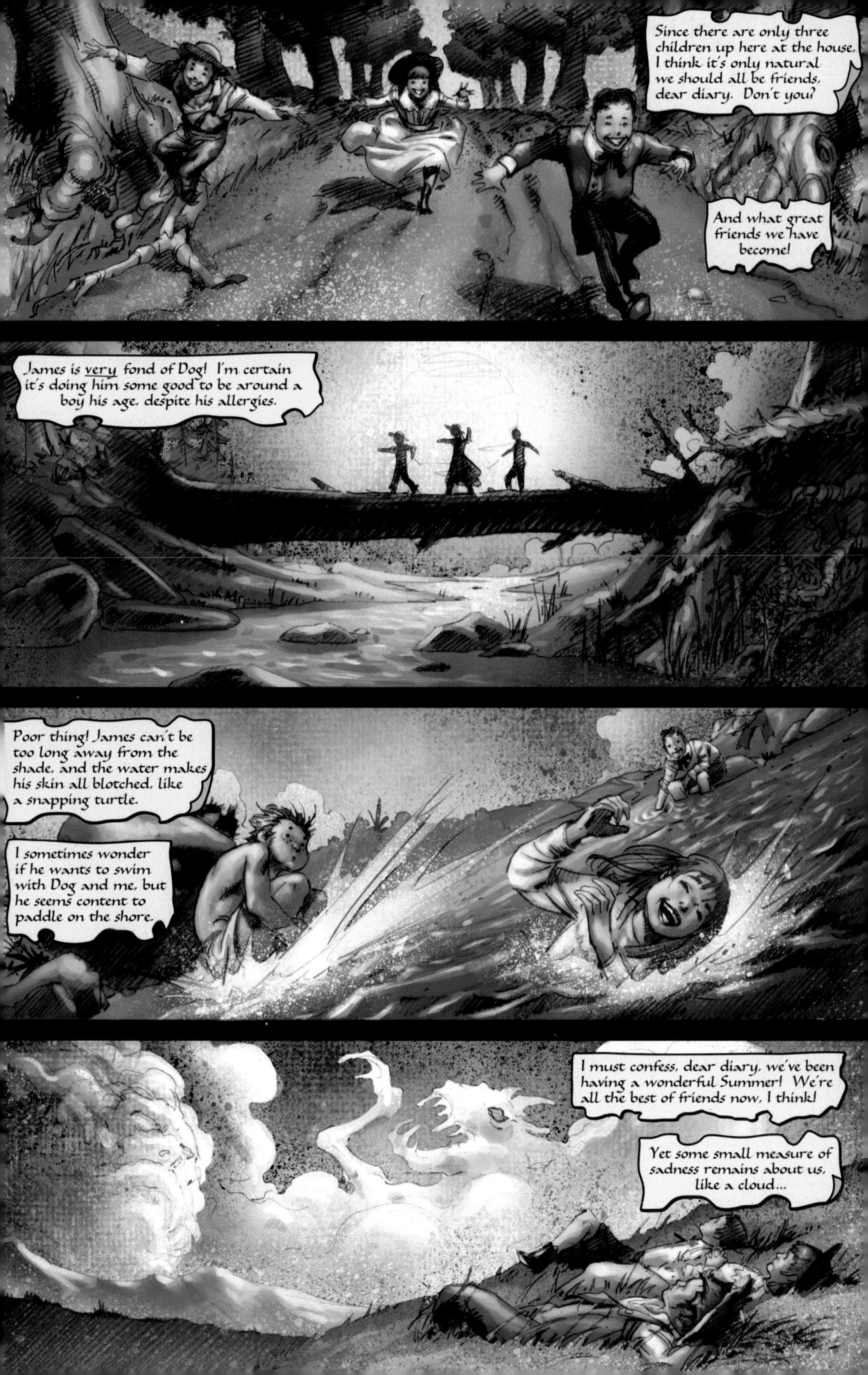
Since there are only three children up here at the house, I think it's only natural we should all be friends, dear diary. Don't you?
And what great friends we have become!
James is very fond of Dog! I'm certain it's doing him some good to be around a boy his age, despite his allergies.
Poor thing! James can't be too long away from the shade, and the water makes his skin all blotched, like a snapping turtle.
I sometimes wonder if he wants to swim with Dog and me, but he seems content to paddle on the shore.
I must confess, dear diary, we've been having a wonderful Summer! We're all the best of friends now, I think!
Yet some small measure of sadness remains about us, like a cloud...

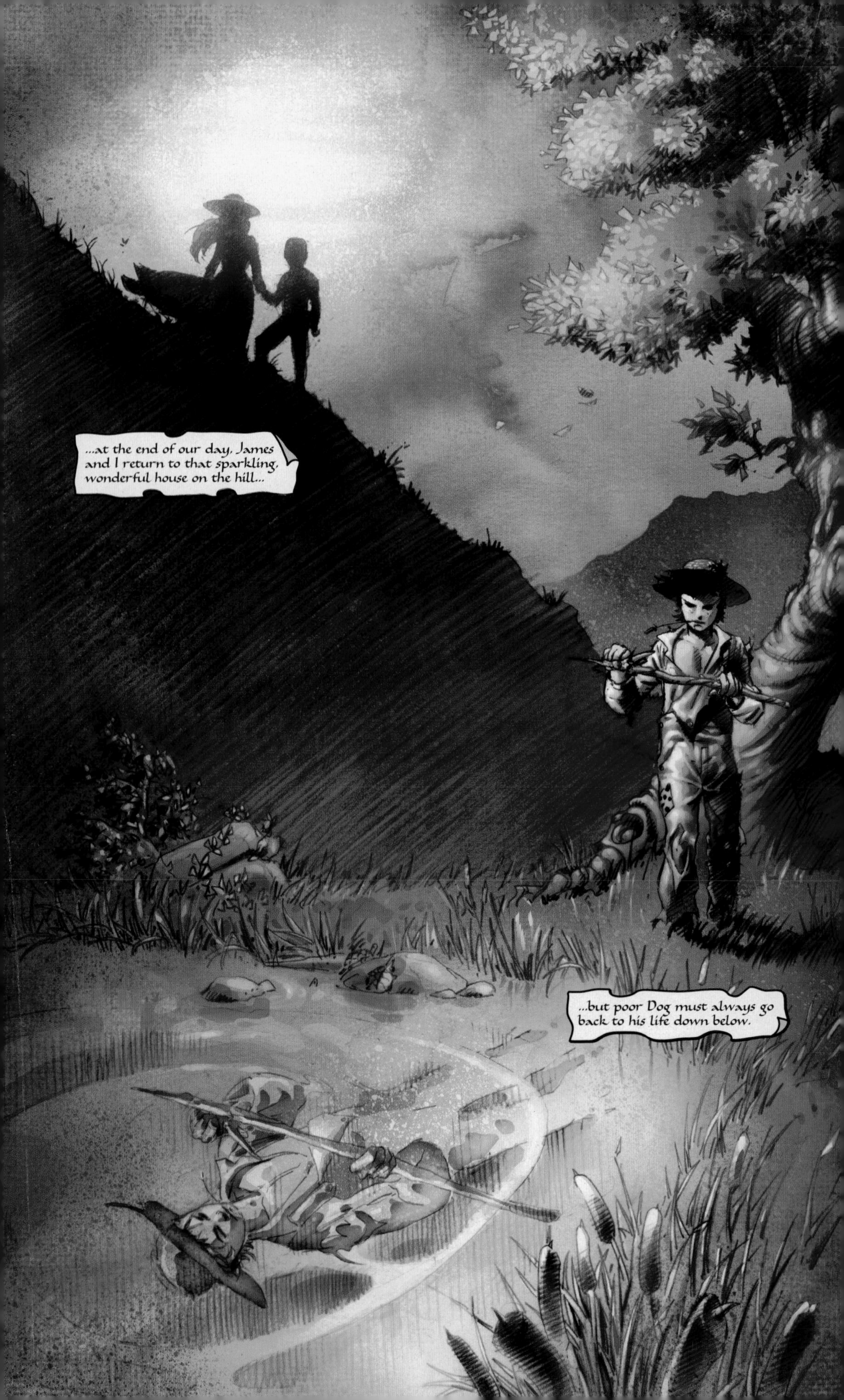

...at the end of our day, James and I return to that sparkling, wonderful house on the hill...
...but poor Dog must always go back to his life down below.

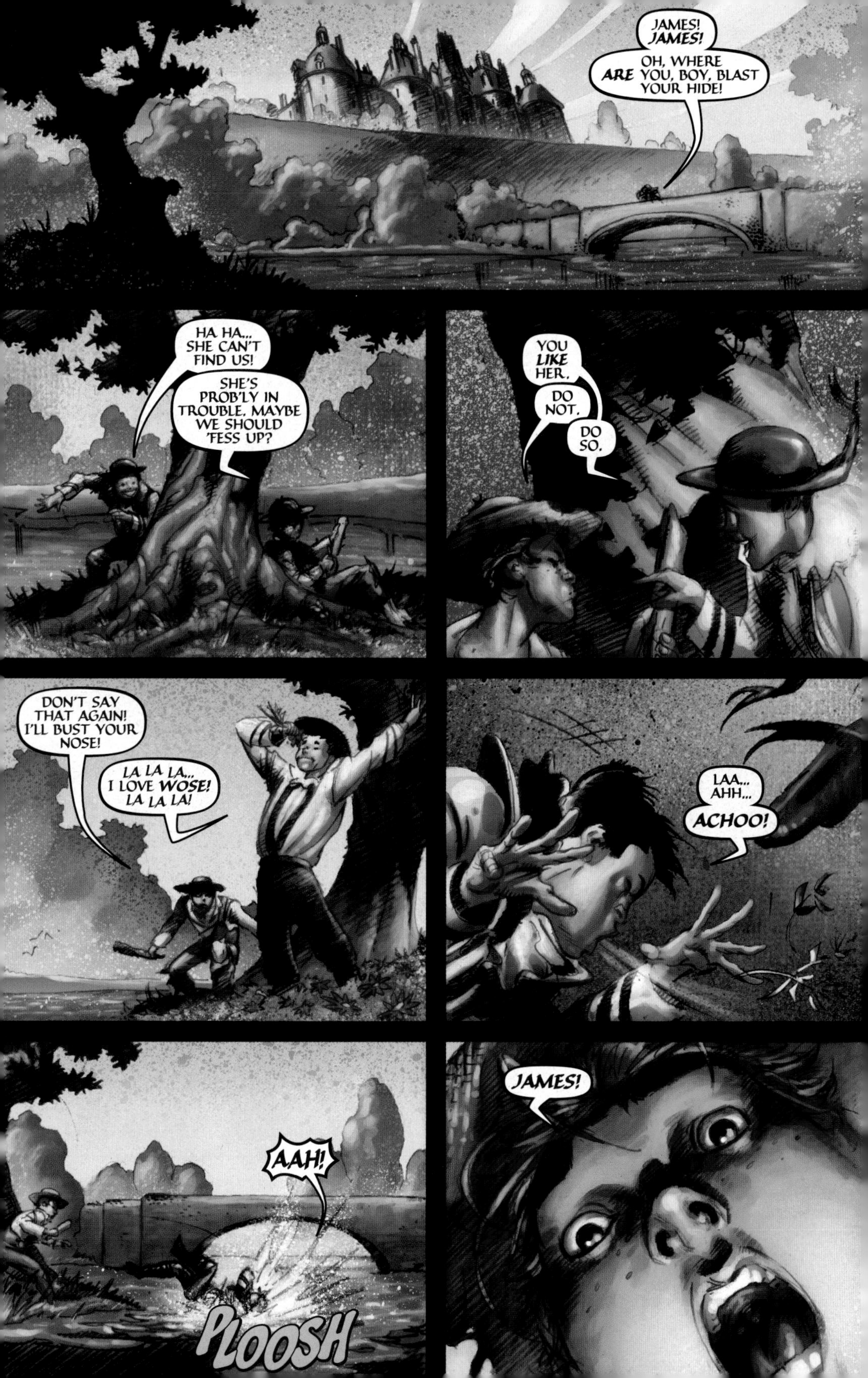
JAMES! JAMES!
OH, WHERE ARE YOU, BOY, BLAST YOUR HIDE!
HA HA... SHE CAN'T FIND US!
SHE'S PROB'LY IN TROUBLE. MAYBE WE SHOULD 'FESS UP?
YOU LIKE HER.
DO NOT.
DO SO.
DON'T SAY THAT AGAIN! I'LL BUST YOUR NOSE!
LA LA LA... I LOVE WOSE! LA LA LA!
LAA... AHH... ACHOO!
AAH!
PLOOSH
JAMES!

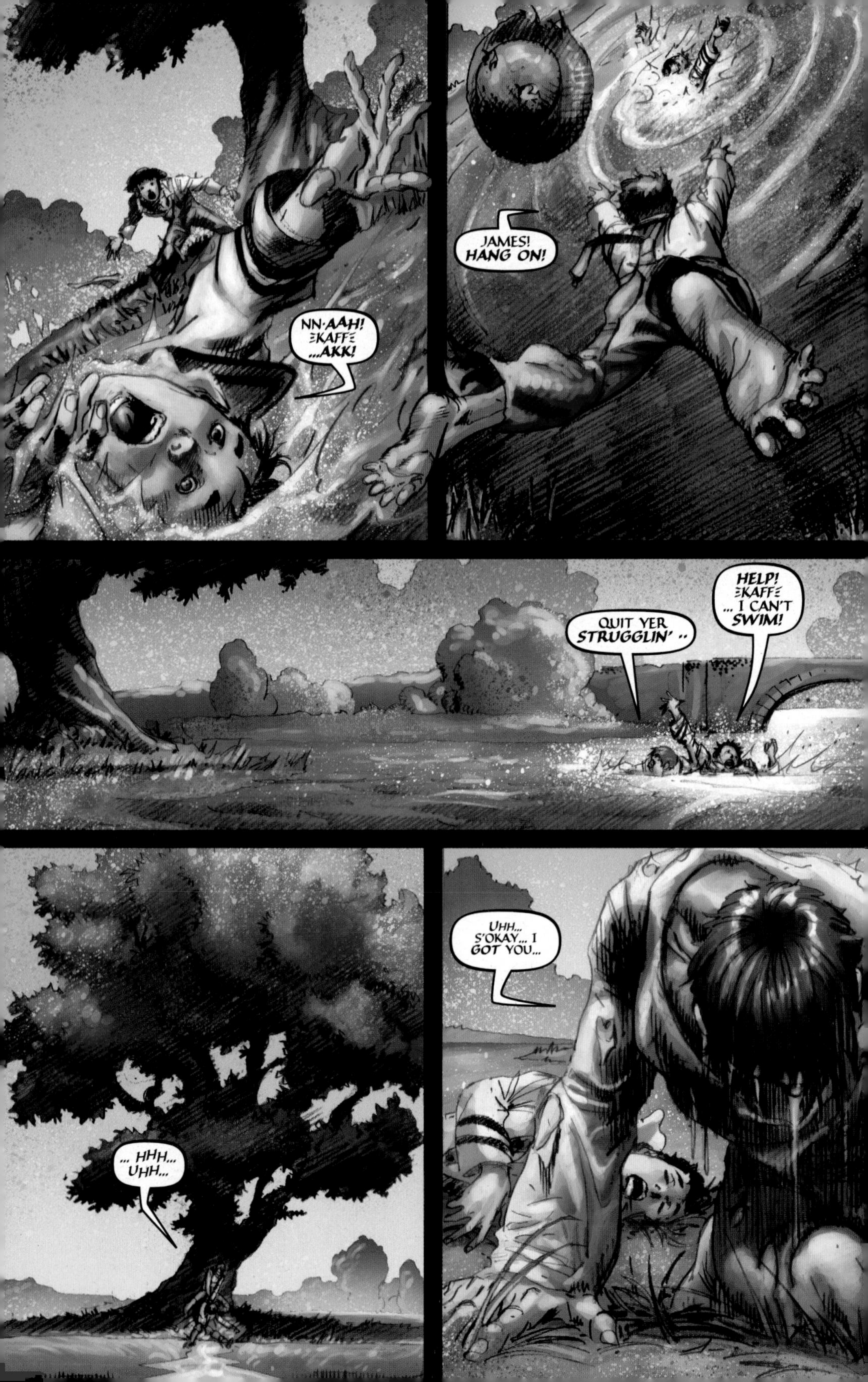
NN·AAH! ≡KAFF≡ ...AKK!
JAMES! HANG ON!
QUIT YER STRUGGLIN' ..
HELP! ≡KAFF≡ ... I CAN'T SWIM!
... HHH... UHH...
UHH... S'OKAY... I GOT YOU...

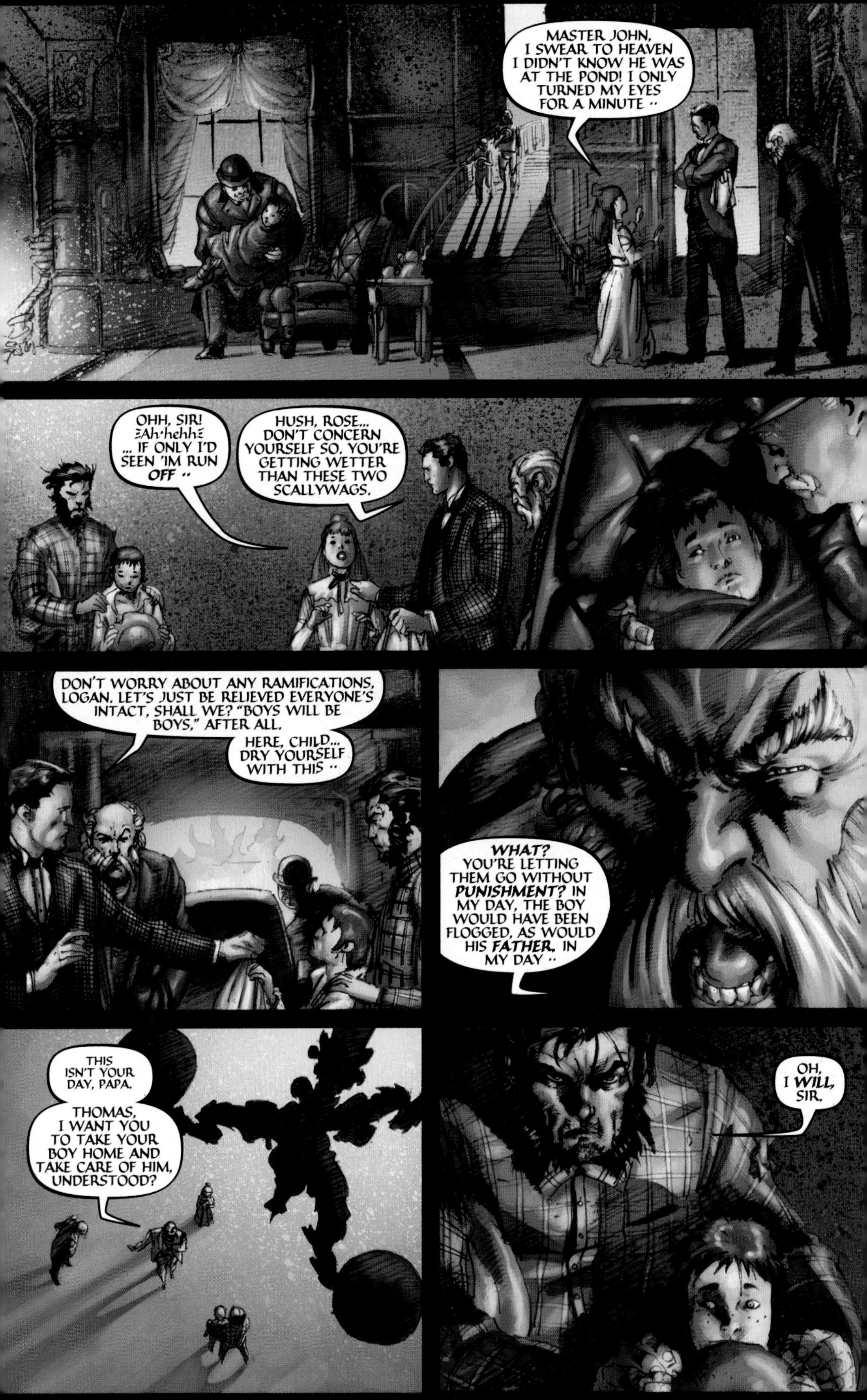
MASTER JOHN, I SWEAR TO HEAVEN I DIDN'T KNOW HE WAS AT THE POND! I ONLY TURNED MY EYES FOR A MINUTE ..
OHH, SIR! Ah-hehh ... IF ONLY I'D SEEN 'IM RUN OFF ..
HUSH, ROSE... DON'T CONCERN YOURSELF SO. YOU'RE GETTING WETTER THAN THESE TWO SCALLYWAGS.
DON'T WORRY ABOUT ANY RAMIFICATIONS, LOGAN. LET'S JUST BE RELIEVED EVERYONE'S INTACT, SHALL WE? "BOYS WILL BE BOYS," AFTER ALL.
HERE, CHILD... DRY YOURSELF WITH THIS ..
WHAT? YOU'RE LETTING THEM GO WITHOUT PUNISHMENT? IN MY DAY, THE BOY WOULD HAVE BEEN FLOGGED, AS WOULD HIS FATHER, IN MY DAY ..
THIS ISN'T YOUR DAY, PAPA.
THOMAS, I WANT YOU TO TAKE YOUR BOY HOME AND TAKE CARE OF HIM, UNDERSTOOD?
OH, I WILL, SIR.

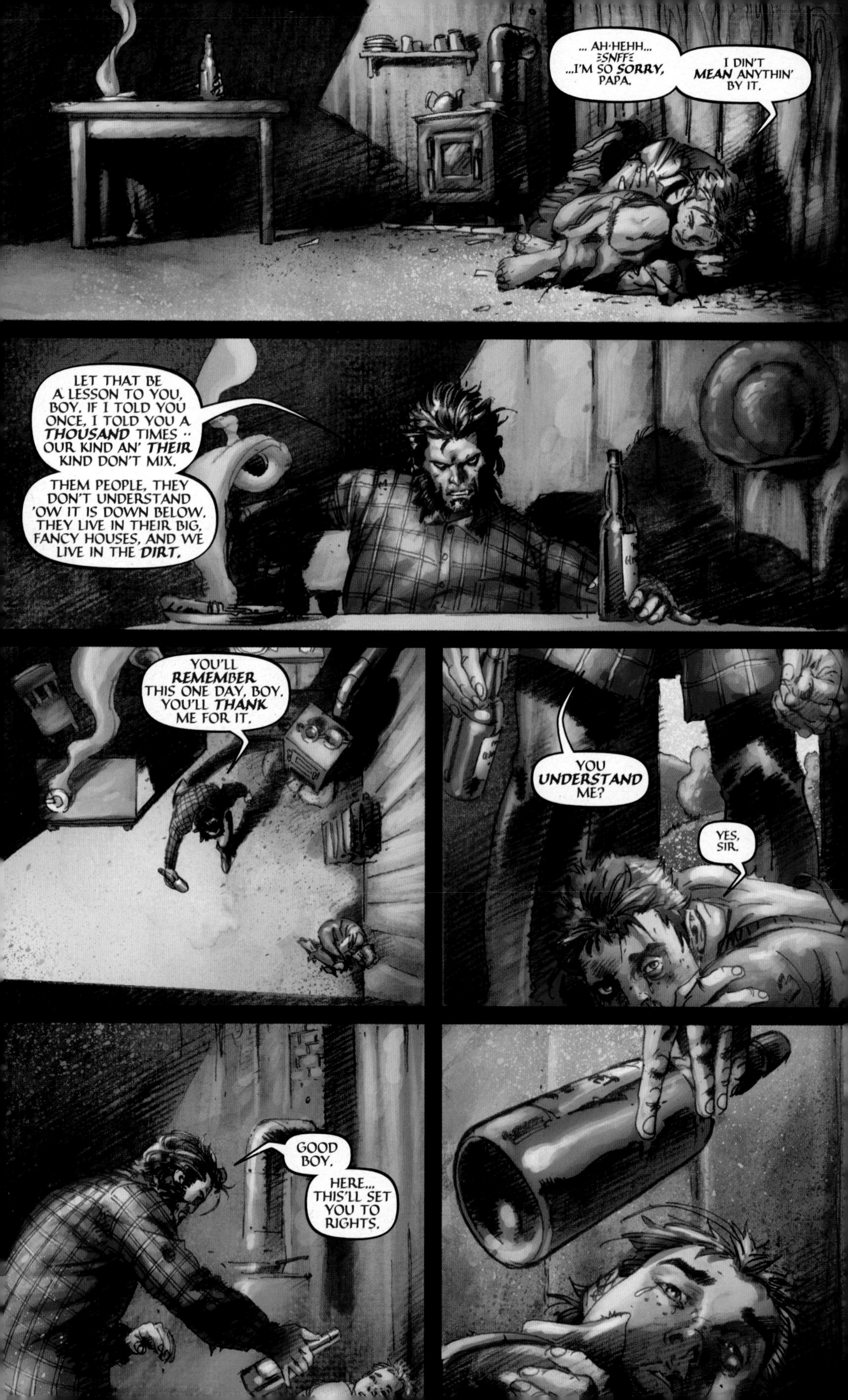

... AH·HEHH... ≡SNFF≡ ...I'M SO SORRY, PAPA.
I DIN'T MEAN ANYTHIN' BY IT.
LET THAT BE A LESSON TO YOU, BOY. IF I TOLD YOU ONCE, I TOLD YOU A THOUSAND TIMES -- OUR KIND AN' THEIR KIND DON'T MIX.
THEM PEOPLE, THEY DON'T UNDERSTAND 'OW IT IS DOWN BELOW. THEY LIVE IN THEIR BIG, FANCY HOUSES, AND WE LIVE IN THE DIRT.
YOU'LL REMEMBER THIS ONE DAY, BOY. YOU'LL THANK ME FOR IT.
YOU UNDERSTAND ME?
YES, SIR.
GOOD BOY.
HERE... THIS'LL SET YOU TO RIGHTS.

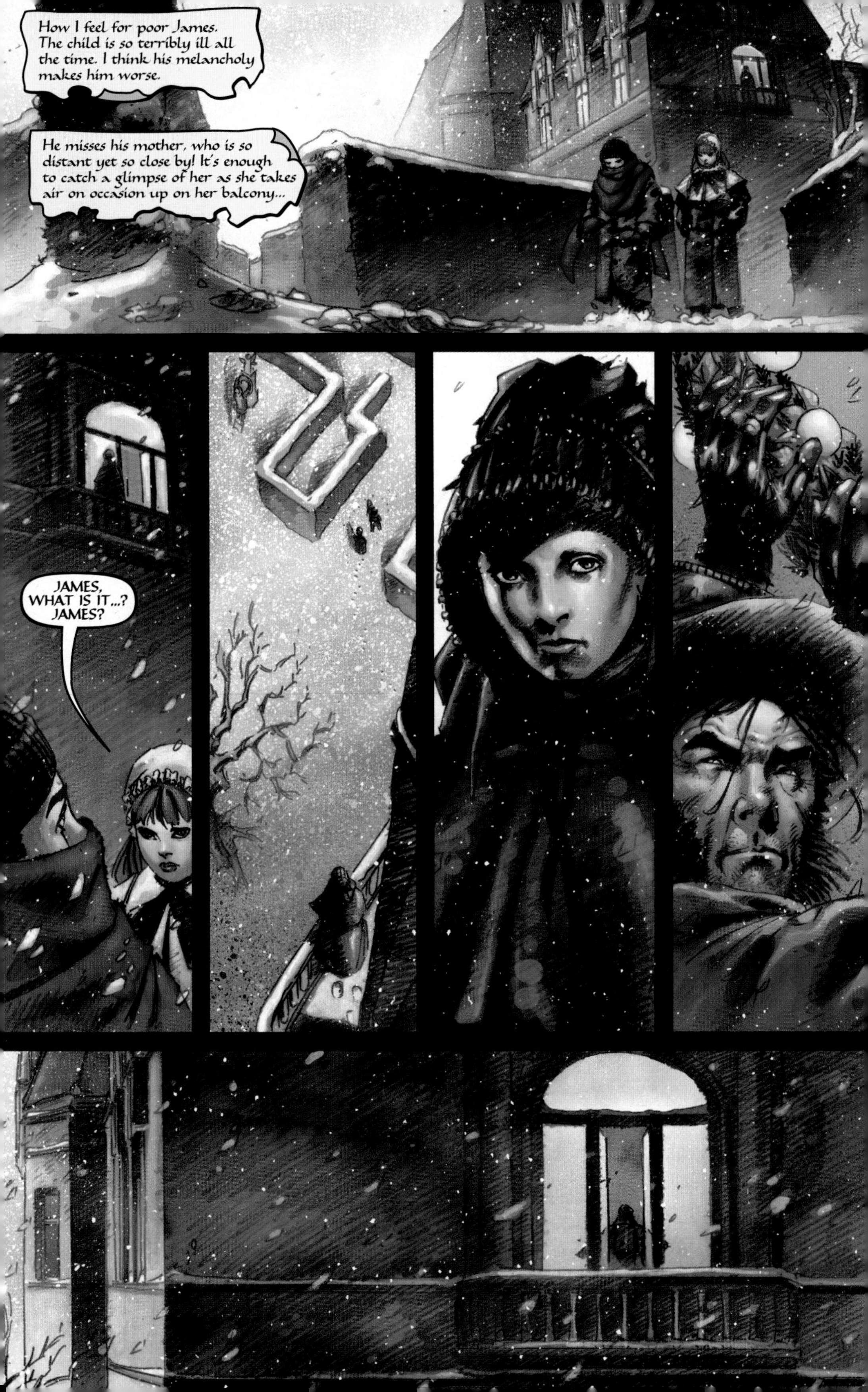
How I feel for poor James. The child is so terribly ill all the time. I think his melancholy makes him worse.
He misses his mother, who is so distant yet so close by! It's enough to catch a glimpse of her as she takes air on occasion up on her balcony...
JAMES, WHAT IS IT...? JAMES?

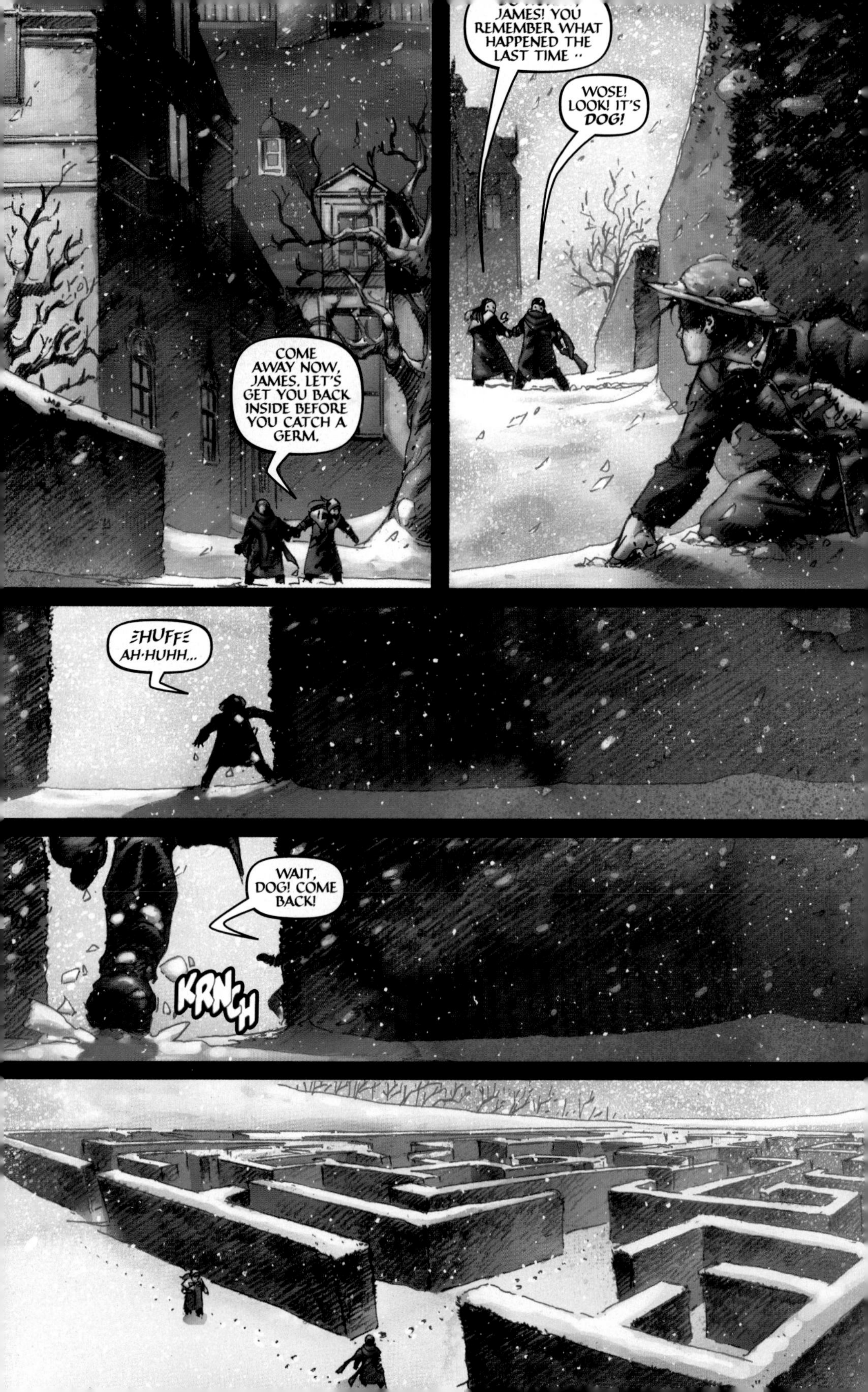
COME AWAY NOW, JAMES, LET'S GET YOU BACK INSIDE BEFORE YOU CATCH A GERM.
JAMES! YOU REMEMBER WHAT HAPPENED THE LAST TIME ..
WOSE! LOOK! IT'S *DOG!*
HUFF AH·HUHH...
WAIT, DOG! COME BACK!
KRNCH

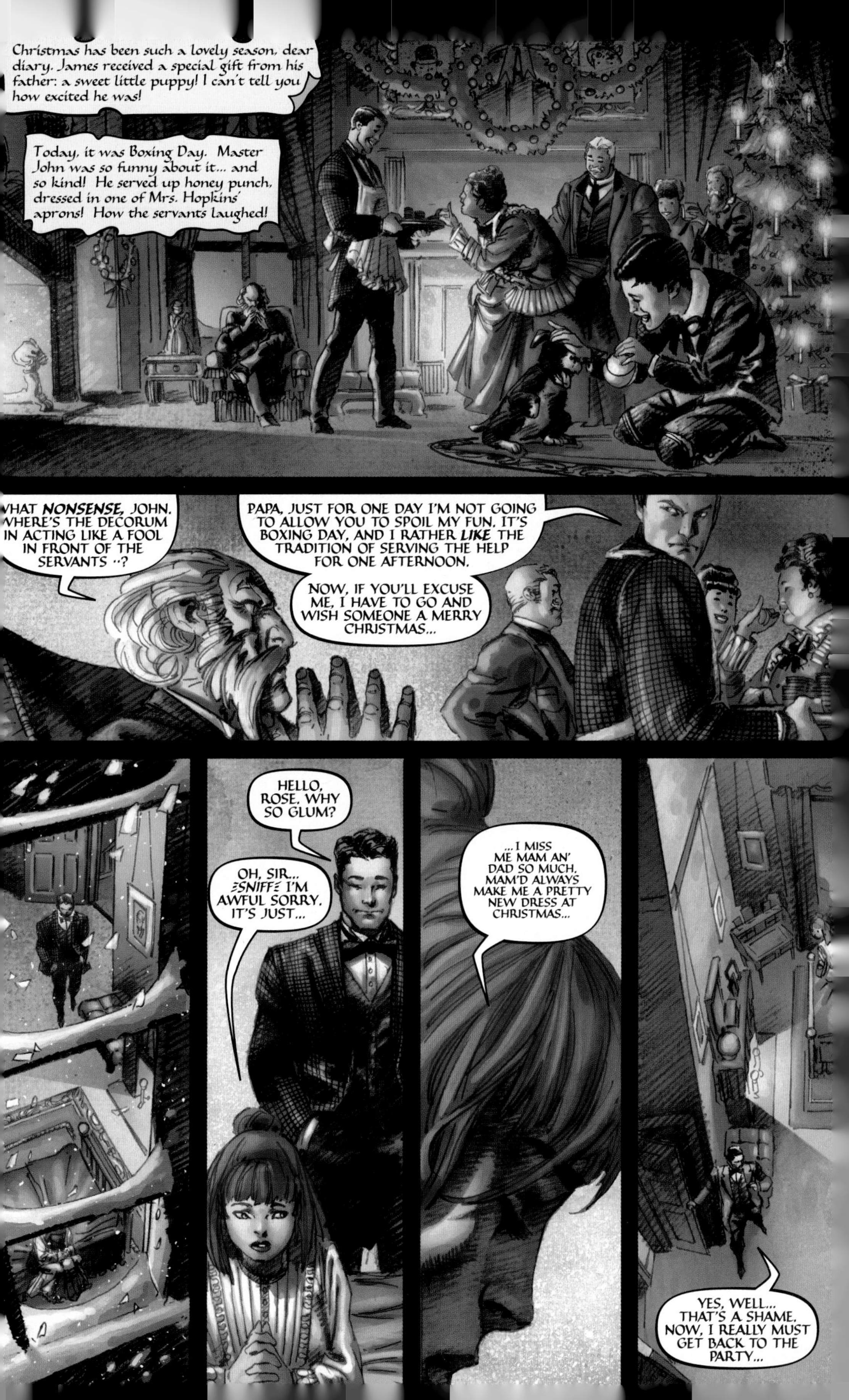

Christmas has been such a lovely season, dear diary. James received a special gift from his father: a sweet little puppy! I can't tell you how excited he was!
Today, it was Boxing Day. Master John was so funny about it... and so kind! He served up honey punch, dressed in one of Mrs. Hopkins' aprons! How the servants laughed!
WHAT NONSENSE, JOHN. WHERE'S THE DECORUM IN ACTING LIKE A FOOL IN FRONT OF THE SERVANTS ..?
PAPA, JUST FOR ONE DAY I'M NOT GOING TO ALLOW YOU TO SPOIL MY FUN. IT'S BOXING DAY, AND I RATHER LIKE THE TRADITION OF SERVING THE HELP FOR ONE AFTERNOON.
NOW, IF YOU'LL EXCUSE ME, I HAVE TO GO AND WISH SOMEONE A MERRY CHRISTMAS...
HELLO, ROSE. WHY SO GLUM?
OH, SIR... ≡SNIFF≡ I'M AWFUL SORRY. IT'S JUST...
...I MISS ME MAM AN' DAD SO MUCH. MAM'D ALWAYS MAKE ME A PRETTY NEW DRESS AT CHRISTMAS...
YES, WELL... THAT'S A SHAME. NOW, I REALLY MUST GET BACK TO THE PARTY...

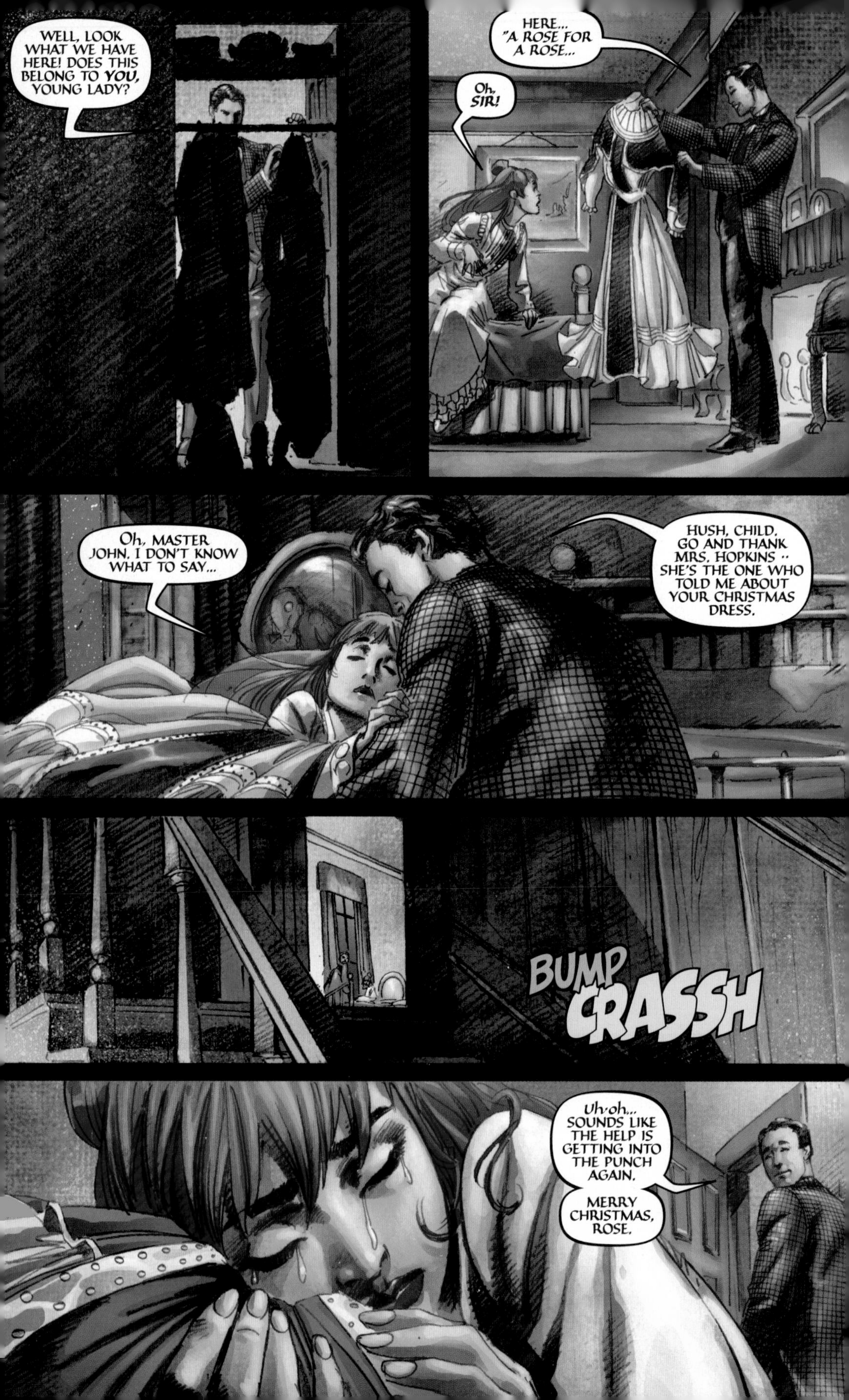
WELL, LOOK WHAT WE HAVE HERE! DOES THIS BELONG TO YOU, YOUNG LADY?
HERE... "A ROSE FOR A ROSE...
Oh, SIR!
Oh, MASTER JOHN, I DON'T KNOW WHAT TO SAY...
HUSH, CHILD. GO AND THANK MRS. HOPKINS -- SHE'S THE ONE WHO TOLD ME ABOUT YOUR CHRISTMAS DRESS.
BUMP
CRASSH
Uh-oh... SOUNDS LIKE THE HELP IS GETTING INTO THE PUNCH AGAIN.
MERRY CHRISTMAS, ROSE.

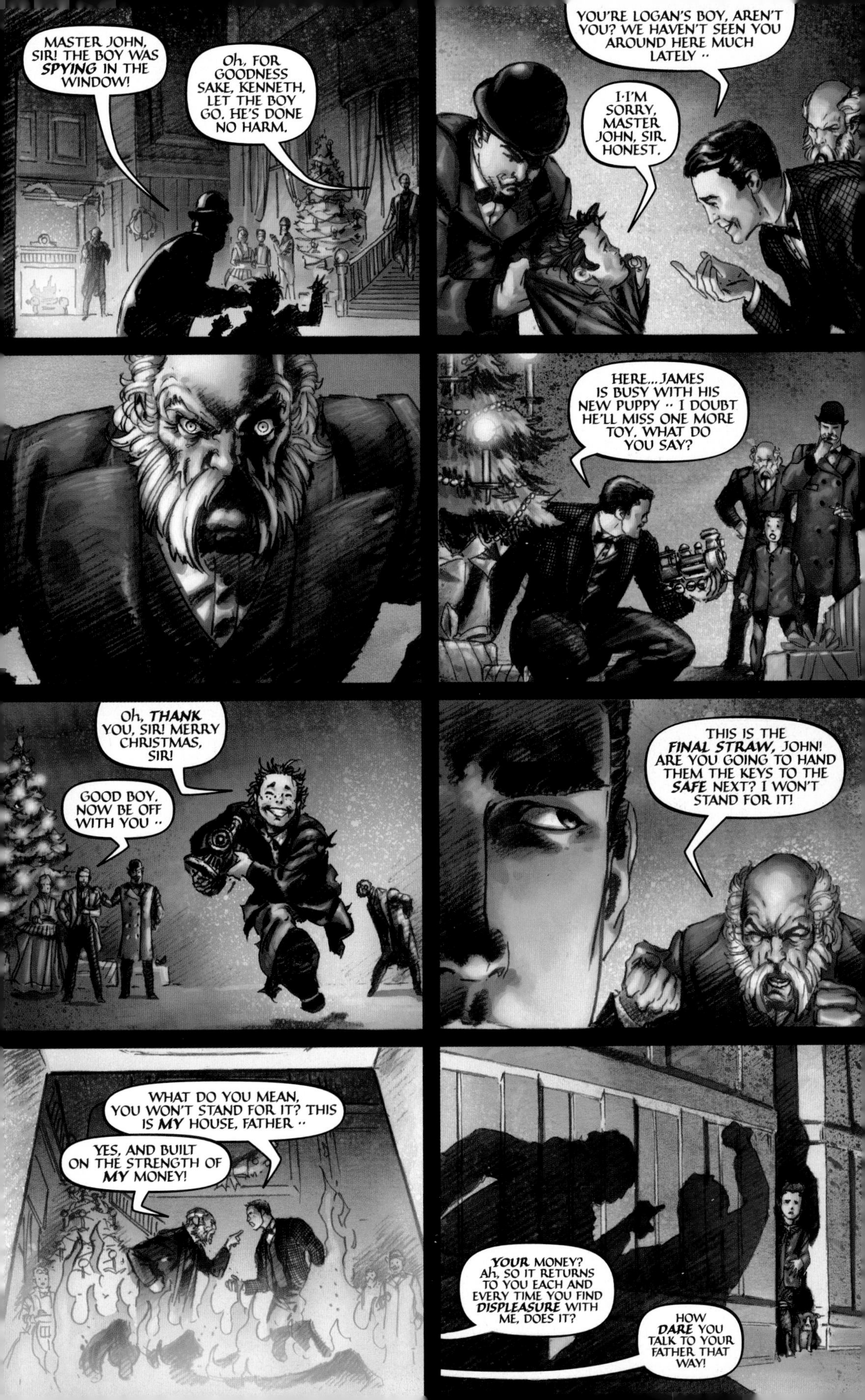
MASTER JOHN, SIR! THE BOY WAS SPYING IN THE WINDOW!
Oh, FOR GOODNESS SAKE, KENNETH, LET THE BOY GO, HE'S DONE NO HARM.
YOU'RE LOGAN'S BOY, AREN'T YOU? WE HAVEN'T SEEN YOU AROUND HERE MUCH LATELY ..
I-I'M SORRY, MASTER JOHN, SIR. HONEST.
HERE... JAMES IS BUSY WITH HIS NEW PUPPY .. I DOUBT HE'LL MISS ONE MORE TOY. WHAT DO YOU SAY?
Oh, THANK YOU, SIR! MERRY CHRISTMAS, SIR!
GOOD BOY. NOW BE OFF WITH YOU ..
THIS IS THE FINAL STRAW, JOHN! ARE YOU GOING TO HAND THEM THE KEYS TO THE SAFE NEXT? I WON'T STAND FOR IT!
WHAT DO YOU MEAN, YOU WON'T STAND FOR IT? THIS IS MY HOUSE, FATHER ..
YES, AND BUILT ON THE STRENGTH OF MY MONEY!
YOUR MONEY? Ah, SO IT RETURNS TO YOU EACH AND EVERY TIME YOU FIND DISPLEASURE WITH ME, DOES IT?
HOW DARE YOU TALK TO YOUR FATHER THAT WAY!

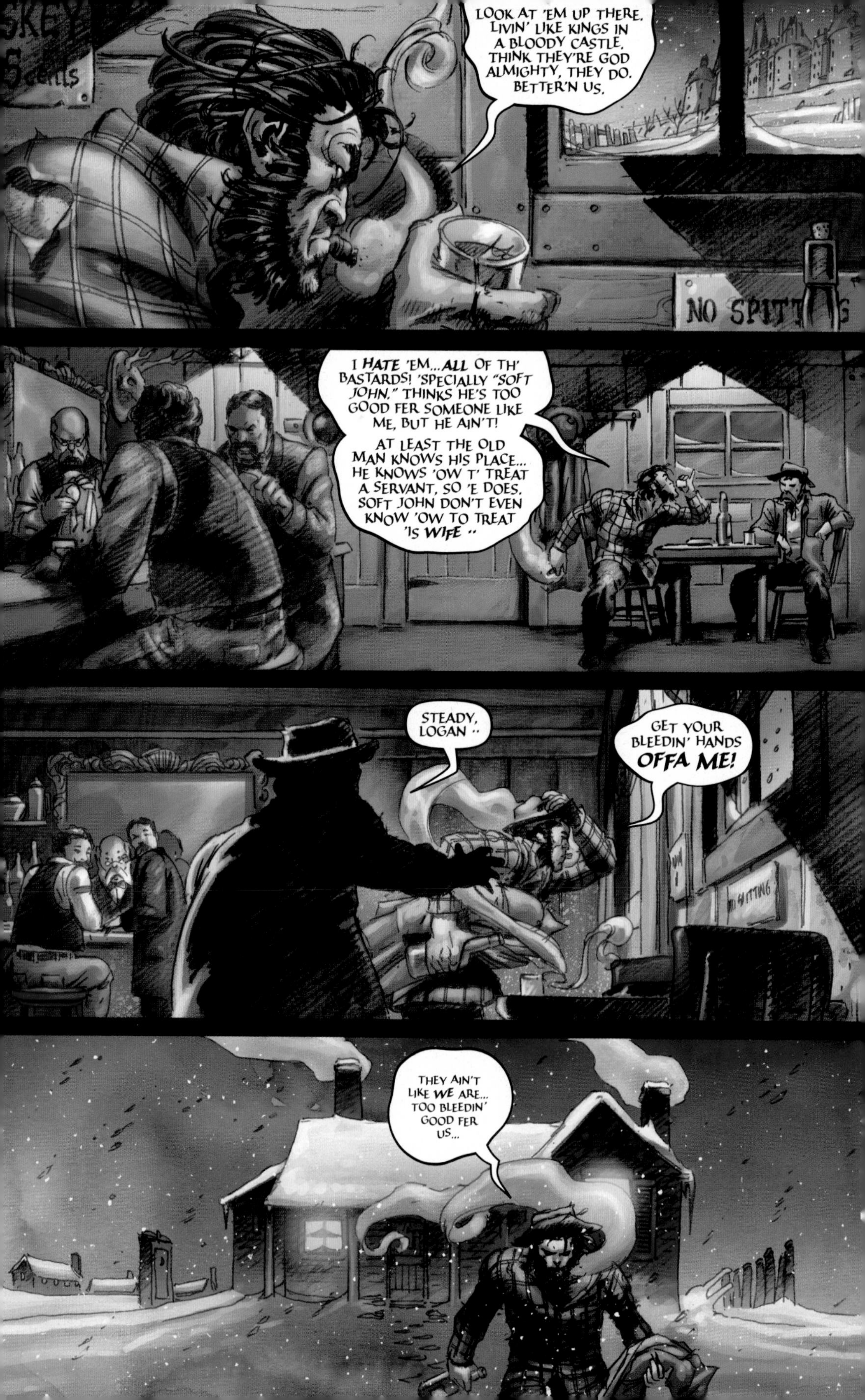

SKEY
5 cents
LOOK AT 'EM UP THERE, LIVIN' LIKE KINGS IN A BLOODY CASTLE. THINK THEY'RE GOD ALMIGHTY, THEY DO. BETTER'N US.
NO SPITT
I HATE 'EM...ALL OF TH' BASTARDS! 'SPECIALLY "SOFT JOHN." THINKS HE'S TOO GOOD FER SOMEONE LIKE ME, BUT HE AIN'T!
AT LEAST THE OLD MAN KNOWS HIS PLACE... HE KNOWS 'OW T' TREAT A SERVANT, SO 'E DOES. SOFT JOHN DON'T EVEN KNOW 'OW TO TREAT 'IS WIFE --
STEADY, LOGAN --
GET YOUR BLEEDIN' HANDS OFFA ME!
THEY AIN'T LIKE WE ARE... TOO BLEEDIN' GOOD FER US...

POPPA! *POPPA!*
LOOK WHAT MASTER
HOWLETT ··

·· *GAVE*
ME.

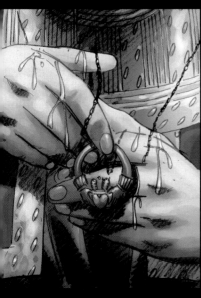

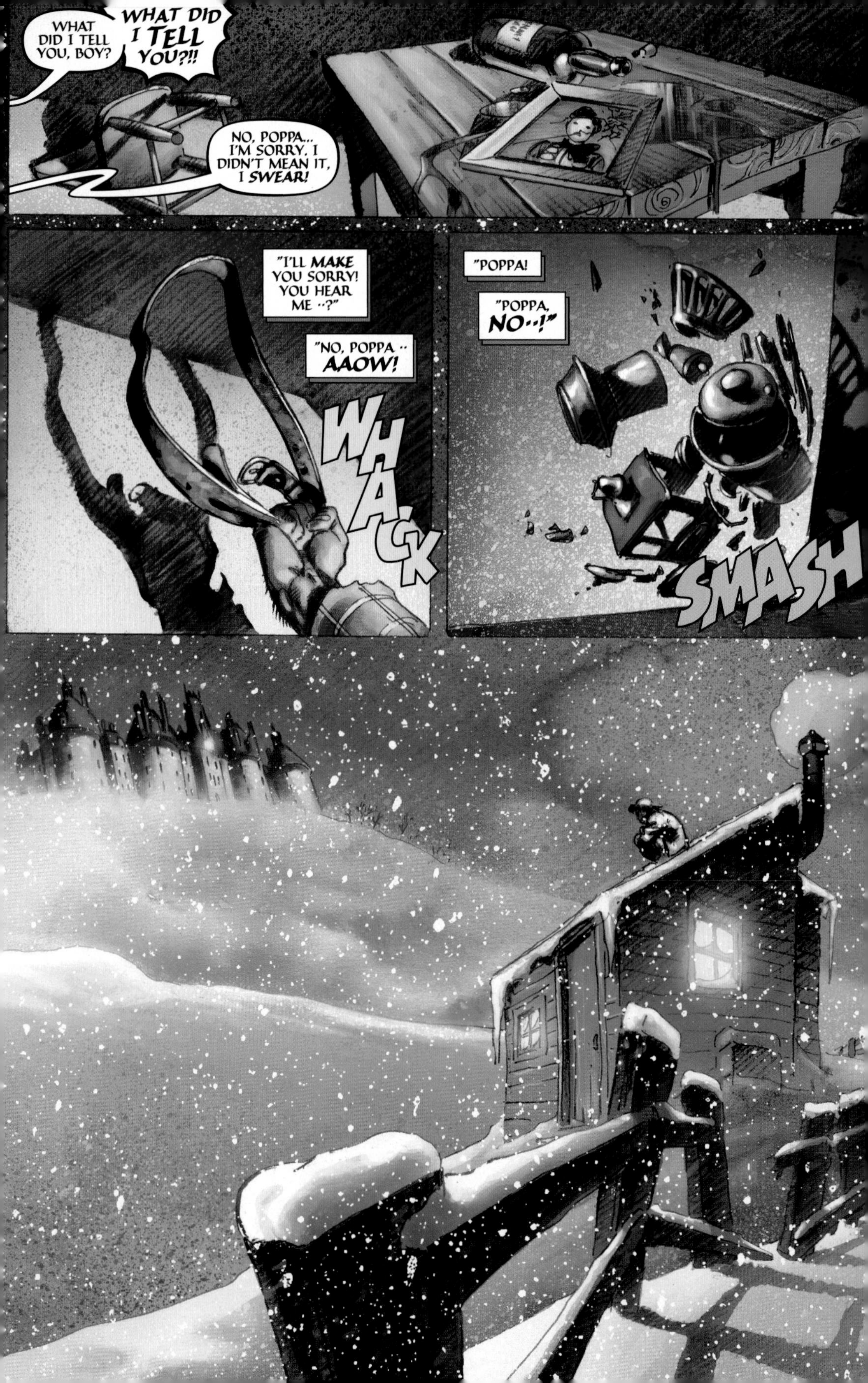
WHAT DID I TELL YOU, BOY?
WHAT DID I TELL YOU?!!
NO, POPPA... I'M SORRY. I DIDN'T MEAN IT, I SWEAR!
"I'LL MAKE YOU SORRY! YOU HEAR ME ..?"
"NO, POPPA .. AAOW!
WHACK
"POPPA!
"POPPA, NO..!"
SMASH

QUESADA
-2001-
ISANOVE

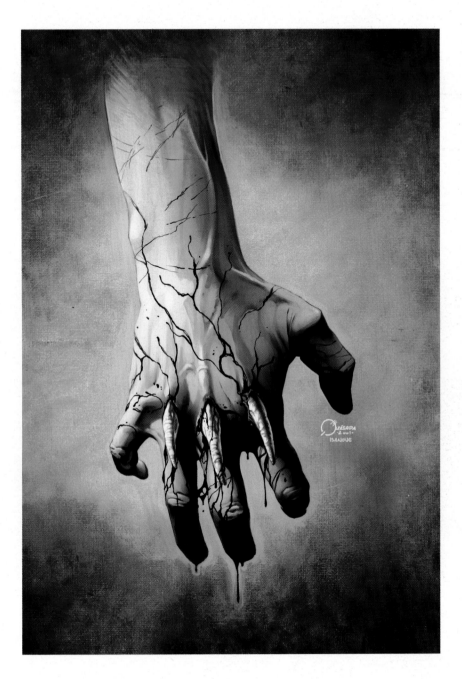

PART II

INNER CHILD

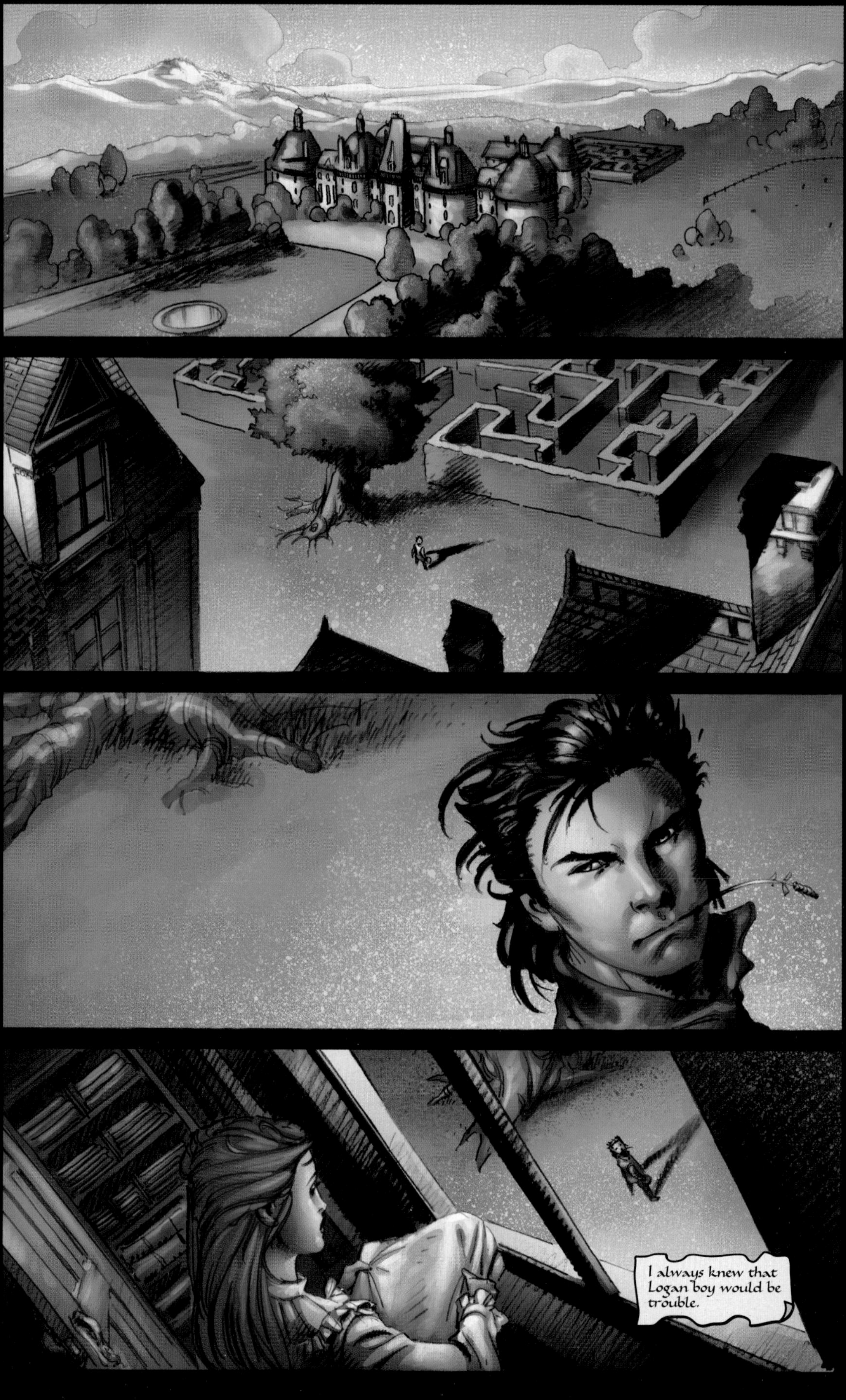
I always knew that Logan boy would be trouble.

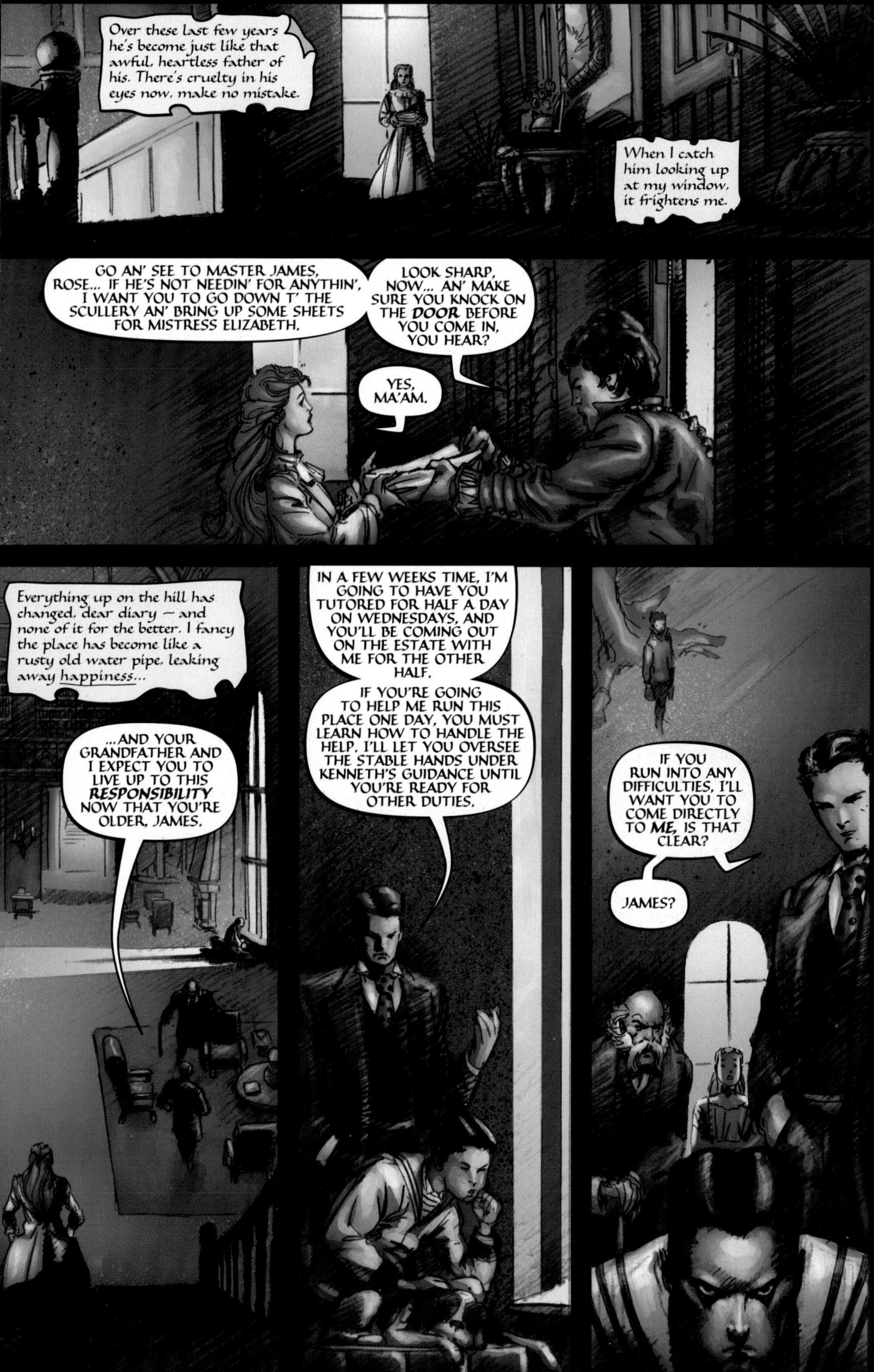

Over these last few years he's become just like that awful, heartless father of his. There's cruelty in his eyes now, make no mistake.
When I catch him looking up at my window, it frightens me.
GO AN' SEE TO MASTER JAMES, ROSE... IF HE'S NOT NEEDIN' FOR ANYTHIN', I WANT YOU TO GO DOWN T' THE SCULLERY AN' BRING UP SOME SHEETS FOR MISTRESS ELIZABETH.
LOOK SHARP, NOW... AN' MAKE SURE YOU KNOCK ON THE DOOR BEFORE YOU COME IN, YOU HEAR?
YES, MA'AM.
Everything up on the hill has changed, dear diary — and none of it for the better. I fancy the place has become like a rusty old water pipe, leaking away happiness...
...AND YOUR GRANDFATHER AND I EXPECT YOU TO LIVE UP TO THIS RESPONSIBILITY NOW THAT YOU'RE OLDER, JAMES.
IN A FEW WEEKS TIME, I'M GOING TO HAVE YOU TUTORED FOR HALF A DAY ON WEDNESDAYS, AND YOU'LL BE COMING OUT ON THE ESTATE WITH ME FOR THE OTHER HALF.
IF YOU'RE GOING TO HELP ME RUN THIS PLACE ONE DAY, YOU MUST LEARN HOW TO HANDLE THE HELP. I'LL LET YOU OVERSEE THE STABLE HANDS UNDER KENNETH'S GUIDANCE UNTIL YOU'RE READY FOR OTHER DUTIES.
IF YOU RUN INTO ANY DIFFICULTIES, I'LL WANT YOU TO COME DIRECTLY TO ME, IS THAT CLEAR?
JAMES?

JAMES, I'M *TALKING* TO YOU, BOY. HAVE YOU REGISTERED EVEN A *SINGLE* WORD I'VE SAID?

YES, PAPA.

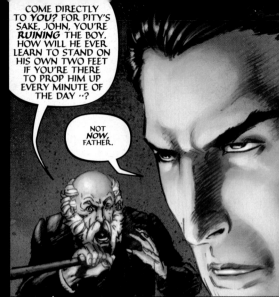

COME DIRECTLY TO *YOU?* FOR PITY'S SAKE, JOHN, YOU'RE *RUINING* THE BOY. HOW WILL HE EVER LEARN TO STAND ON HIS OWN TWO FEET IF YOU'RE THERE TO PROP HIM UP EVERY MINUTE OF THE DAY ..?

NOT *NOW*, FATHER.

DON'T *"NOT NOW"* ME, JOHN HOWLETT! YOU'RE TURNING HIM INTO A LESSER VERSION OF *YOURSELF!* MAYBE YOU'VE FORGOTTEN THAT YOU LOST YOUR *ELDER* CHILD, BUT *I* HAVEN'T. DO YOU REALLY WANT TO LOSE *ANOTHER* ONE?

≡AHEM≡

WHAT DO YOU *WANT*, GIRL? SPIT IT OUT!

IF IT PLEASE YOU, SIR... I WAS SENT DOWN TO ASK AFTER YOUNG MASTER JAMES.

JAMES WILL BE FINE WHERE HE IS FOR THE MOMENT, ROSE. YOU MAY GO ABOUT YOUR DUTIES, THANK YOU.

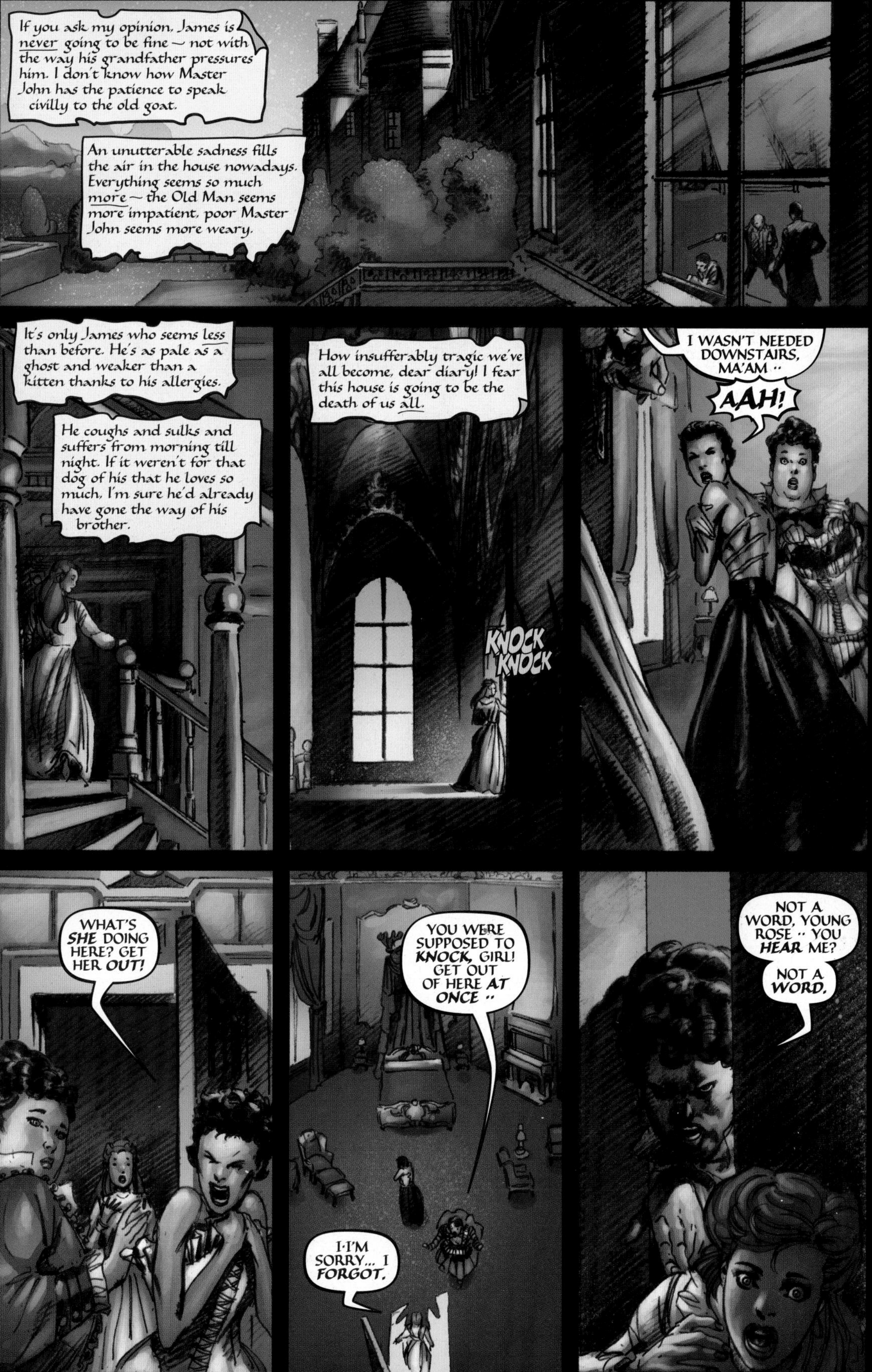
If you ask my opinion, James is never going to be fine ~ not with the way his grandfather pressures him. I don't know how Master John has the patience to speak civilly to the old goat.
An unutterable sadness fills the air in the house nowadays. Everything seems so much more ~ the Old Man seems more impatient, poor Master John seems more weary.
It's only James who seems less than before. He's as pale as a ghost and weaker than a kitten thanks to his allergies.
He coughs and sulks and suffers from morning till night. If it weren't for that dog of his that he loves so much, I'm sure he'd already have gone the way of his brother.
How insufferably tragic we've all become, dear diary! I fear this house is going to be the death of us all.
KNOCK KNOCK
I WASN'T NEEDED DOWNSTAIRS, MA'AM ..
AAH!
WHAT'S SHE DOING HERE? GET HER OUT!
YOU WERE SUPPOSED TO KNOCK, GIRL! GET OUT OF HERE AT ONCE ..
I-I'M SORRY... I FORGOT.
NOT A WORD, YOUNG ROSE .. YOU HEAR ME?
NOT A WORD.

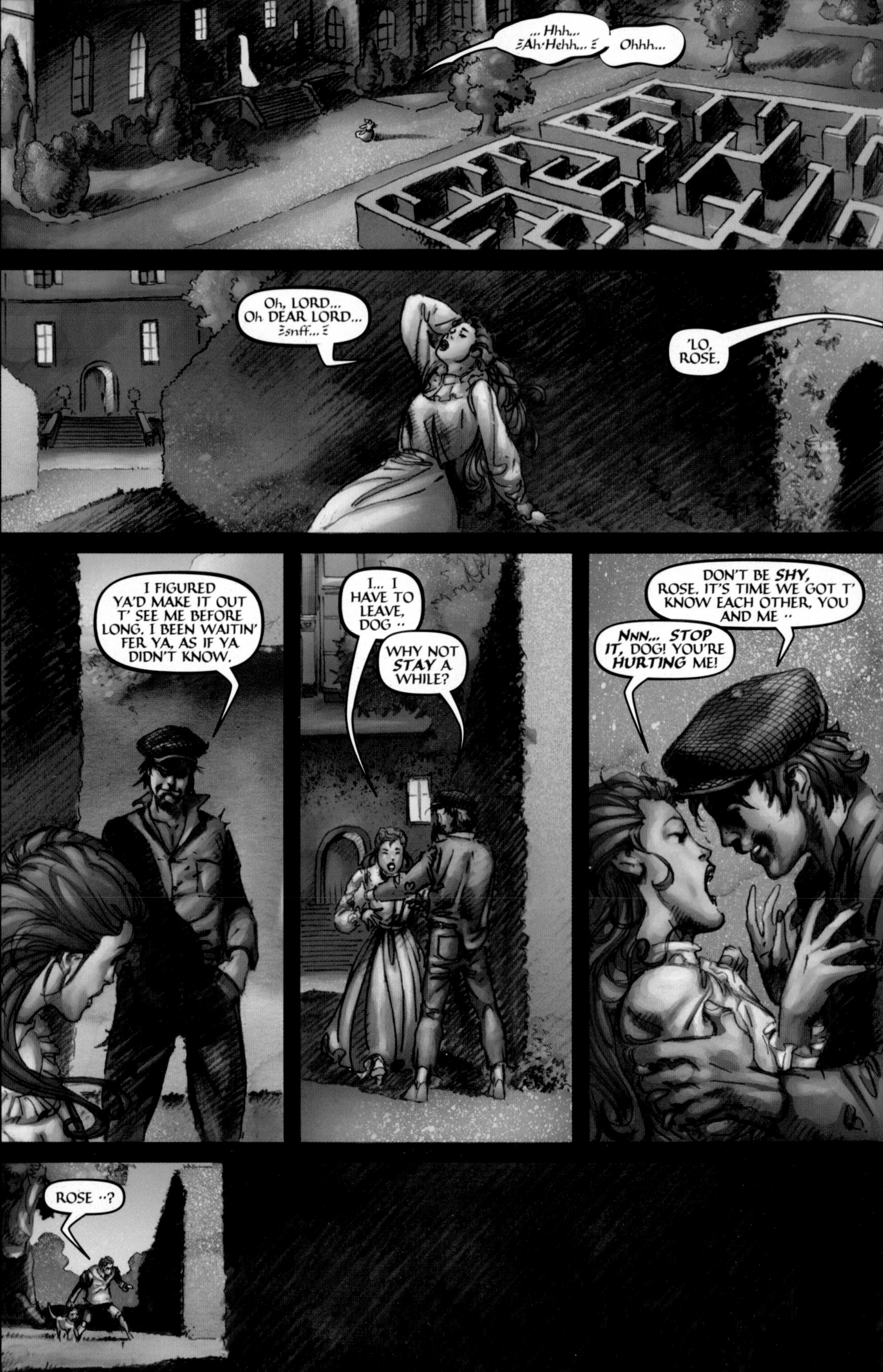

... Hhh...
Ah-Hehh...
Ohhh...
Oh, LORD... Oh DEAR LORD... snff...
'LO, ROSE.
I FIGURED YA'D MAKE IT OUT T' SEE ME BEFORE LONG. I BEEN WAITIN' FER YA, AS IF YA DIDN'T KNOW.
I... I HAVE TO LEAVE, DOG ..
WHY NOT STAY A WHILE?
DON'T BE SHY, ROSE. IT'S TIME WE GOT T' KNOW EACH OTHER, YOU AND ME ..
NNN... STOP IT, DOG! YOU'RE HURTING ME!
ROSE ..?

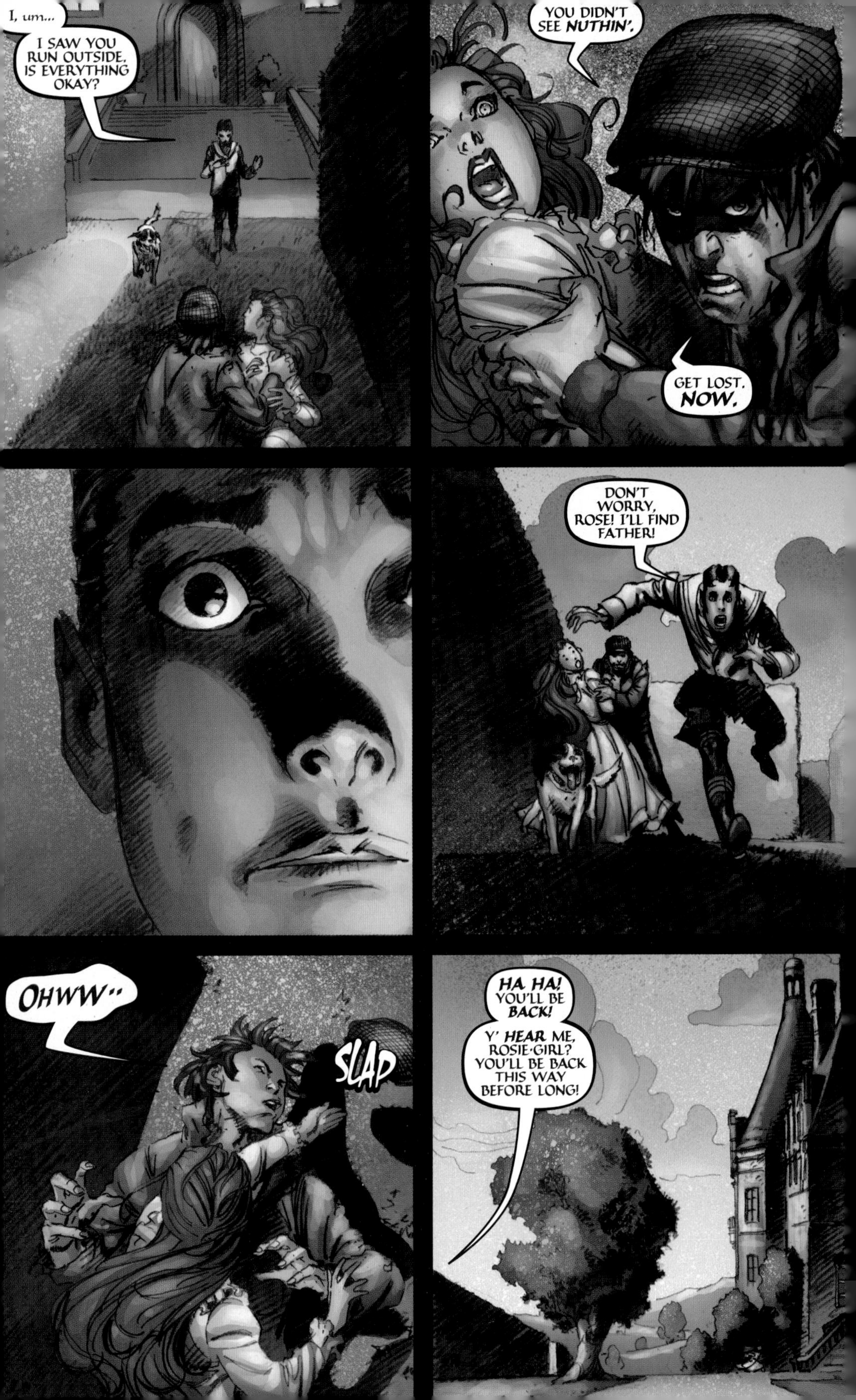
I, um...
I SAW YOU RUN OUTSIDE, IS EVERYTHING OKAY?
YOU DIDN'T SEE NUTHIN'.
GET LOST. NOW.
DON'T WORRY, ROSE! I'LL FIND FATHER!
OHWW..
SLAP
HA HA! YOU'LL BE BACK!
Y' HEAR ME, ROSIE-GIRL? YOU'LL BE BACK THIS WAY BEFORE LONG!

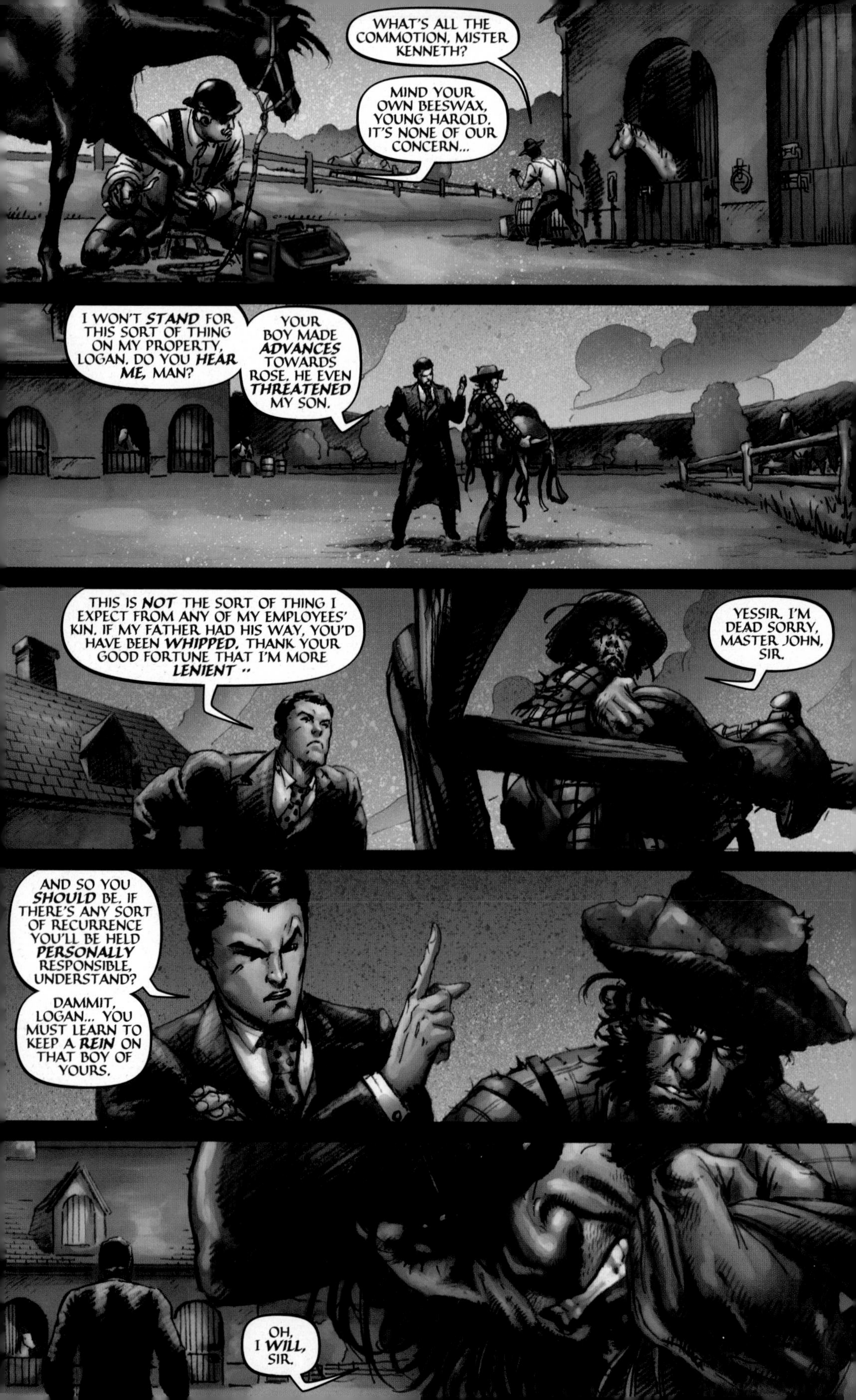
WHAT'S ALL THE COMMOTION, MISTER KENNETH?
MIND YOUR OWN BEESWAX, YOUNG HAROLD. IT'S NONE OF OUR CONCERN...
I WON'T STAND FOR THIS SORT OF THING ON MY PROPERTY, LOGAN. DO YOU HEAR ME, MAN?
YOUR BOY MADE ADVANCES TOWARDS ROSE. HE EVEN THREATENED MY SON.
THIS IS NOT THE SORT OF THING I EXPECT FROM ANY OF MY EMPLOYEES' KIN. IF MY FATHER HAD HIS WAY, YOU'D HAVE BEEN WHIPPED. THANK YOUR GOOD FORTUNE THAT I'M MORE LENIENT --
YESSIR. I'M DEAD SORRY, MASTER JOHN, SIR.
AND SO YOU SHOULD BE. IF THERE'S ANY SORT OF RECURRENCE YOU'LL BE HELD PERSONALLY RESPONSIBLE, UNDERSTAND?
DAMMIT, LOGAN... YOU MUST LEARN TO KEEP A REIN ON THAT BOY OF YOURS.
OH, I WILL, SIR.

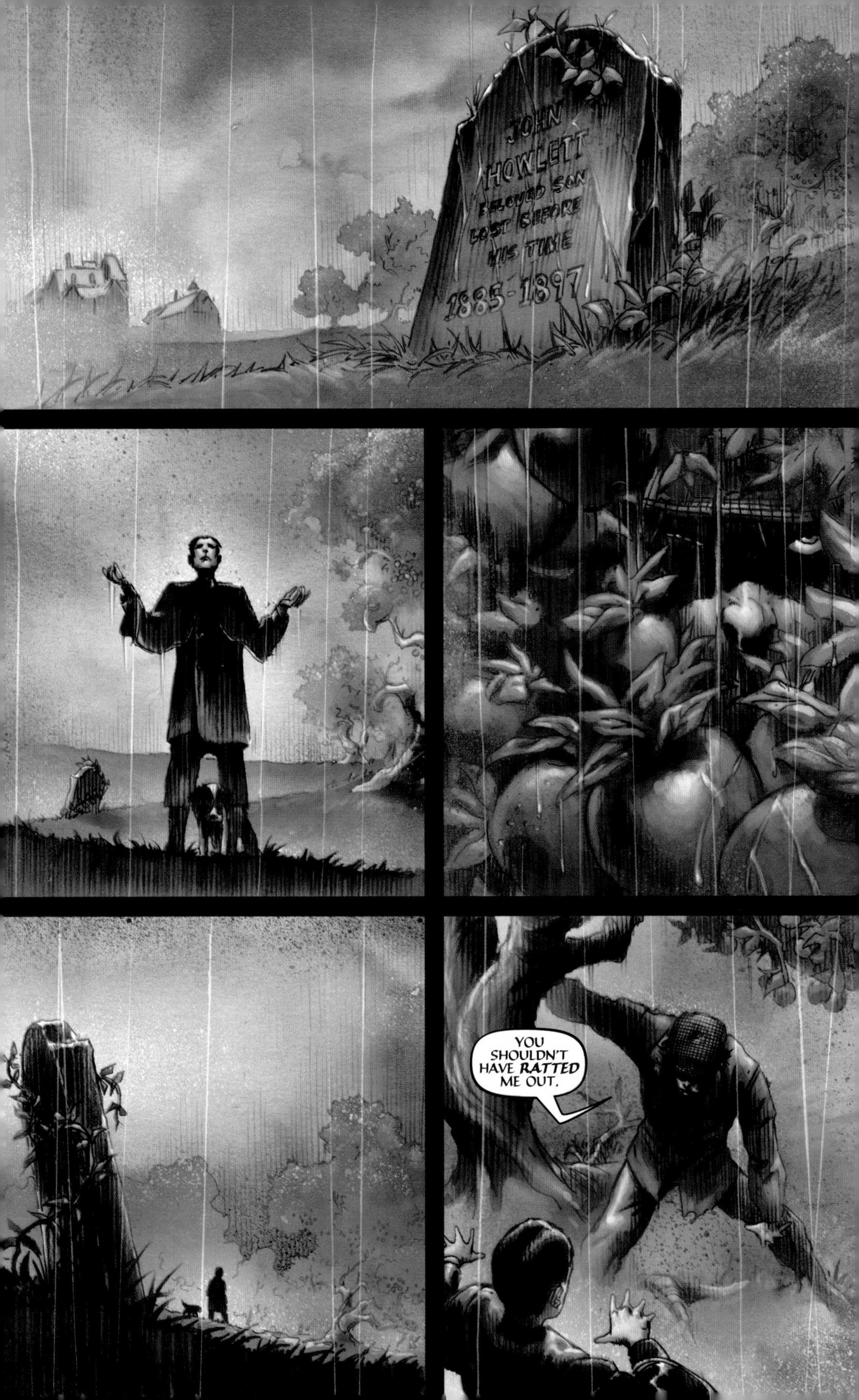
JOHN HOWLETT BELOVED SON LOST BEFORE HIS TIME 1885-1897
YOU SHOULDN'T HAVE RATTED ME OUT.

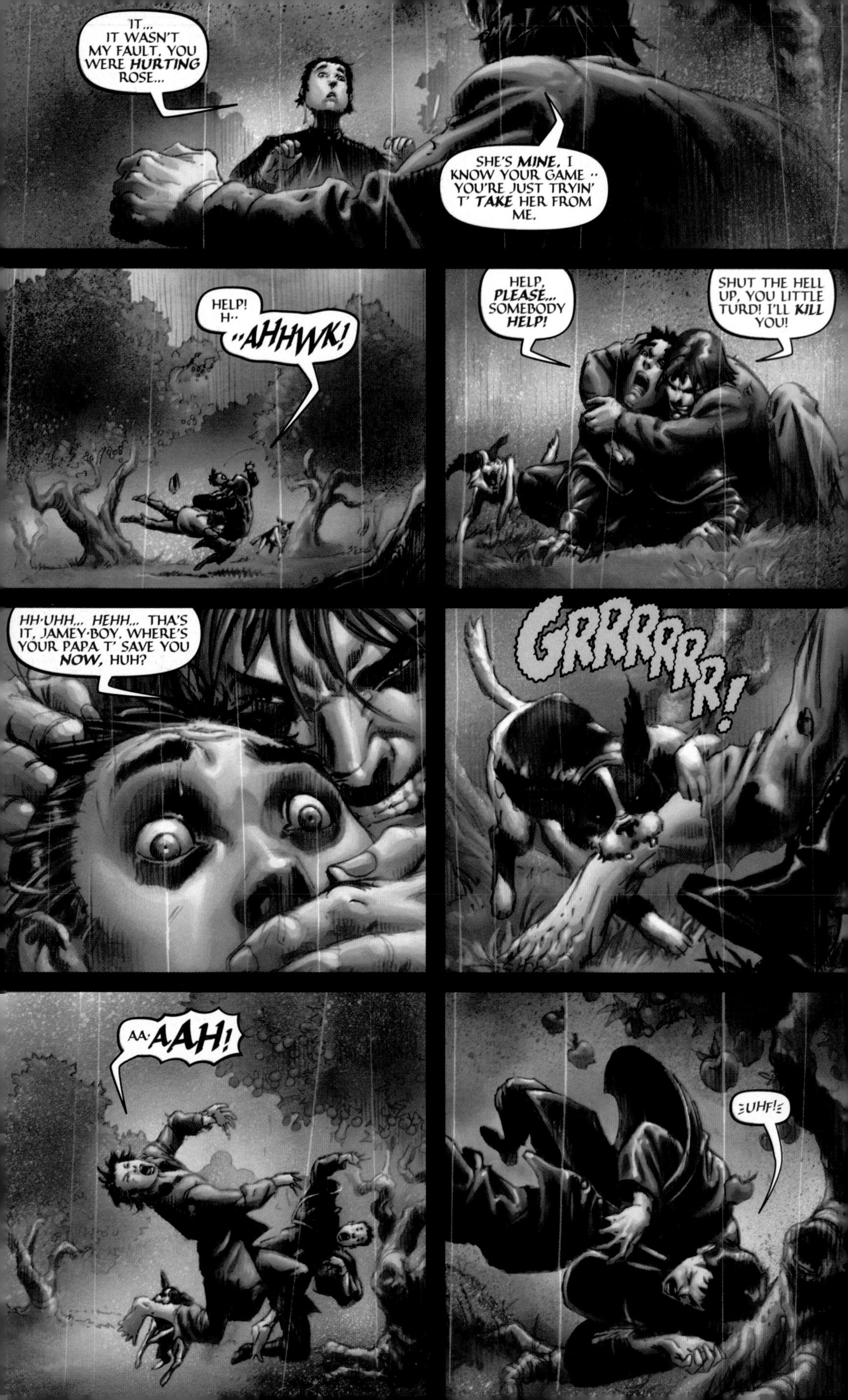
IT... IT WASN'T MY FAULT. YOU WERE HURTING ROSE...
SHE'S MINE. I KNOW YOUR GAME .. YOU'RE JUST TRYIN' T' TAKE HER FROM ME.
HELP! H.. ..AHHWK!
HELP, PLEASE... SOMEBODY HELP!
SHUT THE HELL UP, YOU LITTLE TURD! I'LL KILL YOU!
HH-UHH... HEHH... THA'S IT, JAMEY-BOY. WHERE'S YOUR PAPA T' SAVE YOU NOW, HUH?
GRRRRRR!
AA-AAH!
UHF!

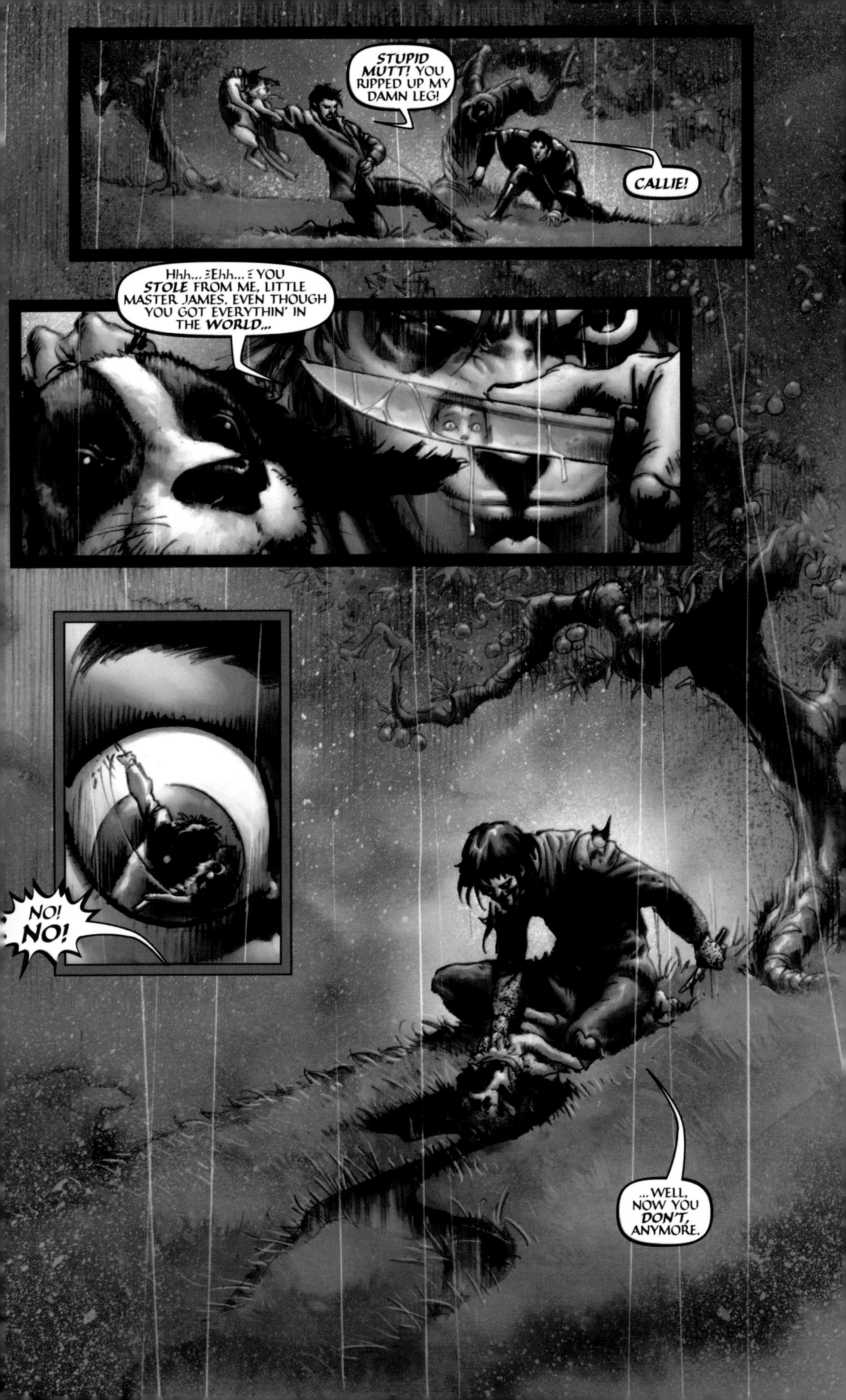
STUPID MUTT! YOU RIPPED UP MY DAMN LEG!
CALLIE!
Hhh... ƎEhh... Ǝ YOU STOLE FROM ME, LITTLE MASTER JAMES, EVEN THOUGH YOU GOT EVERYTHIN' IN THE WORLD...
NO! NO!
...WELL, NOW YOU DON'T, ANYMORE.

DON'T SAY I DIDN'T *WARN* YOU, LOGAN·· I GAVE YOU EVERY CHANCE TO DISCIPLINE THE BOY, HAD YOU BEEN A *SUITABLE* PARENT, THIS WOULD HAVE NEVER HAPPENED.

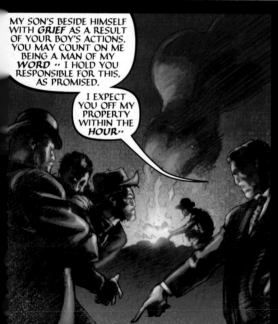

MY SON'S BESIDE HIMSELF WITH *GRIEF* AS A RESULT OF YOUR BOY'S ACTIONS. YOU MAY COUNT ON ME BEING A MAN OF MY *WORD* ·· I HOLD YOU RESPONSIBLE FOR THIS, AS PROMISED.

I EXPECT YOU OFF MY PROPERTY WITHIN THE *HOUR*··

DON'T YOU TALK T' ME LIKE *THAT,* HOWLETT! I SEEN THE WAY Y' ACT AROUND US... YOU THINK YE'RE *BETTER* THAN US!

YA CAN'T *DO* THIS TO ME! I'LL HAVE YOUR BLOODY *HIDE*··

I WON'T *HAVE* YOUR INSOLENCE, DO YOU *HEAR ME,* LOGAN? AFTER THIS, BE THANKFUL I DON'T HAVE YOU BOTH *HUNG!*

NOW, GET THIS MAN OUT OF MY *SIGHT.*

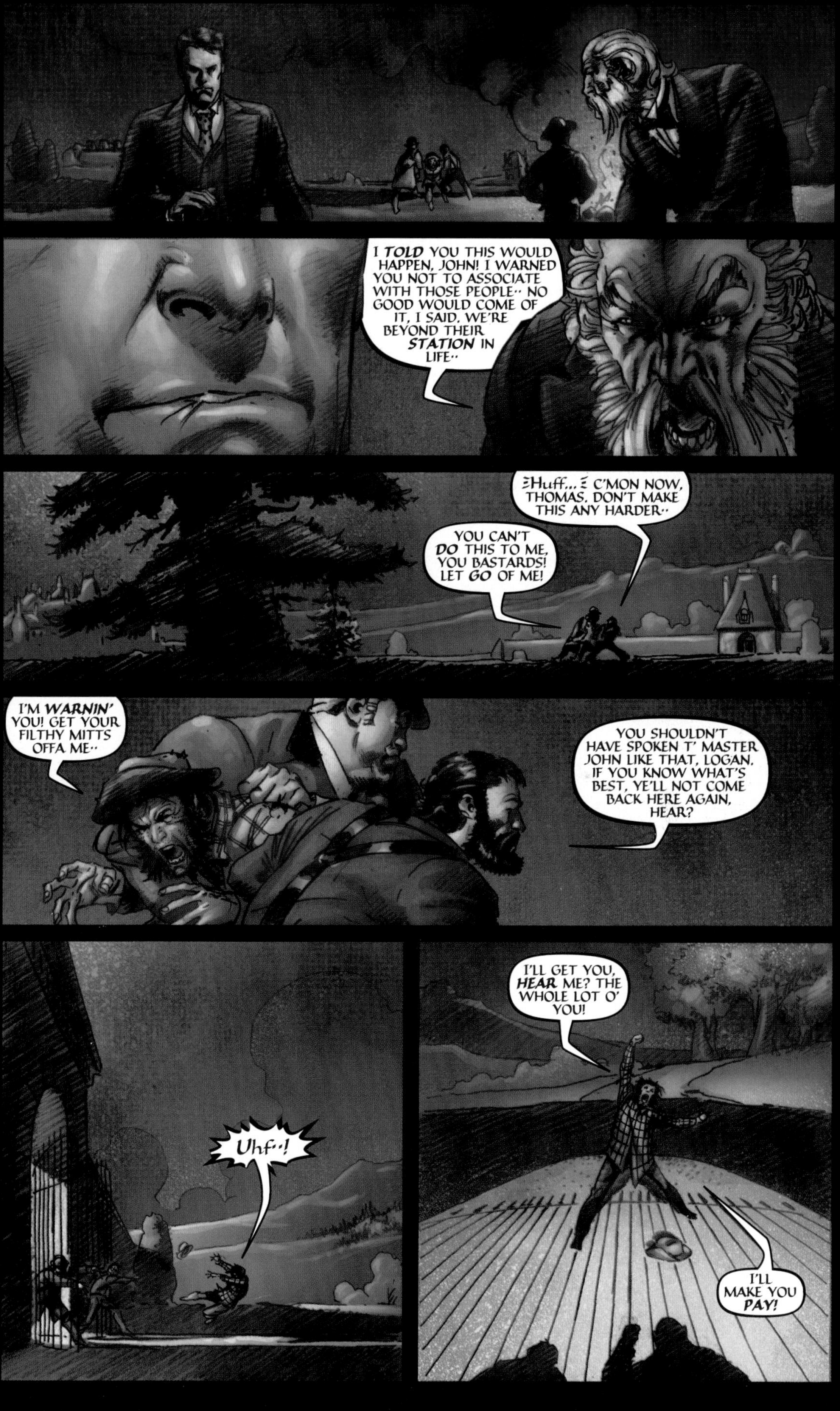
I TOLD YOU THIS WOULD HAPPEN, JOHN! I WARNED YOU NOT TO ASSOCIATE WITH THOSE PEOPLE·· NO GOOD WOULD COME OF IT, I SAID. WE'RE BEYOND THEIR STATION IN LIFE··
Huff... C'MON NOW, THOMAS. DON'T MAKE THIS ANY HARDER··
YOU CAN'T DO THIS TO ME, YOU BASTARDS! LET GO OF ME!
I'M WARNIN' YOU! GET YOUR FILTHY MITTS OFFA ME··
YOU SHOULDN'T HAVE SPOKEN T' MASTER JOHN LIKE THAT, LOGAN. IF YOU KNOW WHAT'S BEST, YE'LL NOT COME BACK HERE AGAIN, HEAR?
Uhf··!
I'LL GET YOU, HEAR ME? THE WHOLE LOT O' YOU!
I'LL MAKE YOU PAY!

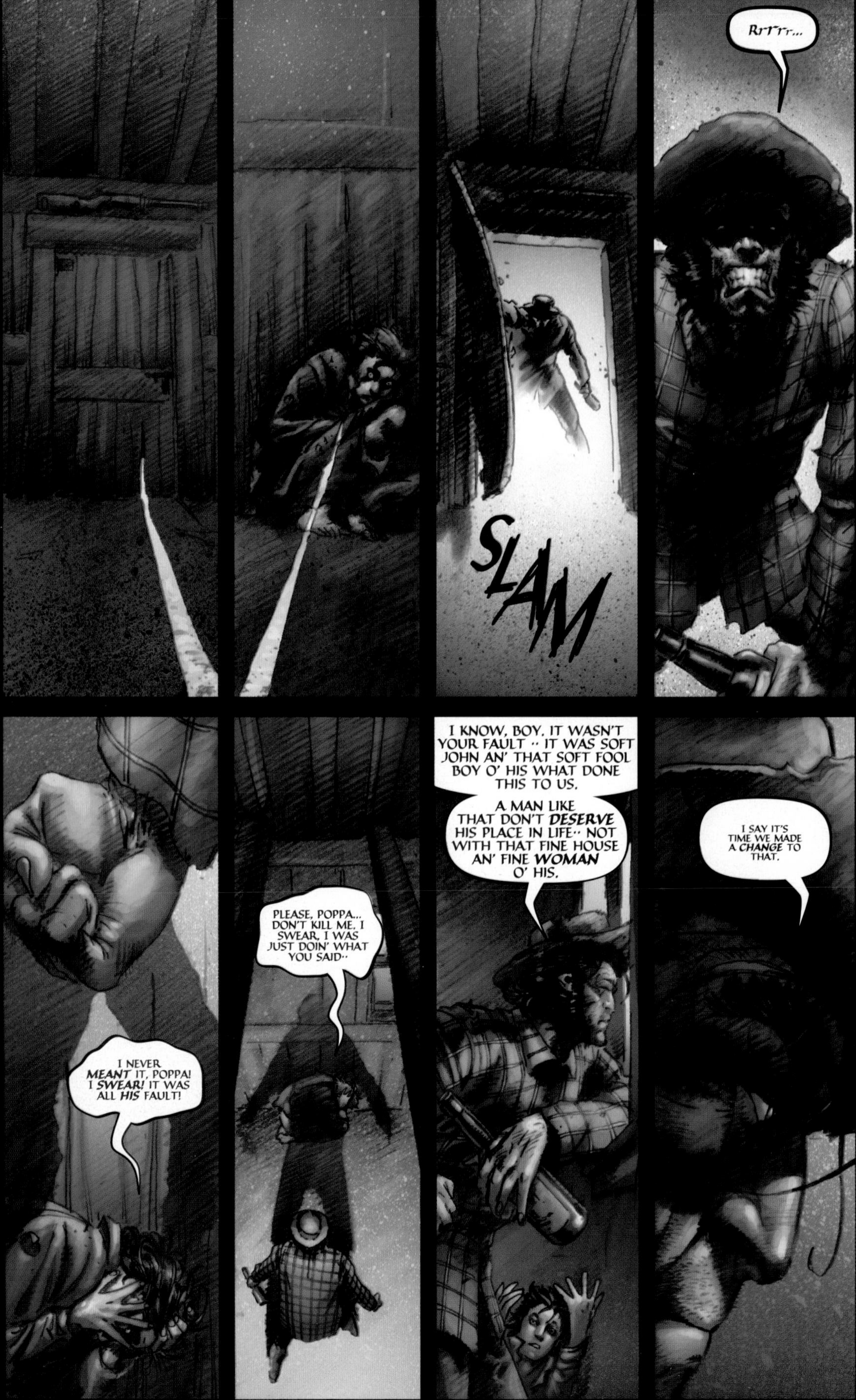
Rrrrr...
SLAM
I NEVER MEANT IT, POPPA! I SWEAR! IT WAS ALL HIS FAULT!
PLEASE, POPPA... DON'T KILL ME, I SWEAR, I WAS JUST DOIN' WHAT YOU SAID..
I KNOW, BOY. IT WASN'T YOUR FAULT .. IT WAS SOFT JOHN AN' THAT SOFT FOOL BOY O' HIS WHAT DONE THIS TO US.
A MAN LIKE THAT DON'T DESERVE HIS PLACE IN LIFE.. NOT WITH THAT FINE HOUSE AN' FINE WOMAN O' HIS.
I SAY IT'S TIME WE MADE A CHANGE TO THAT.

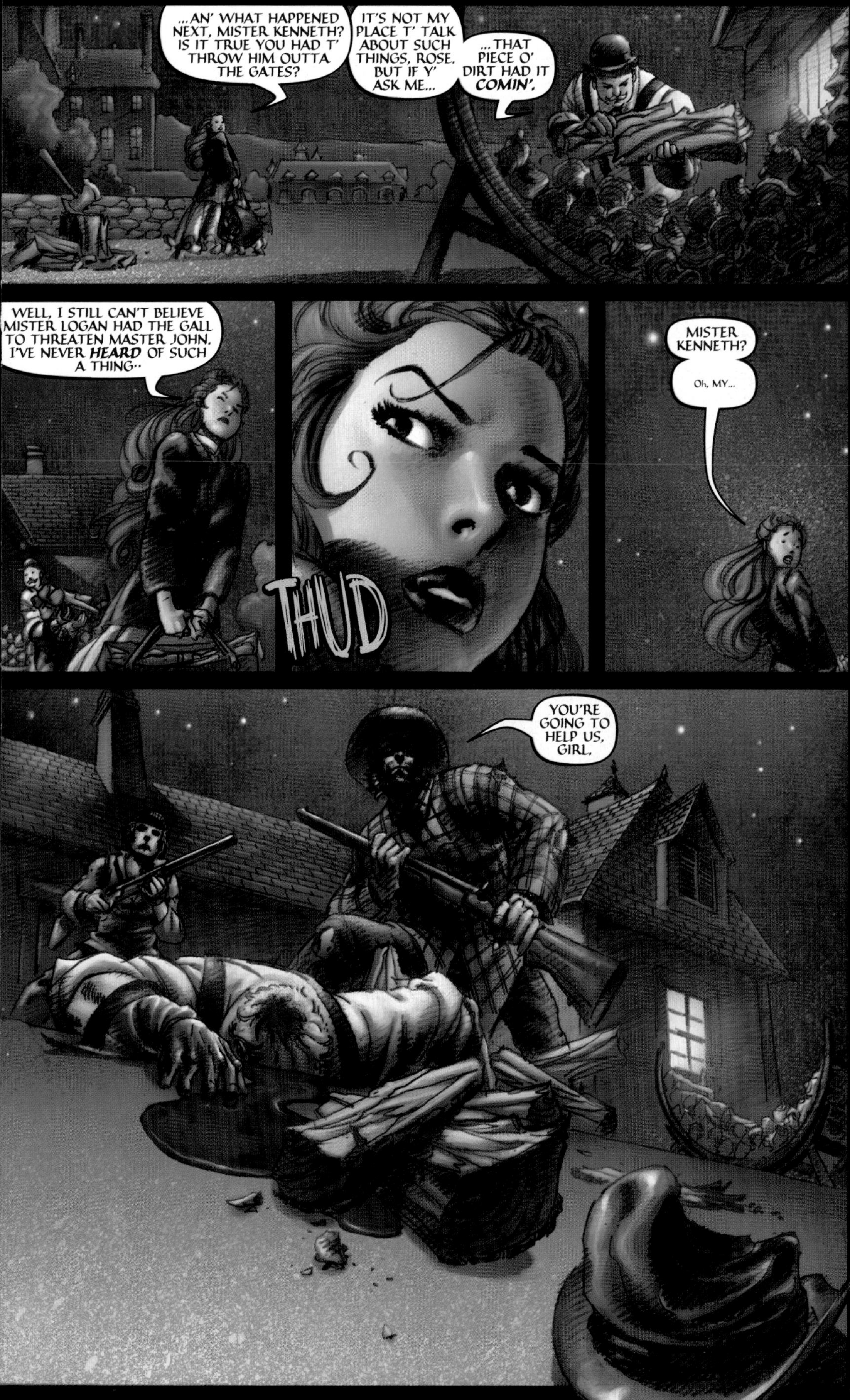
...AN' WHAT HAPPENED NEXT, MISTER KENNETH? IS IT TRUE YOU HAD T' THROW HIM OUTTA THE GATES?
IT'S NOT MY PLACE T' TALK ABOUT SUCH THINGS, ROSE. BUT IF Y' ASK ME...
...THAT PIECE O' DIRT HAD IT COMIN'.
WELL, I STILL CAN'T BELIEVE MISTER LOGAN HAD THE GALL TO THREATEN MASTER JOHN. I'VE NEVER HEARD OF SUCH A THING..
THUD
MISTER KENNETH?
Oh, MY...
YOU'RE GOING TO HELP US, GIRL.

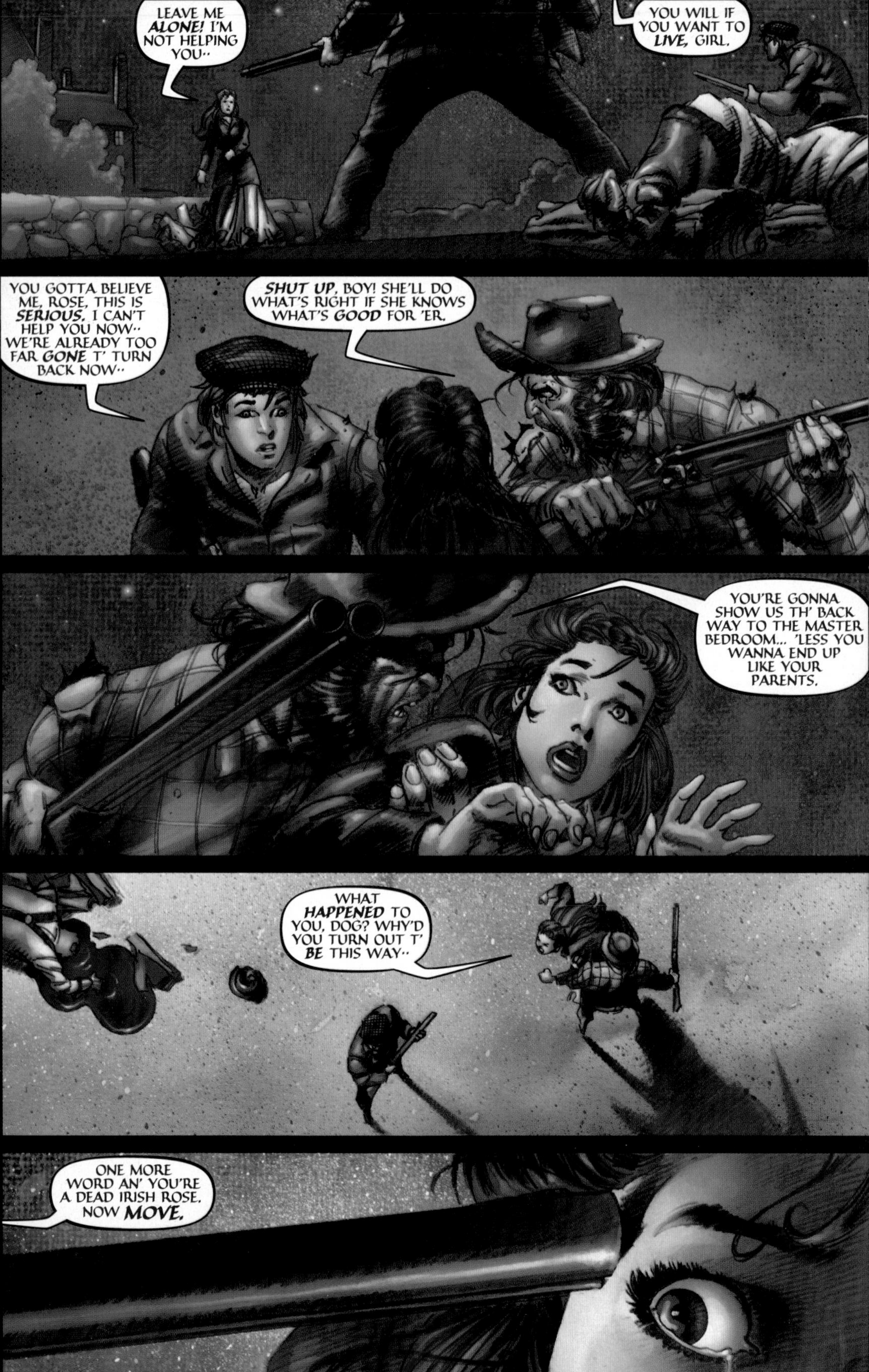

LEAVE ME ALONE! I'M NOT HELPING YOU..
YOU WILL IF YOU WANT TO LIVE, GIRL.
YOU GOTTA BELIEVE ME, ROSE, THIS IS SERIOUS. I CAN'T HELP YOU NOW.. WE'RE ALREADY TOO FAR GONE T' TURN BACK NOW..
SHUT UP, BOY! SHE'LL DO WHAT'S RIGHT IF SHE KNOWS WHAT'S GOOD FOR 'ER.
YOU'RE GONNA SHOW US TH' BACK WAY TO THE MASTER BEDROOM... 'LESS YOU WANNA END UP LIKE YOUR PARENTS.
WHAT HAPPENED TO YOU, DOG? WHY'D YOU TURN OUT T' BE THIS WAY..
ONE MORE WORD AN' YOU'RE A DEAD IRISH ROSE. NOW MOVE.

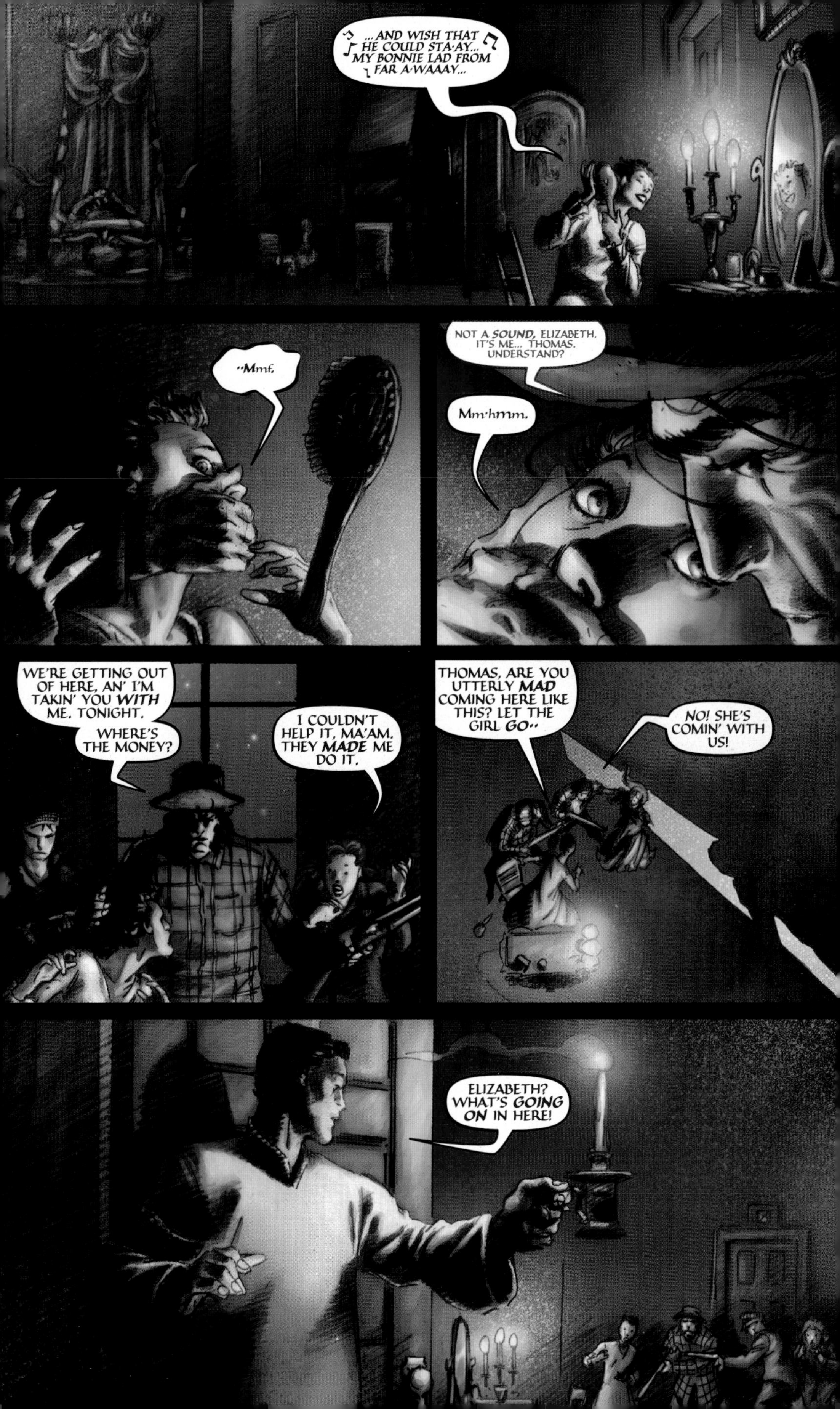
...AND WISH THAT HE COULD STA-AY... MY BONNIE LAD FROM FAR A-WAAAY...
--Mmf.
NOT A SOUND, ELIZABETH. IT'S ME... THOMAS. UNDERSTAND?
Mm-hmm.
WE'RE GETTING OUT OF HERE, AN' I'M TAKIN' YOU WITH ME. TONIGHT.
WHERE'S THE MONEY?
I COULDN'T HELP IT, MA'AM, THEY MADE ME DO IT.
THOMAS, ARE YOU UTTERLY MAD COMING HERE LIKE THIS? LET THE GIRL GO--
NO! SHE'S COMIN' WITH US!
ELIZABETH? WHAT'S GOING ON IN HERE!

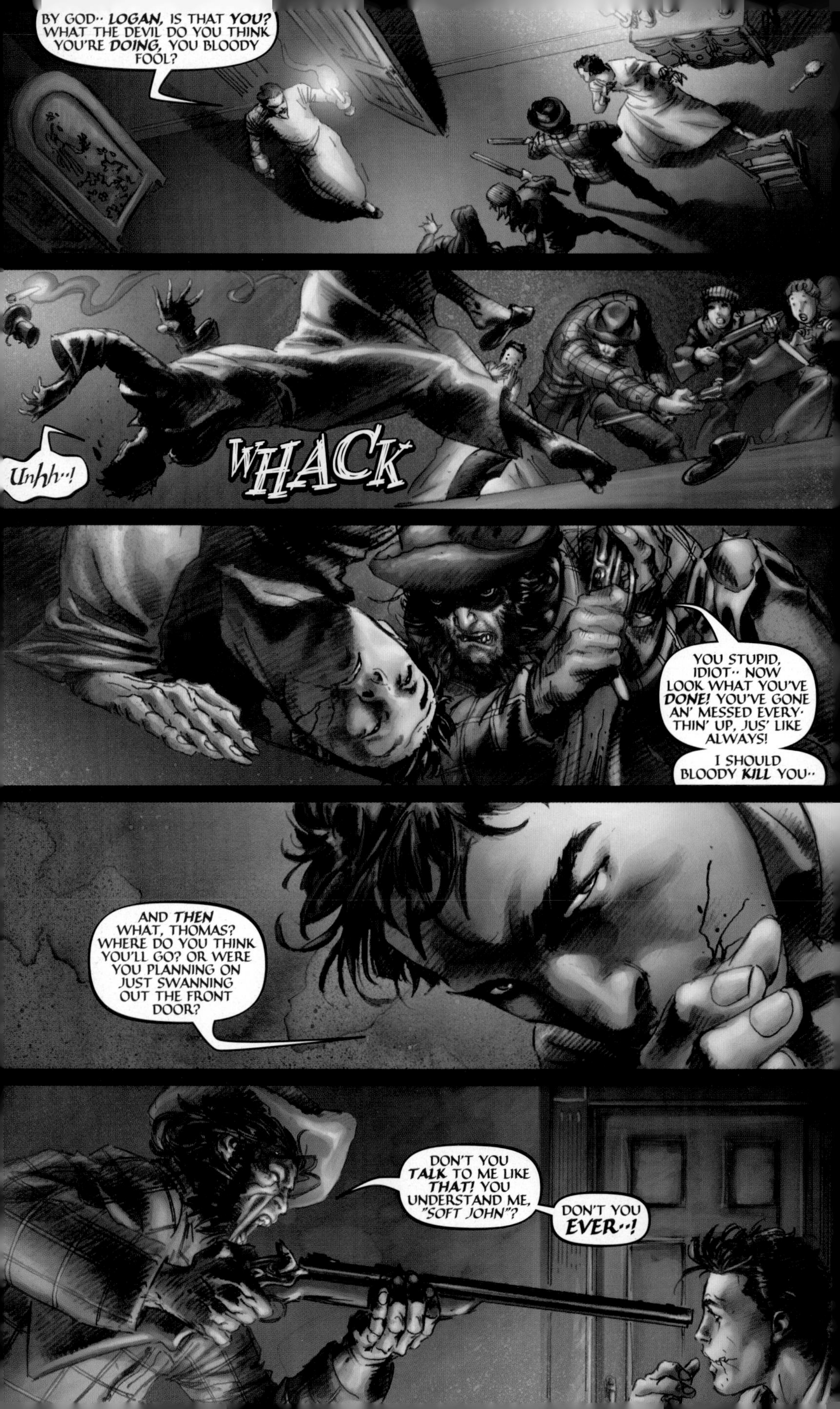
BY GOD·· LOGAN, IS THAT YOU? WHAT THE DEVIL DO YOU THINK YOU'RE DOING, YOU BLOODY FOOL?
Unhh··!
WHACK
YOU STUPID, IDIOT·· NOW LOOK WHAT YOU'VE DONE! YOU'VE GONE AN' MESSED EVERY· THIN' UP, JUS' LIKE ALWAYS!
I SHOULD BLOODY KILL YOU··
AND THEN WHAT, THOMAS? WHERE DO YOU THINK YOU'LL GO? OR WERE YOU PLANNING ON JUST SWANNING OUT THE FRONT DOOR?
DON'T YOU TALK TO ME LIKE THAT! YOU UNDERSTAND ME, "SOFT JOHN"?
DON'T YOU EVER··!

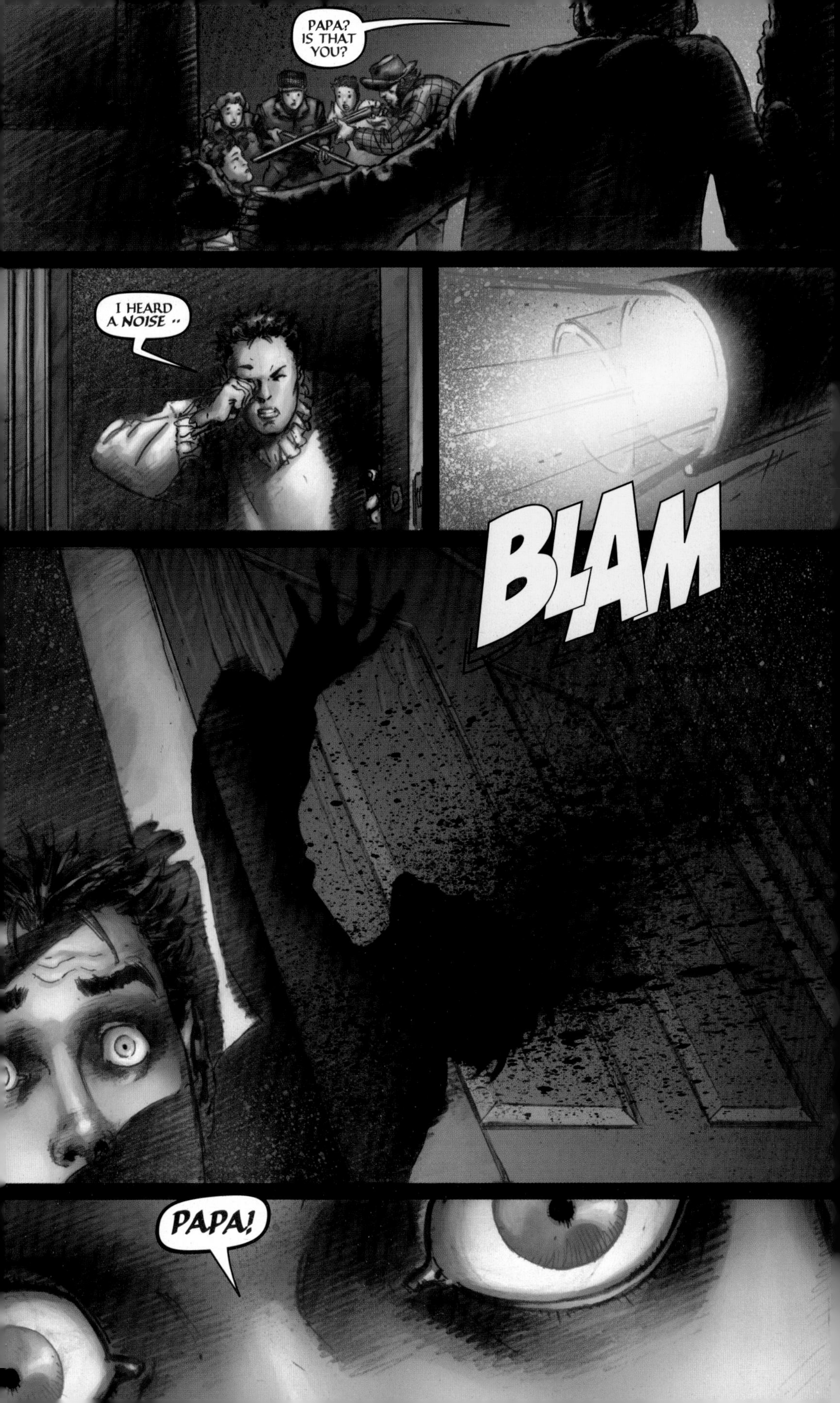
PAPA? IS THAT YOU?
I HEARD A NOISE ..
BLAM
PAPA!

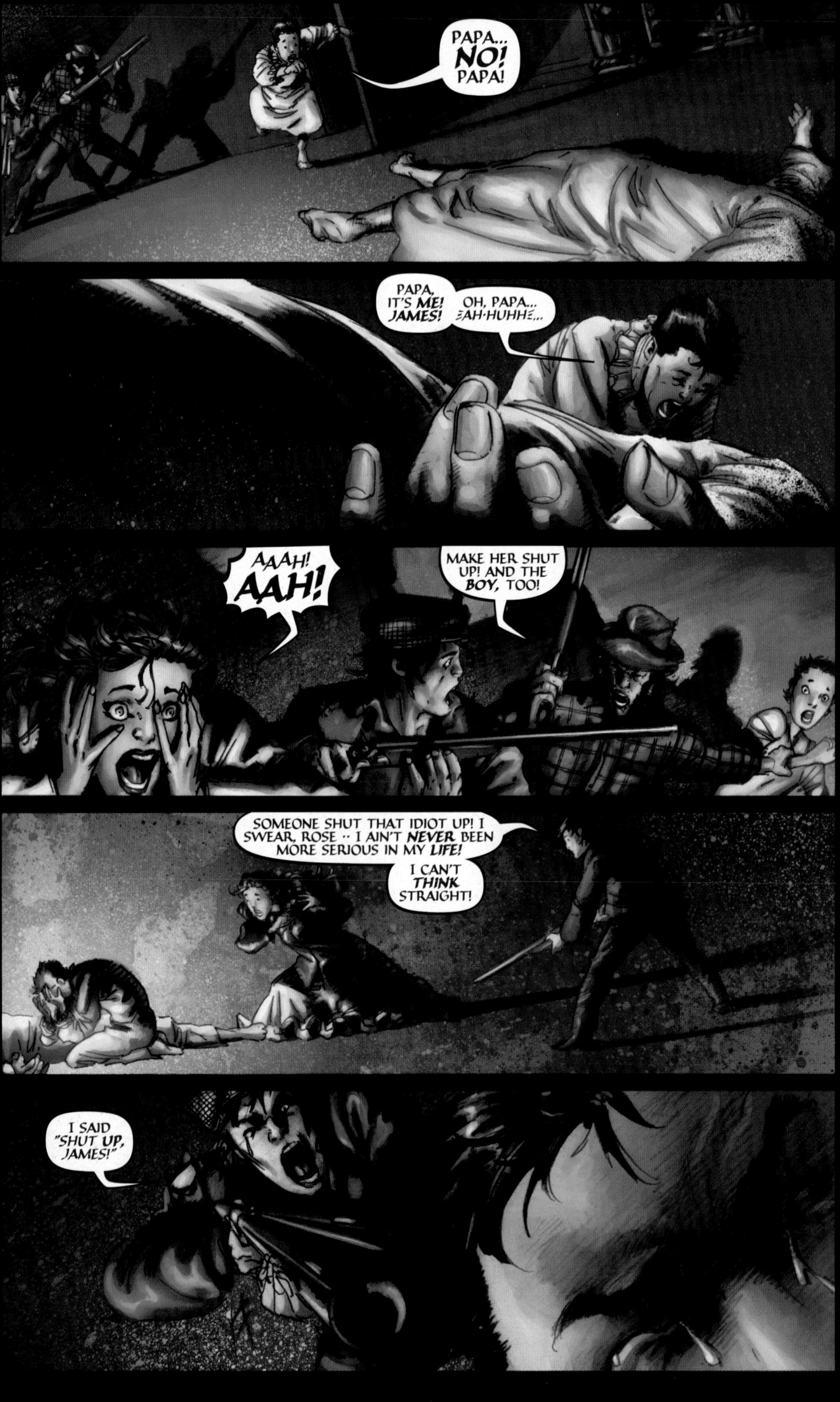
PAPA... NO! PAPA!
PAPA, IT'S ME! JAMES!
OH, PAPA... AH-HUHH...
AAAH! AAH!
MAKE HER SHUT UP! AND THE BOY, TOO!
SOMEONE SHUT THAT IDIOT UP! I SWEAR, ROSE -- I AIN'T NEVER BEEN MORE SERIOUS IN MY LIFE!
I CAN'T THINK STRAIGHT!
I SAID "SHUT UP, JAMES!"

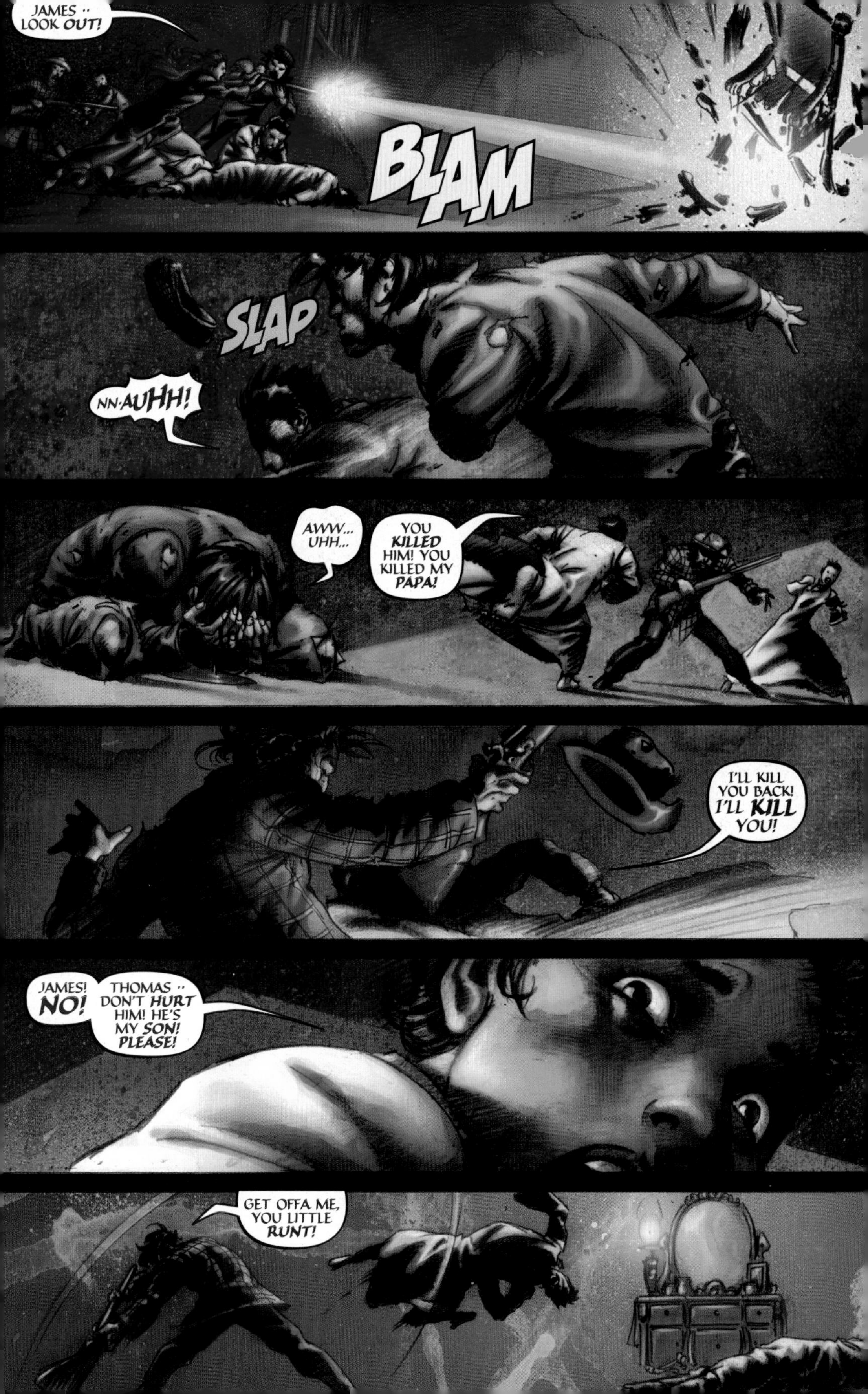
JAMES .. LOOK OUT!
BLAM
SLAP
NN-AUHH!
AWW... UHH...
YOU KILLED HIM! YOU KILLED MY PAPA!
I'LL KILL YOU BACK! I'LL KILL YOU!
JAMES! NO!
THOMAS .. DON'T HURT HIM! HE'S MY SON! PLEASE!
GET OFFA ME, YOU LITTLE RUNT!

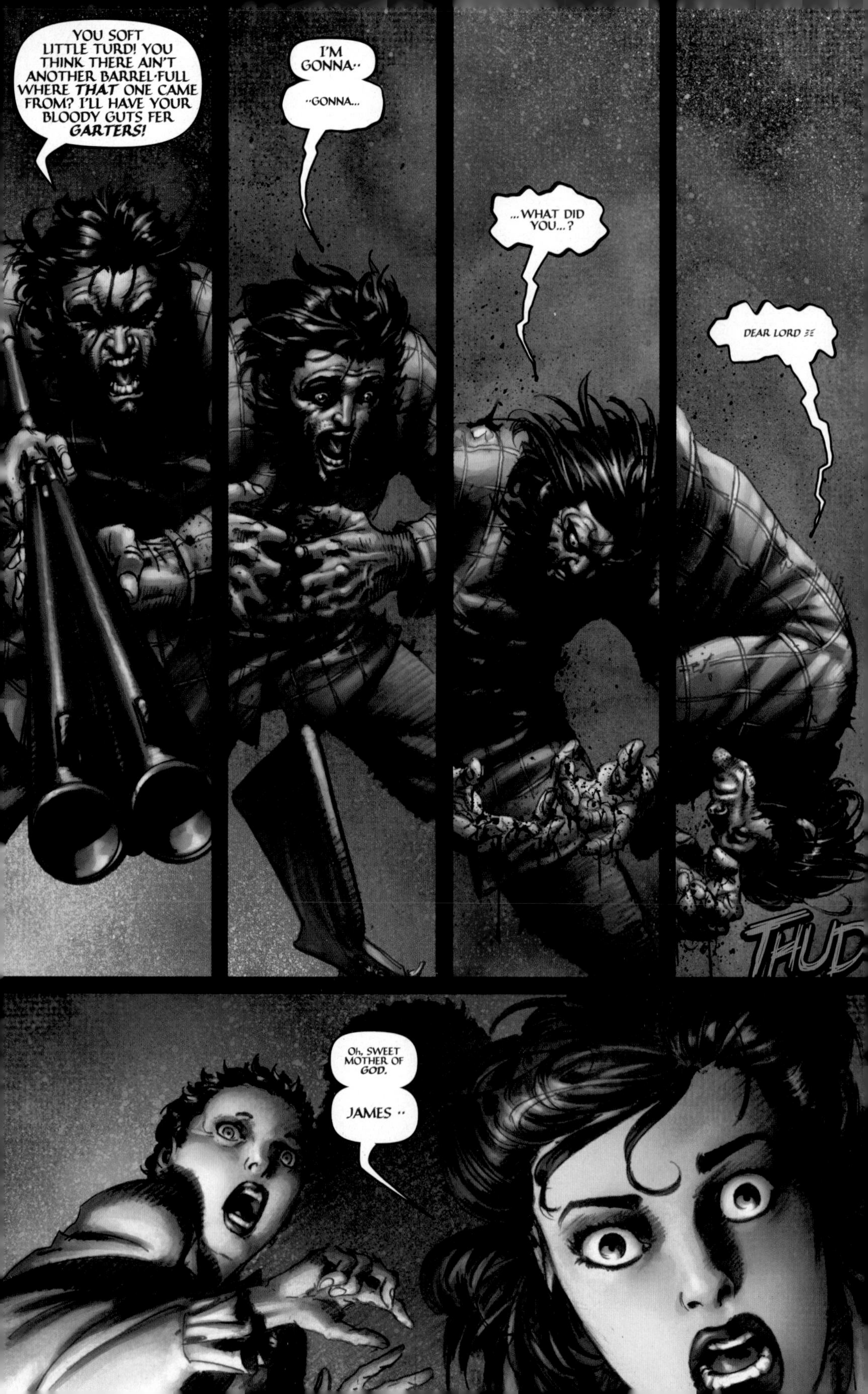
YOU SOFT LITTLE TURD! YOU THINK THERE AIN'T ANOTHER BARREL-FULL WHERE *THAT* ONE CAME FROM? I'LL HAVE YOUR BLOODY GUTS FER *GARTERS!*
I'M GONNA..
..GONNA...
...WHAT DID YOU...?
DEAR LORD
THUD
Oh, SWEET MOTHER OF *GOD.*
JAMES ..

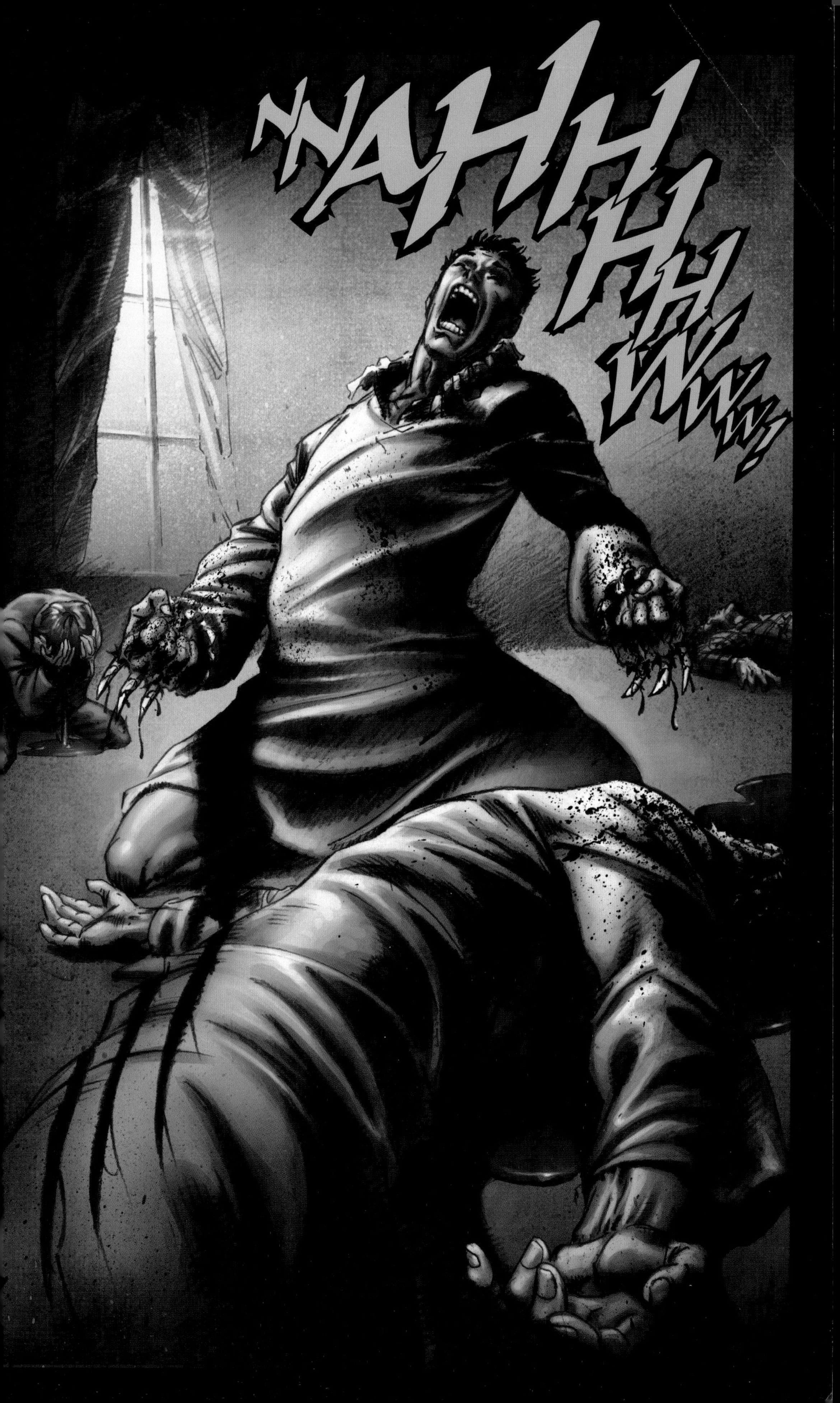
NNAHHHHWWW!

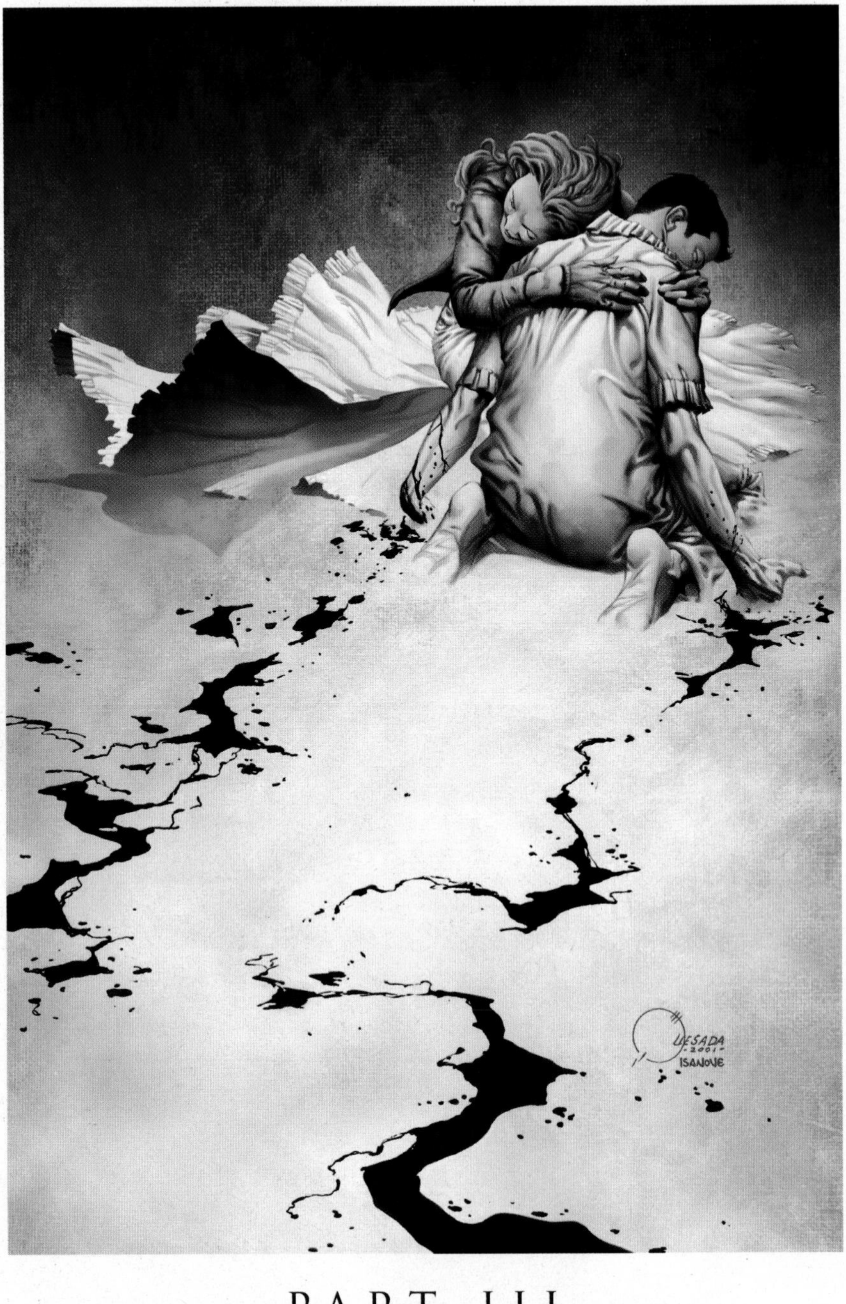
QUESADA
2001
ISANOVE

PART III

THE BEAST WITHIN

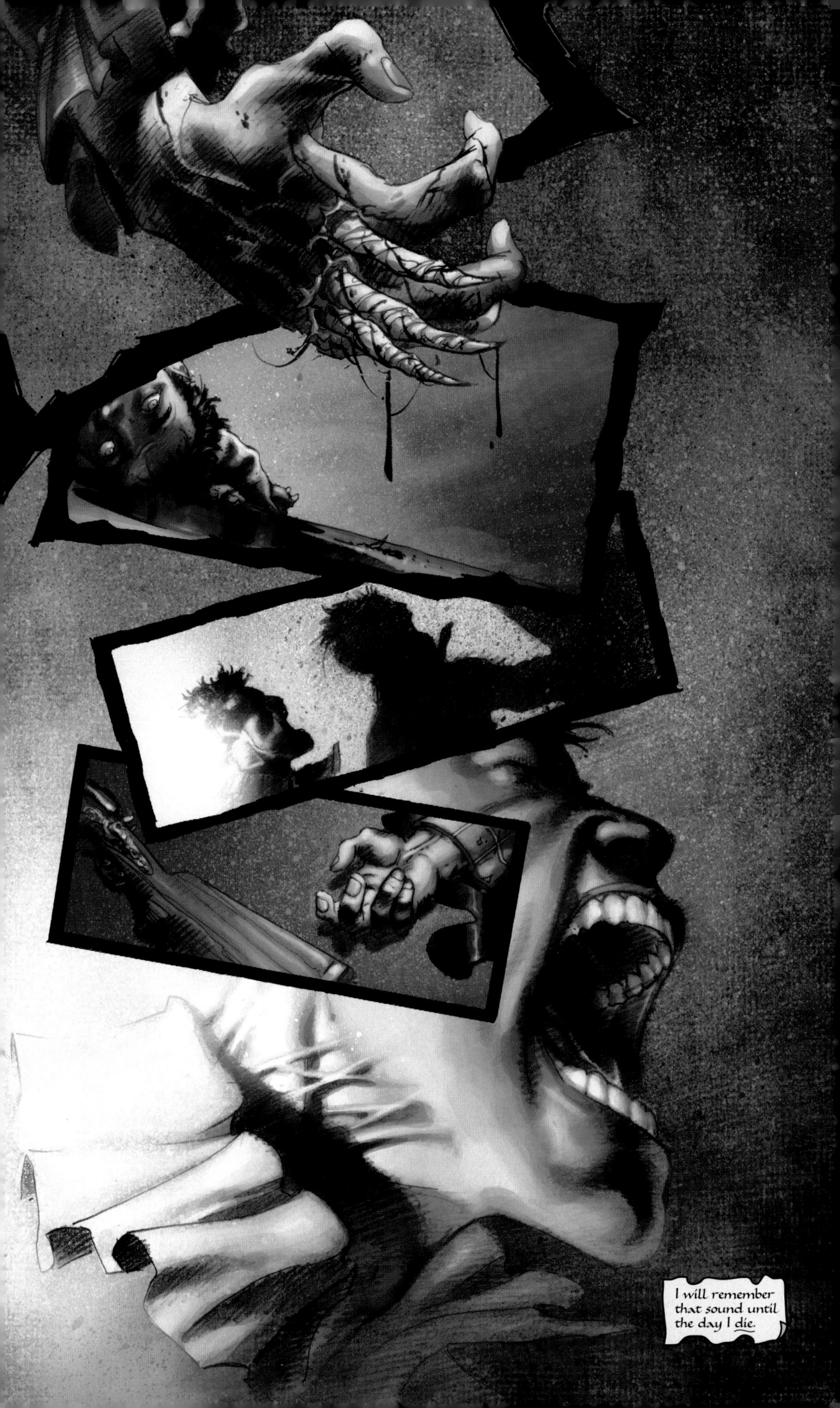
I will remember that sound until the day I die.

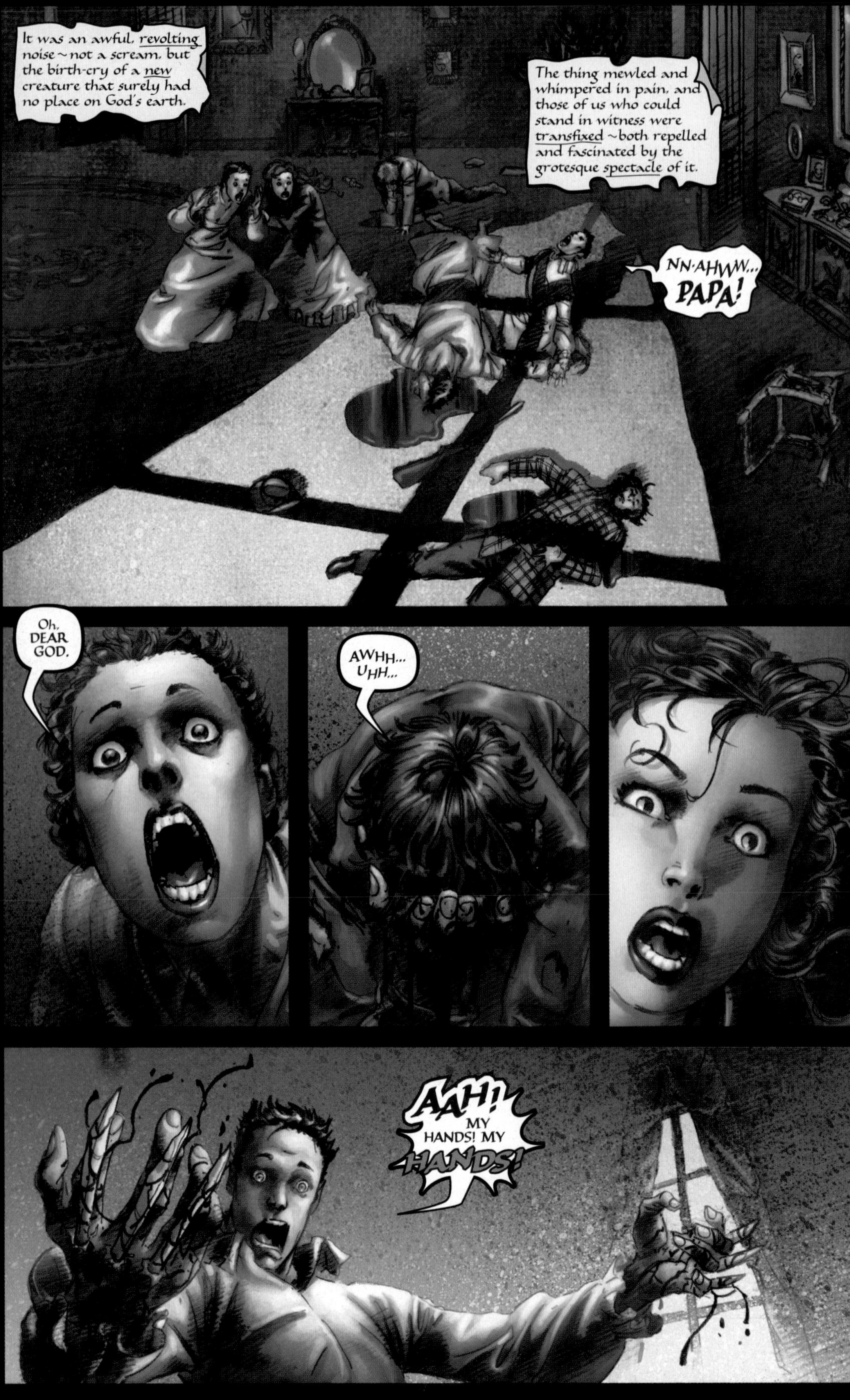
It was an awful, revolting noise ~ not a scream, but the birth-cry of a new creature that surely had no place on God's earth.
The thing mewled and whimpered in pain, and those of us who could stand in witness were transfixed ~ both repelled and fascinated by the grotesque spectacle of it.
NN-AHWW... PAPA!
Oh, DEAR GOD.
AWHH... UHH...
AAH! MY HANDS! MY HANDS!

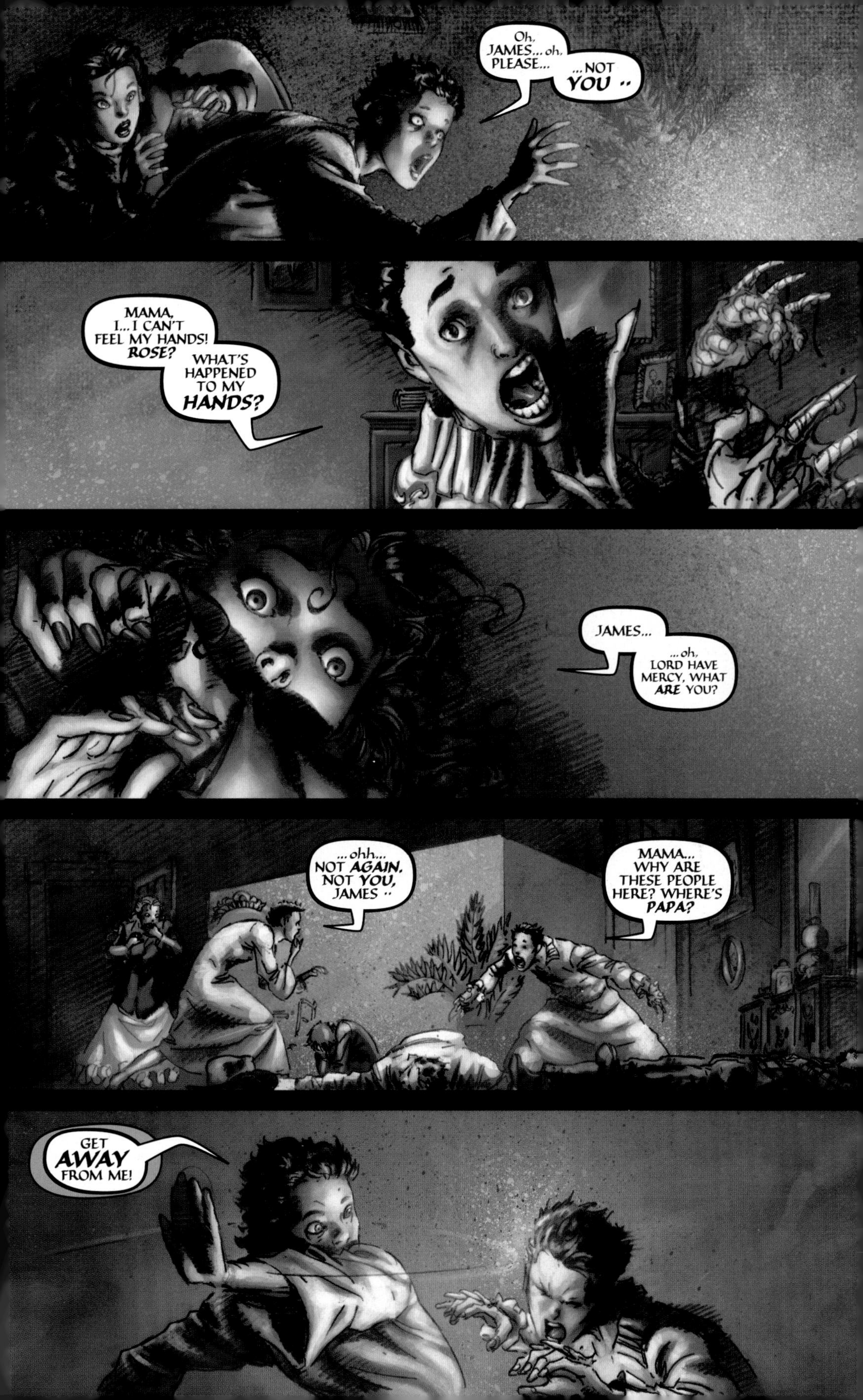

Oh, JAMES... oh, PLEASE...
...NOT YOU ..
MAMA, I... I CAN'T FEEL MY HANDS! ROSE?
WHAT'S HAPPENED TO MY HANDS?
JAMES...
...oh, LORD HAVE MERCY, WHAT ARE YOU?
...ohh... NOT AGAIN, NOT YOU, JAMES ..
MAMA... WHY ARE THESE PEOPLE HERE? WHERE'S PAPA?
GET AWAY FROM ME!

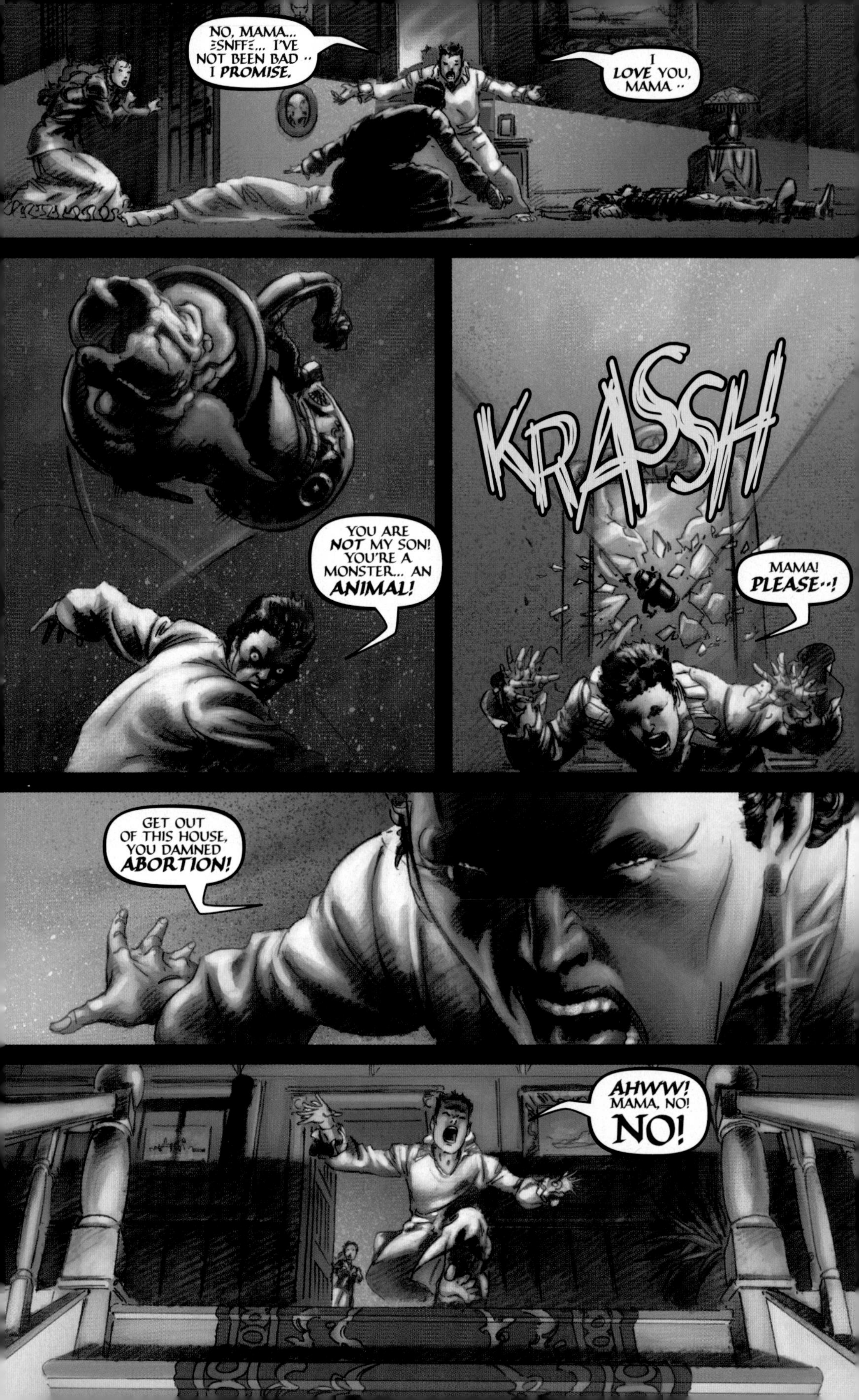
NO, MAMA... SNFF... I'VE NOT BEEN BAD .. I PROMISE.
I LOVE YOU, MAMA ..
YOU ARE NOT MY SON! YOU'RE A MONSTER... AN ANIMAL!
KRASSH
MAMA! PLEASE..!
GET OUT OF THIS HOUSE, YOU DAMNED ABORTION!
AHWW! MAMA, NO! NO!

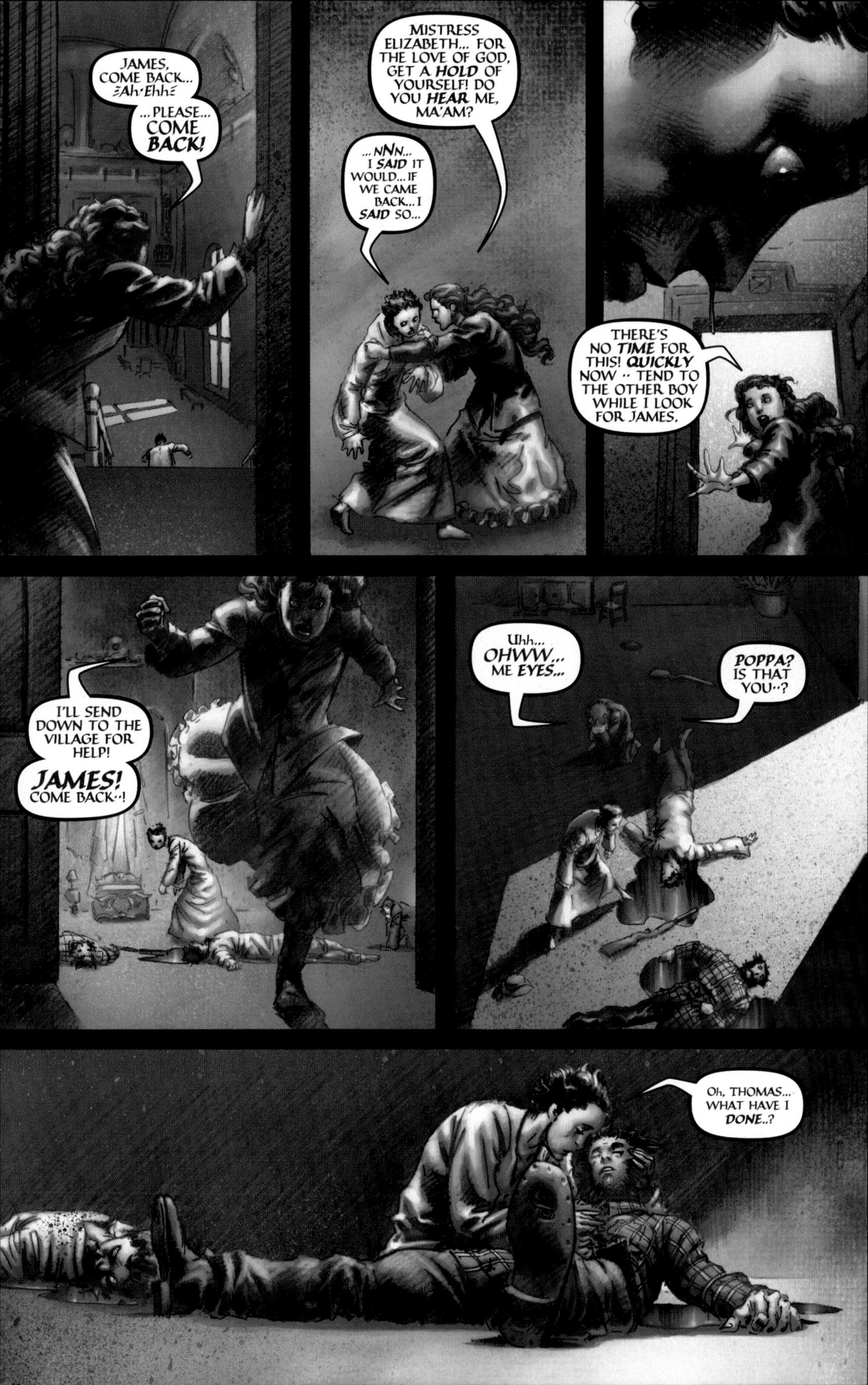
JAMES, COME BACK... Ah-Ehh
...PLEASE... COME BACK!
MISTRESS ELIZABETH... FOR THE LOVE OF GOD, GET A HOLD OF YOURSELF! DO YOU HEAR ME, MA'AM?
...NNN... I SAID IT WOULD... IF WE CAME BACK... I SAID SO...
THERE'S NO TIME FOR THIS! QUICKLY NOW -- TEND TO THE OTHER BOY WHILE I LOOK FOR JAMES.
I'LL SEND DOWN TO THE VILLAGE FOR HELP!
JAMES! COME BACK--!
Uhh... OHWW... ME EYES...
POPPA? IS THAT YOU--?
Oh, THOMAS... WHAT HAVE I DONE..?

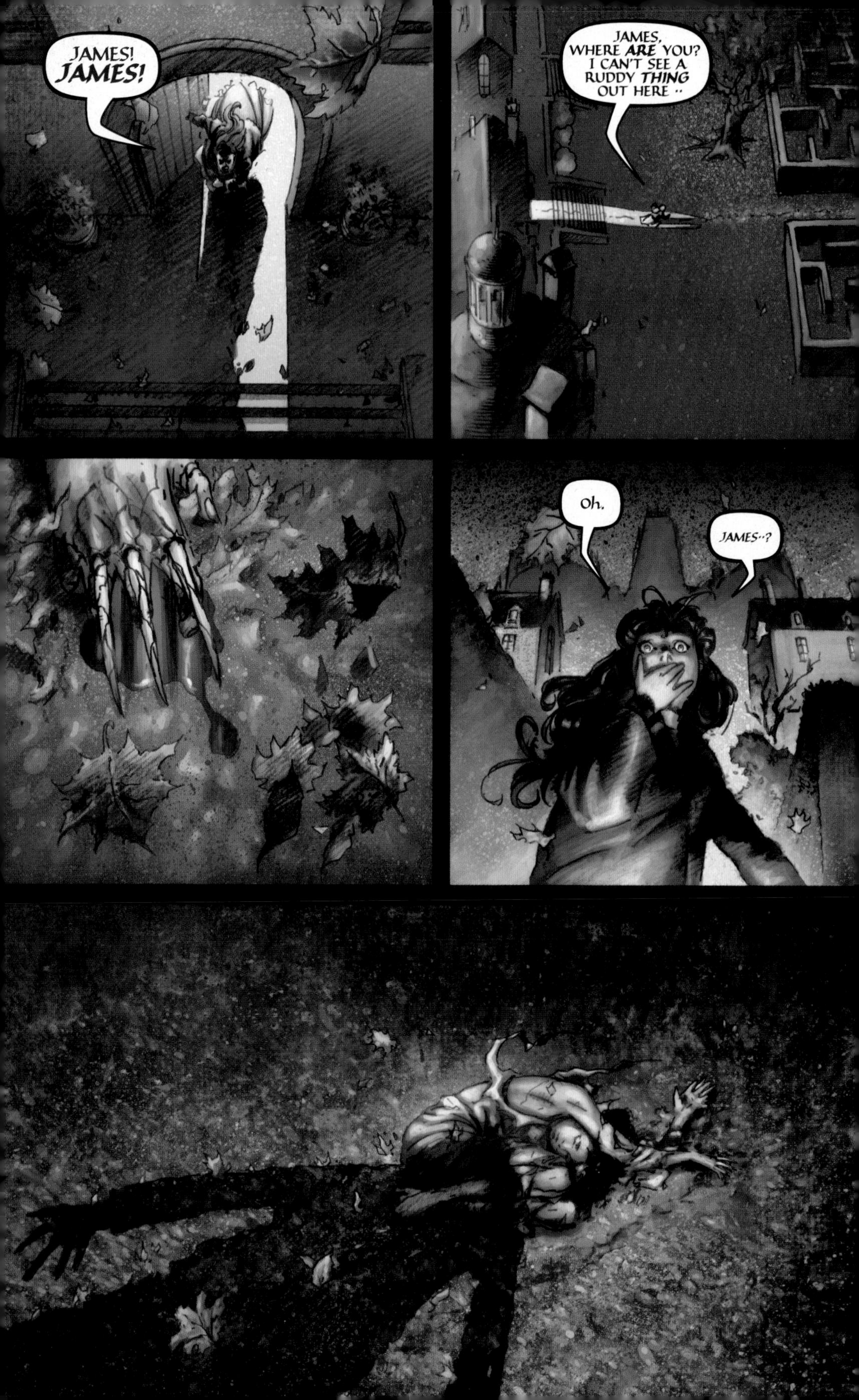
JAMES! JAMES!
JAMES, WHERE ARE YOU? I CAN'T SEE A RUDDY THING OUT HERE ..
Oh.
JAMES..?

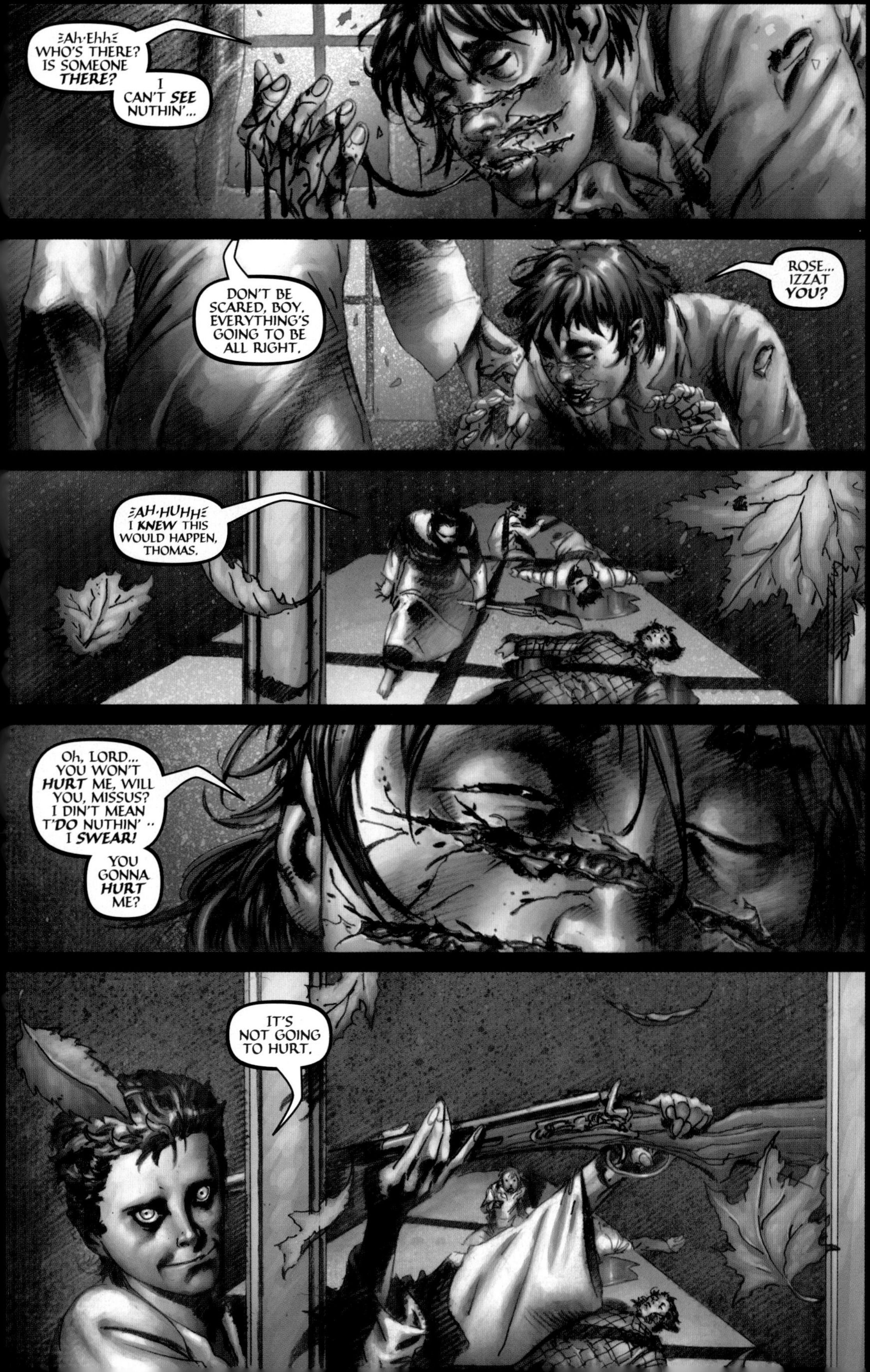

ƎAh·EhhƐ WHO'S THERE? IS SOMEONE THERE?
I CAN'T SEE NUTHIN'...
DON'T BE SCARED, BOY. EVERYTHING'S GOING TO BE ALL RIGHT.
ROSE... IZZAT YOU?
ƎAH·HUHHƐ I KNEW THIS WOULD HAPPEN, THOMAS.
Oh, LORD... YOU WON'T HURT ME, WILL YOU, MISSUS? I DIN'T MEAN T'DO NUTHIN' .. I SWEAR!
YOU GONNA HURT ME?
IT'S NOT GOING TO HURT.

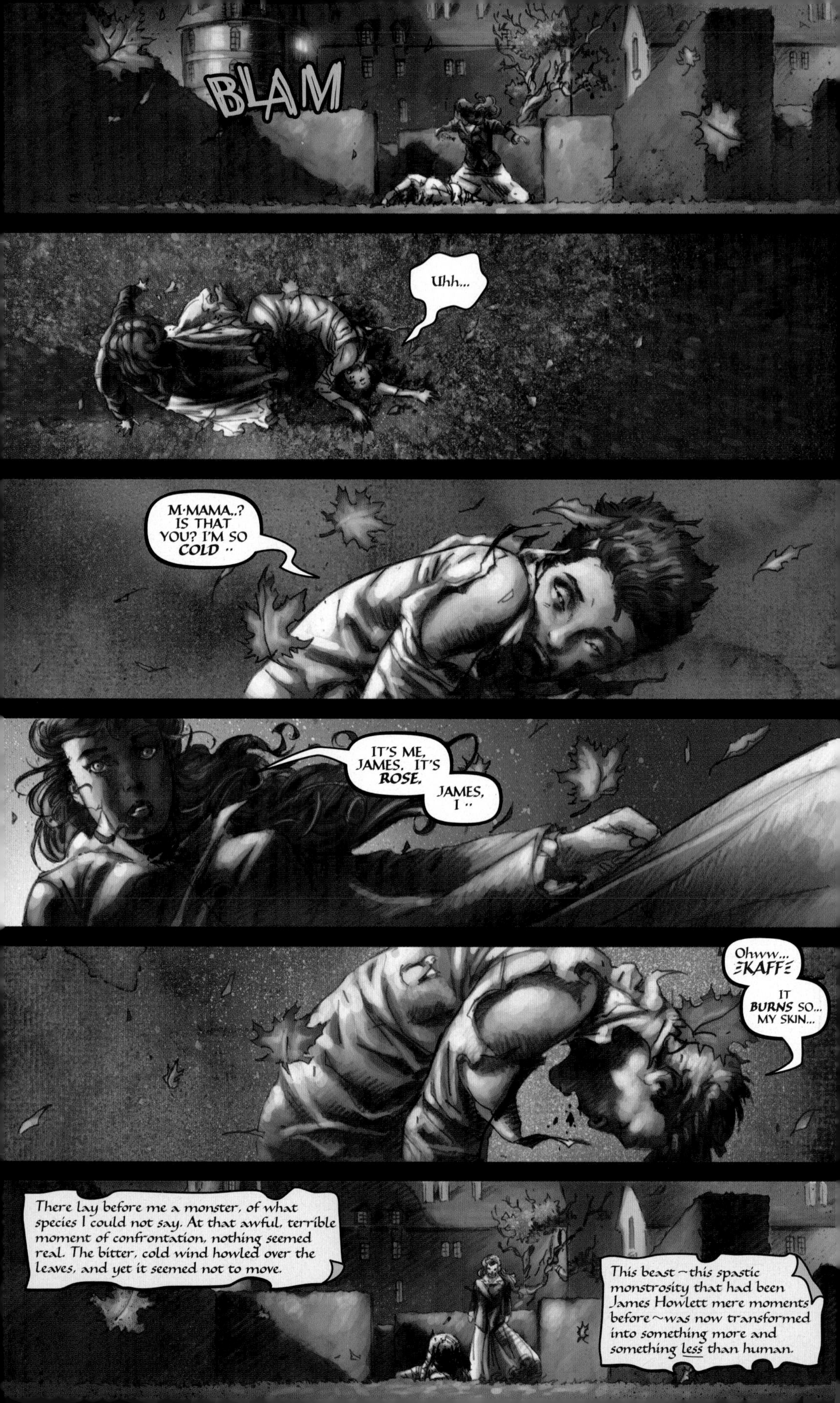
BLAM
Uhh...
M-MAMA..? IS THAT YOU? I'M SO COLD ..
IT'S ME, JAMES. IT'S ROSE.
JAMES, I ..
Ohww... KAFF
IT BURNS SO... MY SKIN...
There lay before me a monster, of what species I could not say. At that awful, terrible moment of confrontation, nothing seemed real. The bitter, cold wind howled over the leaves, and yet it seemed not to move.
This beast ~ this spastic monstrosity that had been James Howlett mere moments before ~ was now transformed into something more and something less than human.

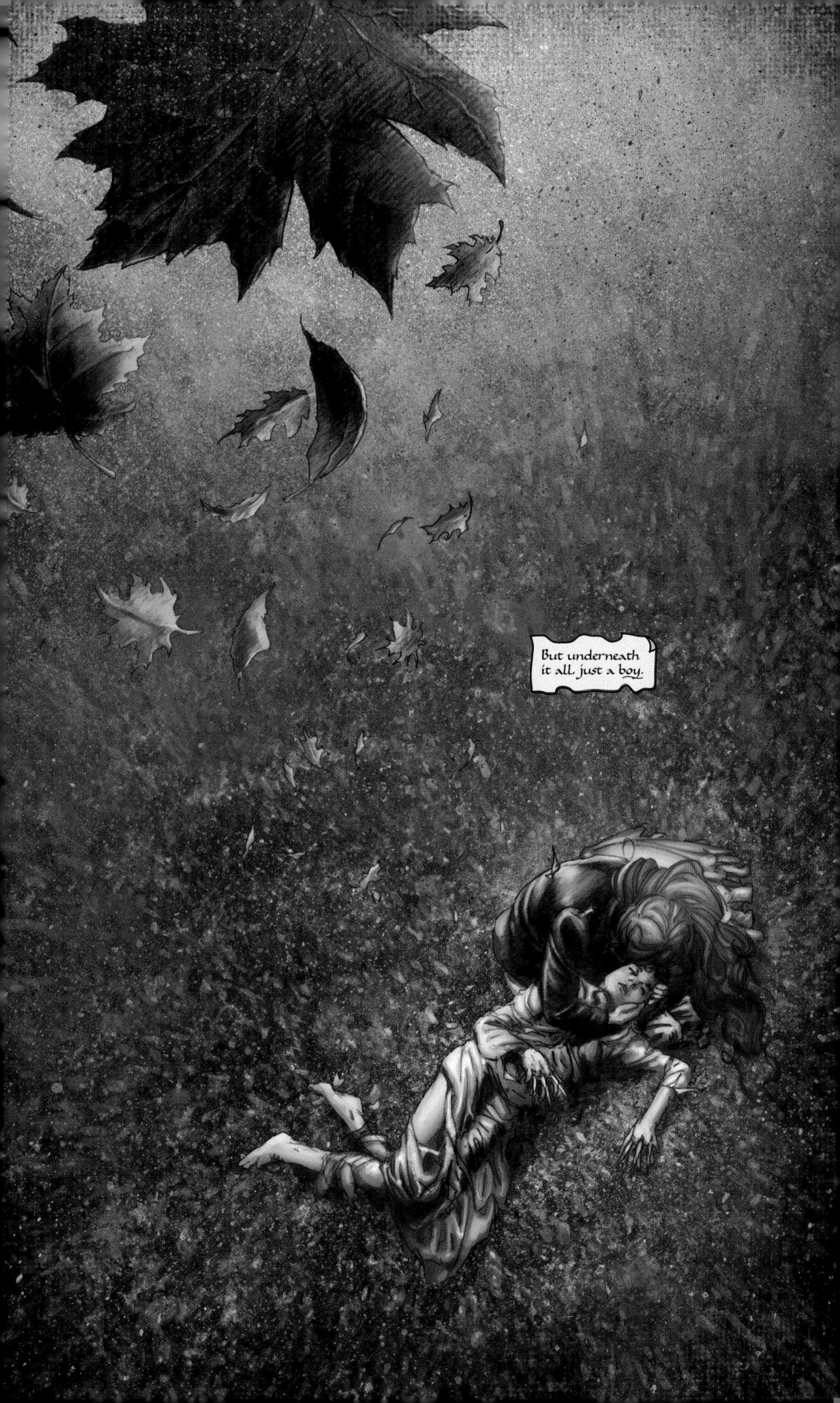
But underneath it all, just a boy.

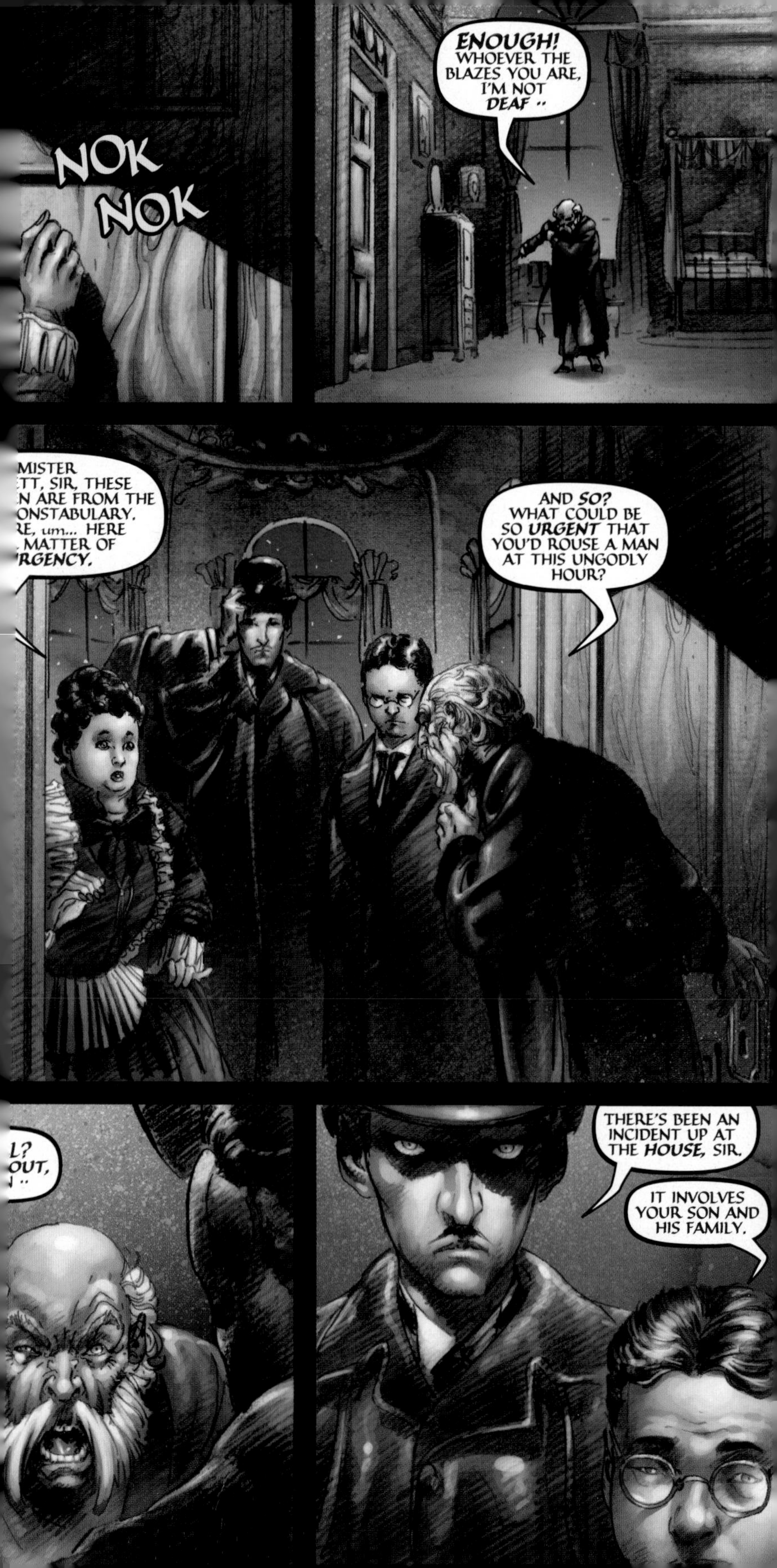
NOK NOK
ENOUGH! WHOEVER THE BLAZES YOU ARE, I'M NOT DEAF ..
MISTER ...TT, SIR, THESE ...N ARE FROM THE ...ONSTABULARY. ...RE, um... HERE ... MATTER OF ...RGENCY.
AND SO? WHAT COULD BE SO URGENT THAT YOU'D ROUSE A MAN AT THIS UNGODLY HOUR?
THERE'S BEEN AN INCIDENT UP AT THE HOUSE, SIR.
IT INVOLVES YOUR SON AND HIS FAMILY.

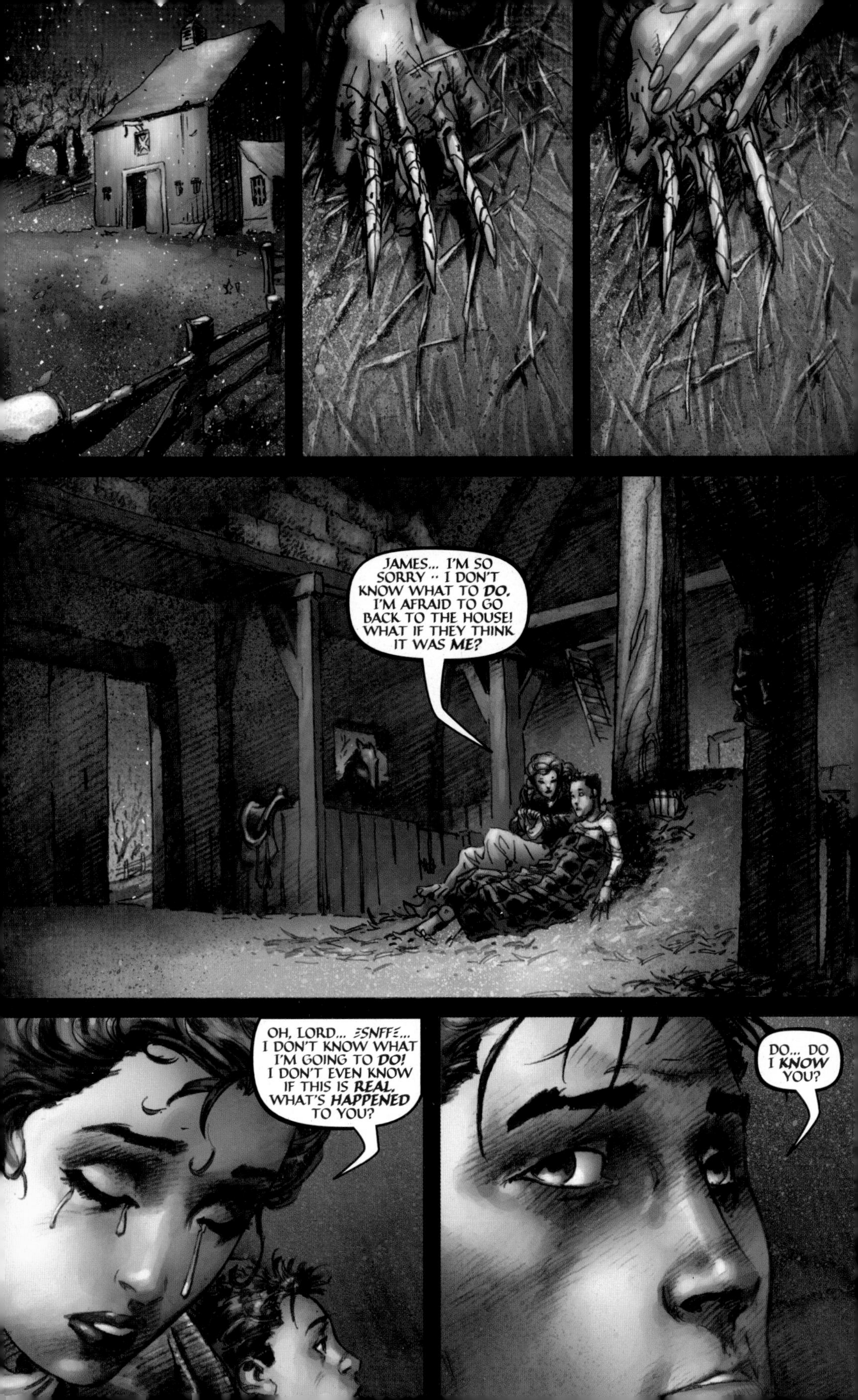
JAMES... I'M SO SORRY -- I DON'T KNOW WHAT TO DO. I'M AFRAID TO GO BACK TO THE HOUSE! WHAT IF THEY THINK IT WAS ME?
OH, LORD... SNFF... I DON'T KNOW WHAT I'M GOING TO DO! I DON'T EVEN KNOW IF THIS IS REAL. WHAT'S HAPPENED TO YOU?
DO... DO I KNOW YOU?

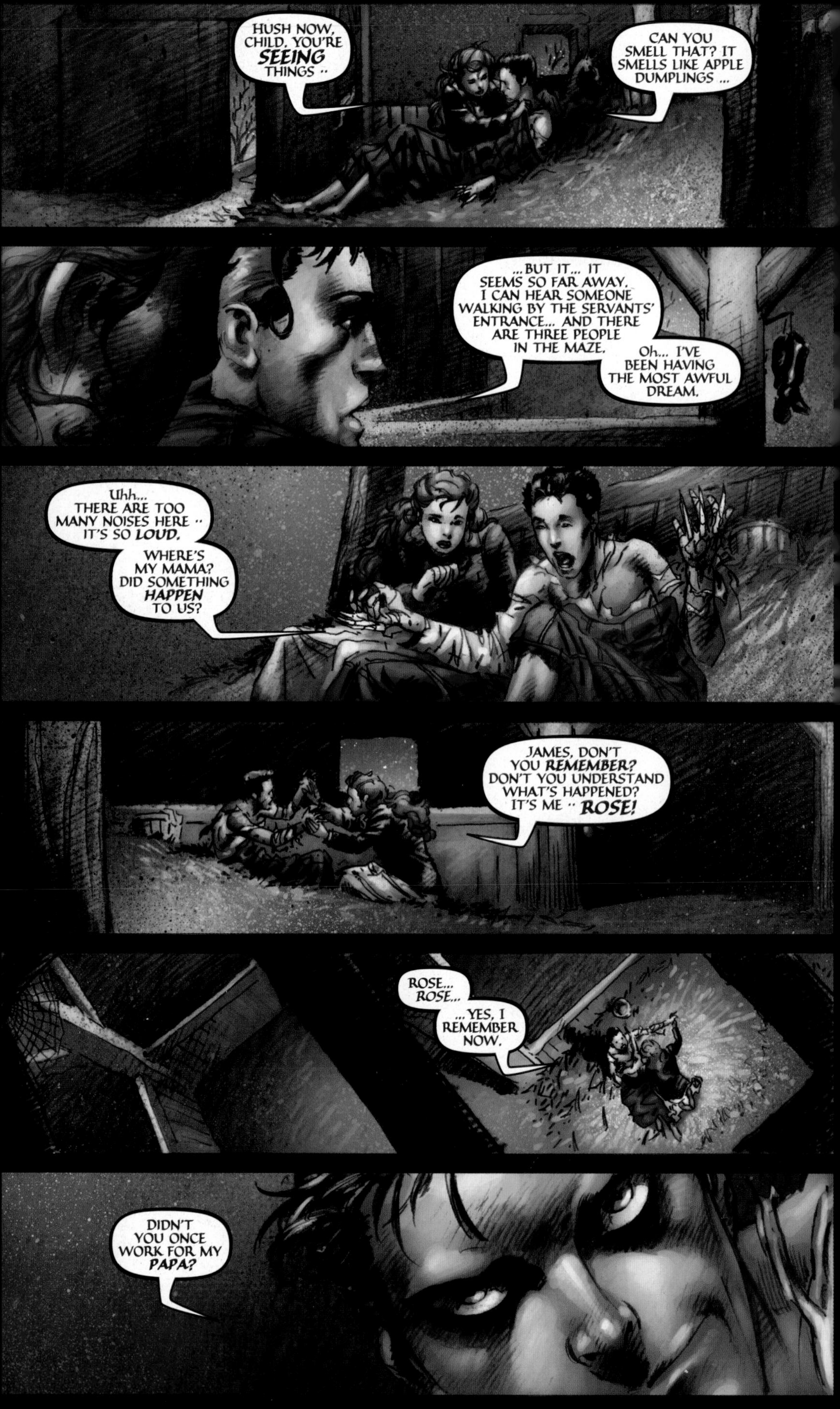
HUSH NOW, CHILD. YOU'RE SEEING THINGS ..
CAN YOU SMELL THAT? IT SMELLS LIKE APPLE DUMPLINGS ...
...BUT IT... IT SEEMS SO FAR AWAY. I CAN HEAR SOMEONE WALKING BY THE SERVANTS' ENTRANCE... AND THERE ARE THREE PEOPLE IN THE MAZE.
Oh... I'VE BEEN HAVING THE MOST AWFUL DREAM.
Uhh... THERE ARE TOO MANY NOISES HERE .. IT'S SO LOUD.
WHERE'S MY MAMA? DID SOMETHING HAPPEN TO US?
JAMES, DON'T YOU REMEMBER? DON'T YOU UNDERSTAND WHAT'S HAPPENED? IT'S ME .. ROSE!
ROSE... ROSE...
...YES, I REMEMBER NOW.
DIDN'T YOU ONCE WORK FOR MY PAPA?

YOU AIN'T GOT A LEG TO *STAND* ON, LAD, AND RIGHT SOON, THAT'LL BE THE *LEAST* OF YOUR WORRIES ·· WE KNOW YOU WERE THERE ·· YOU CARE TO EXPLAIN WHAT YOU WAS *DOIN'* IN THAT BEDROOM?

BEST TO CONFESS *NOW*, BOY. GET IT *OVER* WITH, WHY DON'T YOU ··

I NEVER *DONE* NUTHIN'. I AIN'T GOT NUTHIN' T' SAY TO YOU ··

STAND AWAY, MEN. I'LL HANDLE THIS!

NOW, YOU LISTEN TO ME, BOY, AND LISTEN *WELL* ·· I'VE LOST MY ONLY SON THIS NIGHT, AND MY GRANDSON IS *MISSING*, BELIEVE ME WHEN I TELL YOU, SOMEONE IS GOING TO *PAY*.

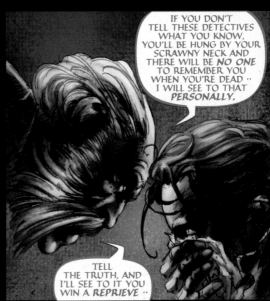

IF YOU DON'T TELL THESE DETECTIVES WHAT YOU KNOW, YOU'LL BE HUNG BY YOUR SCRAWNY NECK AND THERE WILL BE *NO ONE* TO REMEMBER YOU WHEN YOU'RE DEAD ·· I WILL SEE TO THAT *PERSONALLY*.

TELL THE TRUTH, AND I'LL SEE TO IT YOU WIN A *REPRIEVE* ··

IT WAS *ROSE*, SIR... ...SHE HAD A *GUN*.

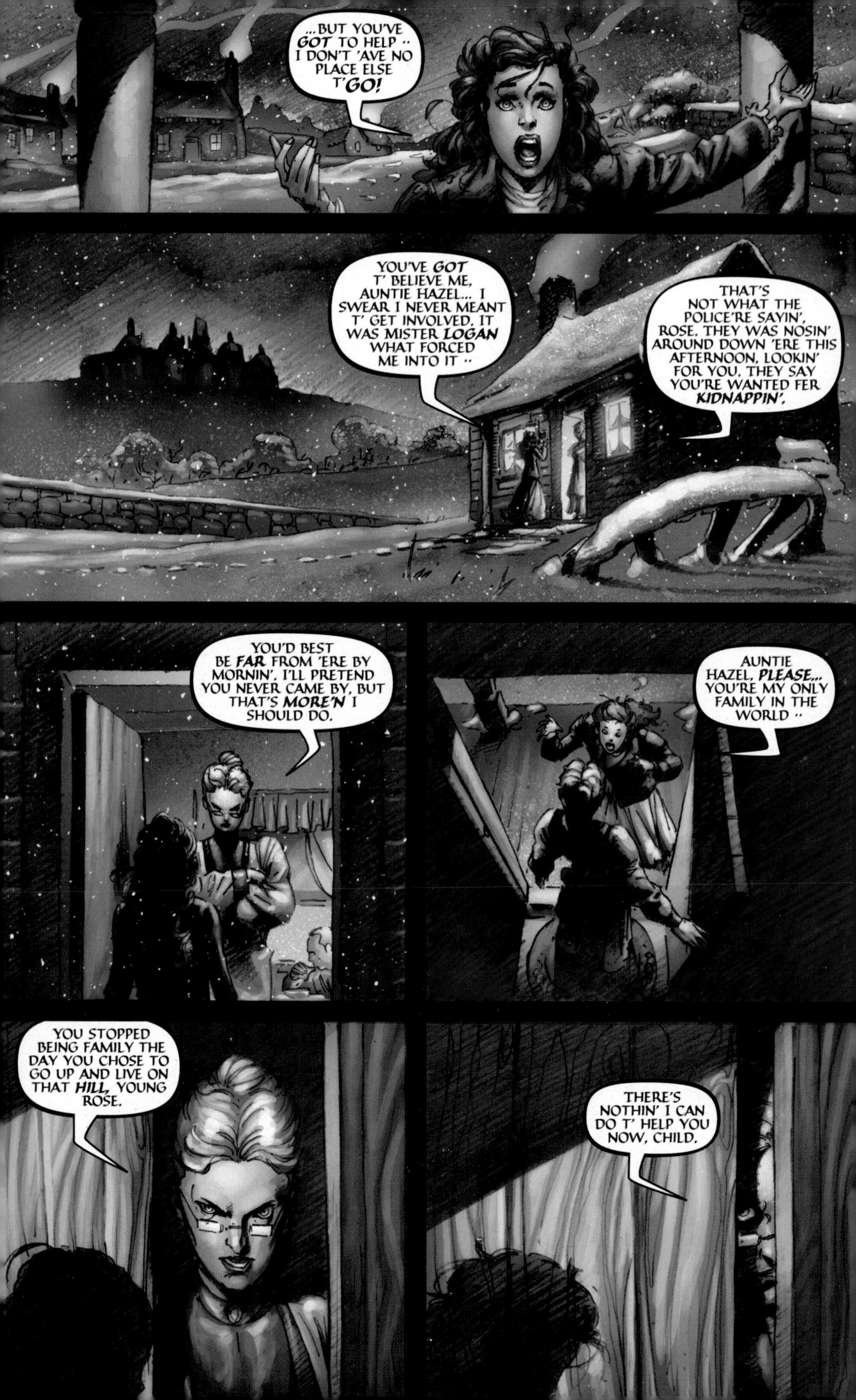
...BUT YOU'VE GOT TO HELP .. I DON'T 'AVE NO PLACE ELSE T'GO!
YOU'VE GOT T' BELIEVE ME, AUNTIE HAZEL... I SWEAR I NEVER MEANT T' GET INVOLVED. IT WAS MISTER LOGAN WHAT FORCED ME INTO IT ..
THAT'S NOT WHAT THE POLICE'RE SAYIN', ROSE. THEY WAS NOSIN' AROUND DOWN 'ERE THIS AFTERNOON, LOOKIN' FOR YOU. THEY SAY YOU'RE WANTED FER KIDNAPPIN'.
YOU'D BEST BE FAR FROM 'ERE BY MORNIN'. I'LL PRETEND YOU NEVER CAME BY, BUT THAT'S MORE'N I SHOULD DO.
AUNTIE HAZEL, PLEASE... YOU'RE MY ONLY FAMILY IN THE WORLD ..
YOU STOPPED BEING FAMILY THE DAY YOU CHOSE TO GO UP AND LIVE ON THAT HILL, YOUNG ROSE.
THERE'S NOTHIN' I CAN DO T' HELP YOU NOW, CHILD.

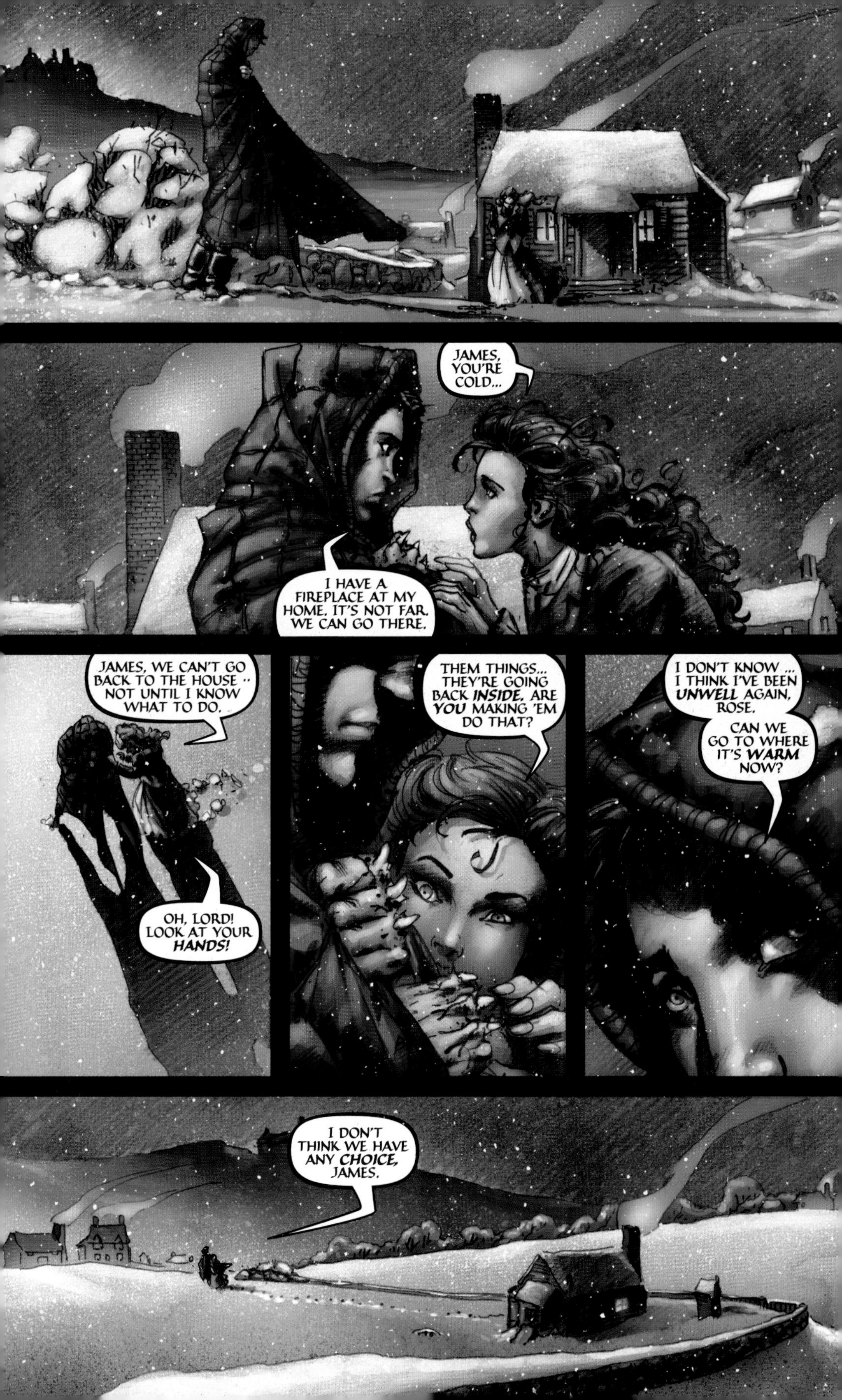
JAMES, YOU'RE COLD...
I HAVE A FIREPLACE AT MY HOME. IT'S NOT FAR. WE CAN GO THERE.
JAMES, WE CAN'T GO BACK TO THE HOUSE -- NOT UNTIL I KNOW WHAT TO DO.
OH, LORD! LOOK AT YOUR *HANDS!*
THEM THINGS... THEY'RE GOING BACK *INSIDE.* ARE *YOU* MAKING 'EM DO THAT?
I DON'T KNOW ... I THINK I'VE BEEN *UNWELL* AGAIN, ROSE.
CAN WE GO TO WHERE IT'S *WARM* NOW?
I DON'T THINK WE HAVE ANY *CHOICE,* JAMES.

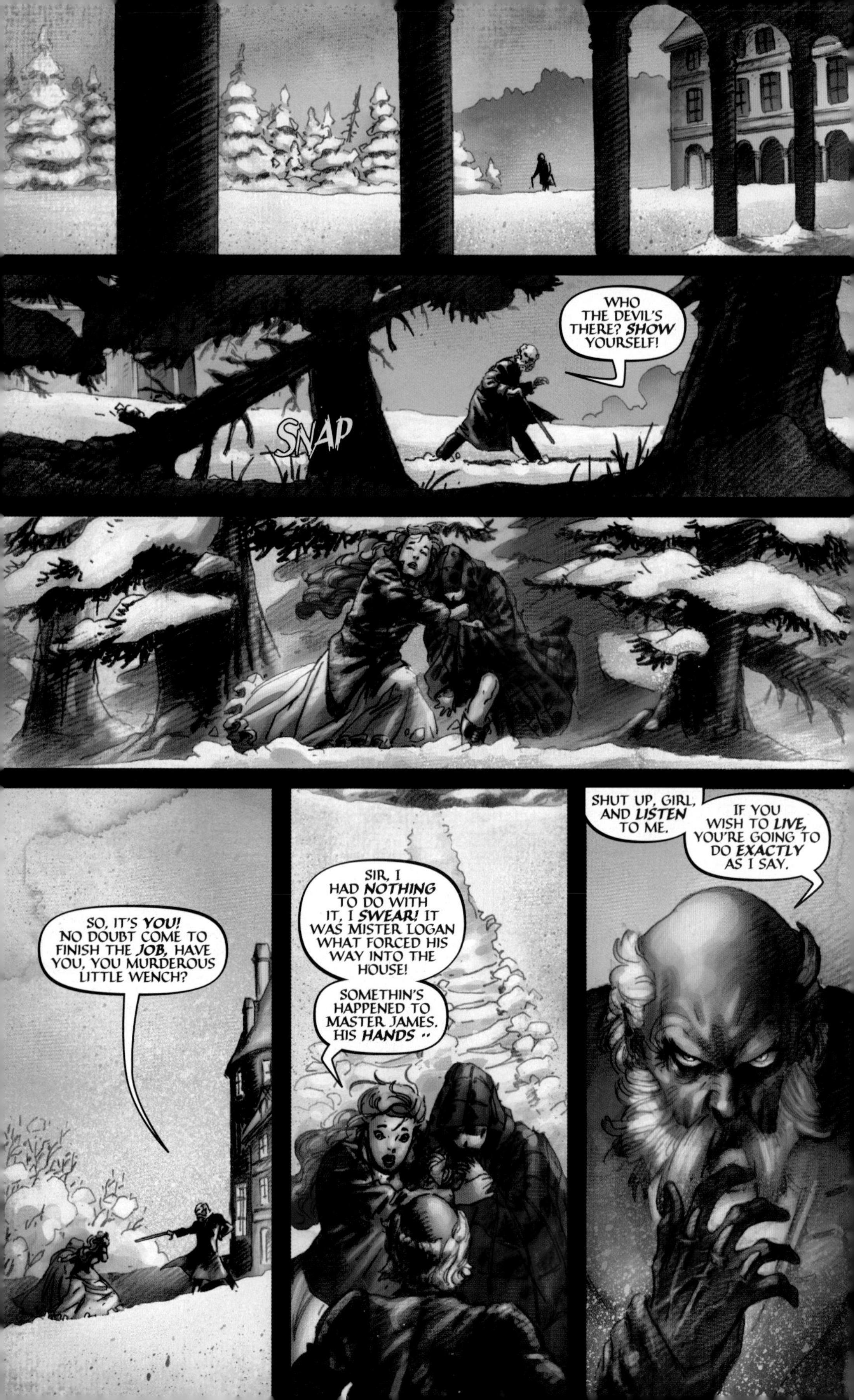
WHO THE DEVIL'S THERE? SHOW YOURSELF!
SNAP
SO, IT'S YOU! NO DOUBT COME TO FINISH THE JOB, HAVE YOU, YOU MURDEROUS LITTLE WENCH?
SIR, I HAD NOTHING TO DO WITH IT, I SWEAR! IT WAS MISTER LOGAN WHAT FORCED HIS WAY INTO THE HOUSE!
SOMETHIN'S HAPPENED TO MASTER JAMES. HIS HANDS --
SHUT UP, GIRL, AND LISTEN TO ME.
IF YOU WISH TO LIVE, YOU'RE GOING TO DO EXACTLY AS I SAY.

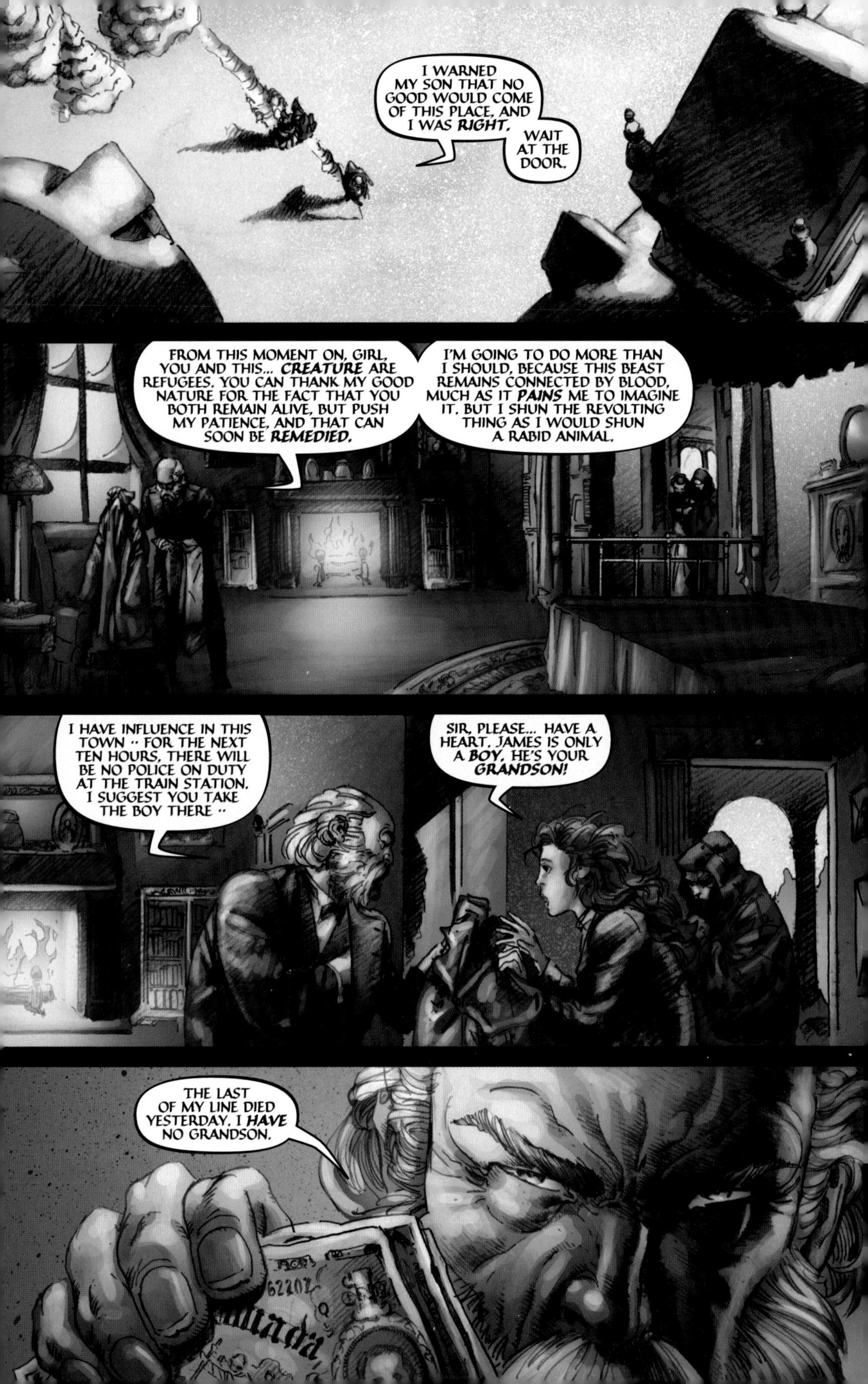
I WARNED MY SON THAT NO GOOD WOULD COME OF THIS PLACE, AND I WAS **RIGHT.**
WAIT AT THE DOOR.
FROM THIS MOMENT ON, GIRL, YOU AND THIS... **CREATURE** ARE REFUGEES. YOU CAN THANK MY GOOD NATURE FOR THE FACT THAT YOU BOTH REMAIN ALIVE, BUT PUSH MY PATIENCE, AND THAT CAN SOON BE **REMEDIED.**
I'M GOING TO DO MORE THAN I SHOULD, BECAUSE THIS BEAST REMAINS CONNECTED BY BLOOD, MUCH AS IT **PAINS** ME TO IMAGINE IT. BUT I SHUN THE REVOLTING THING AS I WOULD SHUN A RABID ANIMAL.
I HAVE INFLUENCE IN THIS TOWN -- FOR THE NEXT TEN HOURS, THERE WILL BE NO POLICE ON DUTY AT THE TRAIN STATION. I SUGGEST YOU TAKE THE BOY THERE --
SIR, PLEASE... HAVE A HEART. JAMES IS ONLY A **BOY.** HE'S YOUR **GRANDSON!**
THE LAST OF MY LINE DIED YESTERDAY. I **HAVE** NO GRANDSON.

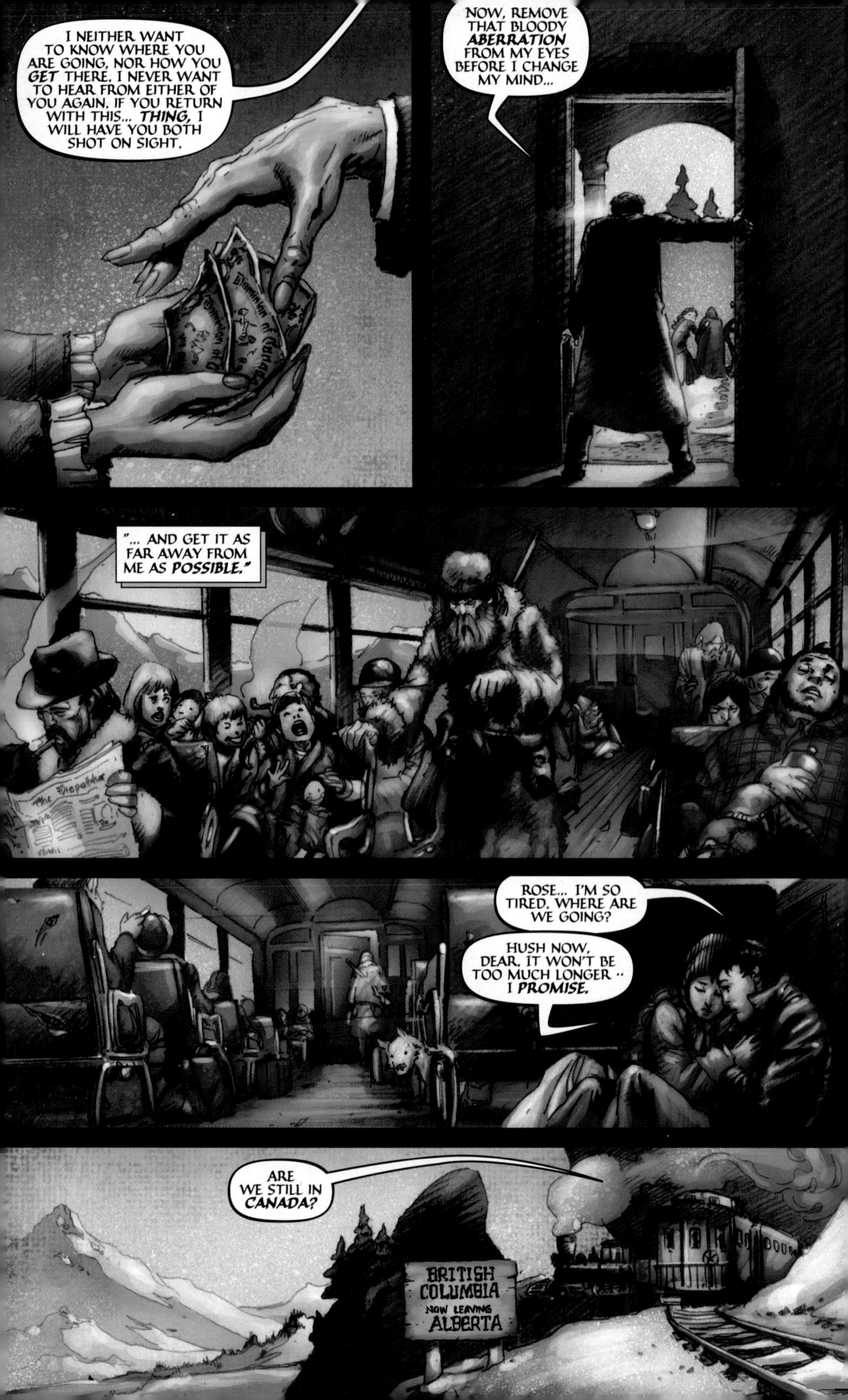
I NEITHER WANT TO KNOW WHERE YOU ARE GOING, NOR HOW YOU GET THERE. I NEVER WANT TO HEAR FROM EITHER OF YOU AGAIN. IF YOU RETURN WITH THIS... THING, I WILL HAVE YOU BOTH SHOT ON SIGHT.
NOW, REMOVE THAT BLOODY ABERRATION FROM MY EYES BEFORE I CHANGE MY MIND...
"... AND GET IT AS FAR AWAY FROM ME AS POSSIBLE."
ROSE... I'M SO TIRED. WHERE ARE WE GOING?
HUSH NOW, DEAR. IT WON'T BE TOO MUCH LONGER .. I PROMISE.
ARE WE STILL IN CANADA?
BRITISH COLUMBIA
NOW LEAVING
ALBERTA

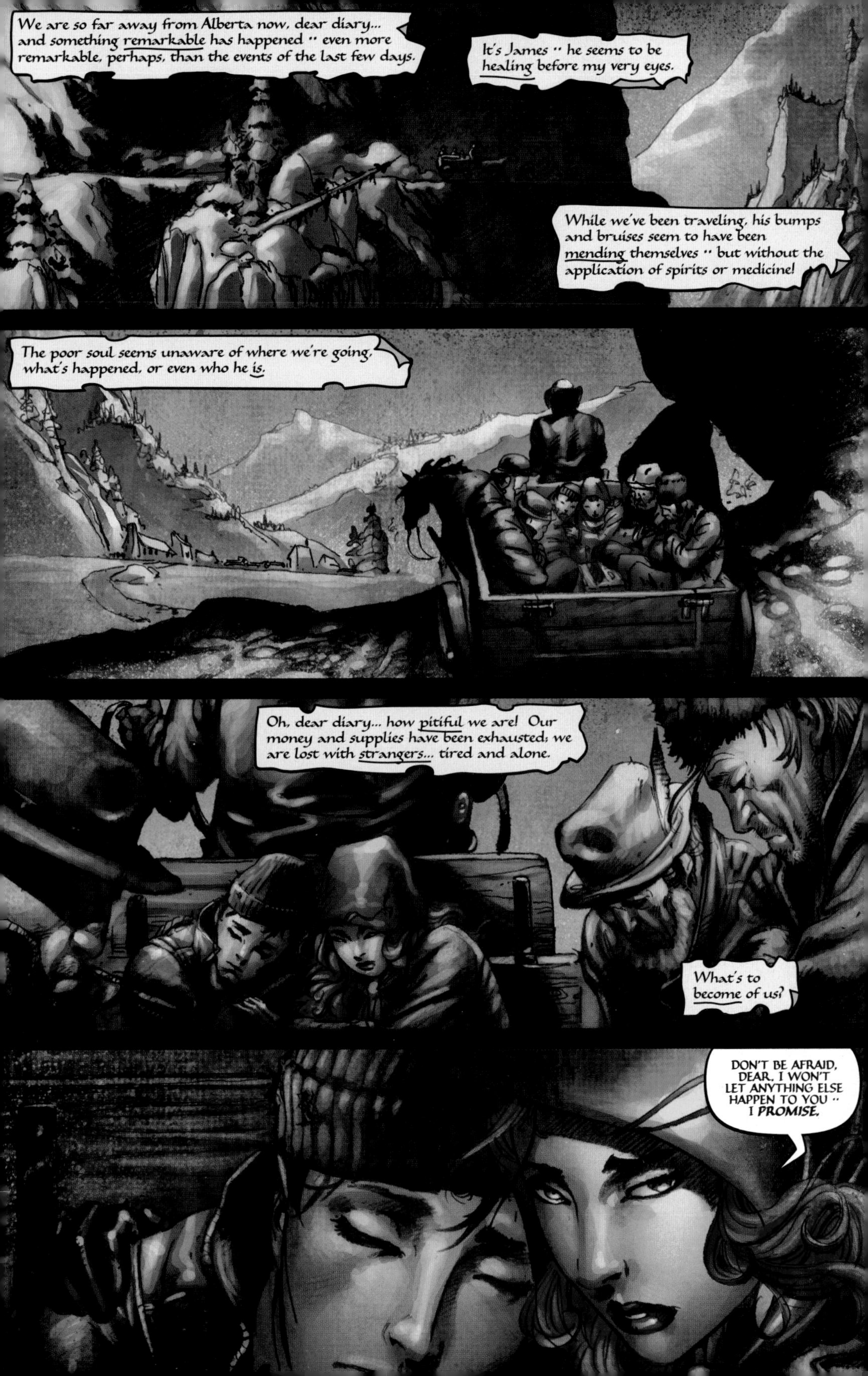
We are so far away from Alberta now, dear diary... and something remarkable has happened -- even more remarkable, perhaps, than the events of the last few days.
It's James -- he seems to be healing before my very eyes.
While we've been traveling, his bumps and bruises seem to have been mending themselves -- but without the application of spirits or medicine!
The poor soul seems unaware of where we're going, what's happened, or even who he is.
Oh, dear diary... how pitiful we are! Our money and supplies have been exhausted; we are lost with strangers... tired and alone.
What's to become of us?
DON'T BE AFRAID, DEAR. I WON'T LET ANYTHING ELSE HAPPEN TO YOU -- I PROMISE.

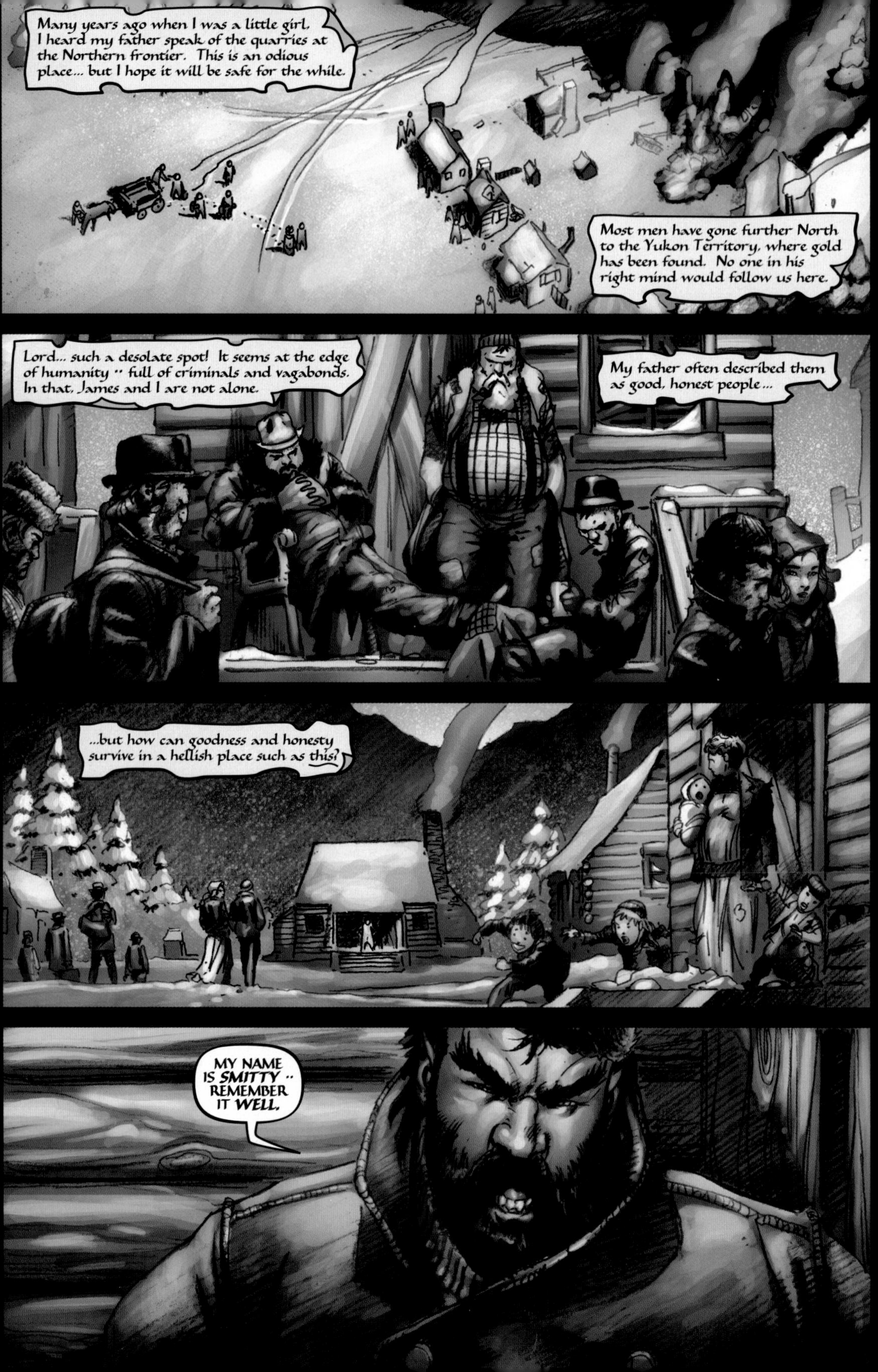
Many years ago when I was a little girl, I heard my father speak of the quarries at the Northern frontier. This is an odious place... but I hope it will be safe for the while.
Most men have gone further North to the Yukon Territory, where gold has been found. No one in his right mind would follow us here.
Lord... such a desolate spot! It seems at the edge of humanity -- full of criminals and vagabonds. In that, James and I are not alone.
My father often described them as good, honest people...
...but how can goodness and honesty survive in a hellish place such as this?
MY NAME IS SMITTY -- REMEMBER IT WELL.

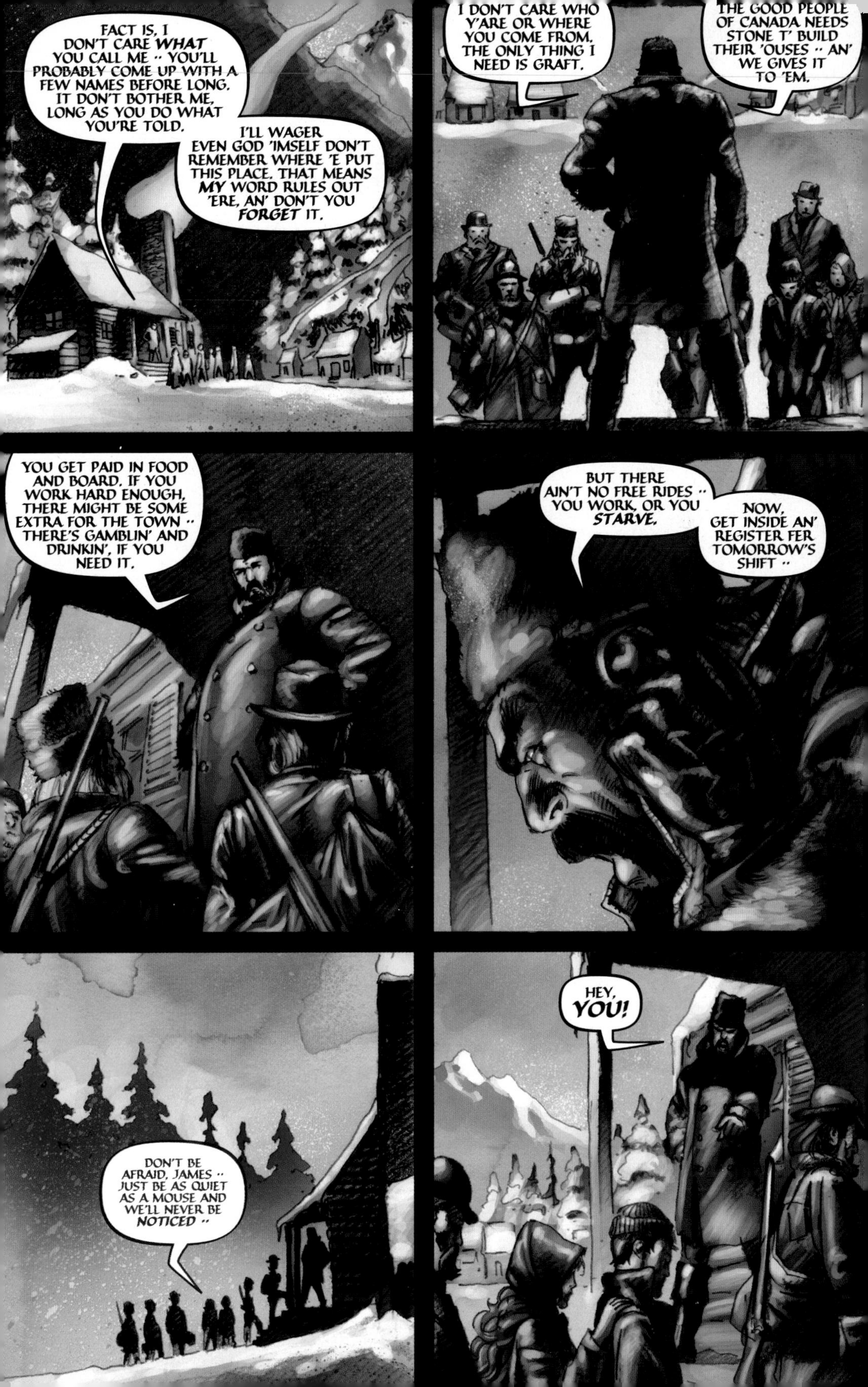
FACT IS, I DON'T CARE WHAT YOU CALL ME .. YOU'LL PROBABLY COME UP WITH A FEW NAMES BEFORE LONG. IT DON'T BOTHER ME, LONG AS YOU DO WHAT YOU'RE TOLD.
I'LL WAGER EVEN GOD 'IMSELF DON'T REMEMBER WHERE 'E PUT THIS PLACE. THAT MEANS MY WORD RULES OUT 'ERE, AN' DON'T YOU FORGET IT.
I DON'T CARE WHO Y'ARE OR WHERE YOU COME FROM. THE ONLY THING I NEED IS GRAFT.
THE GOOD PEOPLE OF CANADA NEEDS STONE T' BUILD THEIR 'OUSES .. AN' WE GIVES IT TO 'EM.
YOU GET PAID IN FOOD AND BOARD. IF YOU WORK HARD ENOUGH, THERE MIGHT BE SOME EXTRA FOR THE TOWN .. THERE'S GAMBLIN' AND DRINKIN', IF YOU NEED IT.
BUT THERE AIN'T NO FREE RIDES .. YOU WORK, OR YOU STARVE.
NOW, GET INSIDE AN' REGISTER FER TOMORROW'S SHIFT ..
DON'T BE AFRAID, JAMES .. JUST BE AS QUIET AS A MOUSE AND WE'LL NEVER BE NOTICED ..
HEY, YOU!

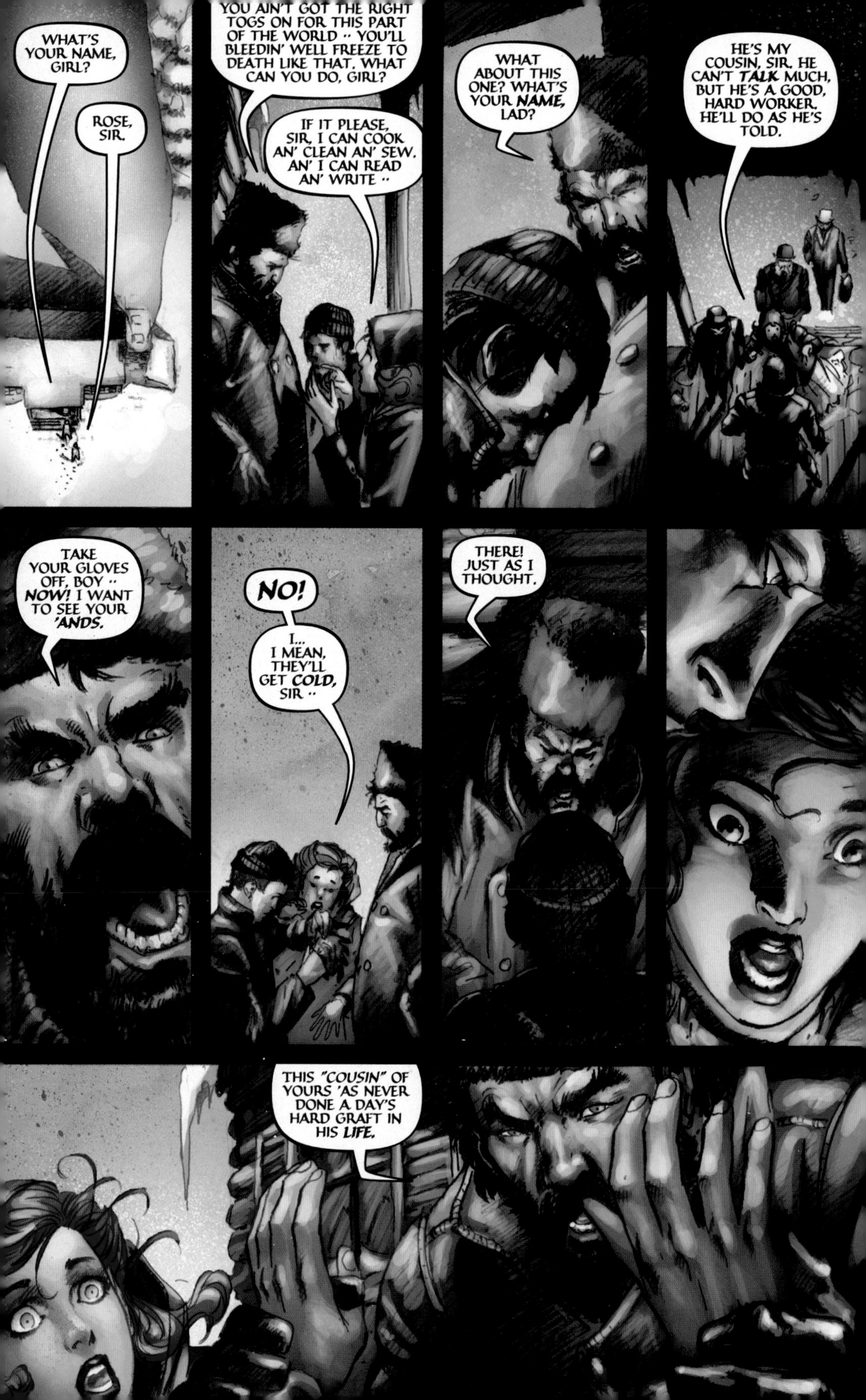
WHAT'S YOUR NAME, GIRL?
ROSE, SIR.
YOU AIN'T GOT THE RIGHT TOGS ON FOR THIS PART OF THE WORLD -- YOU'LL BLEEDIN' WELL FREEZE TO DEATH LIKE THAT. WHAT CAN YOU DO, GIRL?
IF IT PLEASE, SIR, I CAN COOK AN' CLEAN AN' SEW. AN' I CAN READ AN' WRITE --
WHAT ABOUT THIS ONE? WHAT'S YOUR NAME, LAD?
HE'S MY COUSIN, SIR. HE CAN'T TALK MUCH, BUT HE'S A GOOD, HARD WORKER. HE'LL DO AS HE'S TOLD.
TAKE YOUR GLOVES OFF, BOY -- NOW! I WANT TO SEE YOUR 'ANDS.
NO!
I... I MEAN, THEY'LL GET COLD, SIR --
THERE! JUST AS I THOUGHT.
THIS "COUSIN" OF YOURS 'AS NEVER DONE A DAY'S HARD GRAFT IN HIS LIFE.

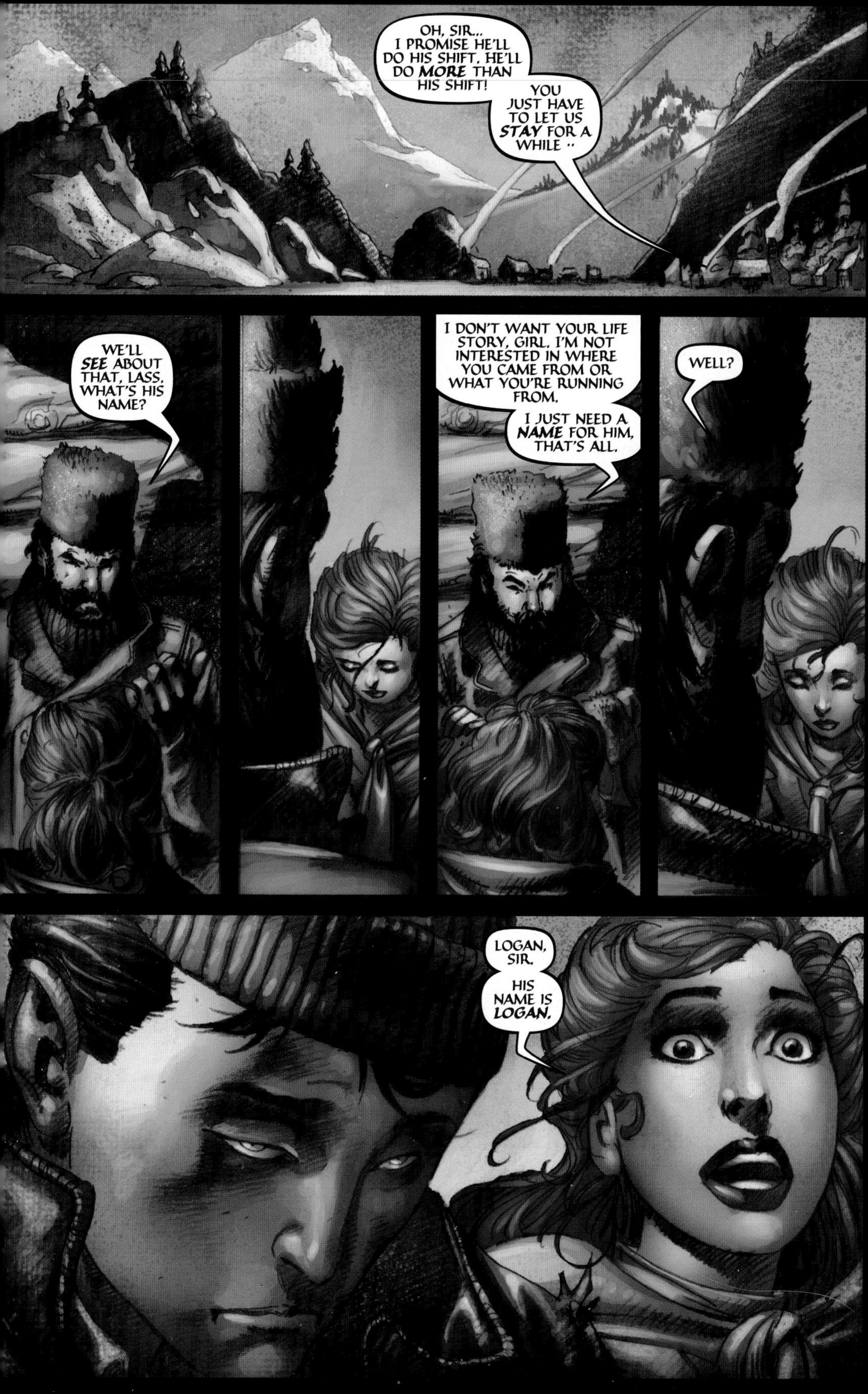

OH, SIR... I PROMISE HE'LL DO HIS SHIFT. HE'LL DO MORE THAN HIS SHIFT!
YOU JUST HAVE TO LET US STAY FOR A WHILE ..
WE'LL SEE ABOUT THAT, LASS. WHAT'S HIS NAME?
I DON'T WANT YOUR LIFE STORY, GIRL. I'M NOT INTERESTED IN WHERE YOU CAME FROM OR WHAT YOU'RE RUNNING FROM.
I JUST NEED A NAME FOR HIM, THAT'S ALL.
WELL?
LOGAN, SIR.
HIS NAME IS LOGAN.

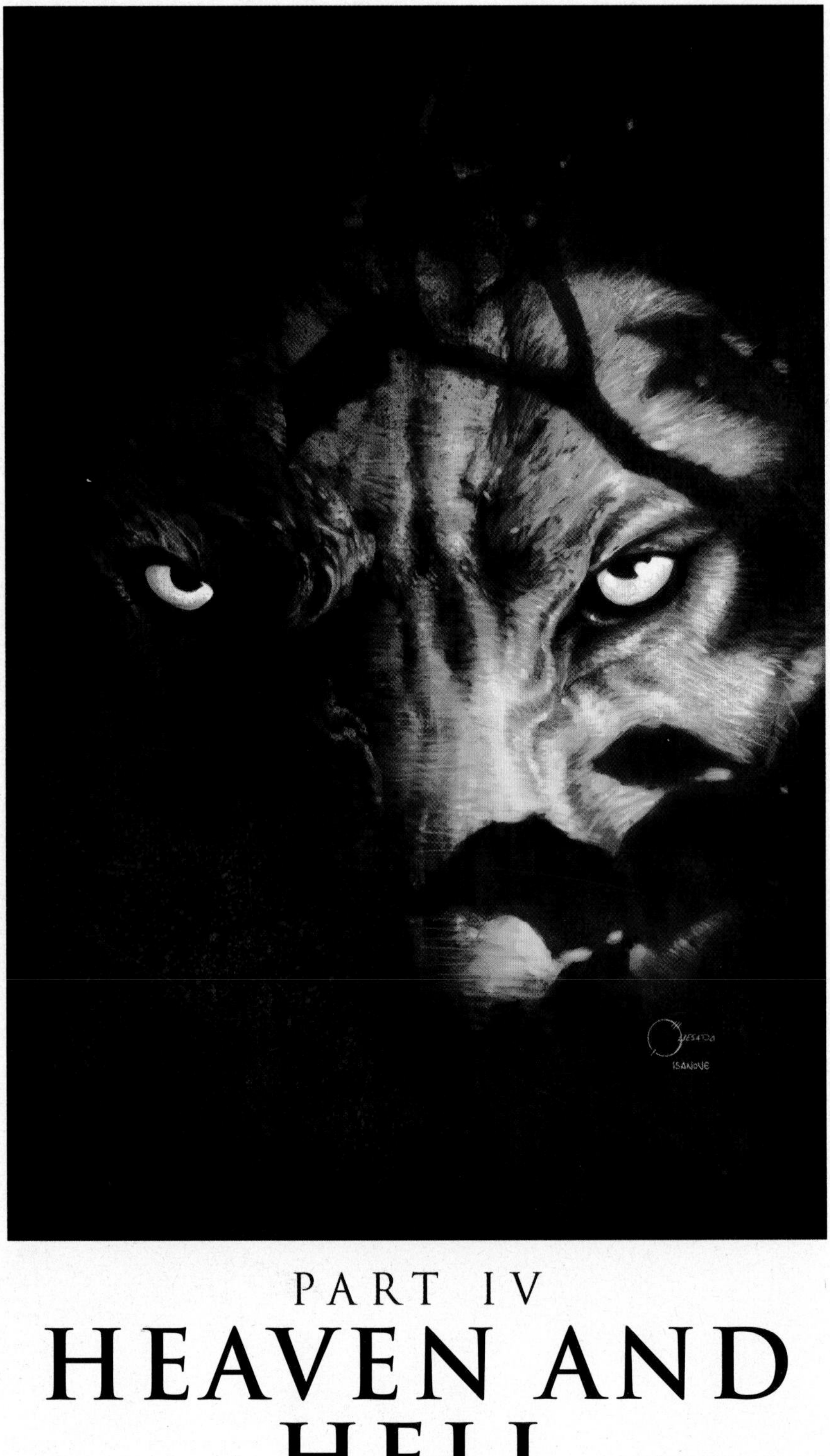

PART IV

HEAVEN AND HELL

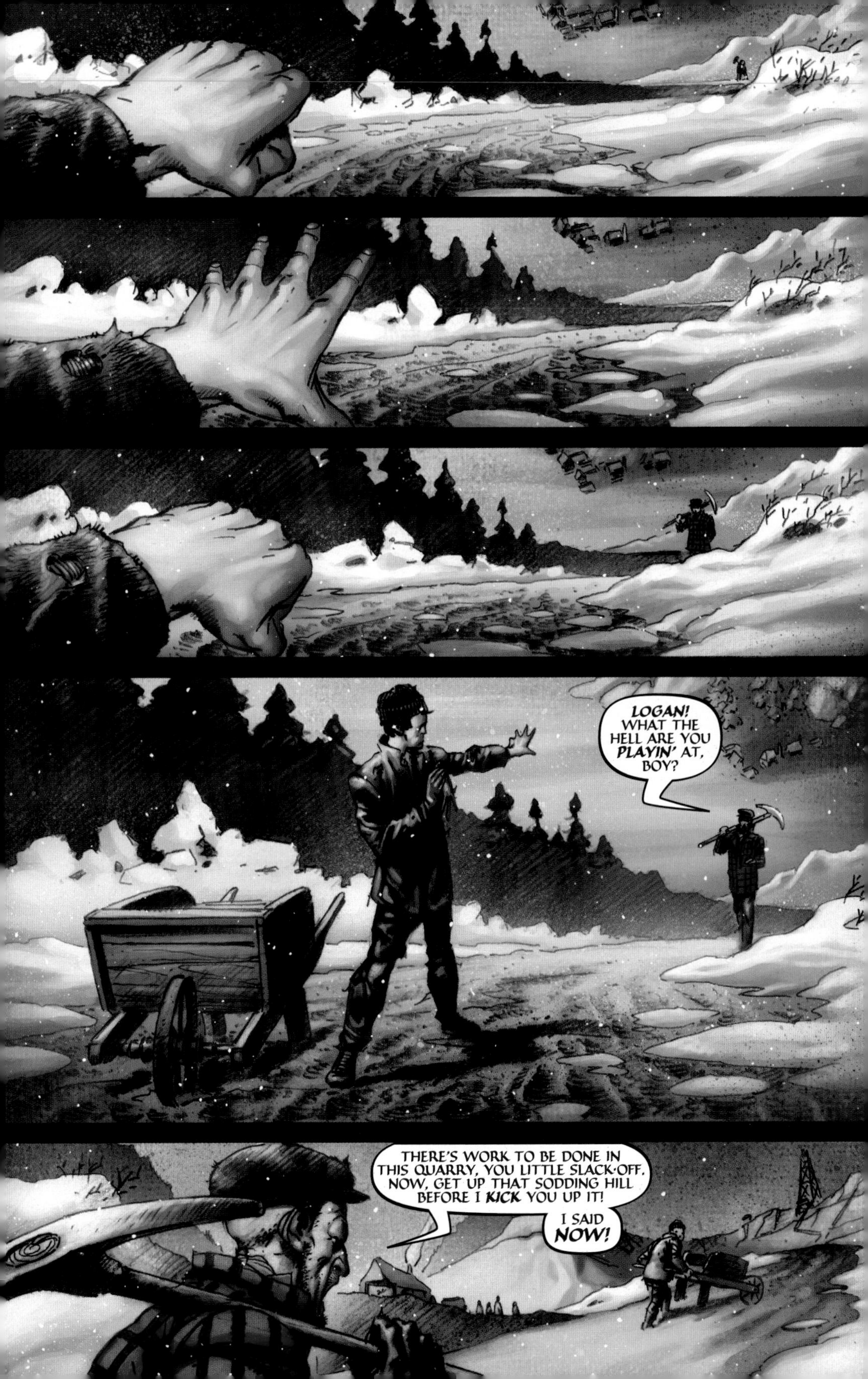
LOGAN! WHAT THE HELL ARE YOU PLAYIN' AT, BOY?
THERE'S WORK TO BE DONE IN THIS QUARRY, YOU LITTLE SLACK-OFF. NOW, GET UP THAT SODDING HILL BEFORE I KICK YOU UP IT!
I SAID NOW!

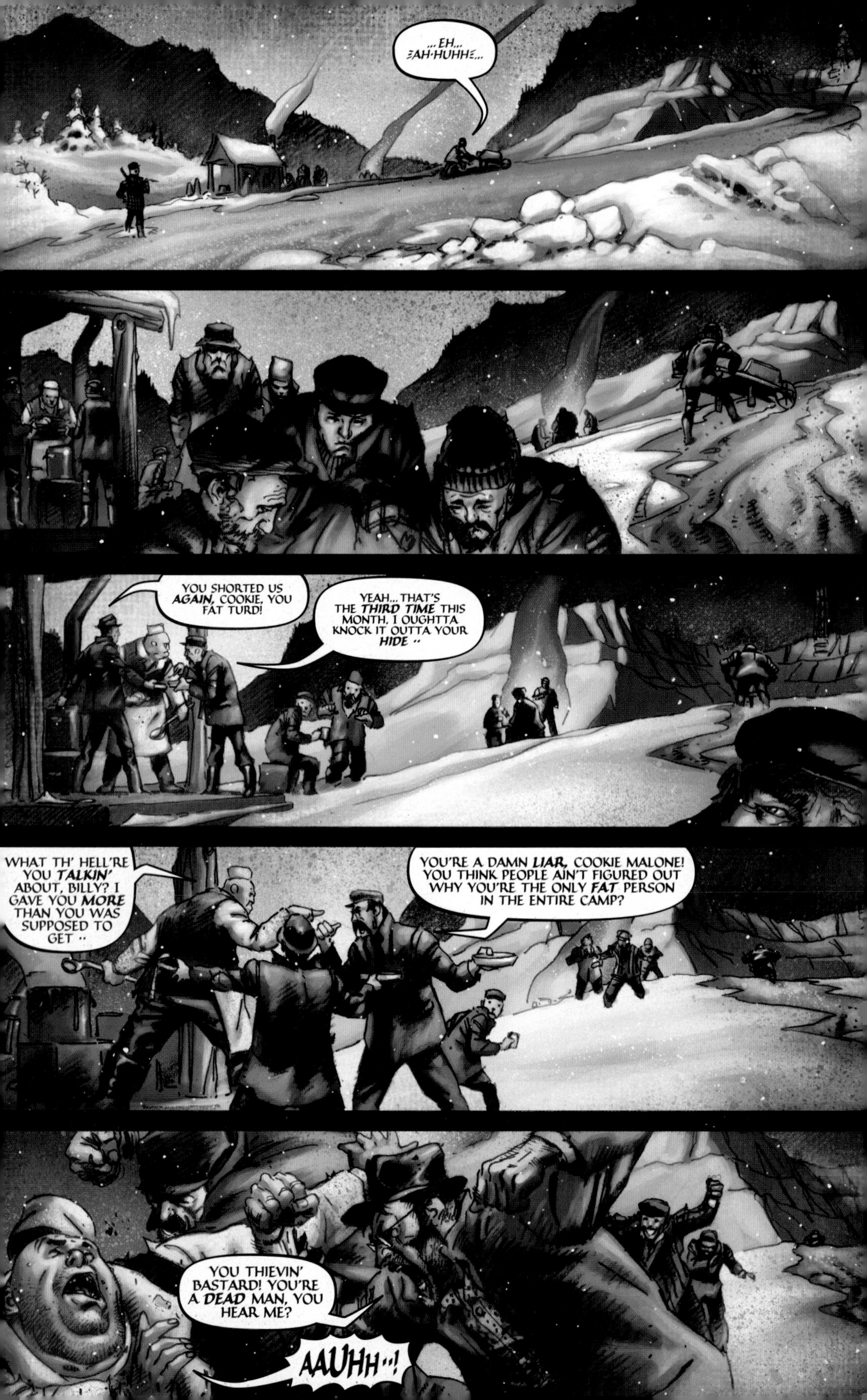
...EH...
AH-HUHH...
YOU SHORTED US AGAIN, COOKIE, YOU FAT TURD!
YEAH... THAT'S THE THIRD TIME THIS MONTH. I OUGHTTA KNOCK IT OUTTA YOUR HIDE --
WHAT TH' HELL'RE YOU TALKIN' ABOUT, BILLY? I GAVE YOU MORE THAN YOU WAS SUPPOSED TO GET --
YOU'RE A DAMN LIAR, COOKIE MALONE! YOU THINK PEOPLE AIN'T FIGURED OUT WHY YOU'RE THE ONLY FAT PERSON IN THE ENTIRE CAMP?
YOU THIEVIN' BASTARD! YOU'RE A DEAD MAN, YOU HEAR ME?
AAUHH --!

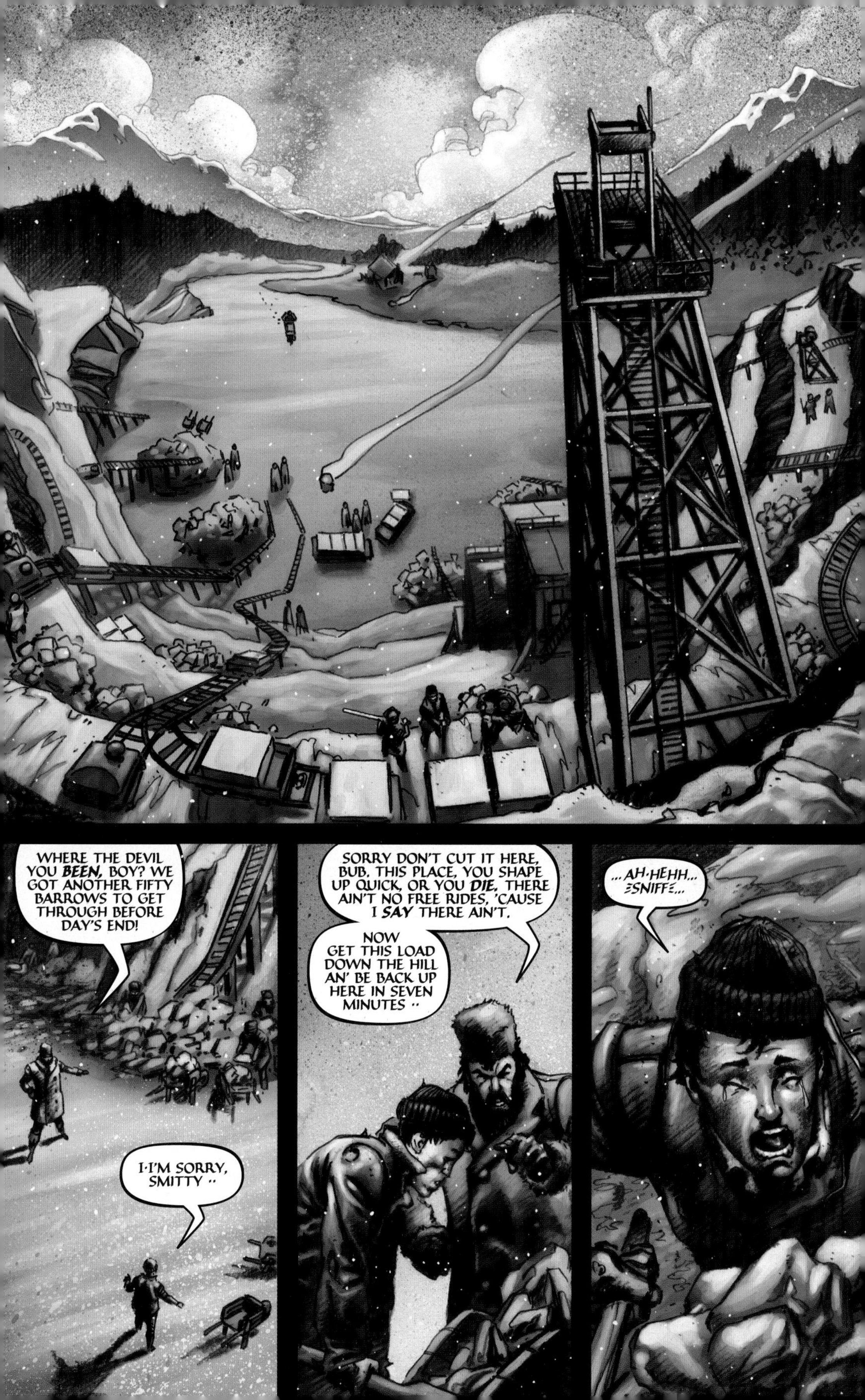
WHERE THE DEVIL YOU BEEN, BOY? WE GOT ANOTHER FIFTY BARROWS TO GET THROUGH BEFORE DAY'S END!
I-I'M SORRY, SMITTY --
SORRY DON'T CUT IT HERE, BUB. THIS PLACE, YOU SHAPE UP QUICK, OR YOU DIE. THERE AIN'T NO FREE RIDES, 'CAUSE I SAY THERE AIN'T.
NOW GET THIS LOAD DOWN THE HILL AN' BE BACK UP HERE IN SEVEN MINUTES --
...AH-HEHH... SNIFF...

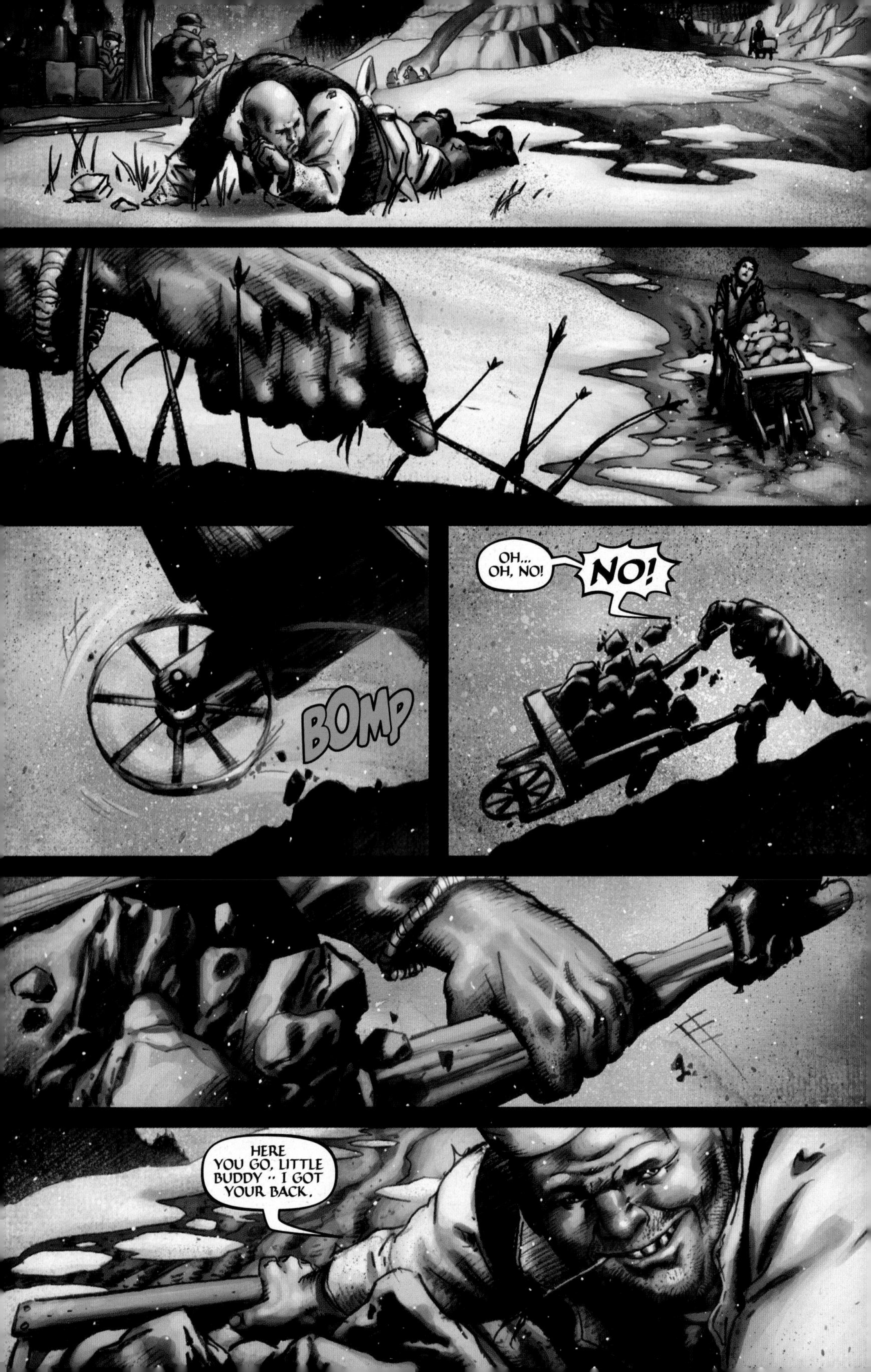
BOMP
OH... OH, NO!
NO!
HERE YOU GO, LITTLE BUDDY -- I GOT YOUR BACK.

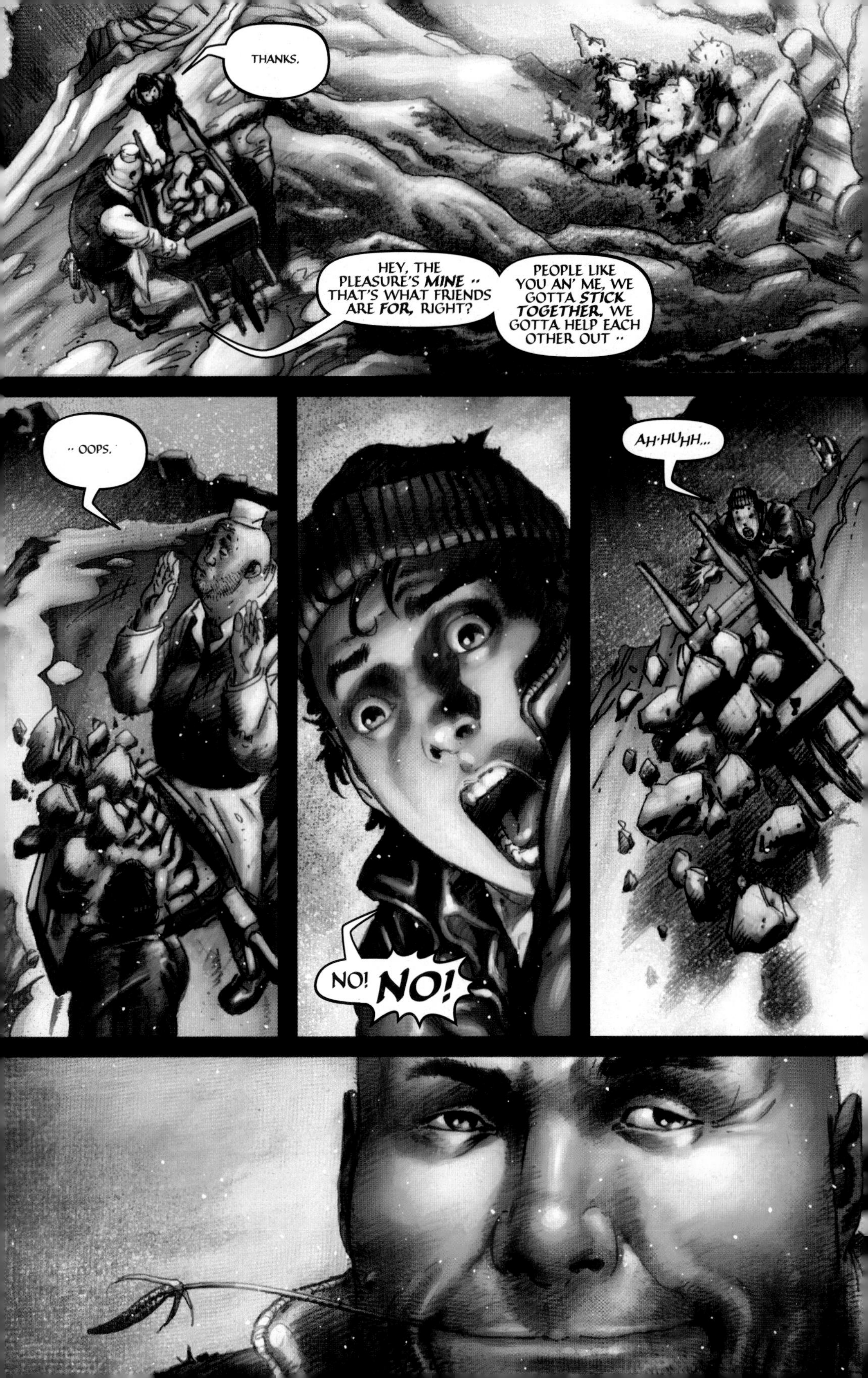
THANKS.
HEY, THE PLEASURE'S **MINE** .. THAT'S WHAT FRIENDS ARE **FOR,** RIGHT?
PEOPLE LIKE YOU AN' ME, WE GOTTA **STICK TOGETHER,** WE GOTTA HELP EACH OTHER OUT ..
.. OOPS.
NO! **NO!**
AH-HUHH...

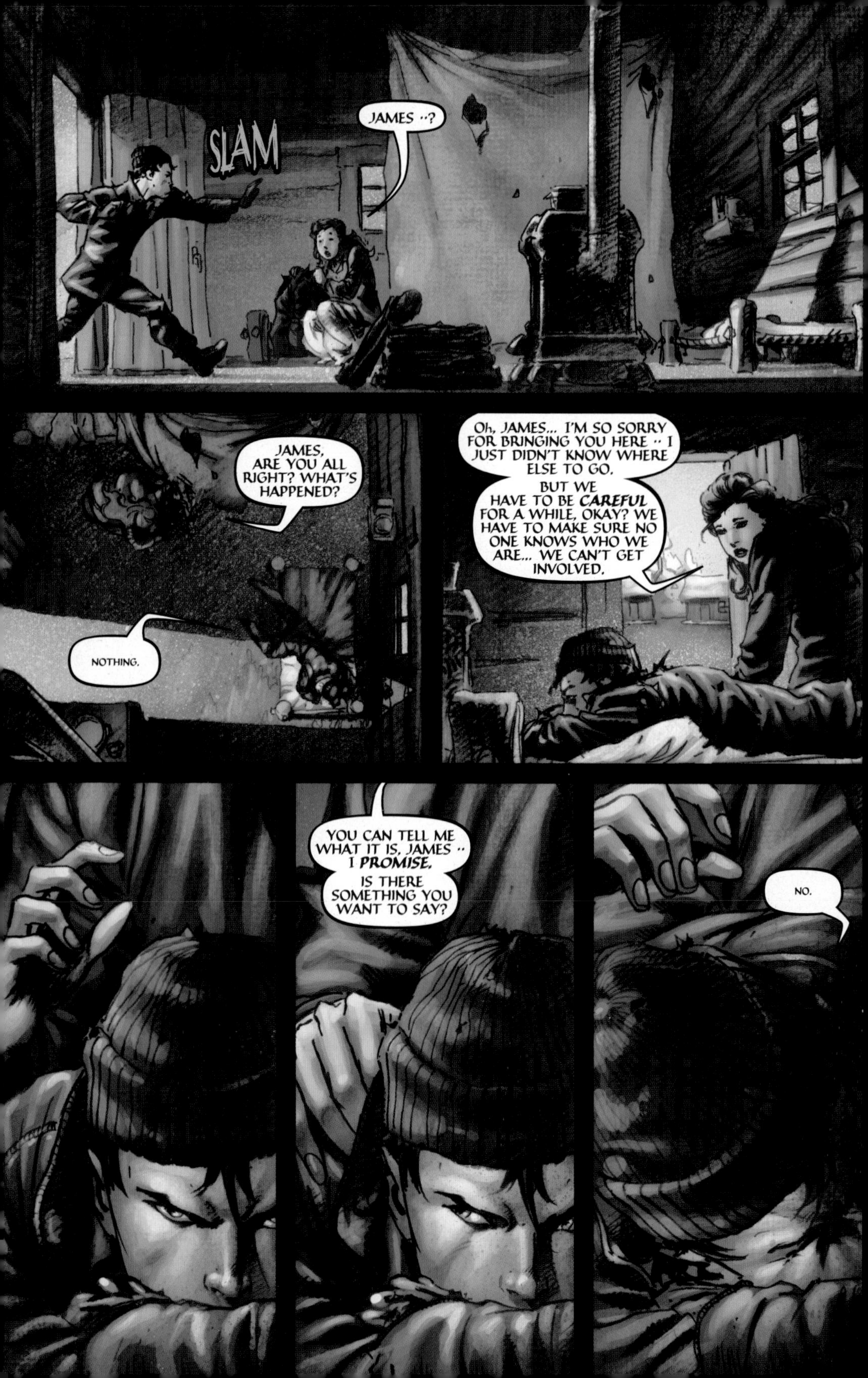
SLAM
JAMES ..?
JAMES, ARE YOU ALL RIGHT? WHAT'S HAPPENED?
NOTHING.
Oh, JAMES... I'M SO SORRY FOR BRINGING YOU HERE .. I JUST DIDN'T KNOW WHERE ELSE TO GO.
BUT WE HAVE TO BE CAREFUL FOR A WHILE, OKAY? WE HAVE TO MAKE SURE NO ONE KNOWS WHO WE ARE... WE CAN'T GET INVOLVED.
YOU CAN TELL ME WHAT IT IS, JAMES .. I PROMISE.
IS THERE SOMETHING YOU WANT TO SAY?
NO.

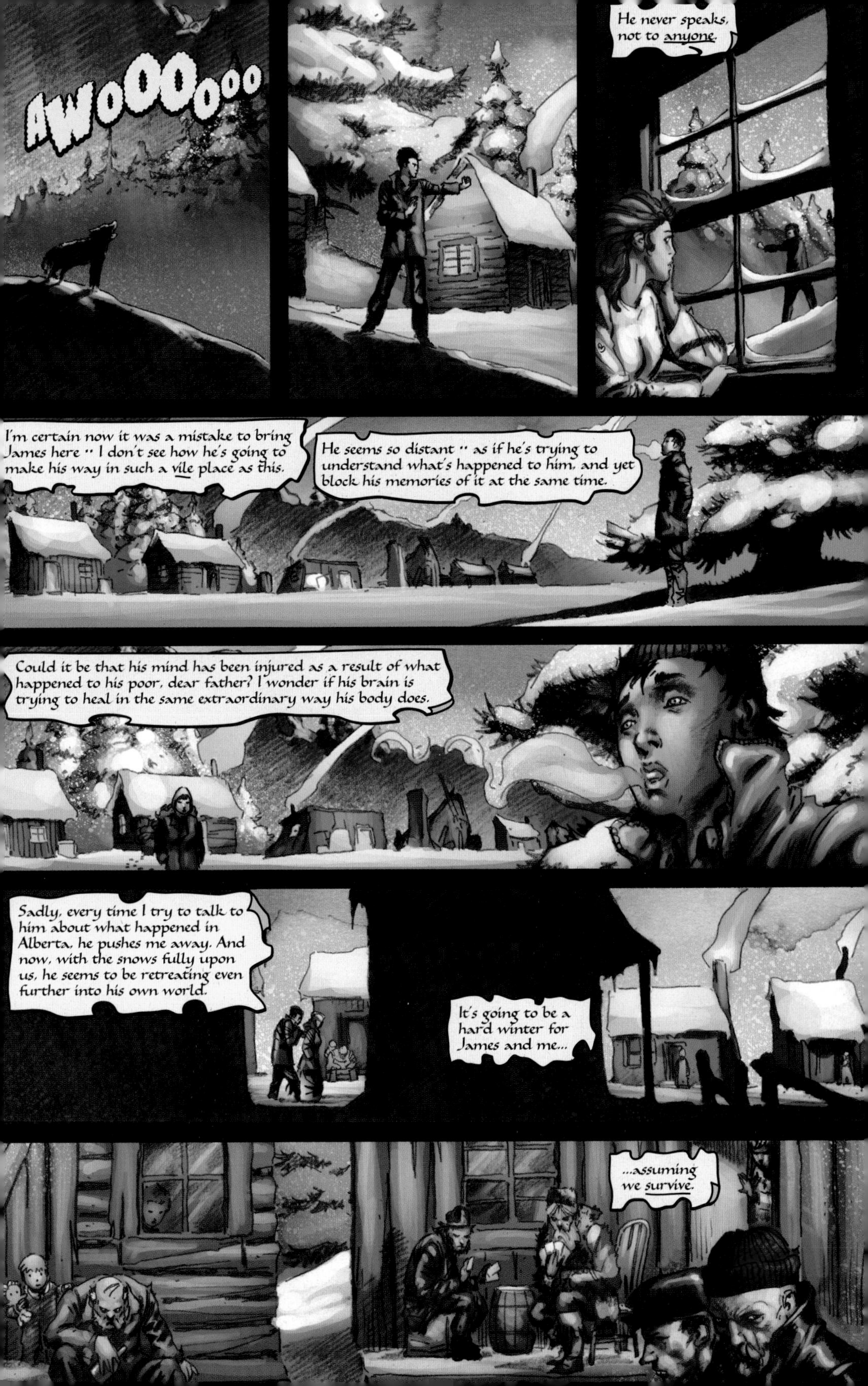
AWoOOOooo
He never speaks, not to anyone.
I'm certain now it was a mistake to bring James here .. I don't see how he's going to make his way in such a vile place as this.
He seems so distant .. as if he's trying to understand what's happened to him, and yet block his memories of it at the same time.
Could it be that his mind has been injured as a result of what happened to his poor, dear father? I wonder if his brain is trying to heal in the same extraordinary way his body does.
Sadly, every time I try to talk to him about what happened in Alberta, he pushes me away. And now, with the snows fully upon us, he seems to be retreating even further into his own world.
It's going to be a hard winter for James and me...
...assuming we survive.

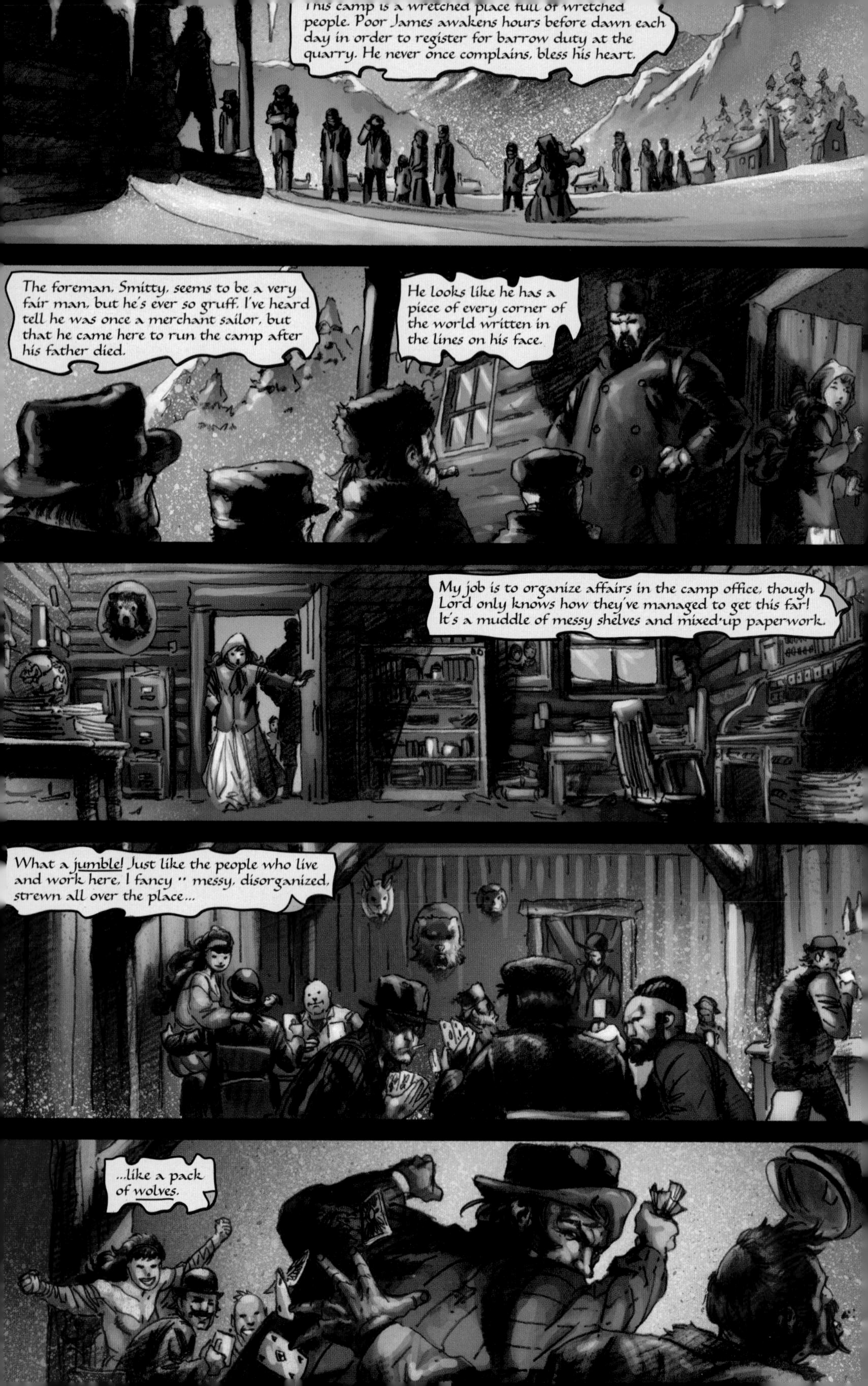
This camp is a wretched place full of wretched people. Poor James awakens hours before dawn each day in order to register for barrow duty at the quarry. He never once complains, bless his heart.
The foreman, Smitty, seems to be a very fair man, but he's ever so gruff. I've heard tell he was once a merchant sailor, but that he came here to run the camp after his father died.
He looks like he has a piece of every corner of the world written in the lines on his face.
My job is to organize affairs in the camp office, though Lord only knows how they've managed to get this far! It's a muddle of messy shelves and mixed-up paperwork.
What a jumble! Just like the people who live and work here, I fancy -- messy, disorganized, strewn all over the place...
...like a pack of wolves.

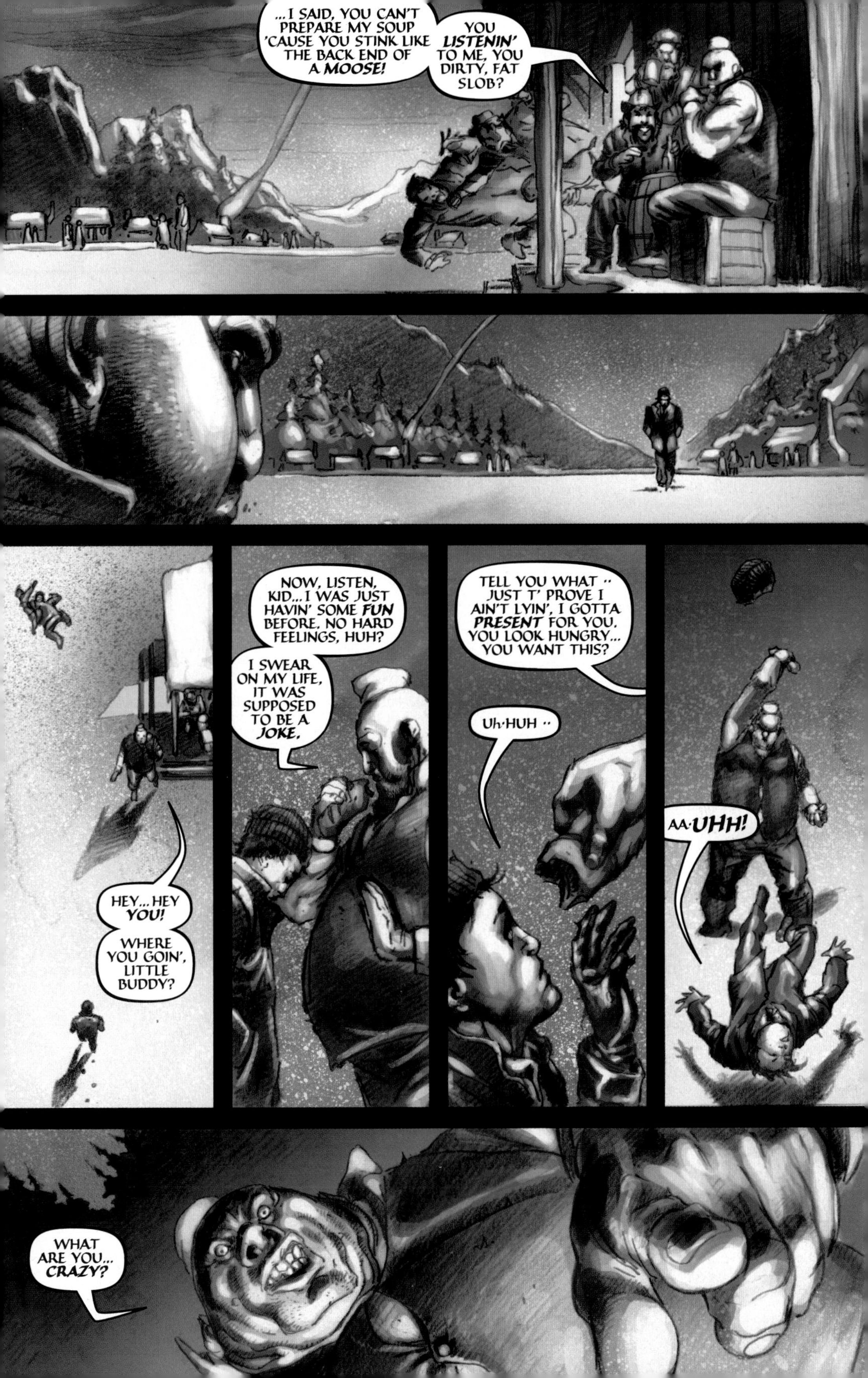
...I SAID, YOU CAN'T PREPARE MY SOUP 'CAUSE YOU STINK LIKE THE BACK END OF A MOOSE!
YOU LISTENIN' TO ME, YOU DIRTY, FAT SLOB?
HEY... HEY YOU!
WHERE YOU GOIN', LITTLE BUDDY?
NOW, LISTEN, KID... I WAS JUST HAVIN' SOME FUN BEFORE. NO HARD FEELINGS, HUH?
I SWEAR ON MY LIFE, IT WAS SUPPOSED TO BE A JOKE.
TELL YOU WHAT .. JUST T' PROVE I AIN'T LYIN', I GOTTA PRESENT FOR YOU. YOU LOOK HUNGRY... YOU WANT THIS?
Uh-HUH ..
AA-UHH!
WHAT ARE YOU... CRAZY?

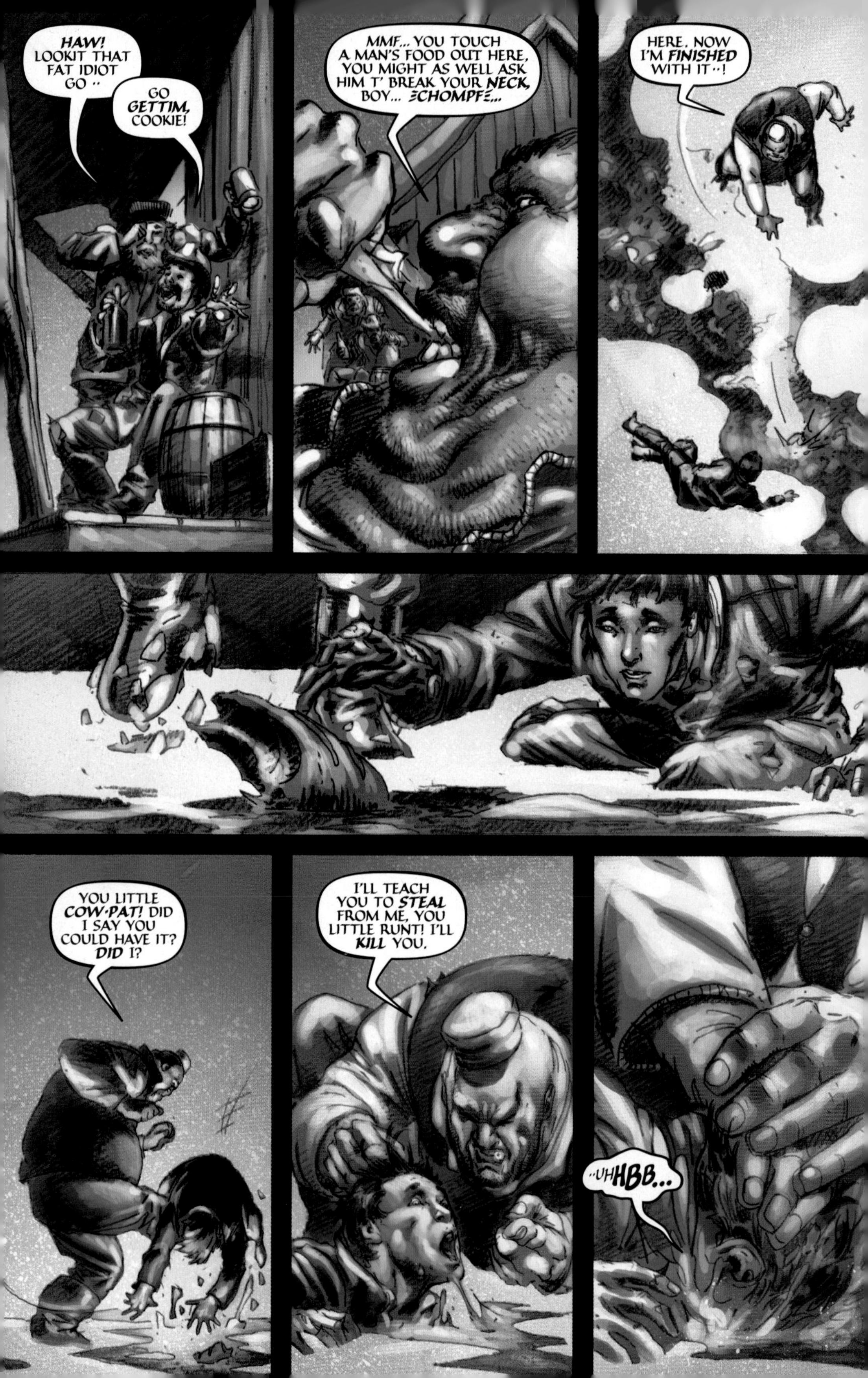
HAW! LOOKIT THAT FAT IDIOT GO ..
GO GETTIM, COOKIE!
MMF... YOU TOUCH A MAN'S FOOD OUT HERE, YOU MIGHT AS WELL ASK HIM T' BREAK YOUR NECK, BOY... CHOMPF...
HERE, NOW I'M FINISHED WITH IT..!
YOU LITTLE COW-PAT! DID I SAY YOU COULD HAVE IT? DID I?
I'LL TEACH YOU TO STEAL FROM ME, YOU LITTLE RUNT! I'LL KILL YOU.
..UHHBB...

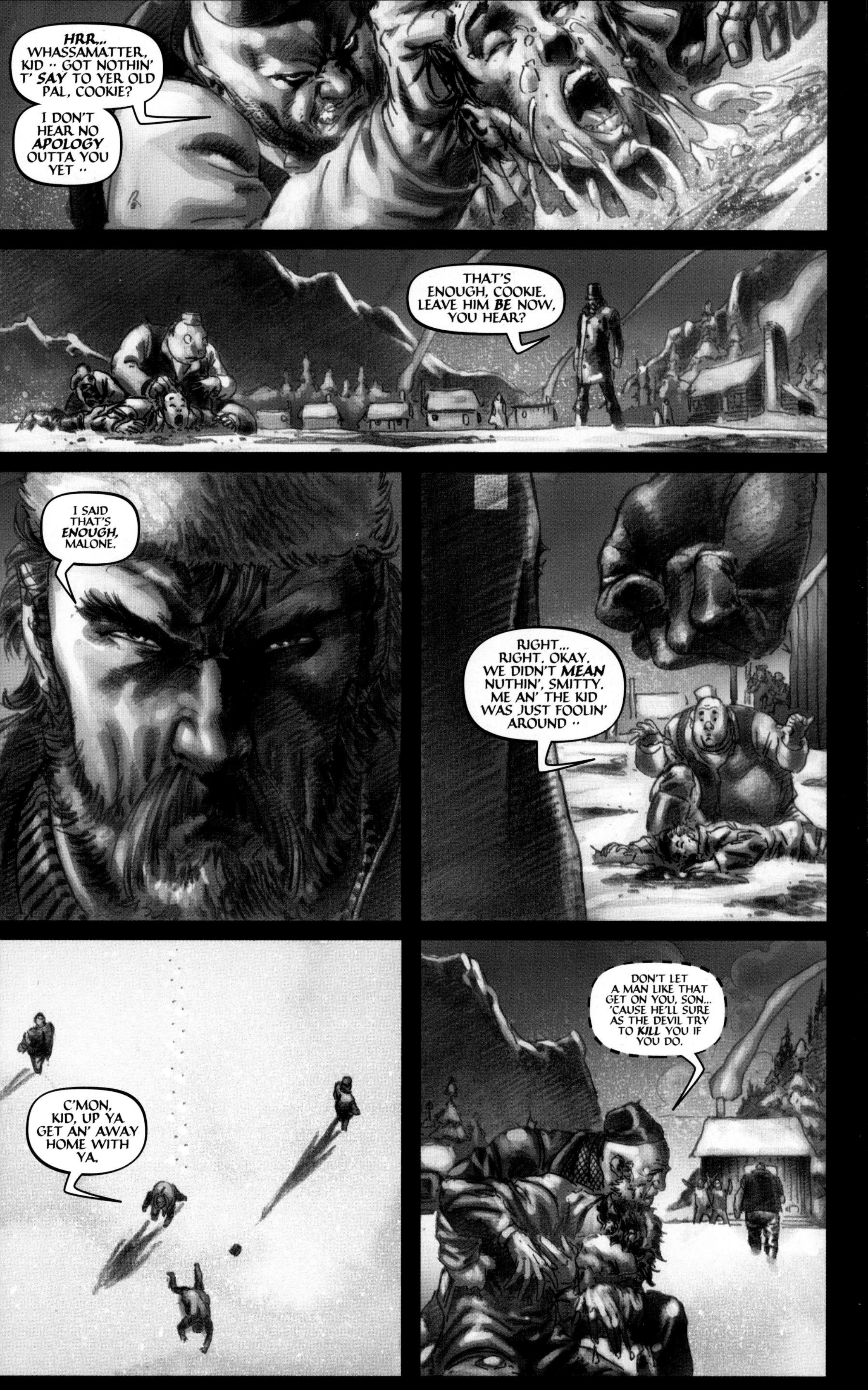
HRR... WHASSAMATTER, KID -- GOT NOTHIN' T' SAY TO YER OLD PAL, COOKIE?
I DON'T HEAR NO APOLOGY OUTTA YOU YET --
THAT'S ENOUGH, COOKIE. LEAVE HIM BE NOW, YOU HEAR?
I SAID THAT'S ENOUGH, MALONE.
RIGHT... RIGHT, OKAY, WE DIDN'T MEAN NUTHIN', SMITTY, ME AN' THE KID WAS JUST FOOLIN' AROUND --
C'MON, KID, UP YA GET AN' AWAY HOME WITH YA.
DON'T LET A MAN LIKE THAT GET ON YOU, SON... 'CAUSE HE'LL SURE AS THE DEVIL TRY TO KILL YOU IF YOU DO.

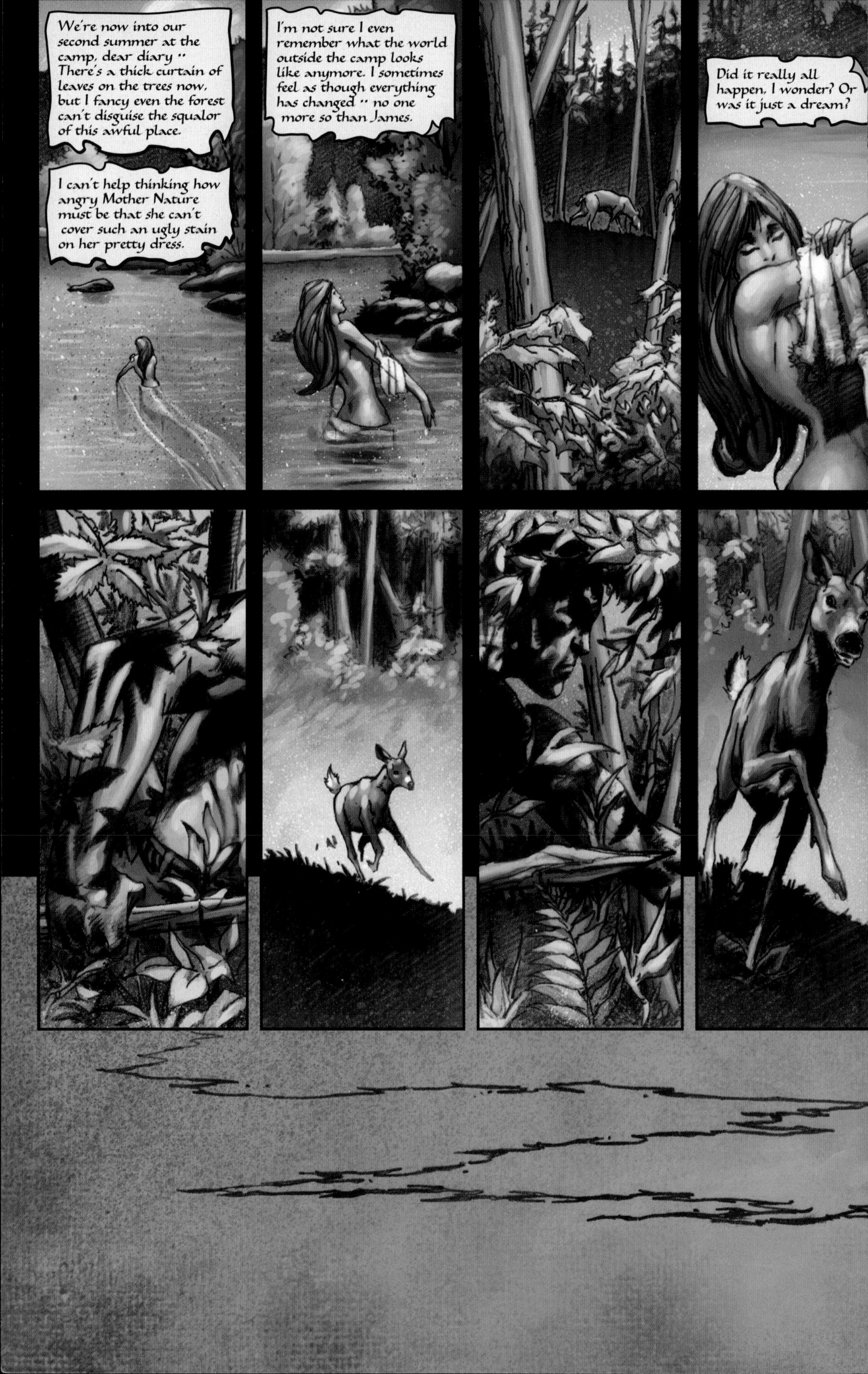
We're now into our second summer at the camp, dear diary -- There's a thick curtain of leaves on the trees now, but I fancy even the forest can't disguise the squalor of this awful place.
I can't help thinking how angry Mother Nature must be that she can't cover such an ugly stain on her pretty dress.
I'm not sure I even remember what the world outside the camp looks like anymore. I sometimes feel as though everything has changed -- no one more so than James.
Did it really all happen, I wonder? Or was it just a dream?

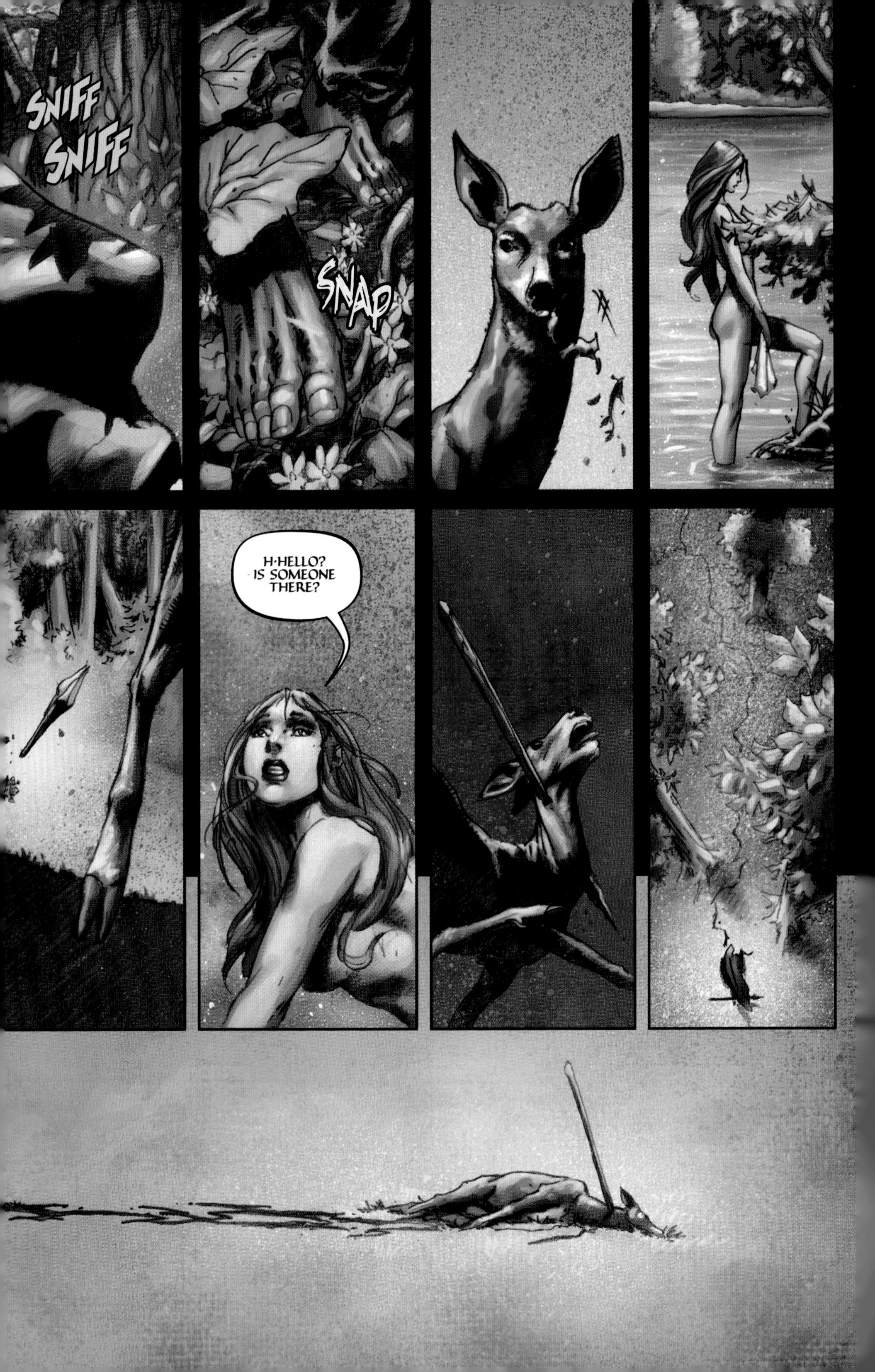
SNIFF SNIFF
SNAP
H-HELLO? IS SOMEONE THERE?

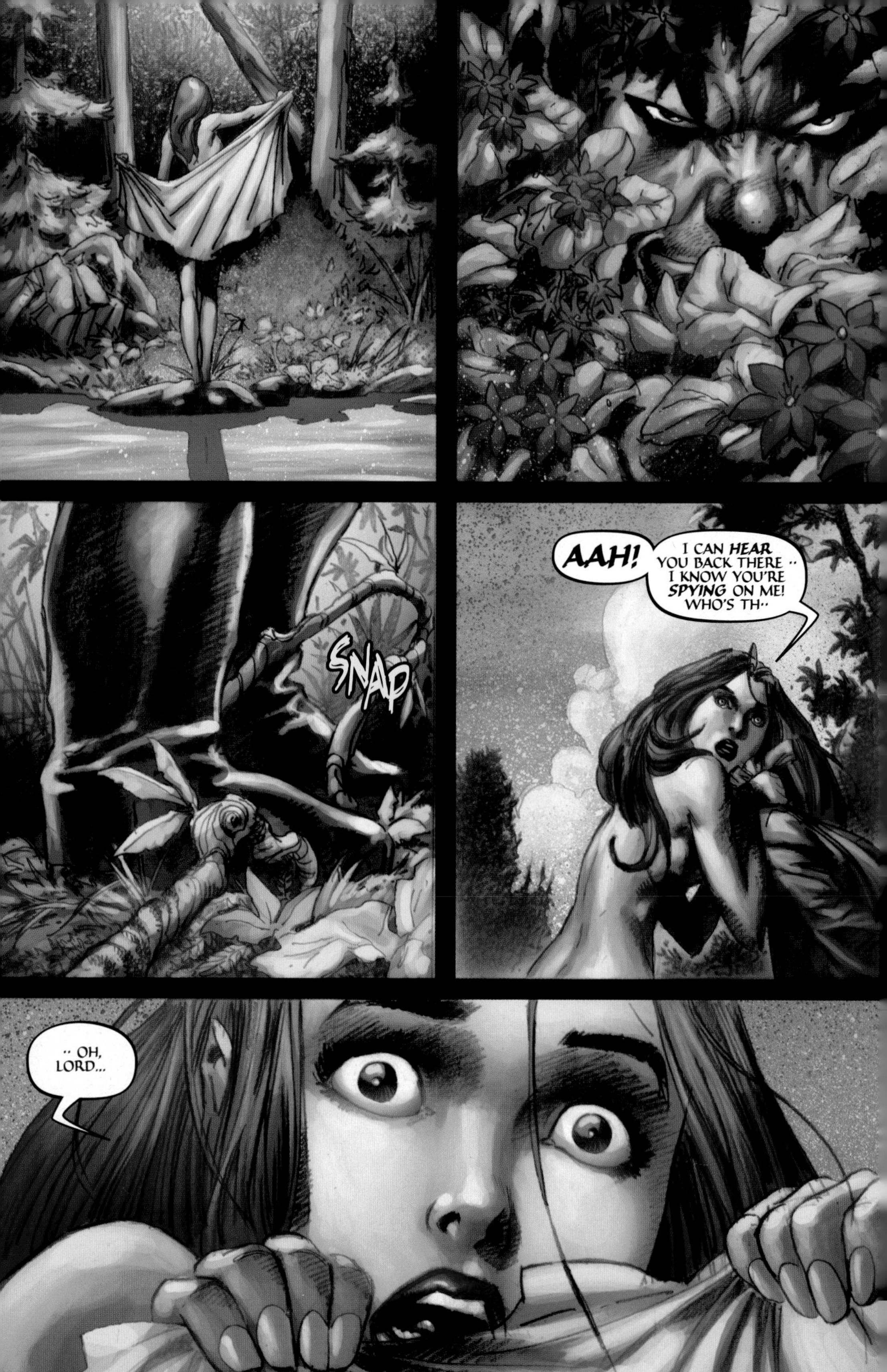
SNAP
AAH!
I CAN HEAR YOU BACK THERE .. I KNOW YOU'RE SPYING ON ME! WHO'S TH..
.. OH, LORD...

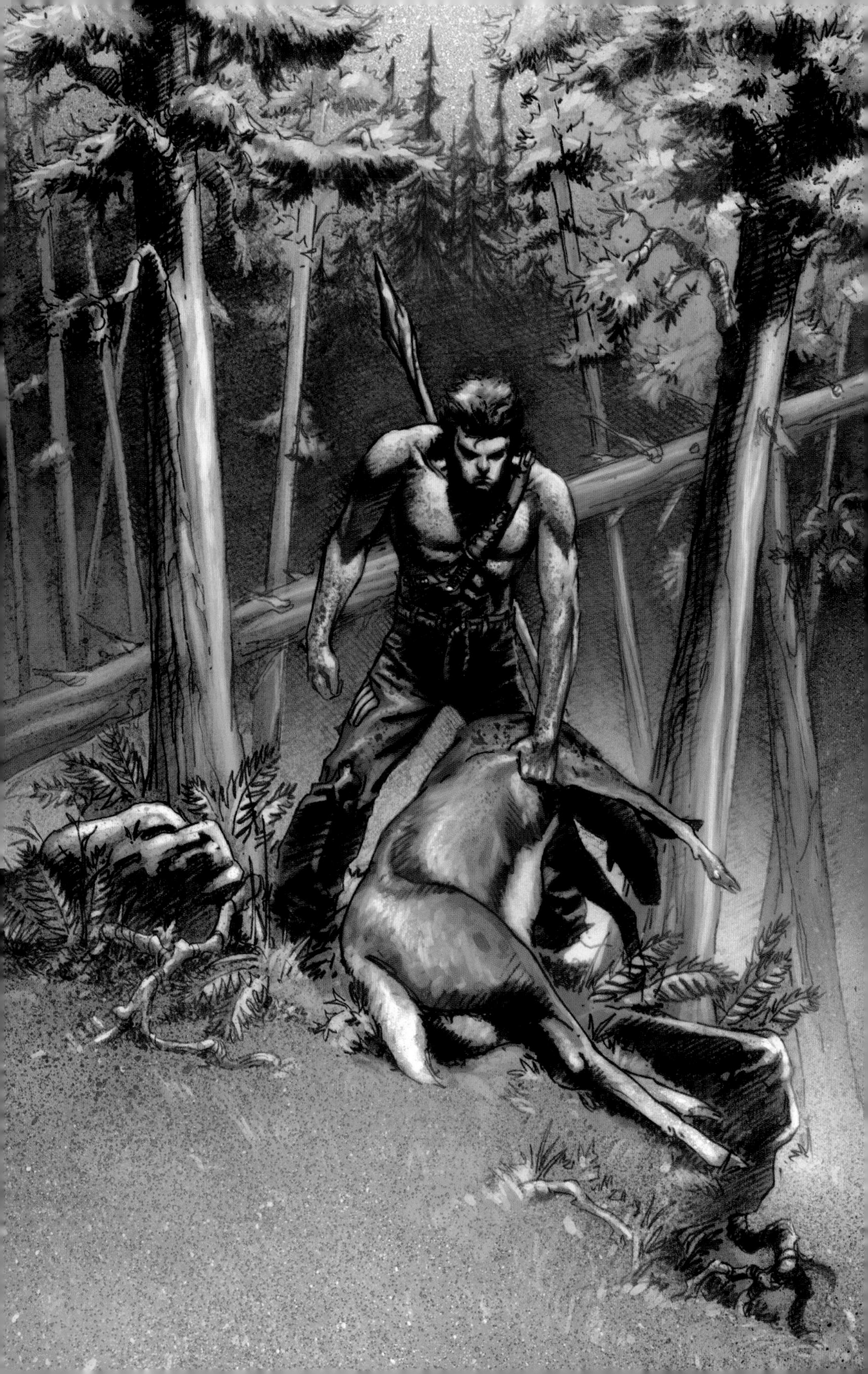

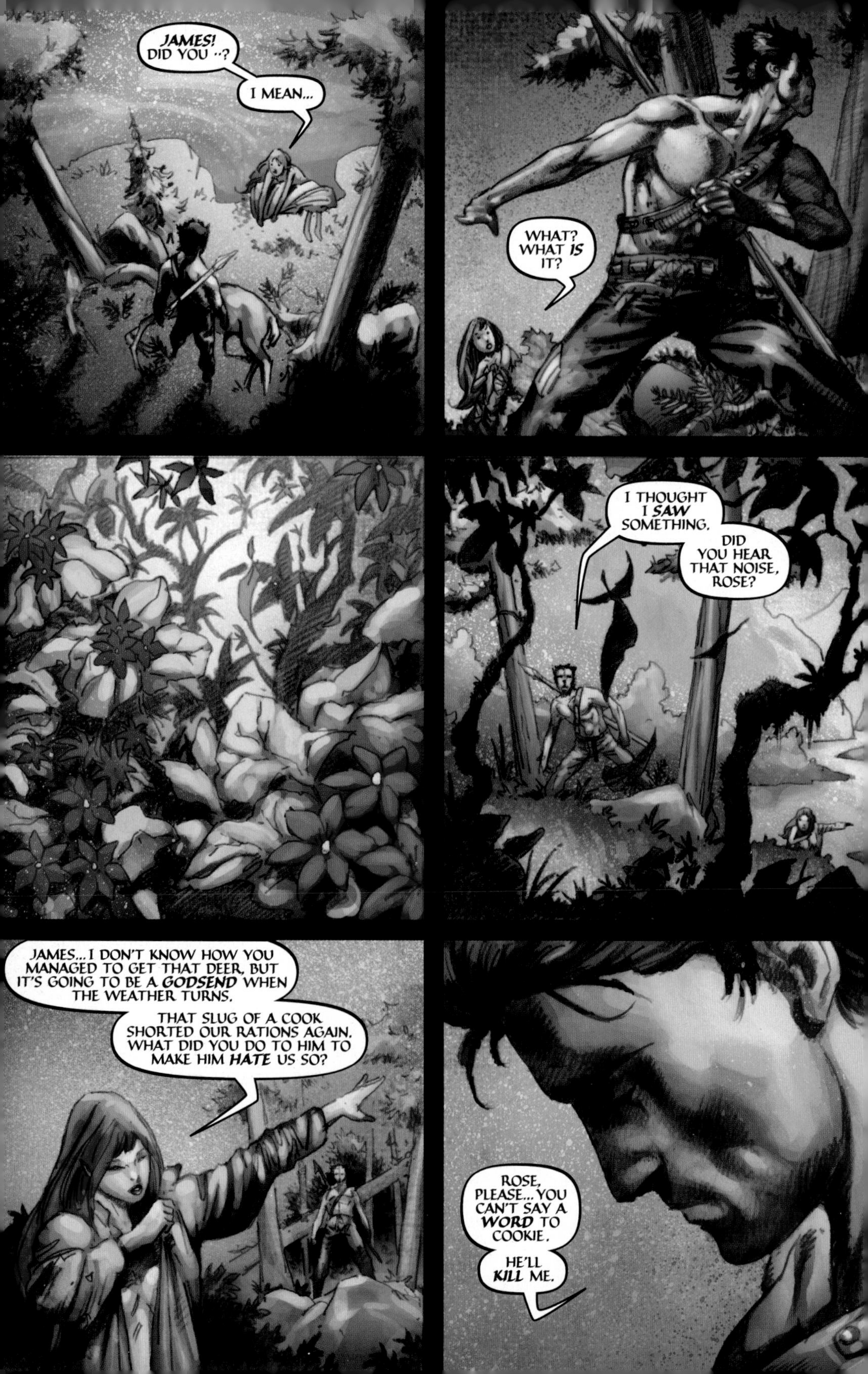
JAMES! DID YOU ..?
I MEAN...
WHAT? WHAT IS IT?
I THOUGHT I SAW SOMETHING.
DID YOU HEAR THAT NOISE, ROSE?
JAMES... I DON'T KNOW HOW YOU MANAGED TO GET THAT DEER, BUT IT'S GOING TO BE A GODSEND WHEN THE WEATHER TURNS.
THAT SLUG OF A COOK SHORTED OUR RATIONS AGAIN. WHAT DID YOU DO TO HIM TO MAKE HIM HATE US SO?
ROSE, PLEASE... YOU CAN'T SAY A WORD TO COOKIE.
HE'LL KILL ME.

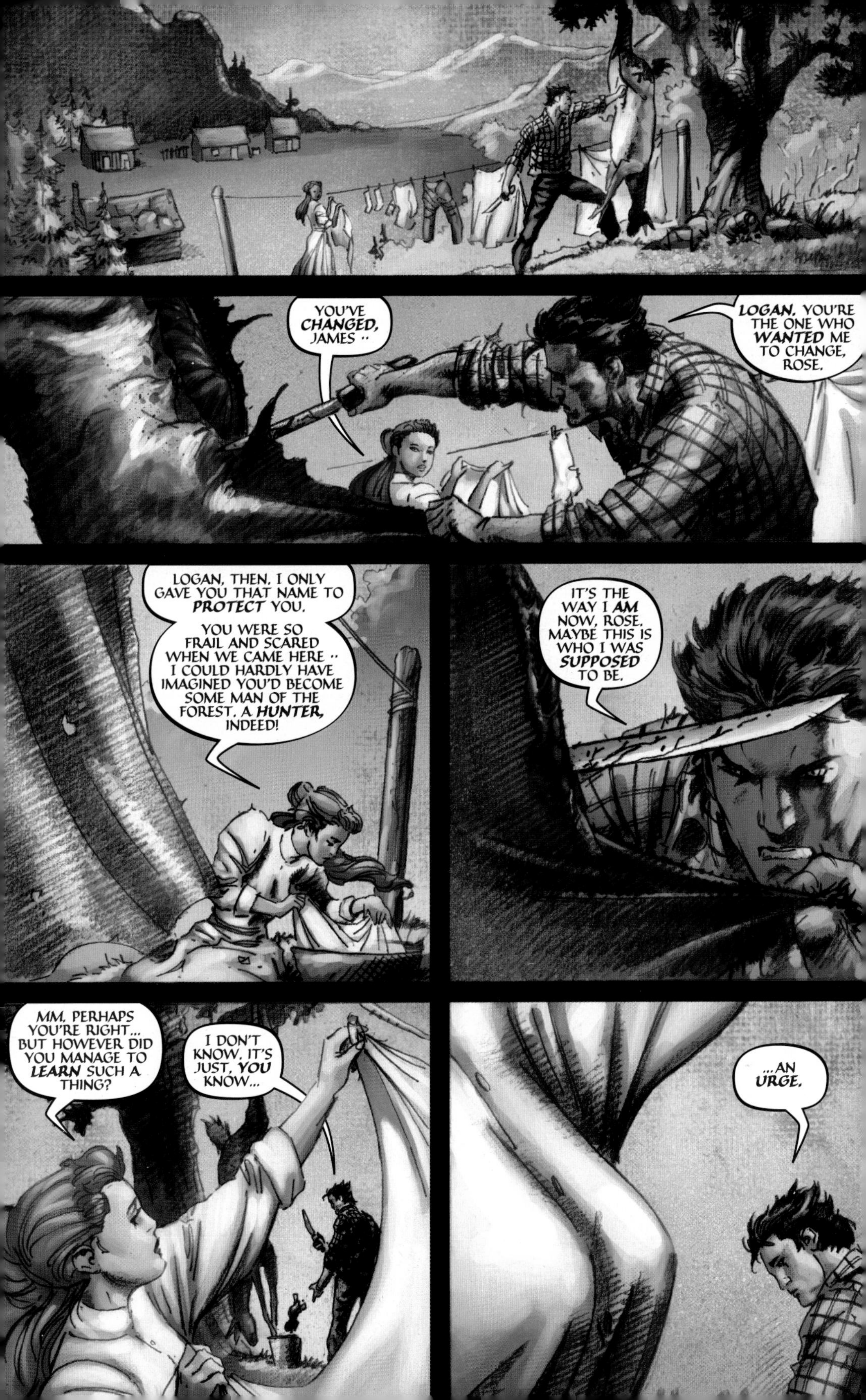

YOU'VE CHANGED, JAMES ..
LOGAN, YOU'RE THE ONE WHO WANTED ME TO CHANGE, ROSE.
LOGAN, THEN. I ONLY GAVE YOU THAT NAME TO PROTECT YOU.
YOU WERE SO FRAIL AND SCARED WHEN WE CAME HERE .. I COULD HARDLY HAVE IMAGINED YOU'D BECOME SOME MAN OF THE FOREST. A HUNTER, INDEED!
IT'S THE WAY I AM NOW, ROSE. MAYBE THIS IS WHO I WAS SUPPOSED TO BE.
MM, PERHAPS YOU'RE RIGHT... BUT HOWEVER DID YOU MANAGE TO LEARN SUCH A THING?
I DON'T KNOW. IT'S JUST, YOU KNOW...
...AN URGE.

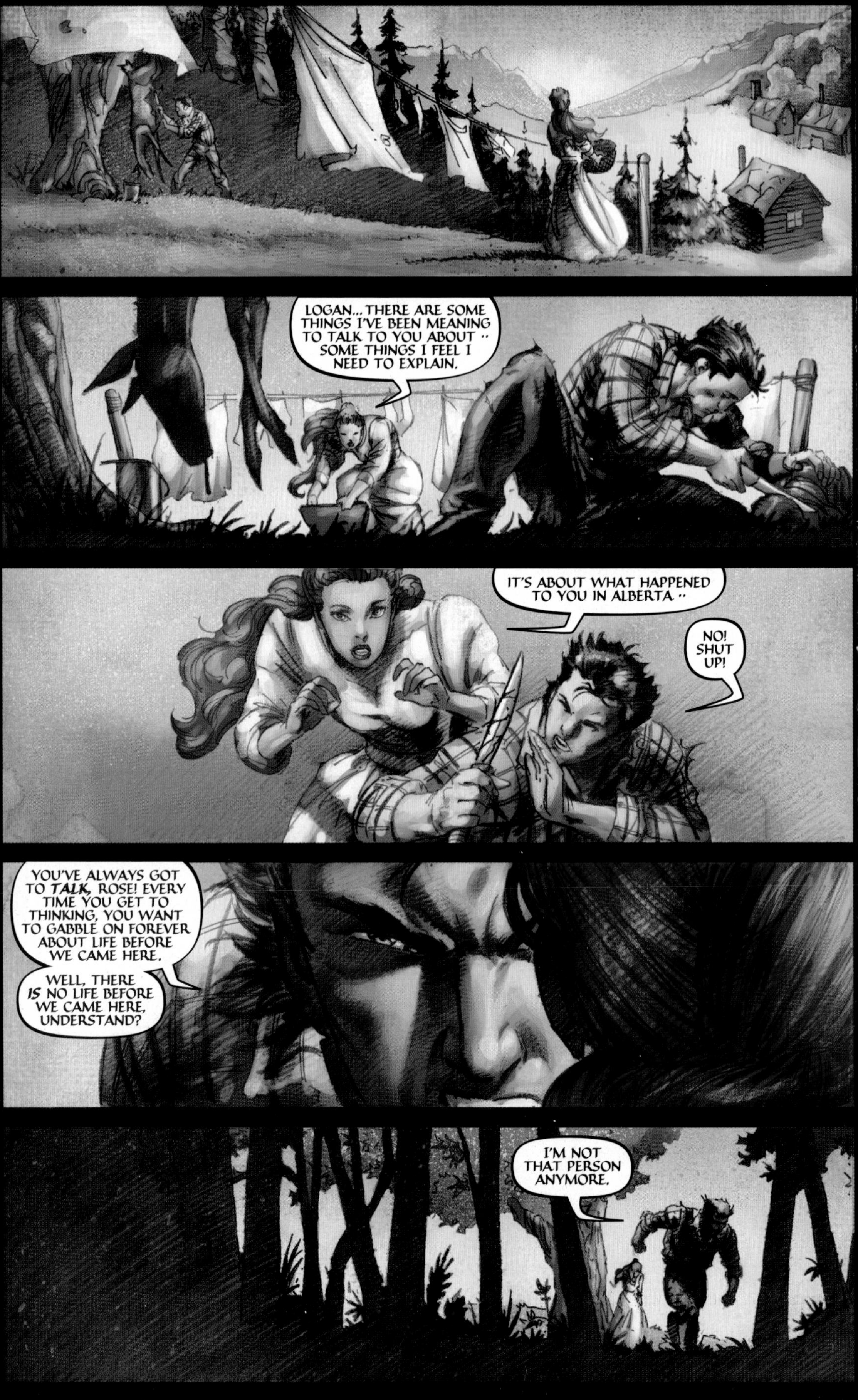
LOGAN... THERE ARE SOME THINGS I'VE BEEN MEANING TO TALK TO YOU ABOUT -- SOME THINGS I FEEL I NEED TO EXPLAIN.
IT'S ABOUT WHAT HAPPENED TO YOU IN ALBERTA --
NO! SHUT UP!
YOU'VE ALWAYS GOT TO *TALK,* ROSE! EVERY TIME YOU GET TO THINKING, YOU WANT TO GABBLE ON FOREVER ABOUT LIFE BEFORE WE CAME HERE.
WELL, THERE *IS* NO LIFE BEFORE WE CAME HERE, UNDERSTAND?
I'M NOT THAT PERSON ANYMORE.

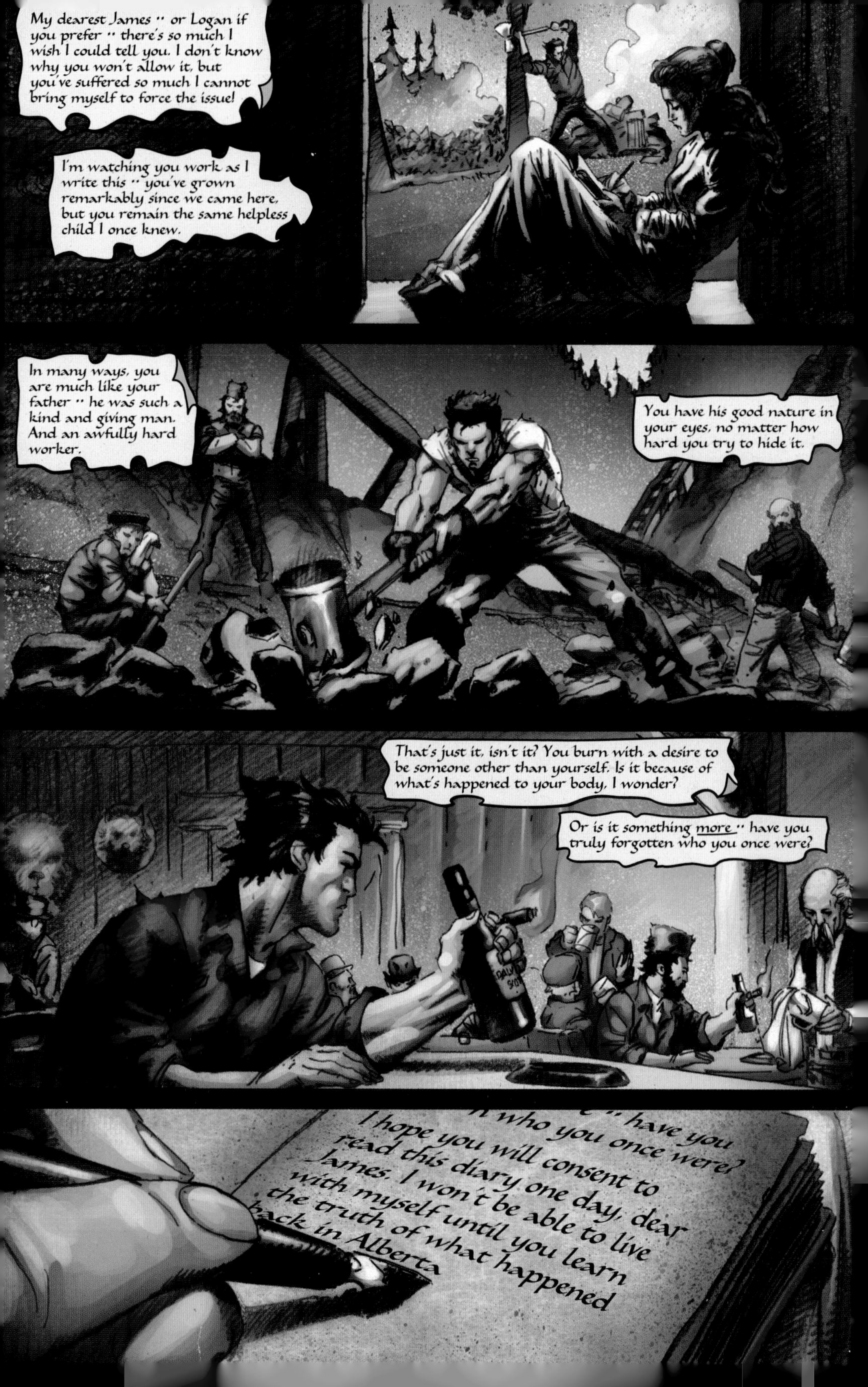
My dearest James -- or Logan if you prefer -- there's so much I wish I could tell you. I don't know why you won't allow it, but you've suffered so much I cannot bring myself to force the issue!
I'm watching you work as I write this -- you've grown remarkably since we came here, but you remain the same helpless child I once knew.
In many ways, you are much like your father -- he was such a kind and giving man. And an awfully hard worker.
You have his good nature in your eyes, no matter how hard you try to hide it.
That's just it, isn't it? You burn with a desire to be someone other than yourself. Is it because of what's happened to your body, I wonder?
Or is it something more -- have you truly forgotten who you once were?
have you
who you once were?
I hope you will consent to
read this diary one day, dear
James. I won't be able to live
with myself until you learn
the truth of what happened
back in Alberta

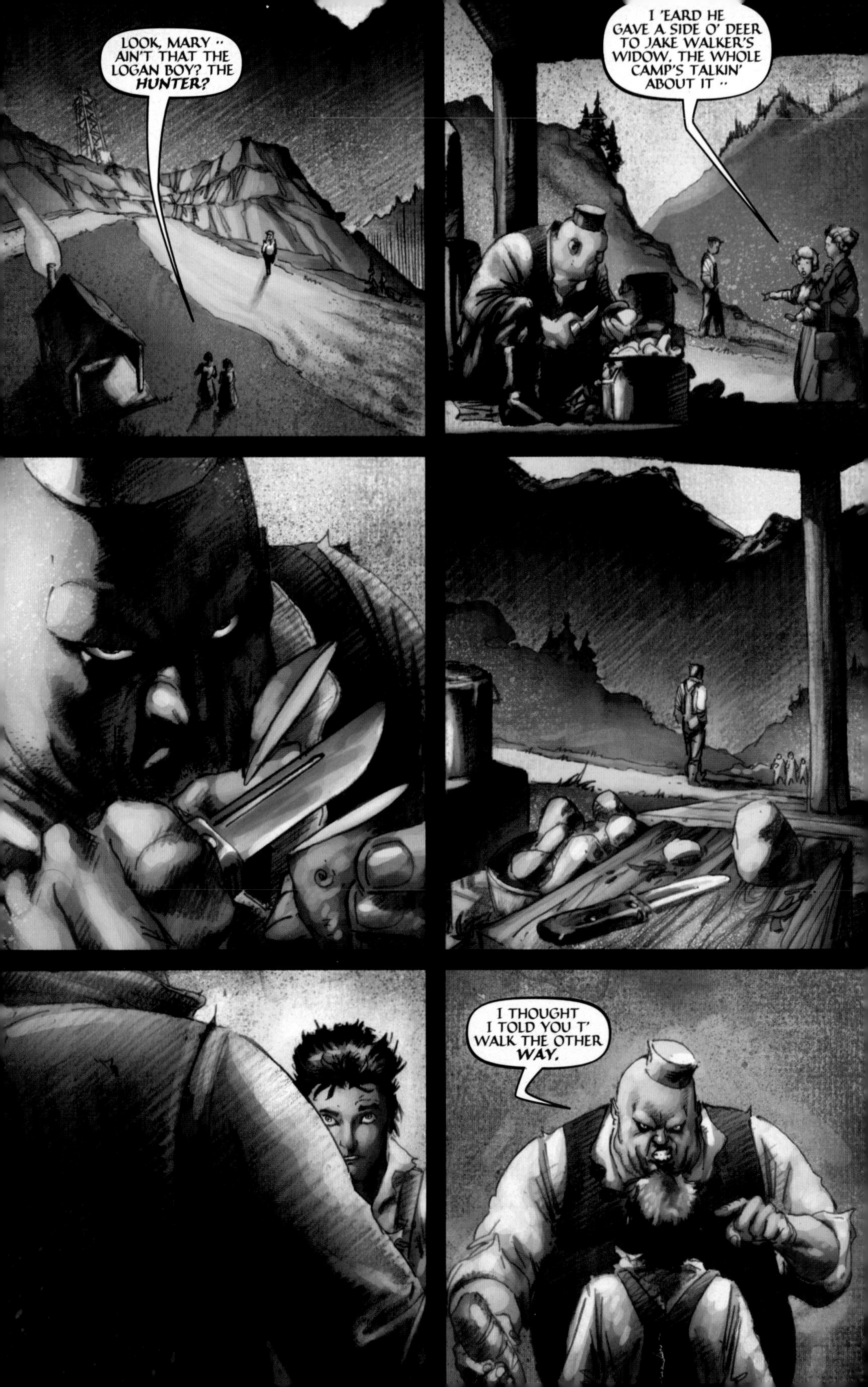
LOOK, MARY .. AIN'T THAT THE LOGAN BOY? THE HUNTER?
I 'EARD HE GAVE A SIDE O' DEER TO JAKE WALKER'S WIDOW. THE WHOLE CAMP'S TALKIN' ABOUT IT ..
I THOUGHT I TOLD YOU T' WALK THE OTHER WAY.

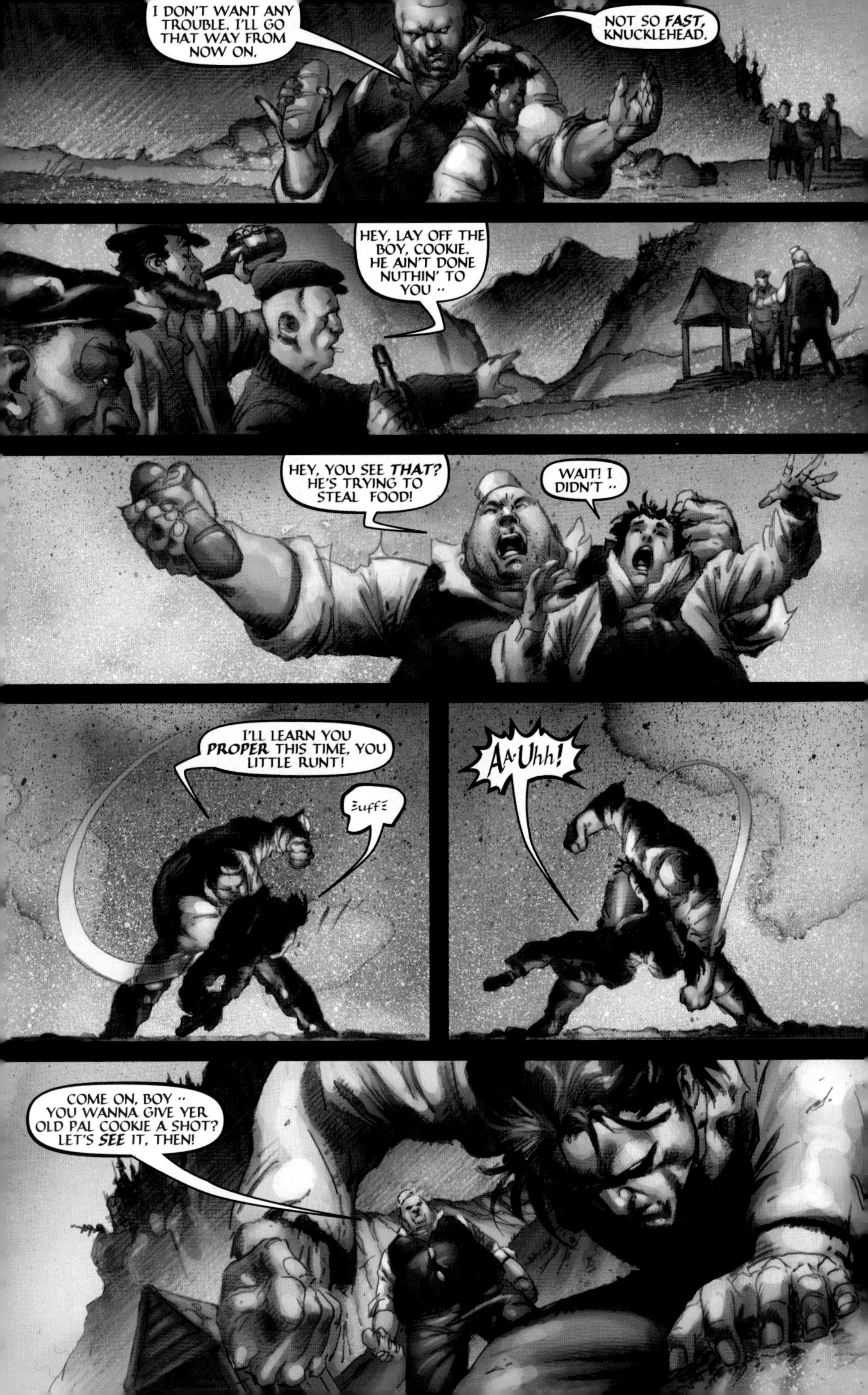
I DON'T WANT ANY TROUBLE. I'LL GO THAT WAY FROM NOW ON.
NOT SO FAST, KNUCKLEHEAD.
HEY, LAY OFF THE BOY, COOKIE. HE AIN'T DONE NUTHIN' TO YOU ..
HEY, YOU SEE THAT? HE'S TRYING TO STEAL FOOD!
WAIT! I DIDN'T ..
I'LL LEARN YOU PROPER THIS TIME, YOU LITTLE RUNT!
uff
AA-Uhh!
COME ON, BOY .. YOU WANNA GIVE YER OLD PAL COOKIE A SHOT? LET'S SEE IT, THEN!

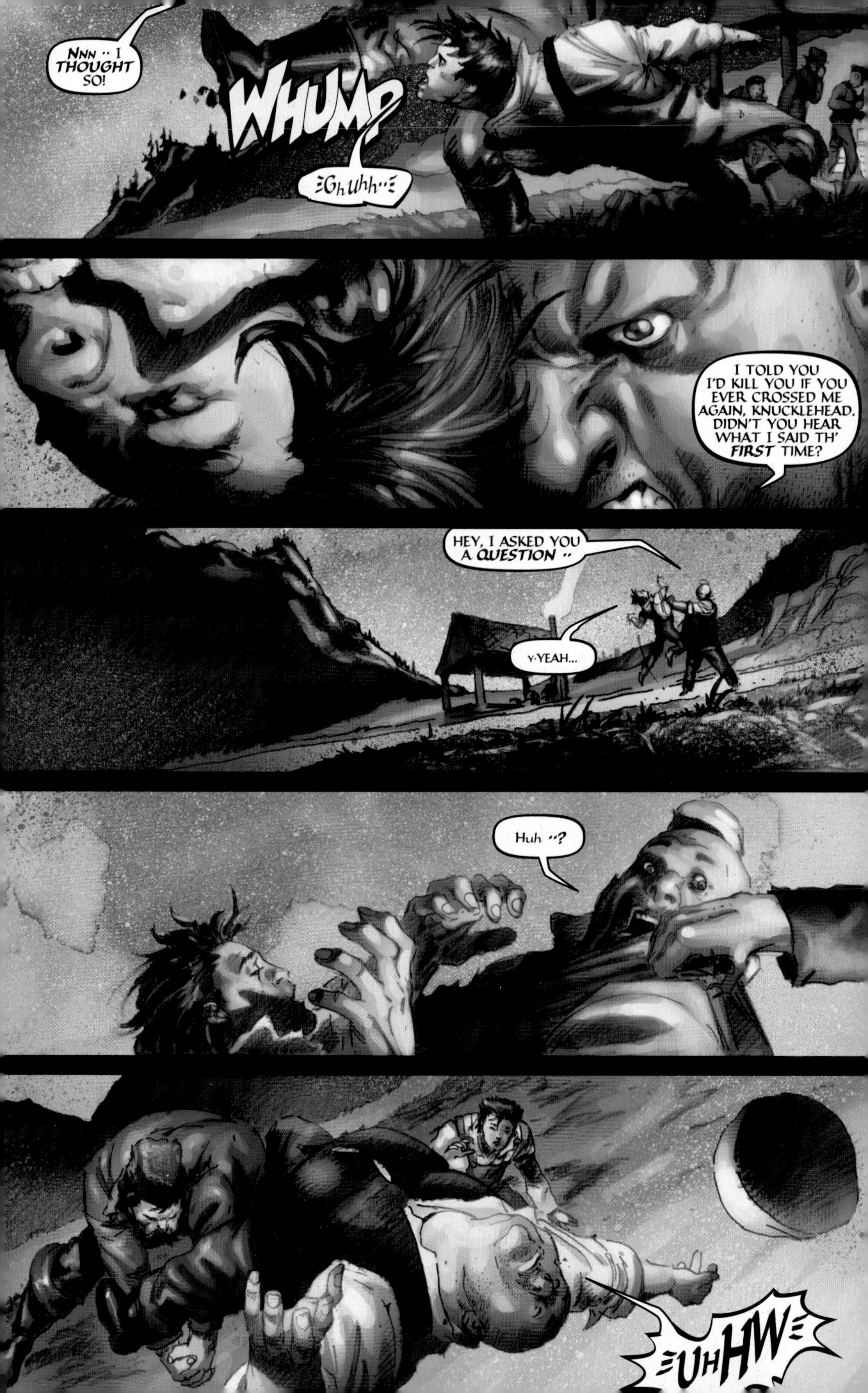
NNN .. I THOUGHT SO!
WHUMP
GHUHH..
I TOLD YOU I'D KILL YOU IF YOU EVER CROSSED ME AGAIN, KNUCKLEHEAD. DIDN'T YOU HEAR WHAT I SAID TH' FIRST TIME?
HEY, I ASKED YOU A QUESTION ..
Y-YEAH...
Huh ..?
UHHW

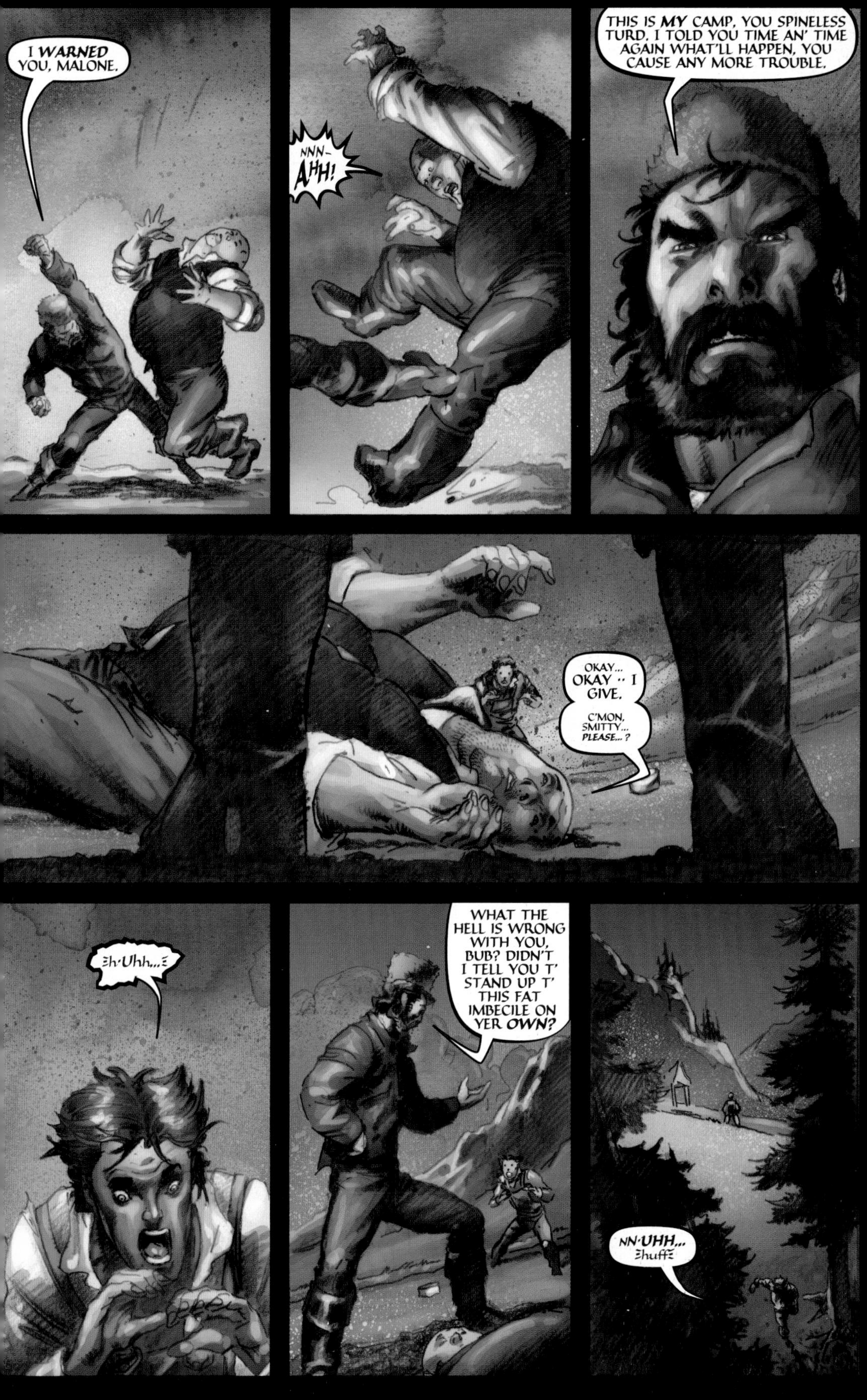
I WARNED YOU, MALONE.
NNN-AHH!
THIS IS MY CAMP, YOU SPINELESS TURD. I TOLD YOU TIME AN' TIME AGAIN WHAT'LL HAPPEN, YOU CAUSE ANY MORE TROUBLE.
OKAY... OKAY -- I GIVE.
C'MON, SMITTY... PLEASE...?
Uhh...
WHAT THE HELL IS WRONG WITH YOU, BUB? DIDN'T I TELL YOU T' STAND UP T' THIS FAT IMBECILE ON YER OWN?
NN-UHH... huff

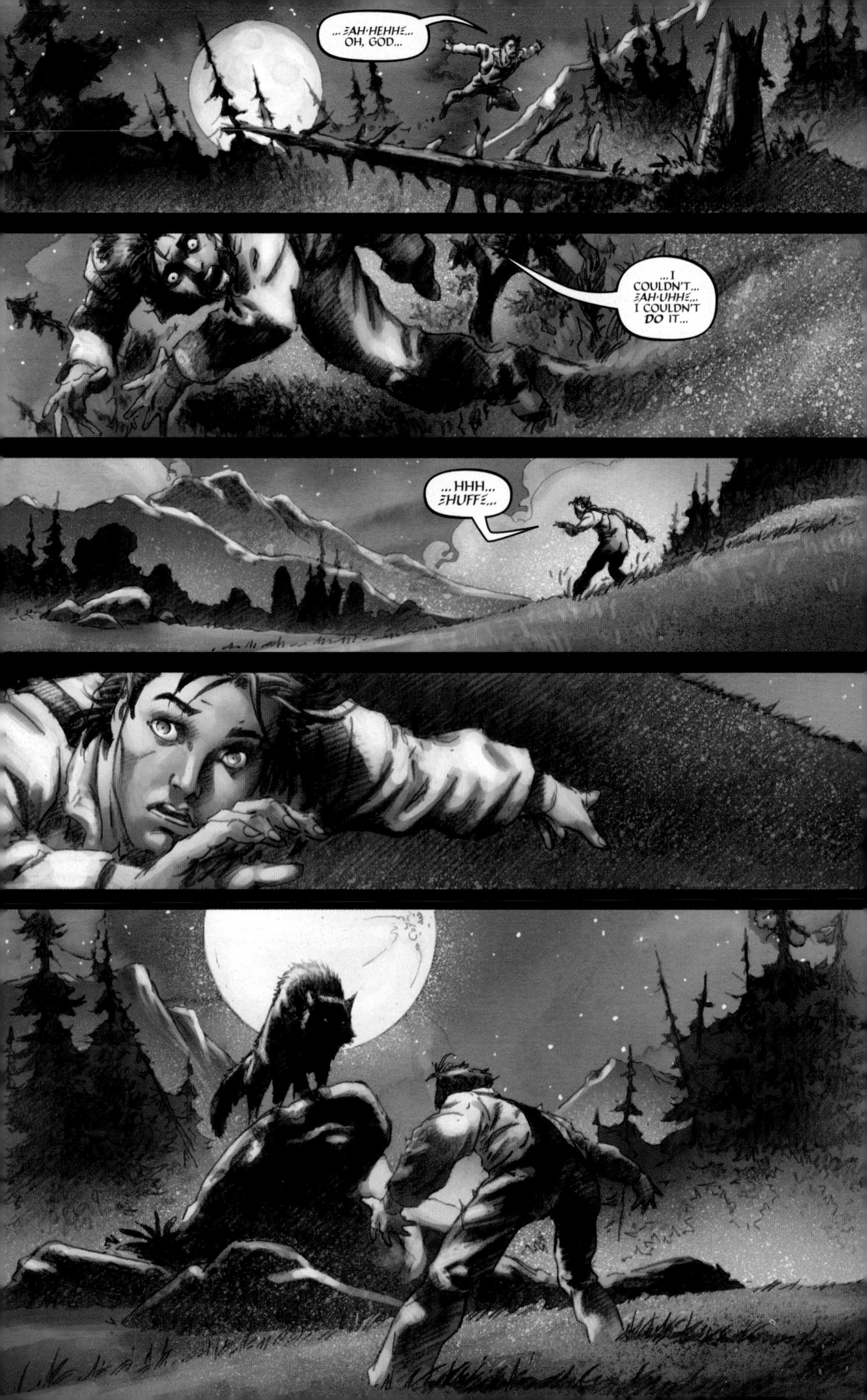
...ƎAH·HEHHƐ... OH, GOD...
...I COULDN'T... ƎAH·UHHƐ... I COULDN'T DO IT...
...HHH... ƎHUFFƐ...

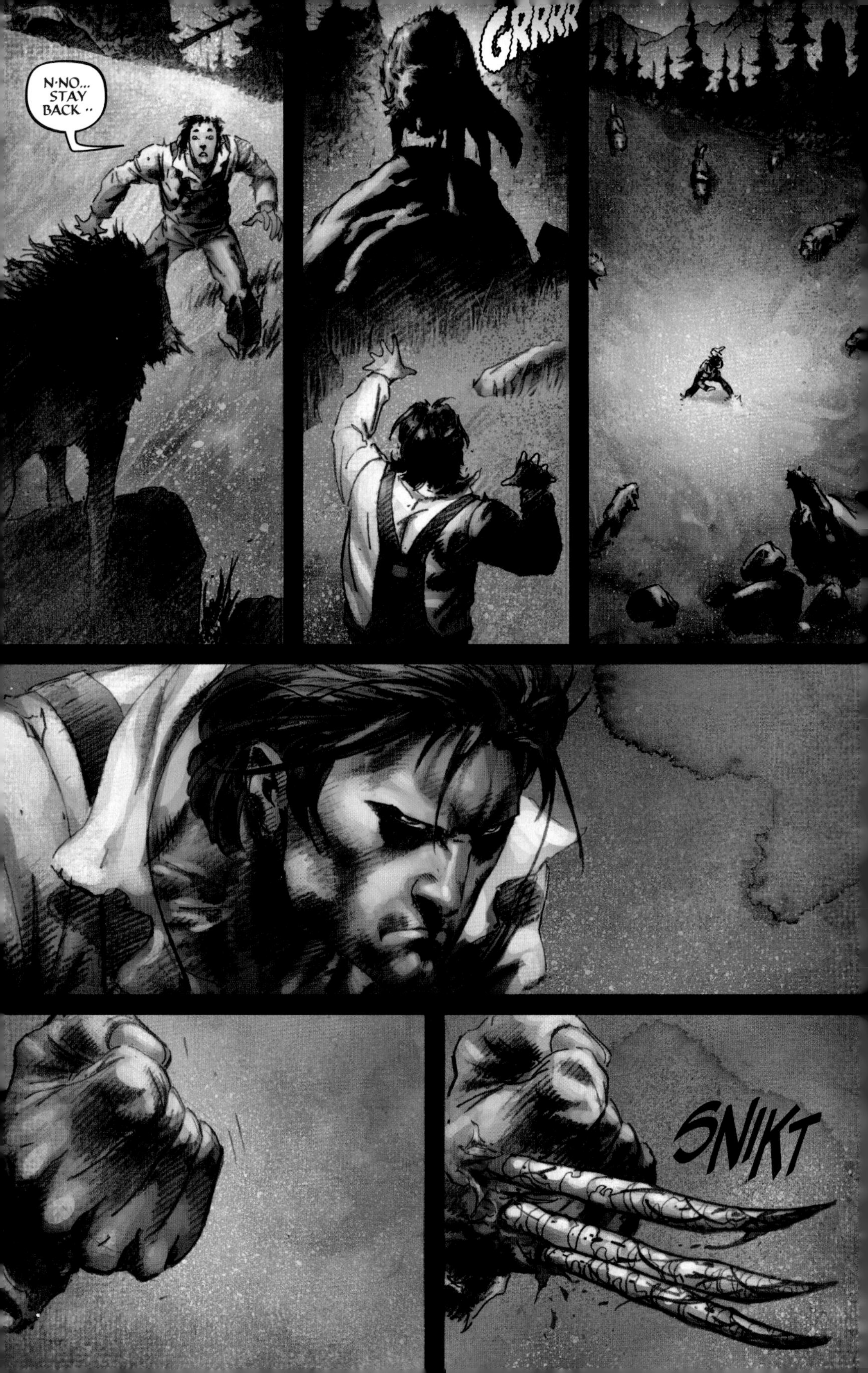
N·NO... STAY BACK ..
GRRRR
SNIKT

GRRRR

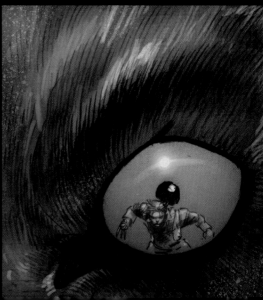

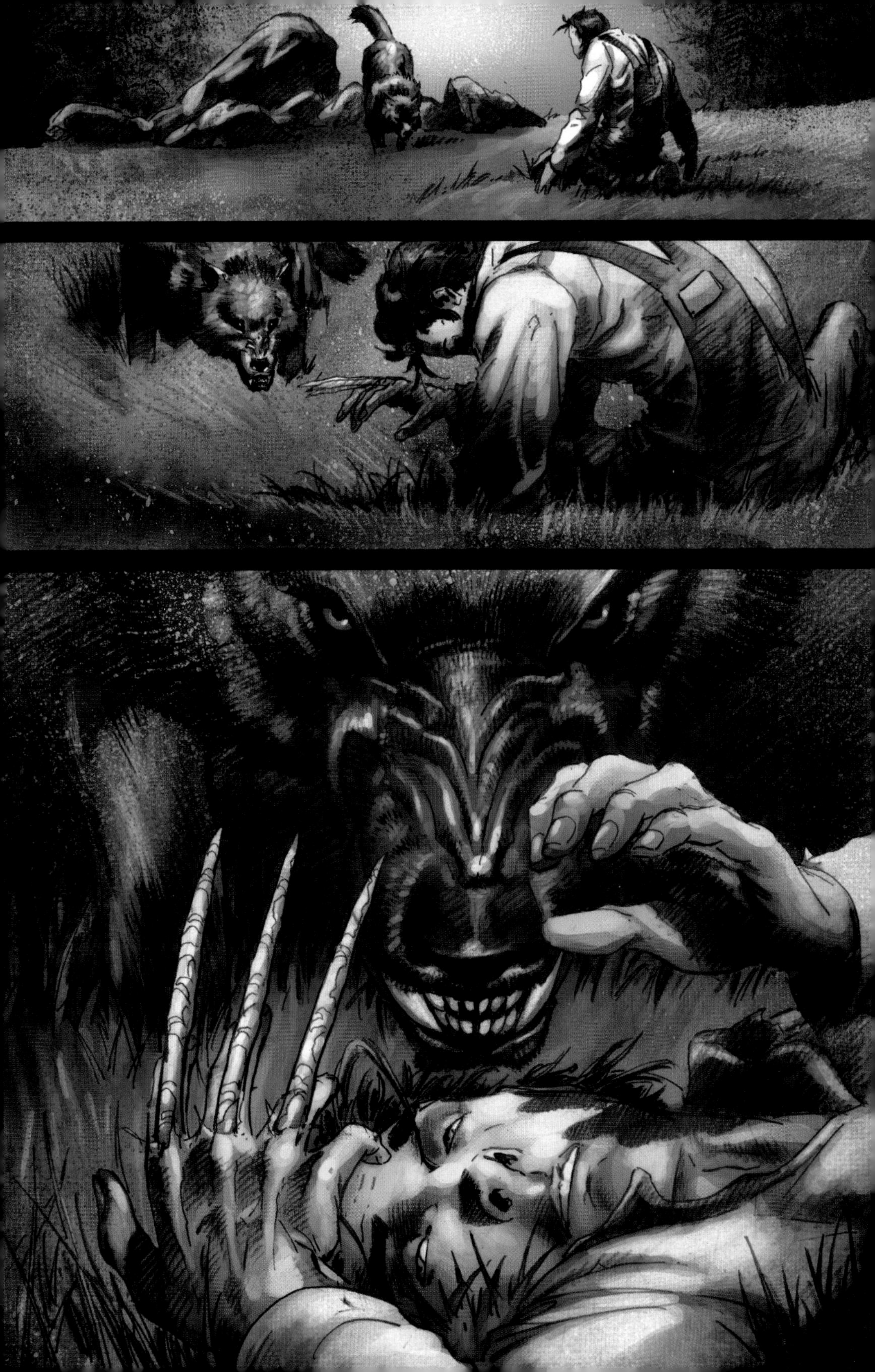

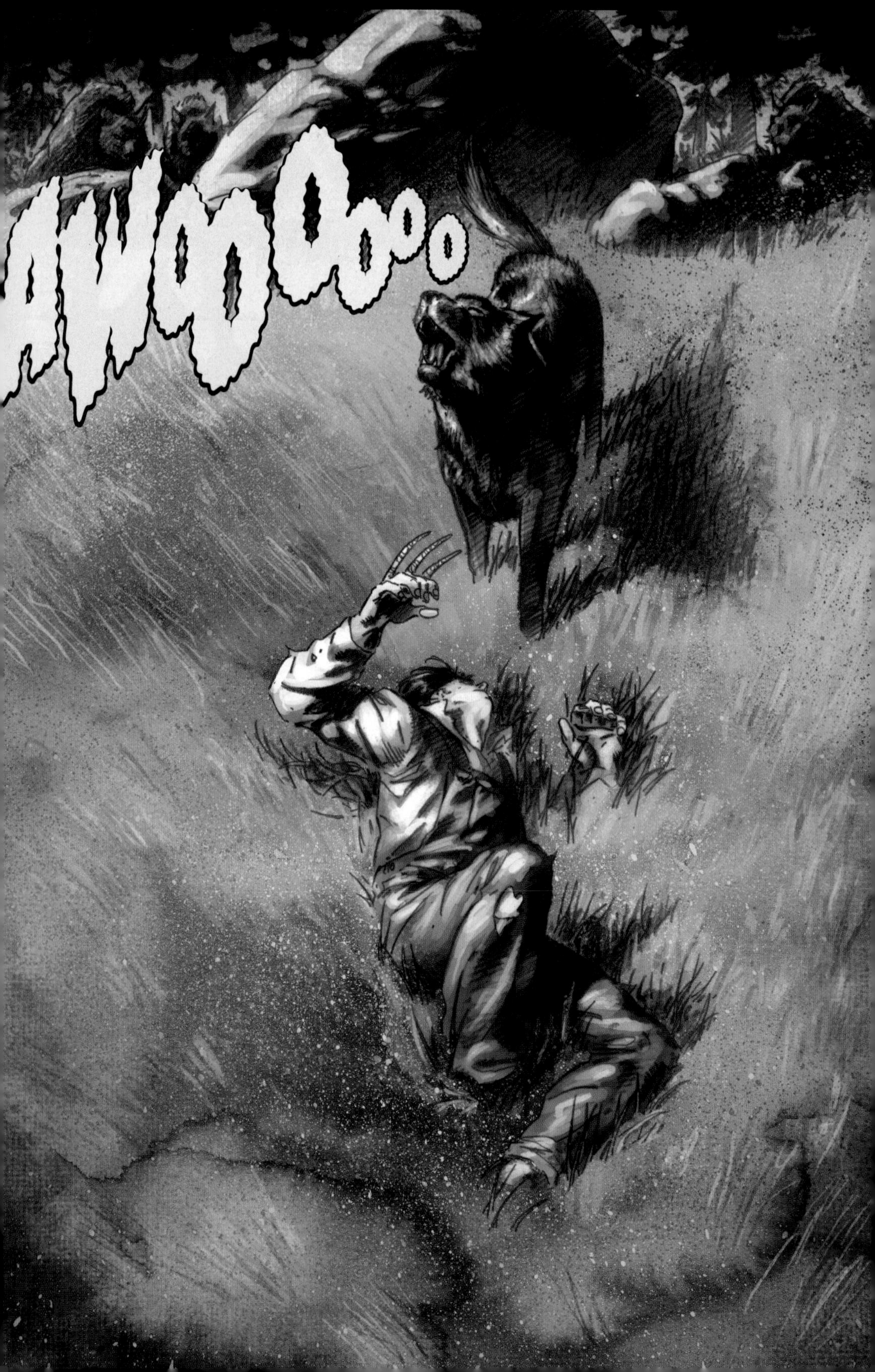
AWOOOooo

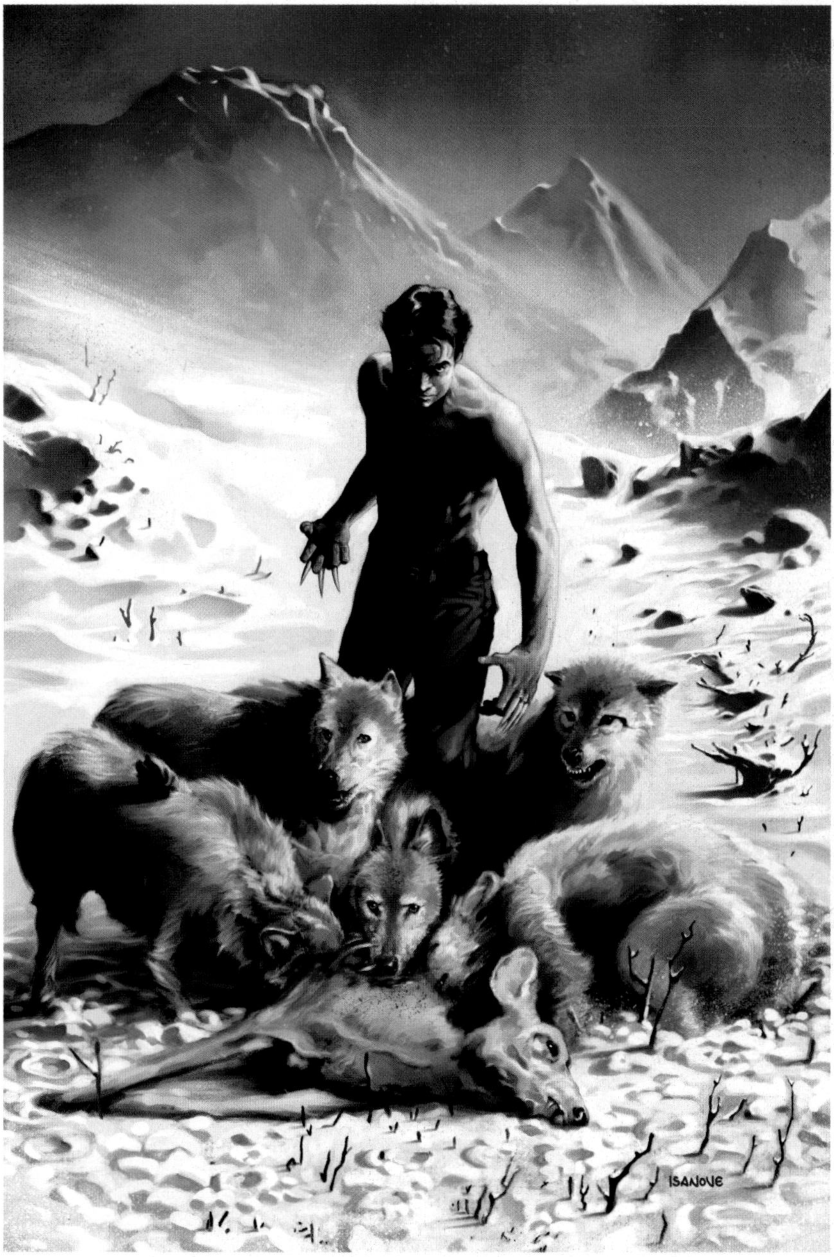
ISANOVE

BY RICHARD ISANOVE

"THE FEAST"

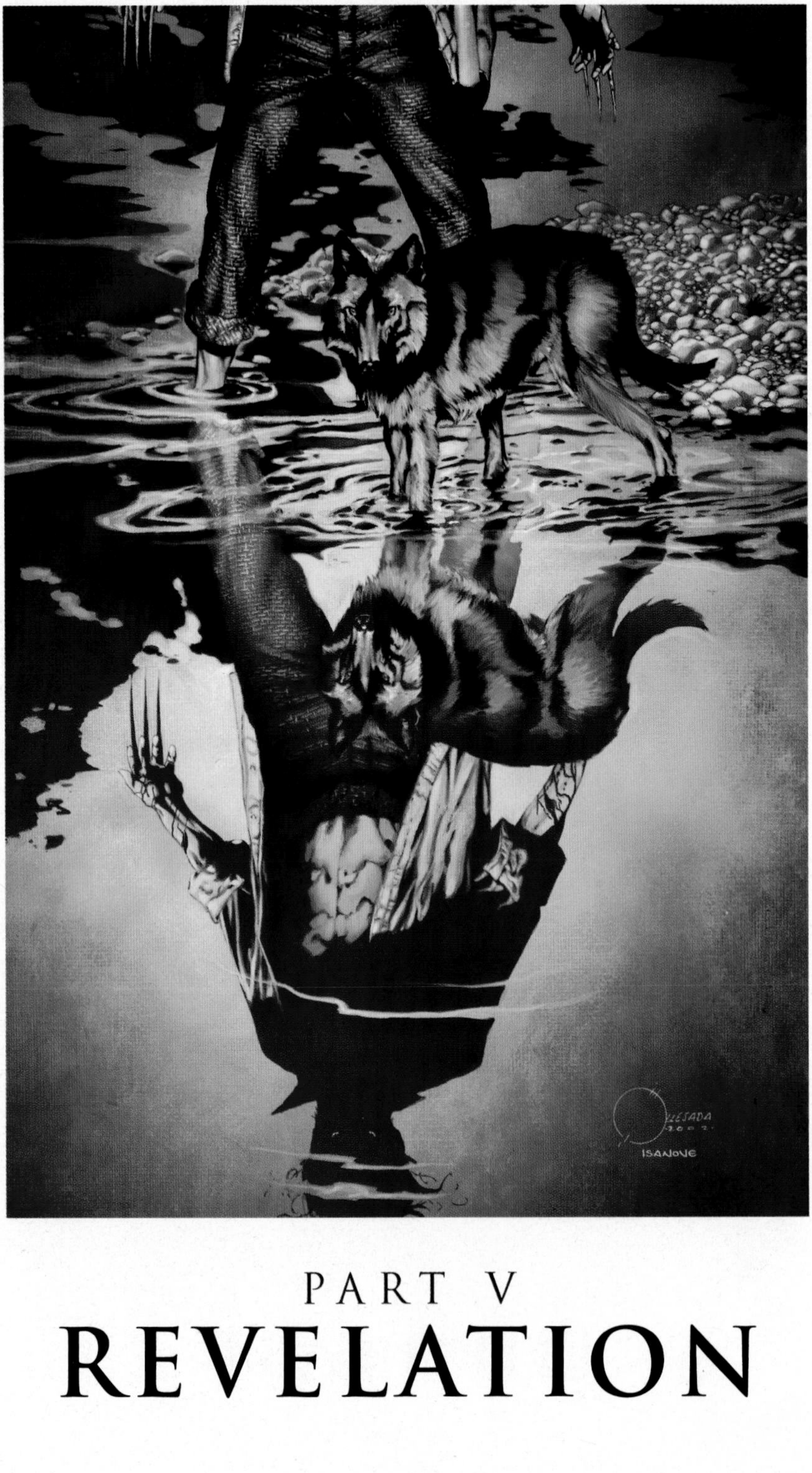
QUESADA
2002
ISANOVE

PART V
REVELATION

TYGER! TYGER! BURNING BRIGHT IN THE FORESTS OF THE NIGHT, WHAT IMMORTAL HAND OR EYE COULD FRAME THY FEARFUL SYMMETRY?

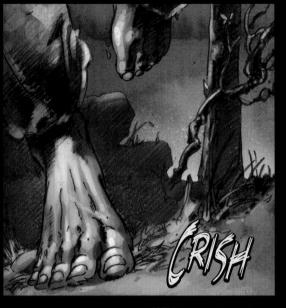

CRISH

"IN WHAT DISTANT DEEPS OR SKIES BURNT THE FIRE OF THINE EYES?

"ON WHAT WINGS DARE HE ASPIRE? WHAT THE HAND DARE SEIZE THE FIRE?

CROOSH

KRIK

"AND WHAT SHOULDER, AND WHAT ART, COULD TWIST THE SINEWS OF THY HEART, AND WHEN THY HEART BEGAN TO BEAT...

"...WHAT DREAD HAND? AND WHAT DREAD FEET?"

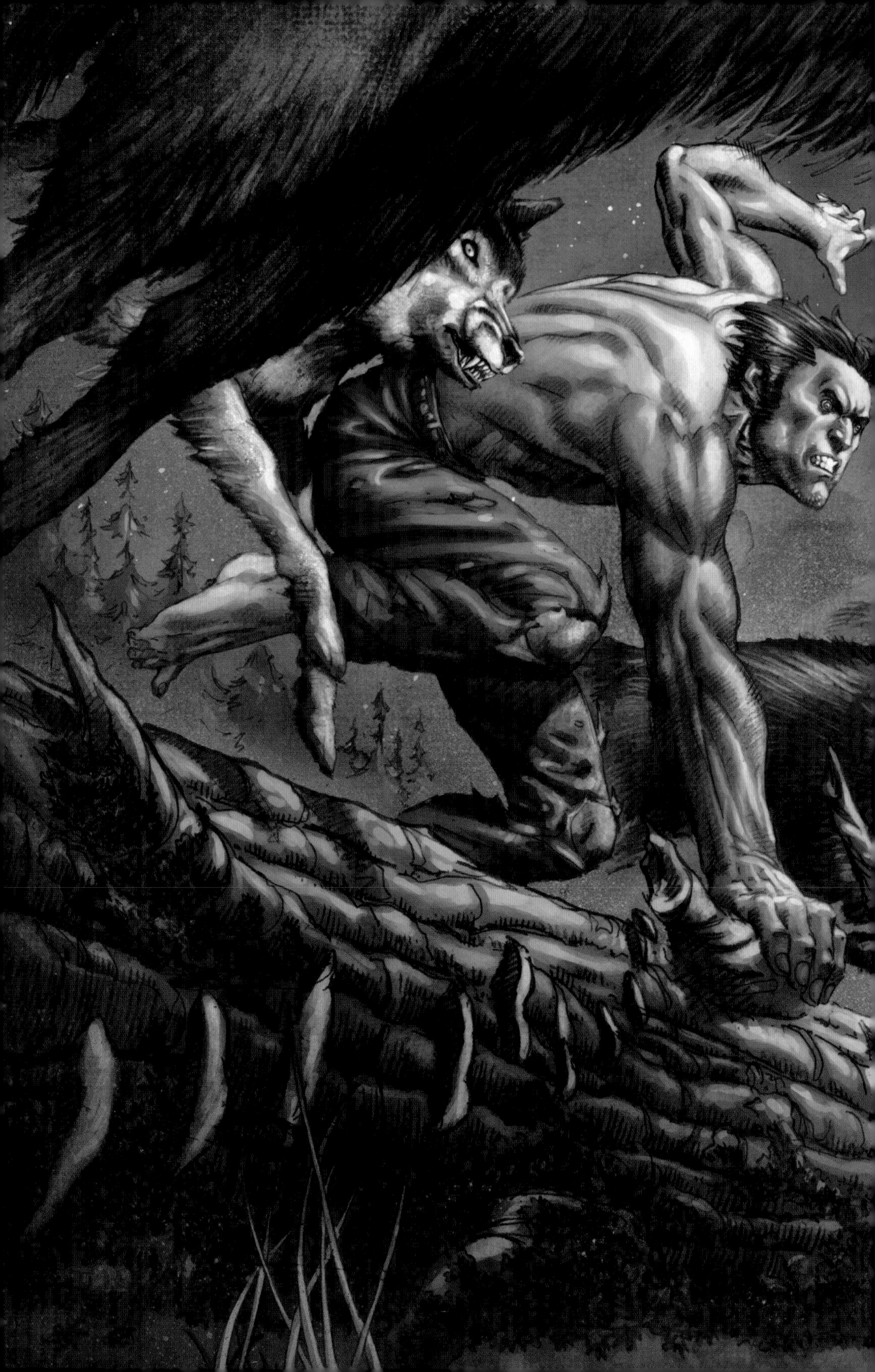

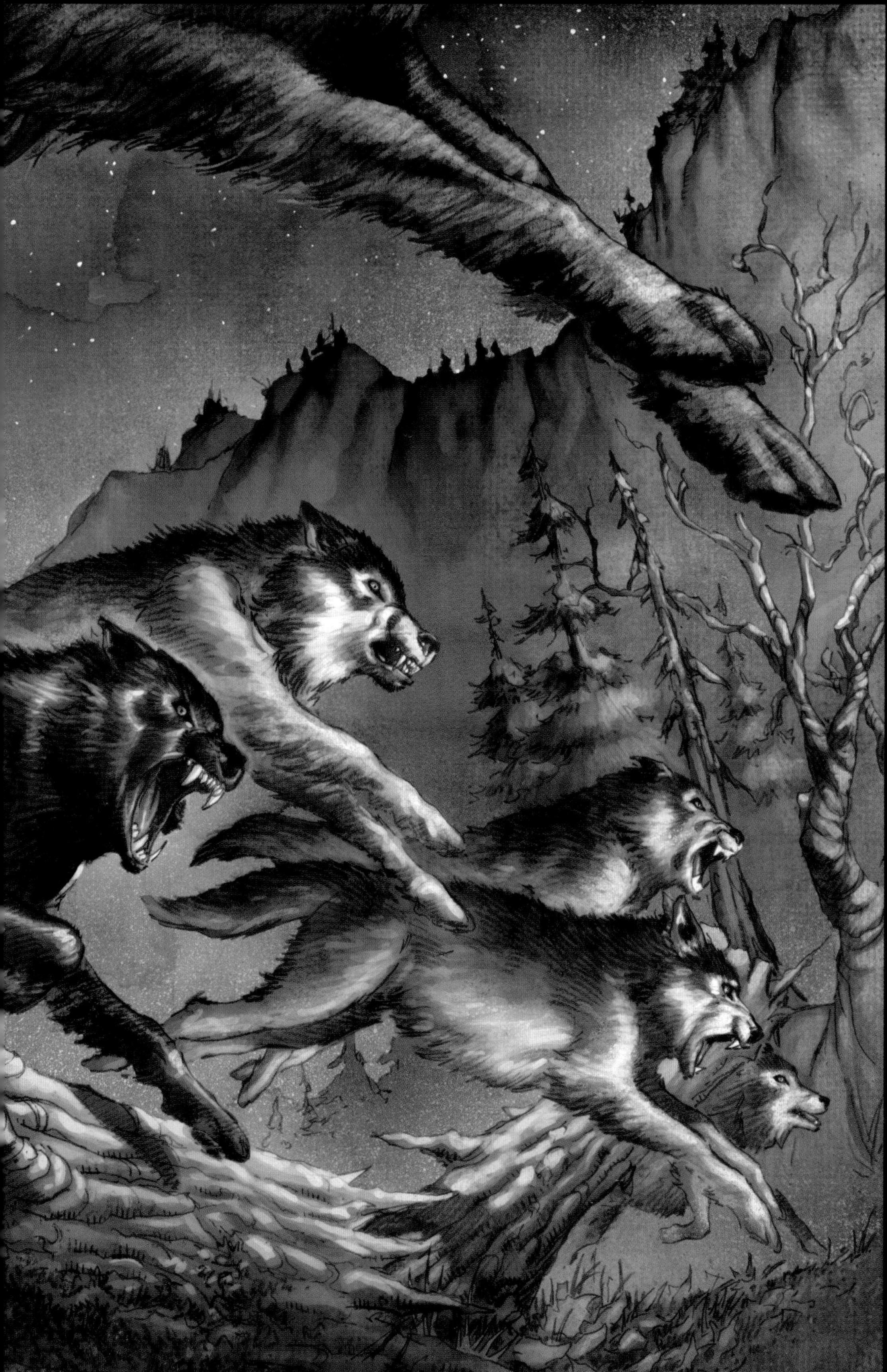

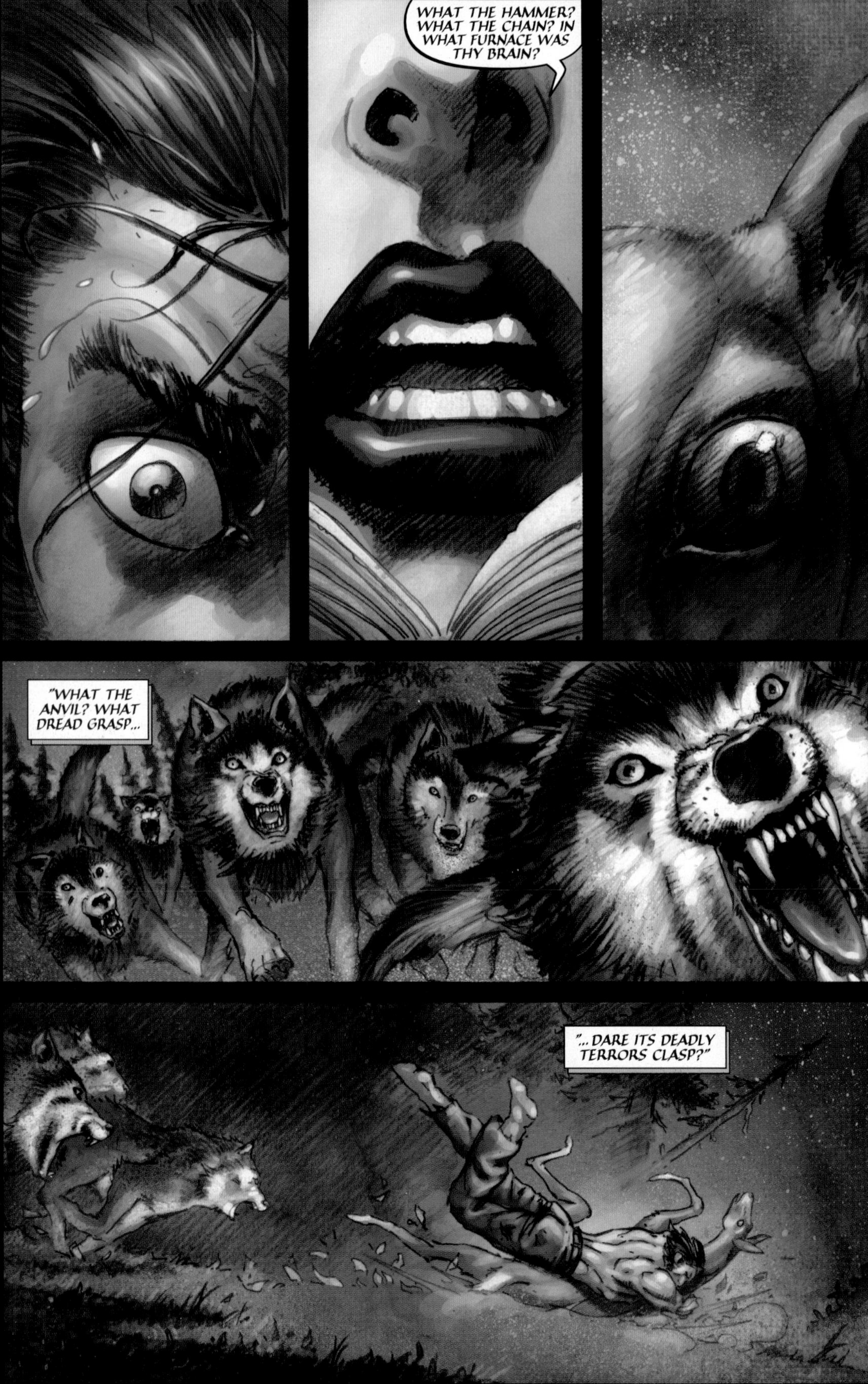
WHAT THE HAMMER? WHAT THE CHAIN? IN WHAT FURNACE WAS THY BRAIN?
"WHAT THE ANVIL? WHAT DREAD GRASP...
"... DARE ITS DEADLY TERRORS CLASP?"

WHEN THE STARS THREW DOWN THEIR SPEARS, AND WATER'D HEAVEN WITH THEIR TEARS, DID HE SMILE HIS WORK TO SEE?

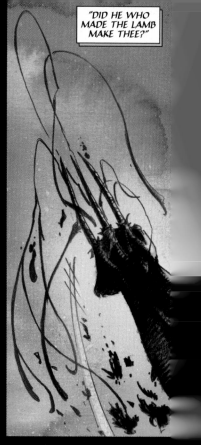

"DID HE WHO MADE THE LAMB MAKE THEE?"

TYGER! TYGER! BURNING BRIGHT, IN THE FORESTS OF THE NIGHT, WHAT IMMORTAL HAND OR EYE...

"...DARE FRAME THY FEARFUL SYMMETRY?"

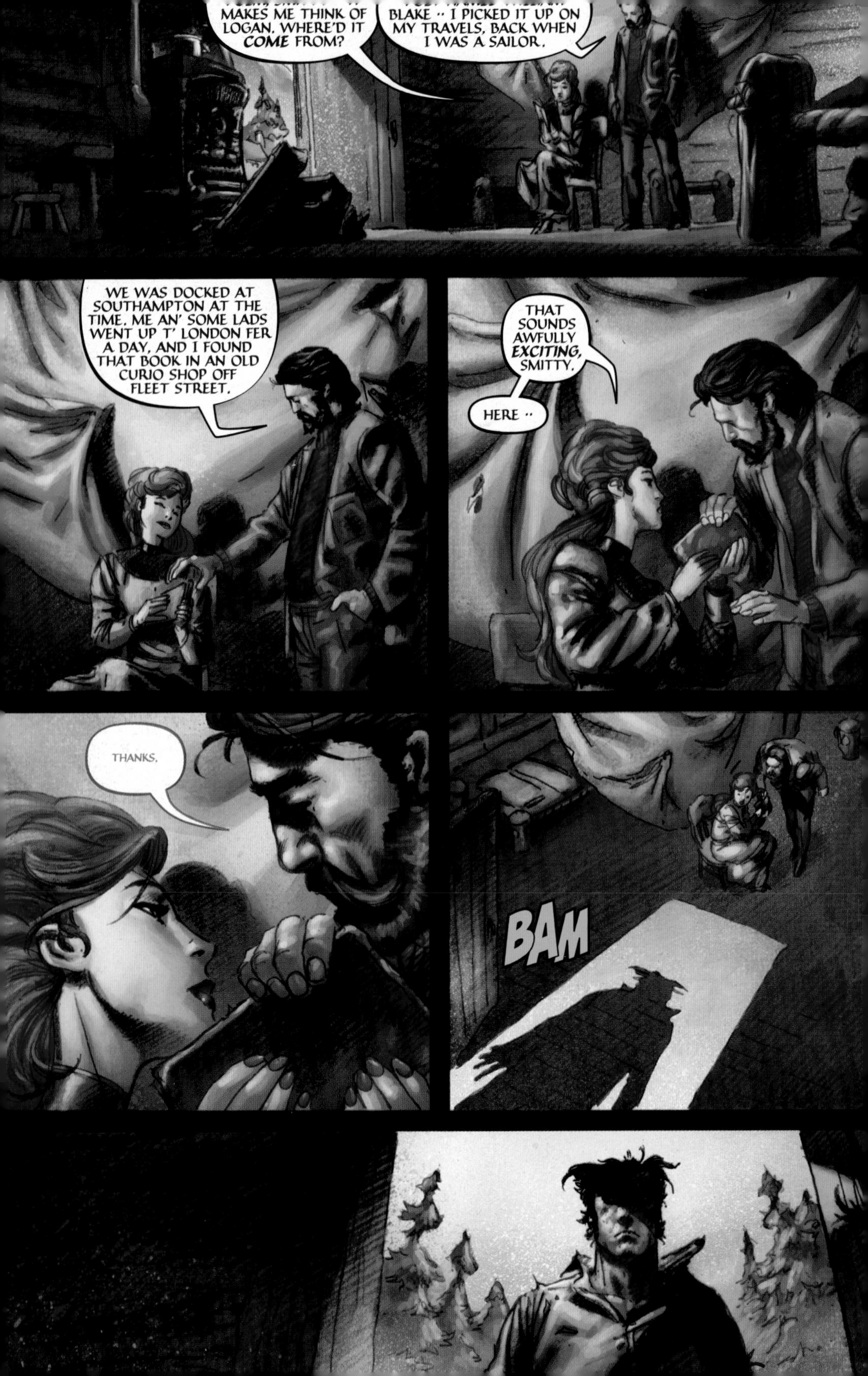
MAKES ME THINK OF LOGAN. WHERE'D IT COME FROM?
BLAKE .. I PICKED IT UP ON MY TRAVELS, BACK WHEN I WAS A SAILOR.
WE WAS DOCKED AT SOUTHAMPTON AT THE TIME. ME AN' SOME LADS WENT UP T' LONDON FER A DAY, AND I FOUND THAT BOOK IN AN OLD CURIO SHOP OFF FLEET STREET.
THAT SOUNDS AWFULLY EXCITING, SMITTY.
HERE ..
THANKS.
BAM

AH-HEM... HELLO, LAD. ME AN' YOUR COUSIN WERE JUST VISITIN' FOR A WHILE TILL YOU CAME BY.

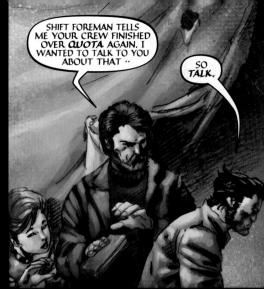

SHIFT FOREMAN TELLS ME YOUR CREW FINISHED OVER QUOTA AGAIN. I WANTED TO TALK TO YOU ABOUT THAT ..

SO TALK.

LOGAN, MISTER SMITH'S BEEN KIND ENOUGH TO BRING BY SOME BOOKS HE PICKED UP FROM HIS DAYS AT SEA. ISN'T THAT KIND OF HIM?

AYE, WELL, LOOK... I REALLY CAME BY T' SEE YOU, LAD. CLEAN YOURSELF UP AN' GET SOME REST TONIGHT.

I'LL WANT YOU TO TAKE THE MORNIN' OFF TOMORROW AN' COME MEET ME UP ON THE HILL, BY THE NEW SEAM.

WHAT FOR?

I GOT A JOB FOR YOU.

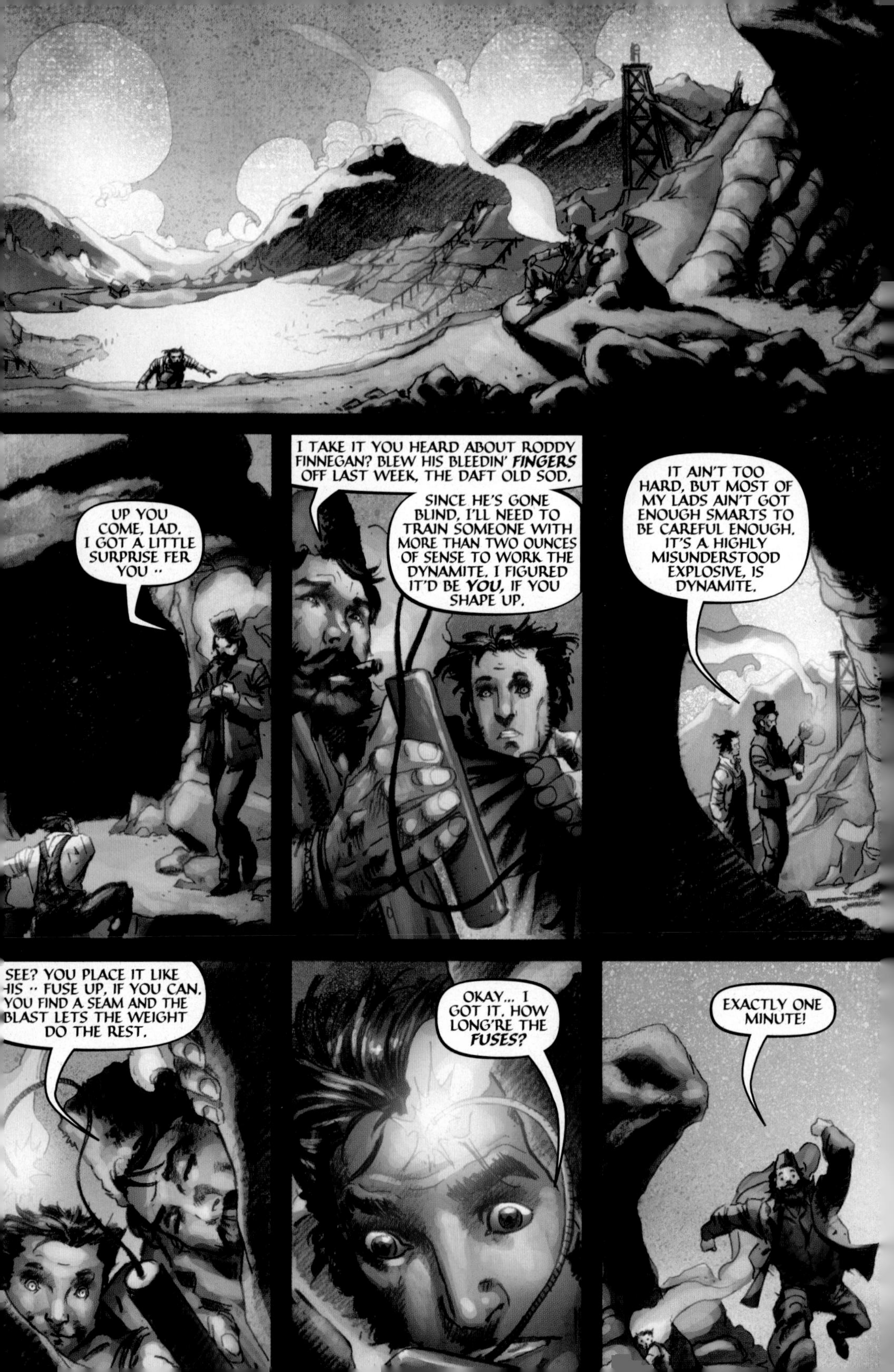
UP YOU COME, LAD. I GOT A LITTLE SURPRISE FER YOU --
I TAKE IT YOU HEARD ABOUT RODDY FINNEGAN? BLEW HIS BLEEDIN' FINGERS OFF LAST WEEK, THE DAFT OLD SOD.
SINCE HE'S GONE BLIND, I'LL NEED TO TRAIN SOMEONE WITH MORE THAN TWO OUNCES OF SENSE TO WORK THE DYNAMITE. I FIGURED IT'D BE YOU, IF YOU SHAPE UP.
IT AIN'T TOO HARD, BUT MOST OF MY LADS AIN'T GOT ENOUGH SMARTS TO BE CAREFUL ENOUGH. IT'S A HIGHLY MISUNDERSTOOD EXPLOSIVE, IS DYNAMITE.
SEE? YOU PLACE IT LIKE HIS -- FUSE UP, IF YOU CAN. YOU FIND A SEAM AND THE BLAST LETS THE WEIGHT DO THE REST.
OKAY... I GOT IT. HOW LONG'RE THE FUSES?
EXACTLY ONE MINUTE!

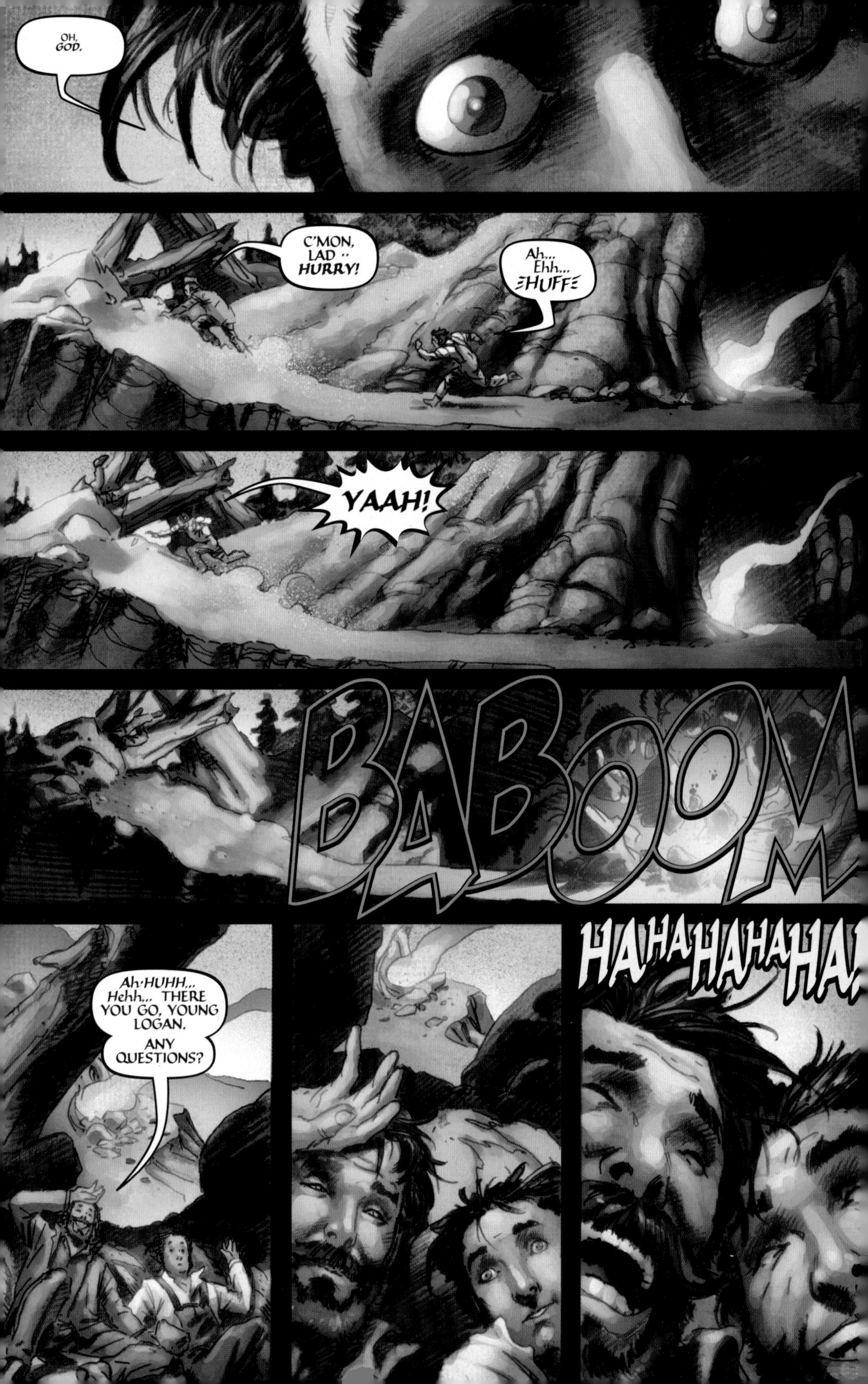
OH, GOD.
C'MON, LAD -- HURRY!
Ah... Ehh... HUFF
YAAH!
BABOOM
Ah-HUHH... Hehh... THERE YOU GO, YOUNG LOGAN.
ANY QUESTIONS?
HAHAHAHAHAHA!

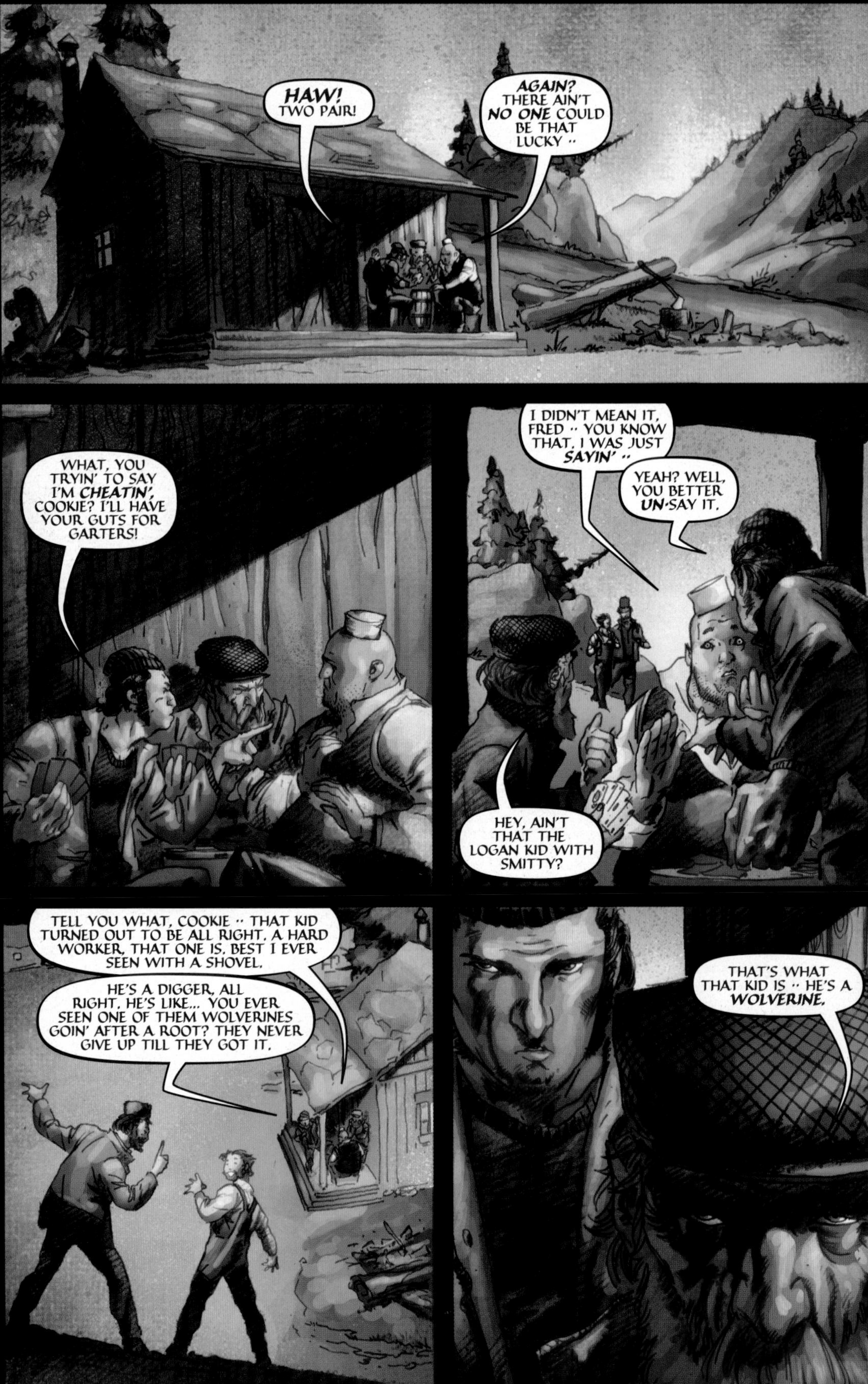
HAW! TWO PAIR!
AGAIN? THERE AIN'T NO ONE COULD BE THAT LUCKY ..
WHAT, YOU TRYIN' TO SAY I'M CHEATIN', COOKIE? I'LL HAVE YOUR GUTS FOR GARTERS!
I DIDN'T MEAN IT, FRED .. YOU KNOW THAT. I WAS JUST SAYIN' ..
YEAH? WELL, YOU BETTER UN-SAY IT.
HEY, AIN'T THAT THE LOGAN KID WITH SMITTY?
TELL YOU WHAT, COOKIE .. THAT KID TURNED OUT TO BE ALL RIGHT. A HARD WORKER, THAT ONE IS. BEST I EVER SEEN WITH A SHOVEL.
HE'S A DIGGER, ALL RIGHT. HE'S LIKE... YOU EVER SEEN ONE OF THEM WOLVERINES GOIN' AFTER A ROOT? THEY NEVER GIVE UP TILL THEY GOT IT.
THAT'S WHAT THAT KID IS .. HE'S A WOLVERINE.

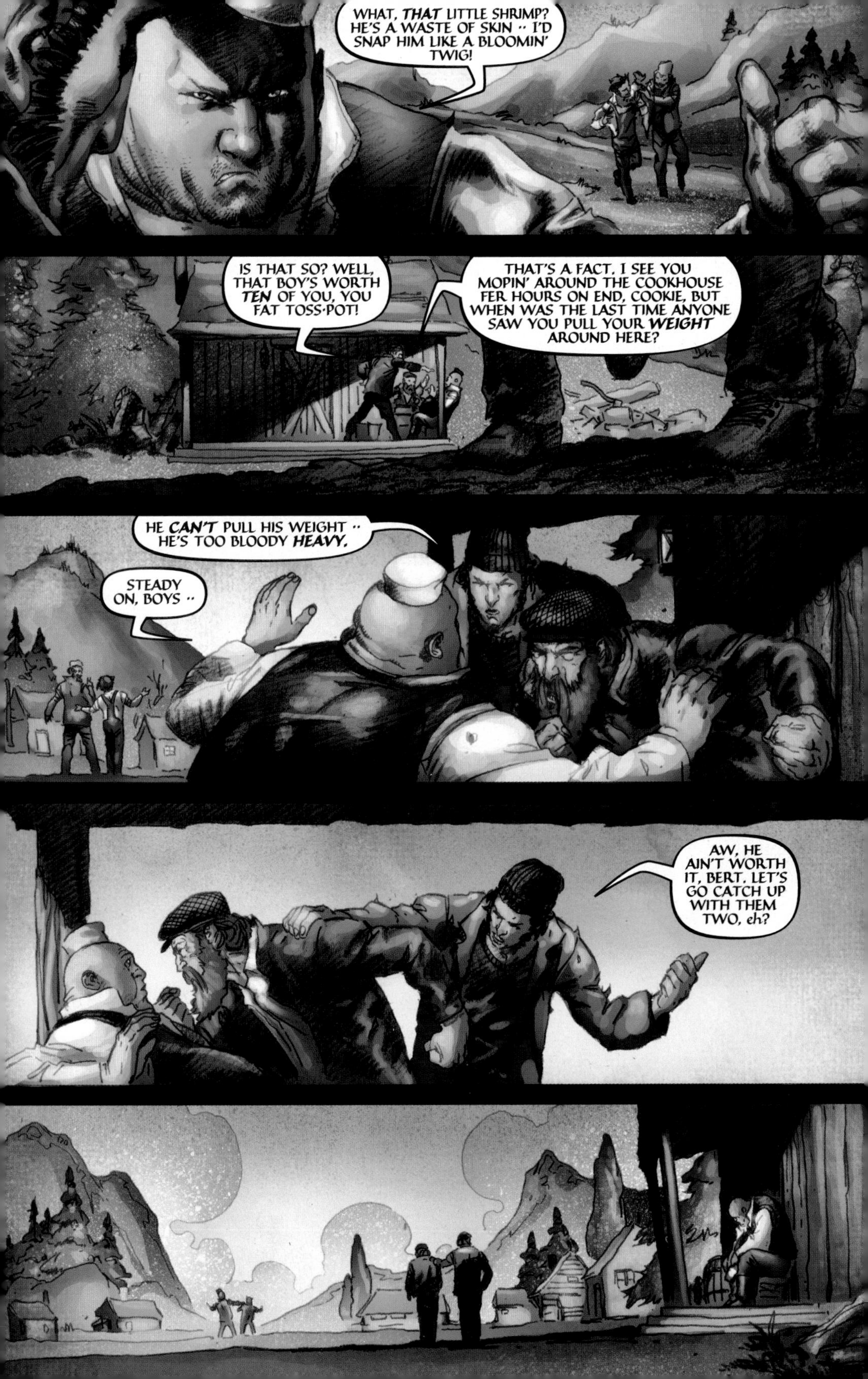
WHAT, THAT LITTLE SHRIMP? HE'S A WASTE OF SKIN -- I'D SNAP HIM LIKE A BLOOMIN' TWIG!
IS THAT SO? WELL, THAT BOY'S WORTH TEN OF YOU, YOU FAT TOSS-POT!
THAT'S A FACT. I SEE YOU MOPIN' AROUND THE COOKHOUSE FER HOURS ON END, COOKIE, BUT WHEN WAS THE LAST TIME ANYONE SAW YOU PULL YOUR WEIGHT AROUND HERE?
HE CAN'T PULL HIS WEIGHT -- HE'S TOO BLOODY HEAVY.
STEADY ON, BOYS --
AW, HE AIN'T WORTH IT, BERT. LET'S GO CATCH UP WITH THEM TWO, eh?

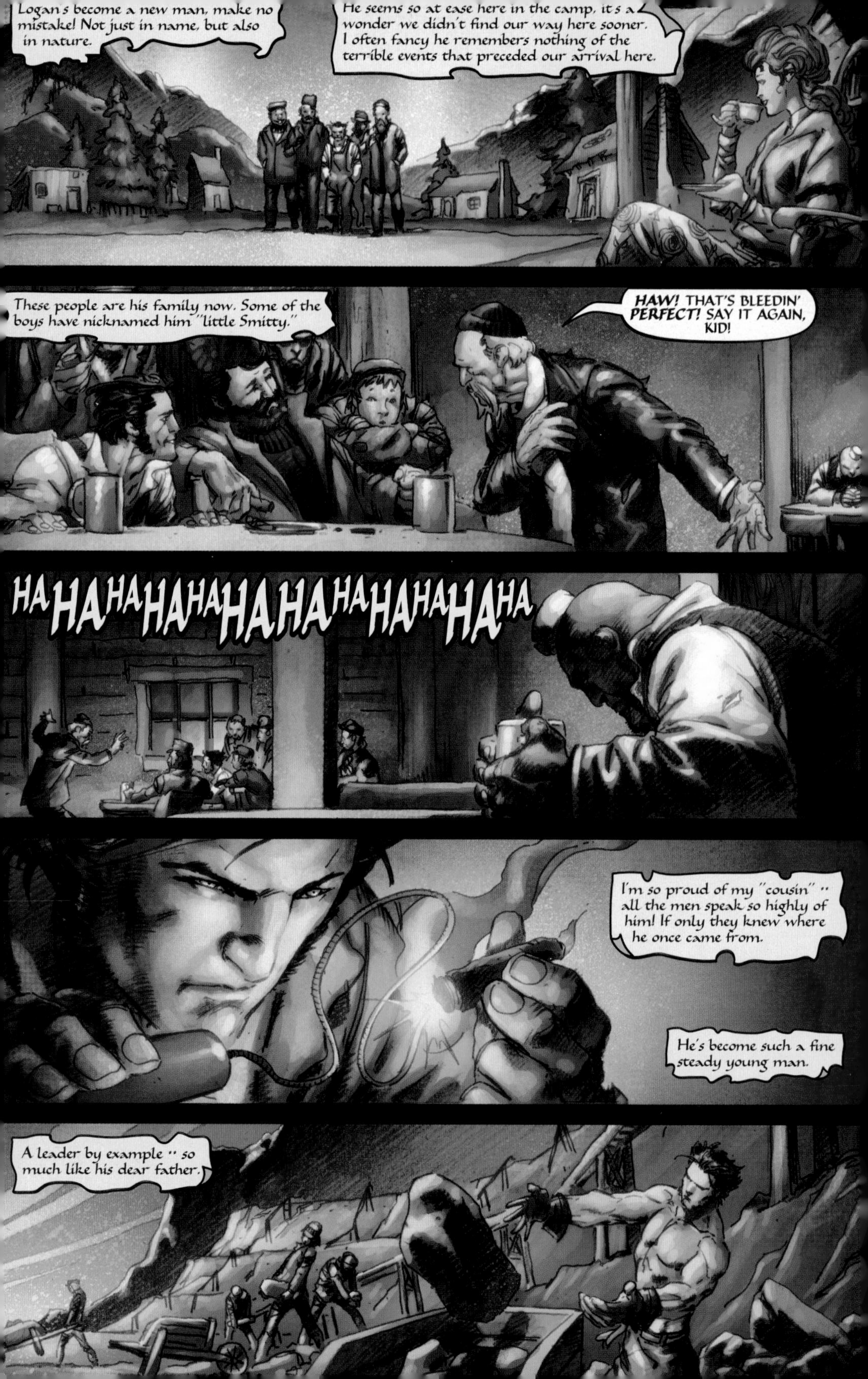
Logan's become a new man, make no mistake! Not just in name, but also in nature.
He seems so at ease here in the camp, it's a wonder we didn't find our way here sooner. I often fancy he remembers nothing of the terrible events that preceded our arrival here.
These people are his family now. Some of the boys have nicknamed him "little Smitty."
HAW! THAT'S BLEEDIN' PERFECT! SAY IT AGAIN, KID!
HA HA HA HA HA HA HA HA HA HA HA HA HA HA
I'm so proud of my "cousin" -- all the men speak so highly of him! If only they knew where he once came from.
He's become such a fine steady young man.
A leader by example -- so much like his dear father.

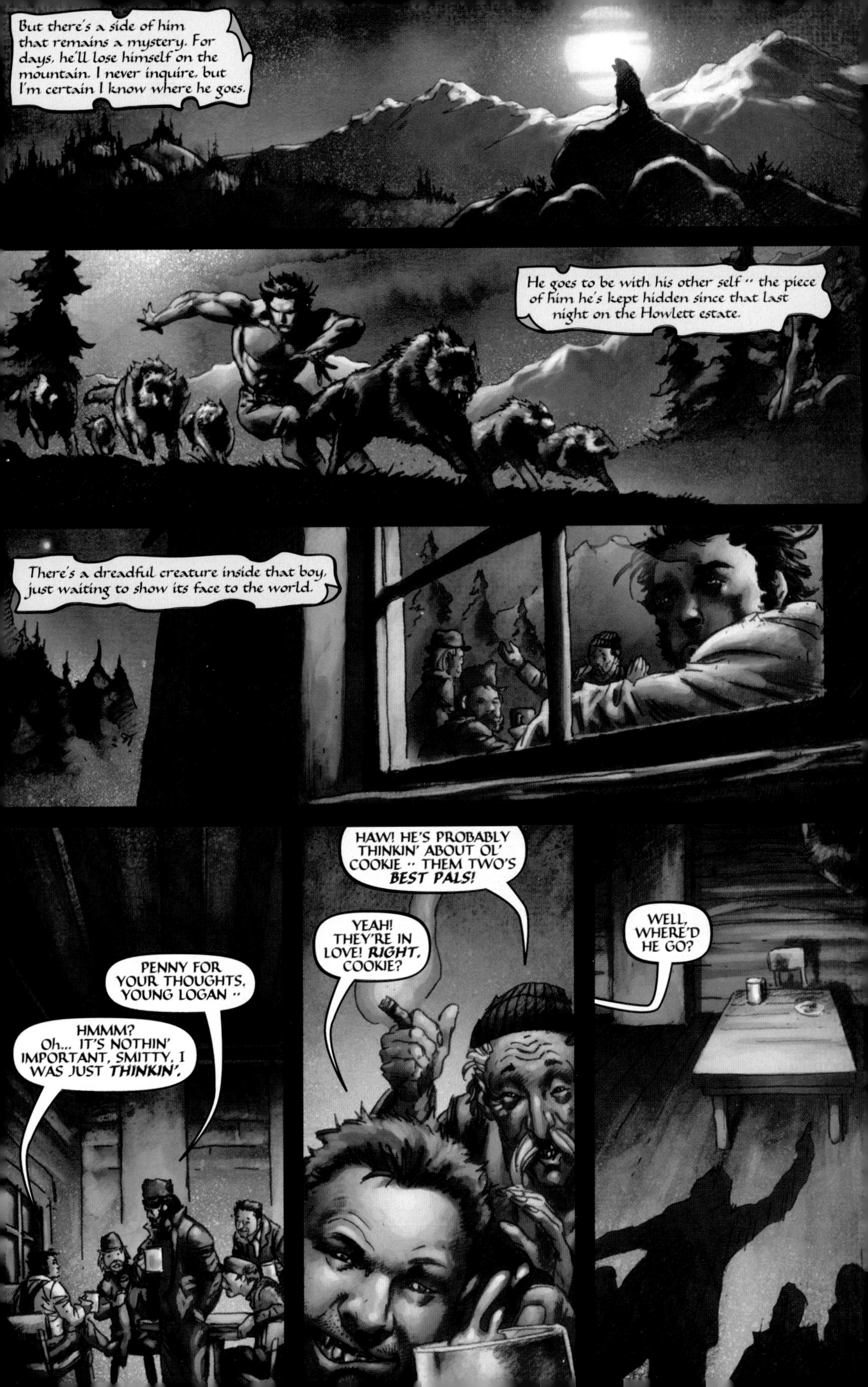

But there's a side of him that remains a mystery. For days, he'll lose himself on the mountain. I never inquire, but I'm certain I know where he goes.
He goes to be with his other self -- the piece of him he's kept hidden since that last night on the Howlett estate.
There's a dreadful creature inside that boy, just waiting to show its face to the world.
PENNY FOR YOUR THOUGHTS, YOUNG LOGAN --
HMMM? Oh... IT'S NOTHIN' IMPORTANT, SMITTY. I WAS JUST THINKIN'.
HAW! HE'S PROBABLY THINKIN' ABOUT OL' COOKIE -- THEM TWO'S BEST PALS!
YEAH! THEY'RE IN LOVE! RIGHT, COOKIE?
WELL, WHERE'D HE GO?

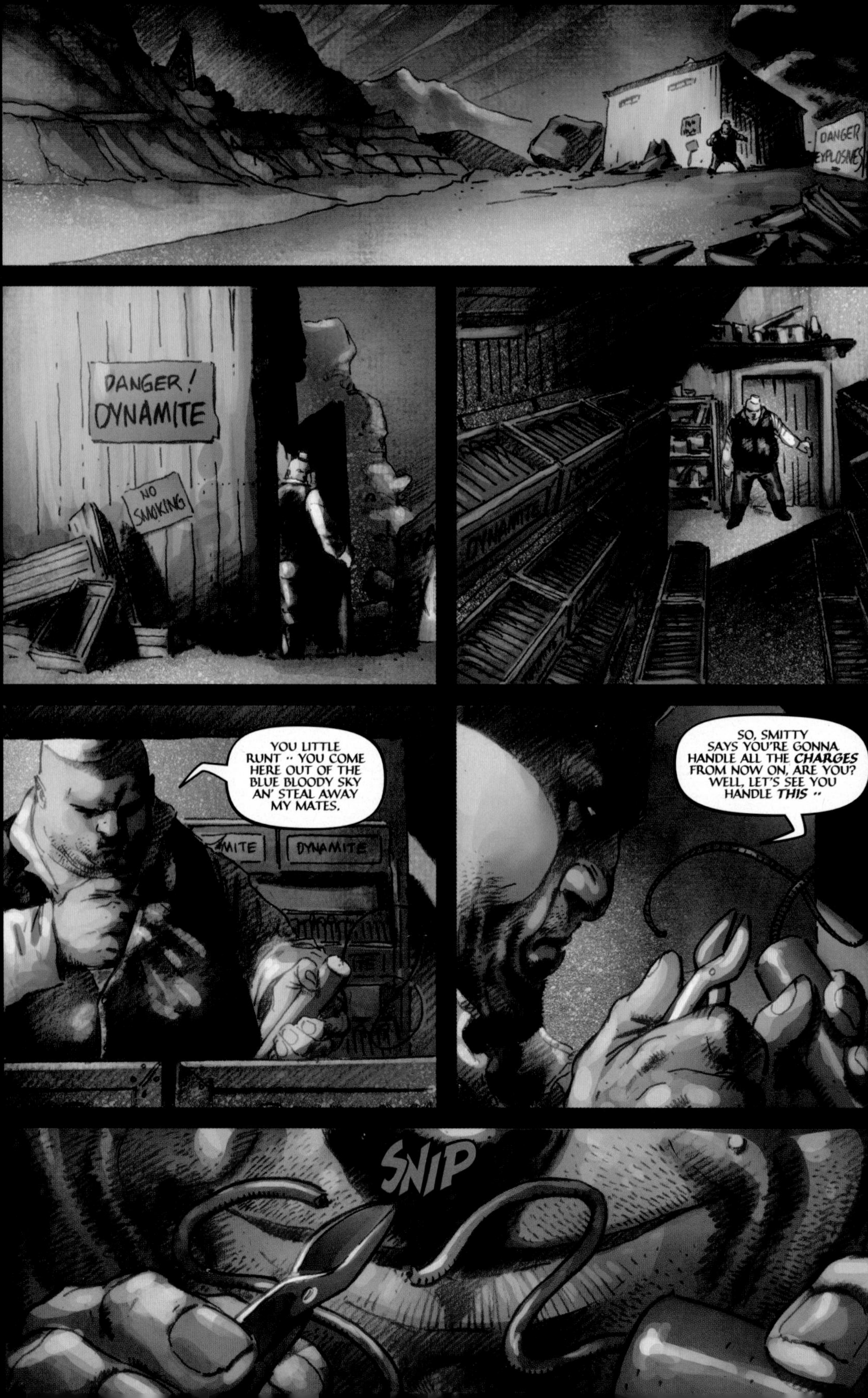
DANGER EXPLOSIVES
DANGER! DYNAMITE
NO SMOKING
DYNAMITE
YOU LITTLE RUNT -- YOU COME HERE OUT OF THE BLUE BLOODY SKY AN' STEAL AWAY MY MATES.
DYNAMITE
SO, SMITTY SAYS YOU'RE GONNA HANDLE ALL THE CHARGES FROM NOW ON, ARE YOU? WELL, LET'S SEE YOU HANDLE THIS --
SNIP

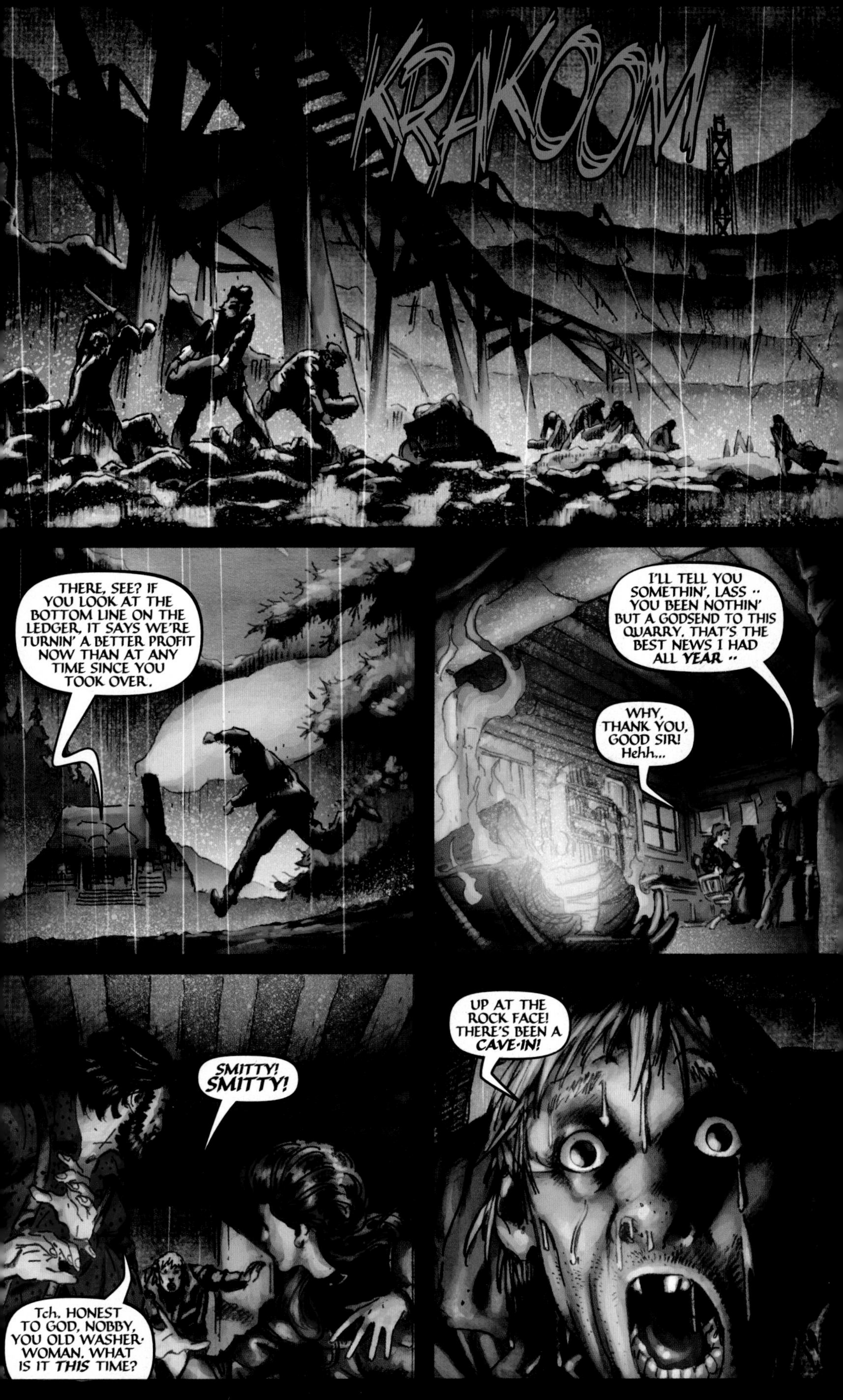
KRAKOOM
THERE, SEE? IF YOU LOOK AT THE BOTTOM LINE ON THE LEDGER, IT SAYS WE'RE TURNIN' A BETTER PROFIT NOW THAN AT ANY TIME SINCE YOU TOOK OVER.
I'LL TELL YOU SOMETHIN', LASS .. YOU BEEN NOTHIN' BUT A GODSEND TO THIS QUARRY. THAT'S THE BEST NEWS I HAD ALL YEAR ..
WHY, THANK YOU, GOOD SIR! Hehh...
SMITTY! SMITTY!
Tch. HONEST TO GOD, NOBBY, YOU OLD WASHER-WOMAN. WHAT IS IT THIS TIME?
UP AT THE ROCK FACE! THERE'S BEEN A CAVE-IN!

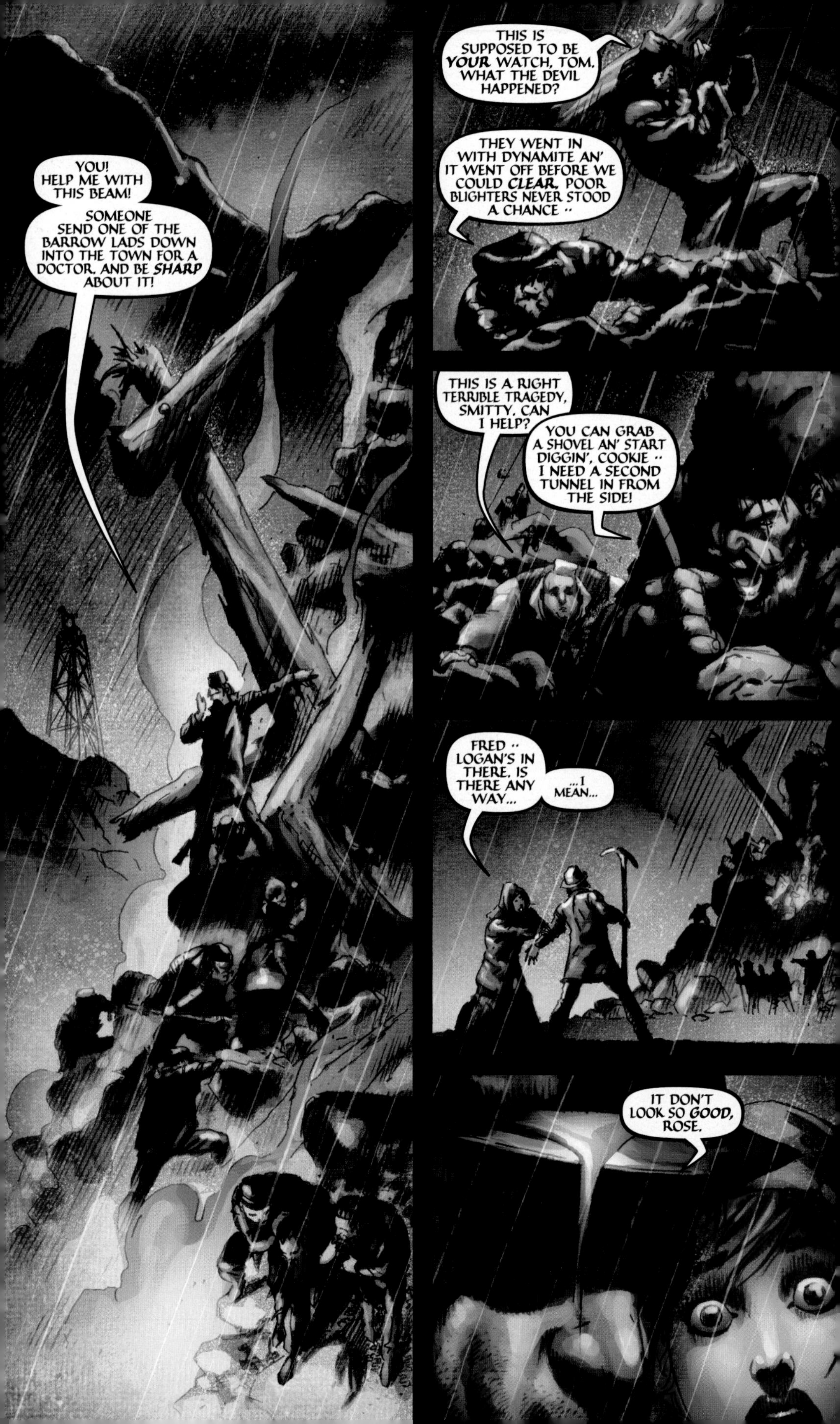
YOU! HELP ME WITH THIS BEAM!
SOMEONE SEND ONE OF THE BARROW LADS DOWN INTO THE TOWN FOR A DOCTOR, AND BE *SHARP* ABOUT IT!
THIS IS SUPPOSED TO BE *YOUR* WATCH, TOM. WHAT THE DEVIL HAPPENED?
THEY WENT IN WITH DYNAMITE AN' IT WENT OFF BEFORE WE COULD *CLEAR.* POOR BLIGHTERS NEVER STOOD A CHANCE --
THIS IS A RIGHT TERRIBLE TRAGEDY, SMITTY. CAN I HELP?
YOU CAN GRAB A SHOVEL AN' START DIGGIN', COOKIE -- I NEED A SECOND TUNNEL IN FROM THE SIDE!
FRED -- LOGAN'S IN THERE. IS THERE ANY WAY...
...I MEAN...
IT DON'T LOOK SO *GOOD,* ROSE.

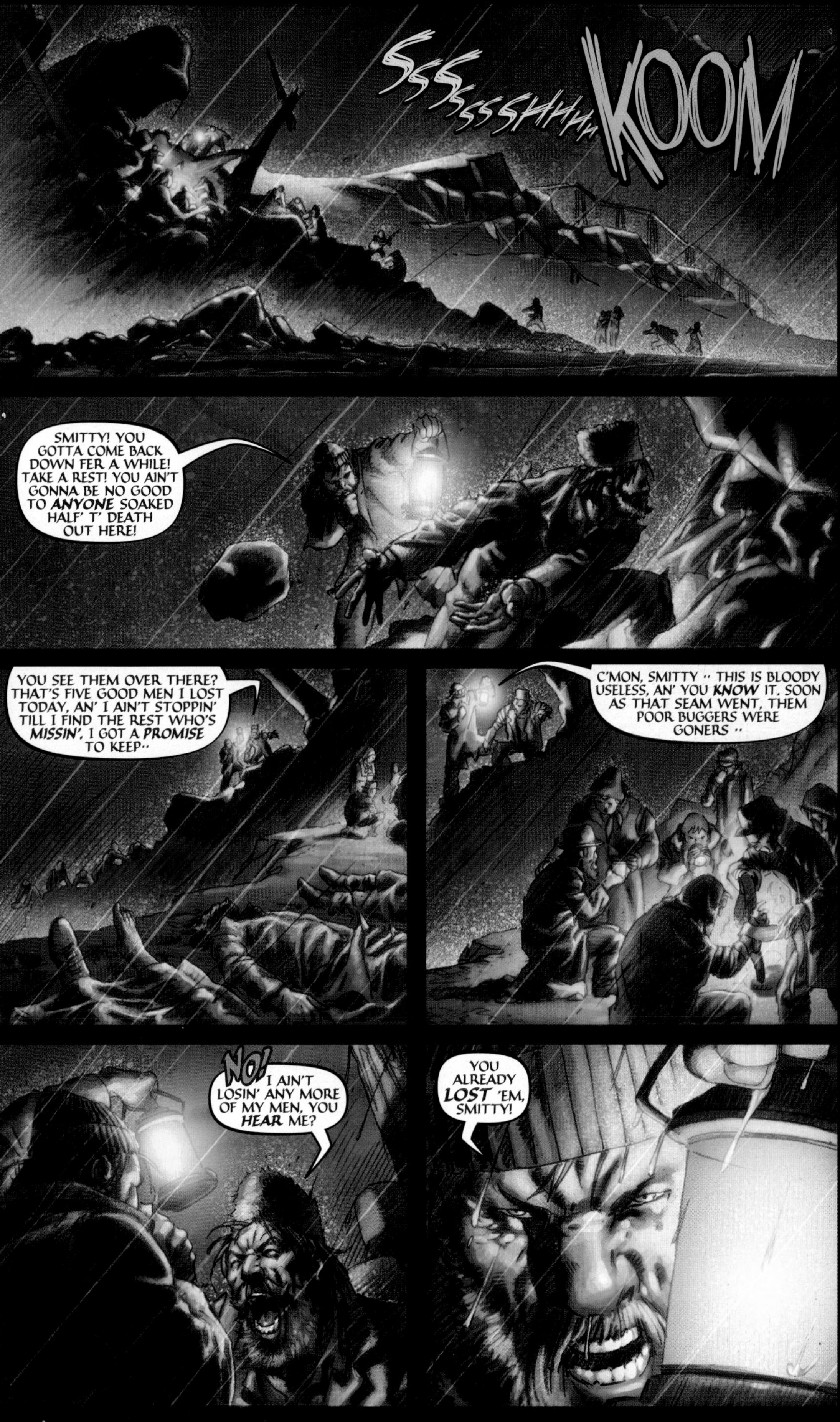
SSSSSSSHHHHHKOOM
SMITTY! YOU GOTTA COME BACK DOWN FER A WHILE! TAKE A REST! YOU AIN'T GONNA BE NO GOOD TO ANYONE SOAKED HALF' T' DEATH OUT HERE!
YOU SEE THEM OVER THERE? THAT'S FIVE GOOD MEN I LOST TODAY, AN' I AIN'T STOPPIN' TILL I FIND THE REST WHO'S MISSIN'. I GOT A PROMISE TO KEEP..
C'MON, SMITTY .. THIS IS BLOODY USELESS, AN' YOU KNOW IT. SOON AS THAT SEAM WENT, THEM POOR BUGGERS WERE GONERS ..
NO! I AIN'T LOSIN' ANY MORE OF MY MEN, YOU HEAR ME?
YOU ALREADY LOST 'EM, SMITTY!

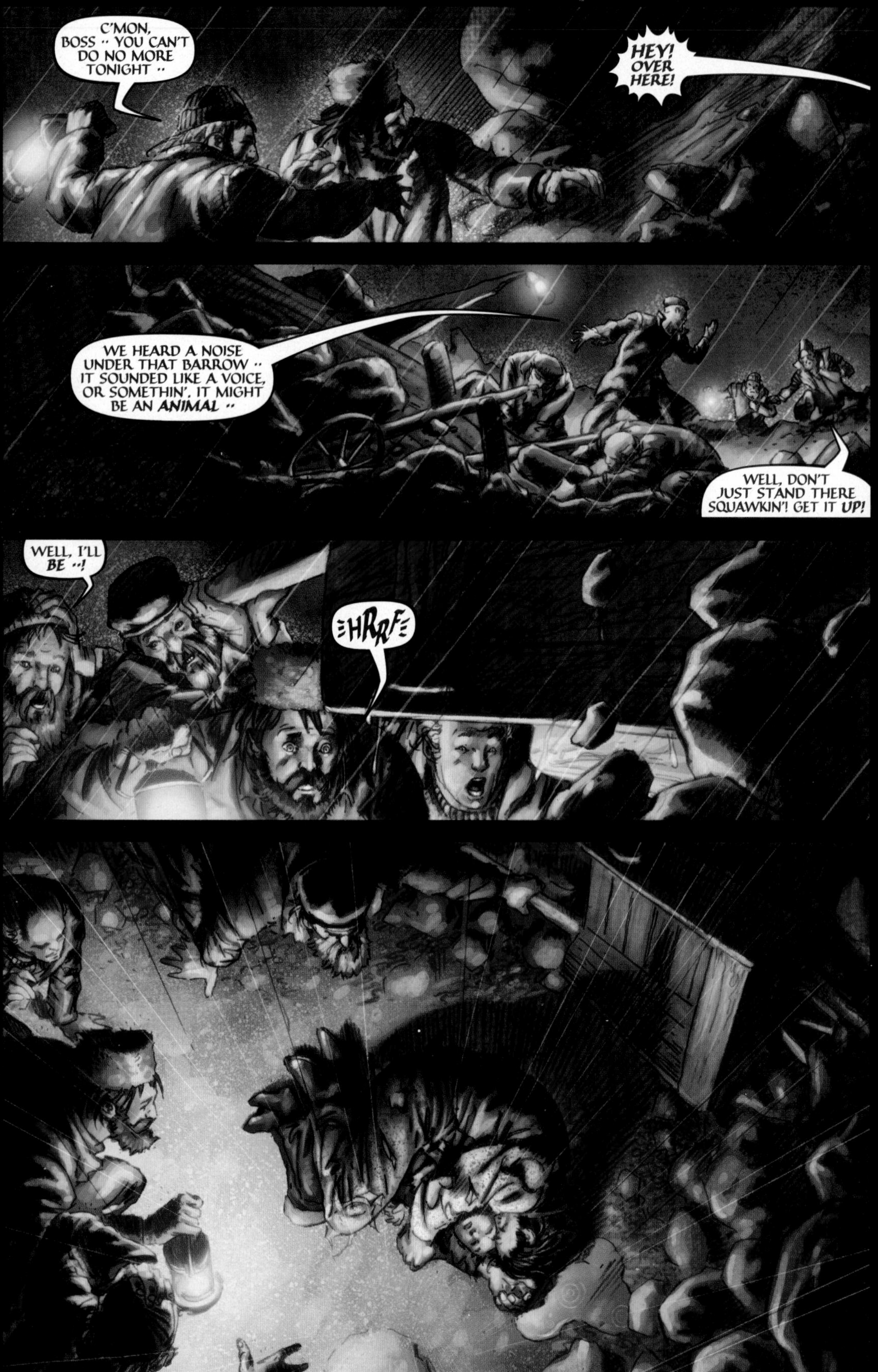

C'MON, BOSS -- YOU CAN'T DO NO MORE TONIGHT --
HEY! OVER HERE!
WE HEARD A NOISE UNDER THAT BARROW -- IT SOUNDED LIKE A VOICE, OR SOMETHIN'. IT MIGHT BE AN ANIMAL --
WELL, DON'T JUST STAND THERE SQUAWKIN'! GET IT UP!
WELL, I'LL BE --!
HRRF

...DAMNDEST THING I EVER SAW. YOU DON'T NEED *ME* TO TELL YOU THAT WAS SOME KIND O' *MIRACLE* OUT THERE LAST NIGHT, LOGAN.

MATTHEW FOWLER'S WIFE LOST HER HUSBAND IN THE SLIDE. SHE WANTED ME TO THANK YOU THAT SHE DIDN'T LOSE HER *SON*, AS WELL.

HERE YOU GO, LAD... THIS IS FOR YOU ··

WHAT IS IT?

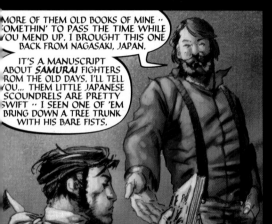

MORE OF THEM OLD BOOKS OF MINE ·· SOMETHIN' TO PASS THE TIME WHILE YOU MEND UP. I BROUGHT THIS ONE BACK FROM NAGASAKI, JAPAN.

IT'S A MANUSCRIPT ABOUT *SAMURAI* FIGHTERS FROM THE OLD DAYS, I'LL TELL YOU... THEM LITTLE JAPANESE SCOUNDRELS ARE PRETTY SWIFT ·· I SEEN ONE OF 'EM BRING DOWN A TREE TRUNK WITH HIS BARE FISTS.

MATTER OF FACT, I LEARNED A LOT FROM THEM... ABOUT THE WORLD AN' ABOUT LIFE. IT'S A STRONG PERSON WHO FOLLOWS HIS OWN PATH, THEY SAY. I SEE THAT STRENGTH IN *YOU*, LOGAN.

YOU SHOULD HAVE *DIED* LAST NIGHT. I DON'T KNOW HOW YOU SAVED THAT BOY, AN' I AIN'T GONNA *PRY*, BUT WHATEVER IT *IS* ABOUT YOU, SON, YOU NEED T' KNOW IT DON'T MAKE NO DIFFERENCE TO ME ONE WAY OR THE OTHER. UNDERSTAND?

ANYWAY, I GOTTA GET BACK T' THE QUARRY.

MISS ROSE ·· CAN I ASK YOU TO WALK WITH ME FOR A FEW MINUTES?

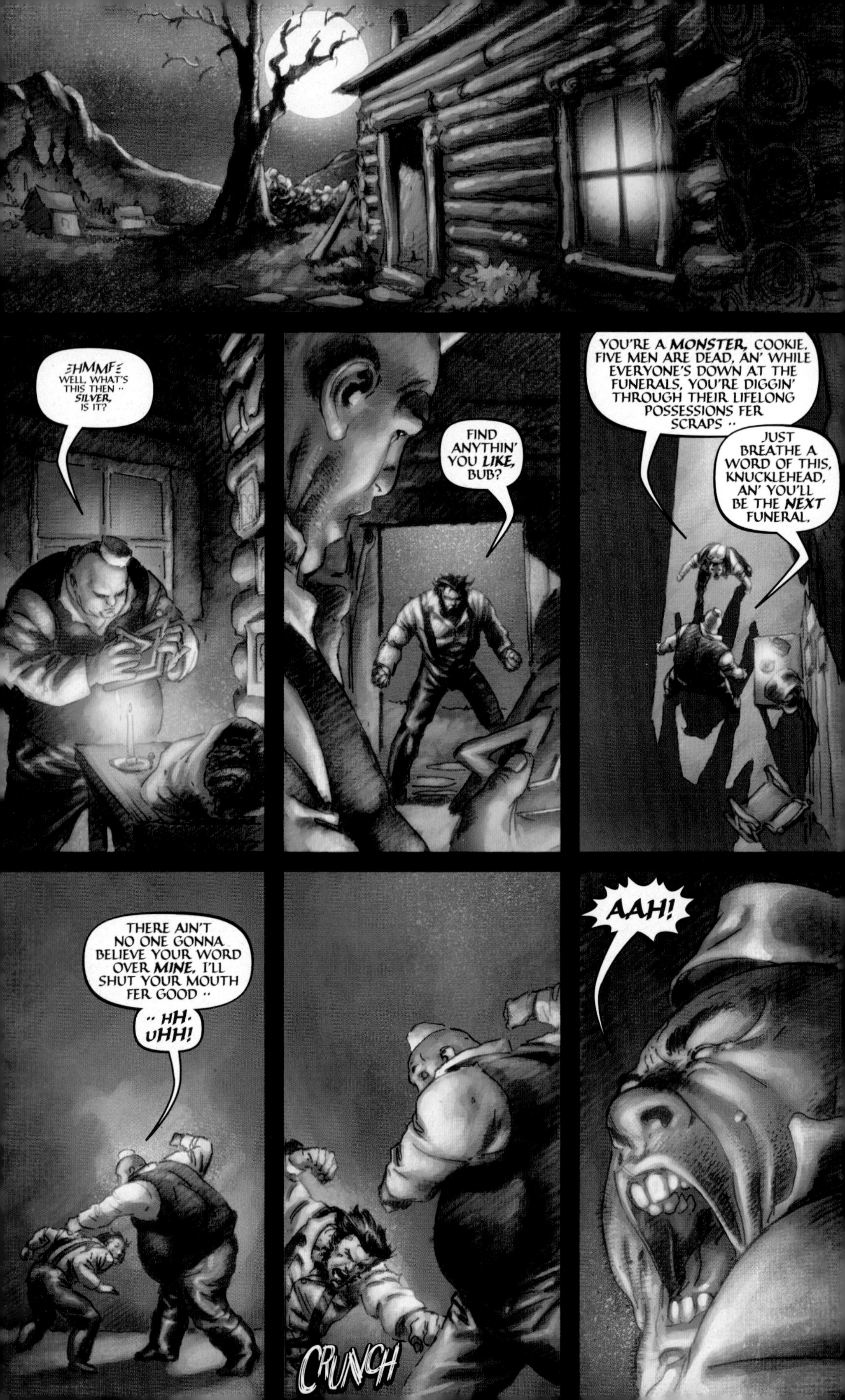

HMMF
WELL, WHAT'S THIS THEN .. SILVER, IS IT?
FIND ANYTHIN' YOU LIKE, BUB?
YOU'RE A MONSTER, COOKIE. FIVE MEN ARE DEAD, AN' WHILE EVERYONE'S DOWN AT THE FUNERALS, YOU'RE DIGGIN' THROUGH THEIR LIFELONG POSSESSIONS FER SCRAPS ..
JUST BREATHE A WORD OF THIS, KNUCKLEHEAD, AN' YOU'LL BE THE NEXT FUNERAL.
THERE AIN'T NO ONE GONNA BELIEVE YOUR WORD OVER MINE. I'LL SHUT YOUR MOUTH FER GOOD ..
.. HH. UHH!
CRUNCH
AAH!

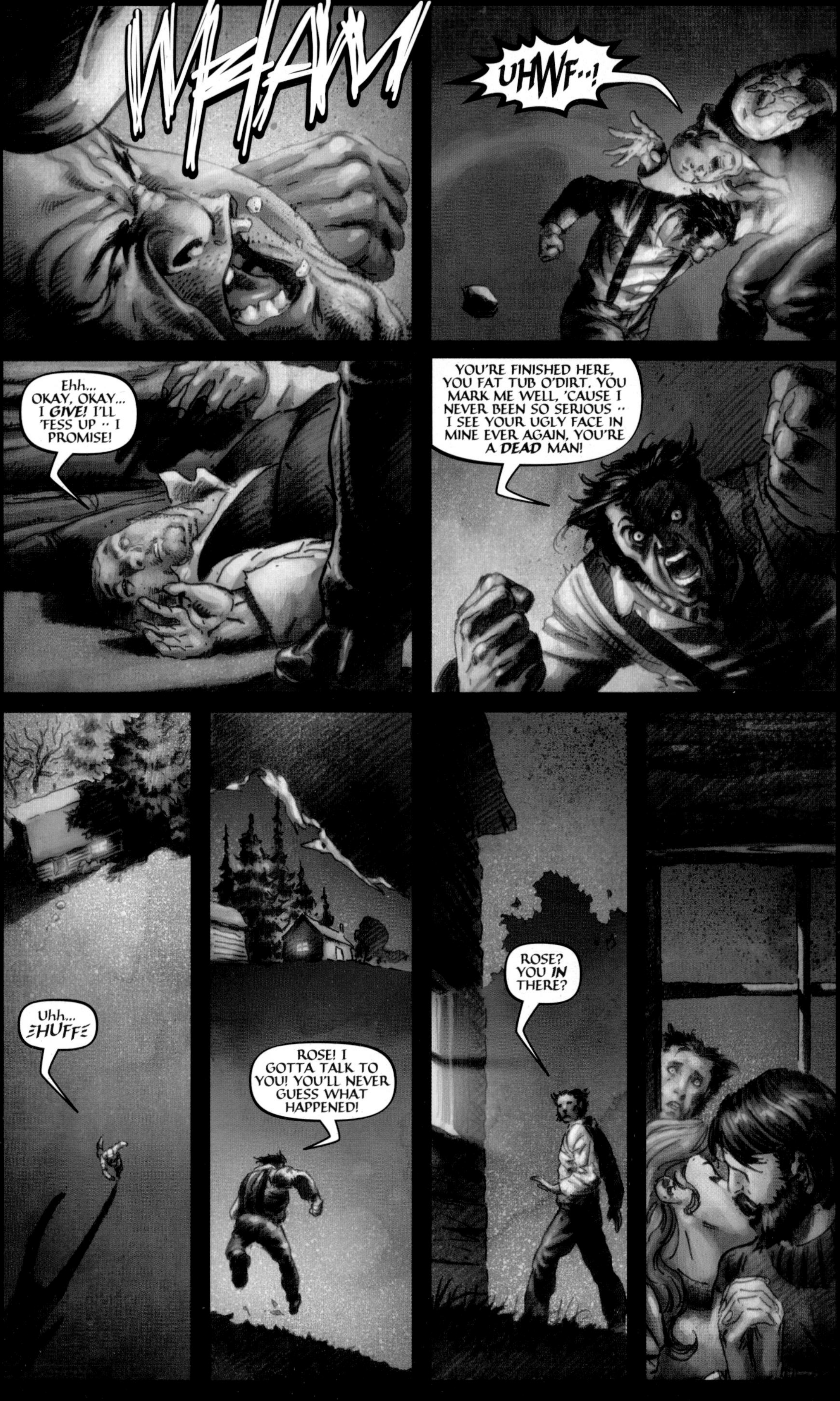
WHAM
UHWF..!
Ehh... OKAY, OKAY... I GIVE! I'LL 'FESS UP .. I PROMISE!
YOU'RE FINISHED HERE, YOU FAT TUB O'DIRT. YOU MARK ME WELL, 'CAUSE I NEVER BEEN SO SERIOUS .. I SEE YOUR UGLY FACE IN MINE EVER AGAIN, YOU'RE A DEAD MAN!
Uhh... HUFF
ROSE! I GOTTA TALK TO YOU! YOU'LL NEVER GUESS WHAT HAPPENED!
ROSE? YOU IN THERE?

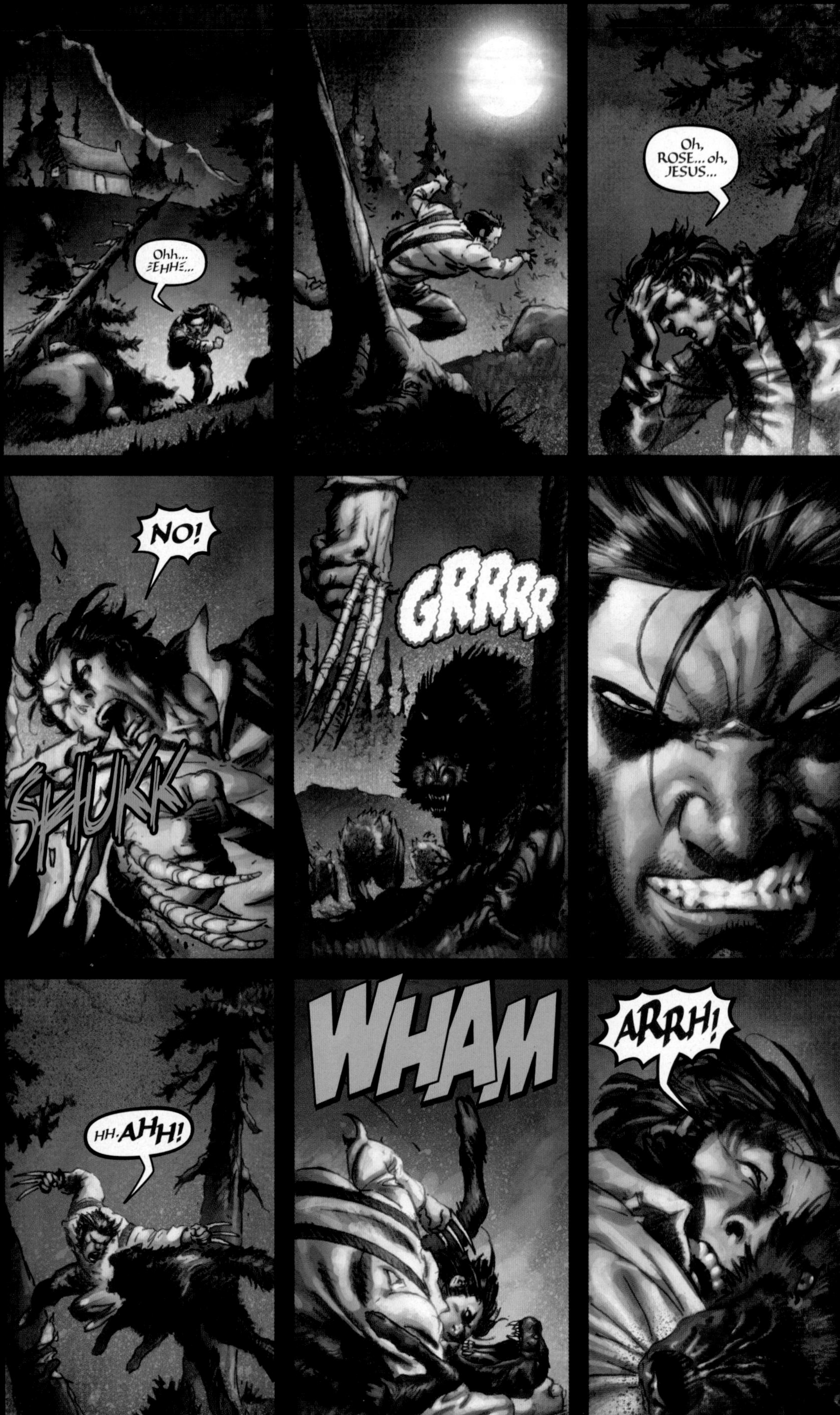

Ohh... EHHE...
Oh, ROSE... oh, JESUS...
NO!
SHUKK
GRRRR
HH, AHH!
WHAM
ARRH!

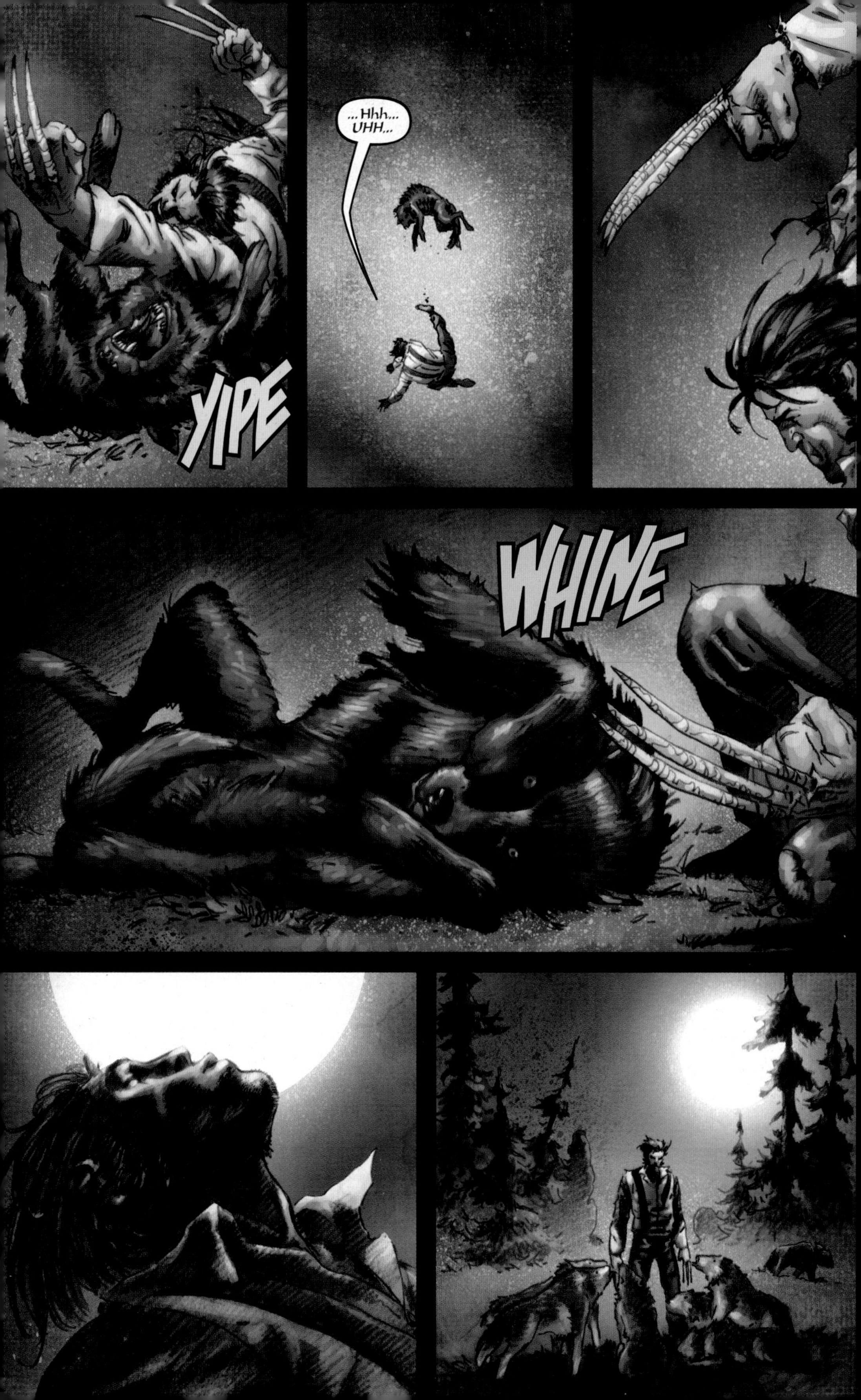
YIPE
...Hhh...
UHH...
WHINE

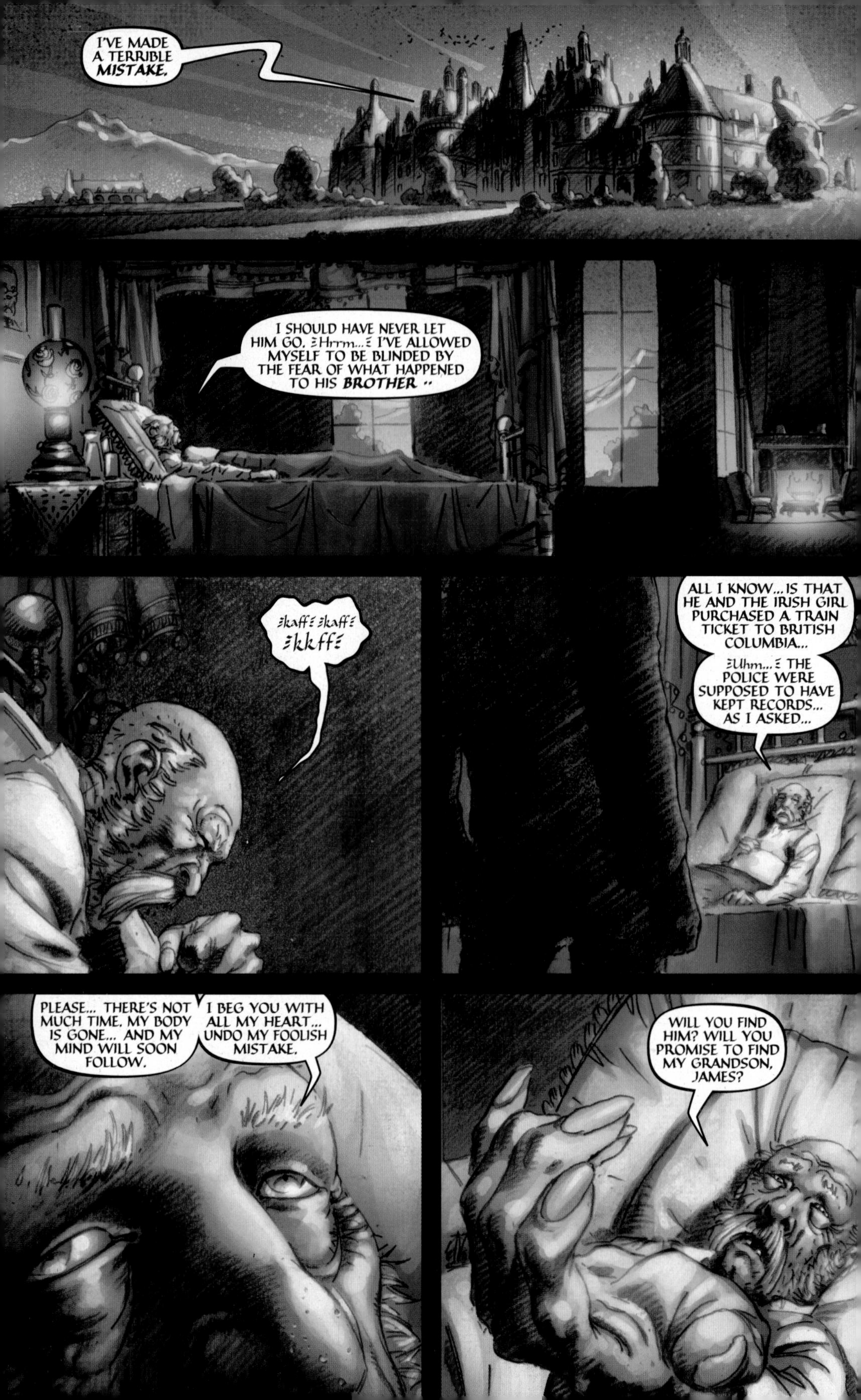
I'VE MADE A TERRIBLE MISTAKE.
I SHOULD HAVE NEVER LET HIM GO. ≷Hrrm...≶ I'VE ALLOWED MYSELF TO BE BLINDED BY THE FEAR OF WHAT HAPPENED TO HIS BROTHER --
≷kaff≶ ≷kaff≶ ≷kkff≶
ALL I KNOW... IS THAT HE AND THE IRISH GIRL PURCHASED A TRAIN TICKET TO BRITISH COLUMBIA...
≷Uhm...≶ THE POLICE WERE SUPPOSED TO HAVE KEPT RECORDS... AS I ASKED...
PLEASE... THERE'S NOT MUCH TIME, MY BODY IS GONE... AND MY MIND WILL SOON FOLLOW.
I BEG YOU WITH ALL MY HEART... UNDO MY FOOLISH MISTAKE.
WILL YOU FIND HIM? WILL YOU PROMISE TO FIND MY GRANDSON, JAMES?

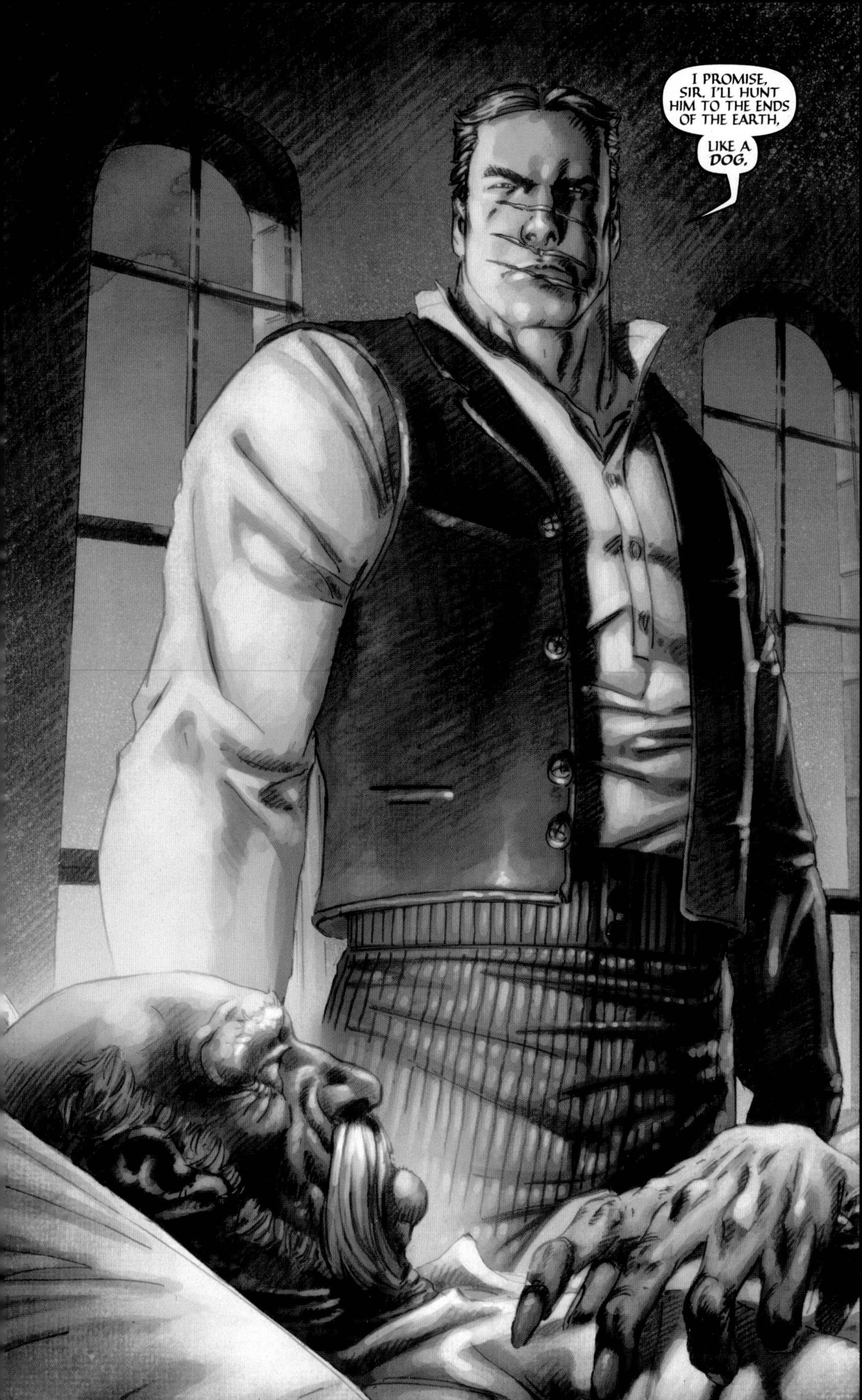
I PROMISE, SIR. I'LL HUNT HIM TO THE ENDS OF THE EARTH,
LIKE A DOG.

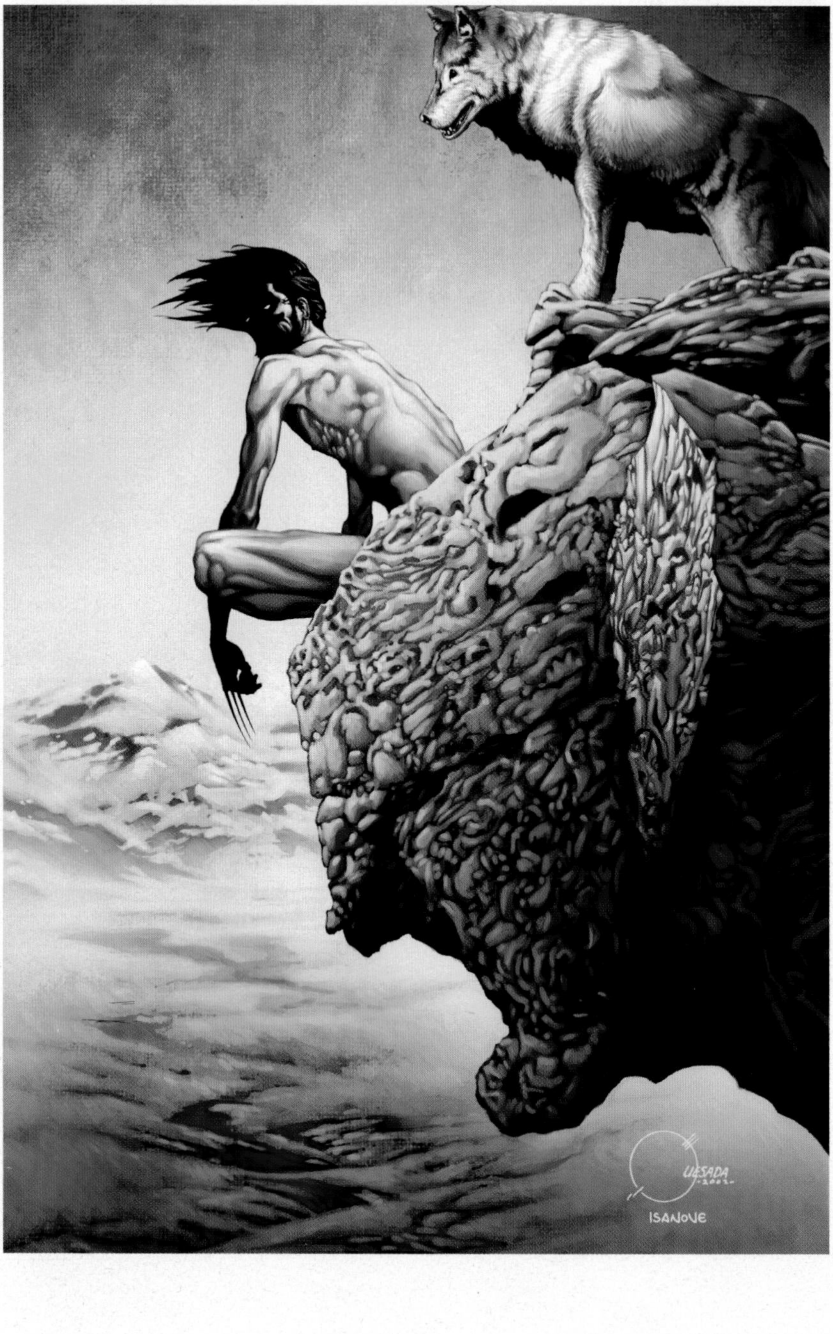
QUESADA
2002
ISANOVE

PART VI

DUST TO DUST

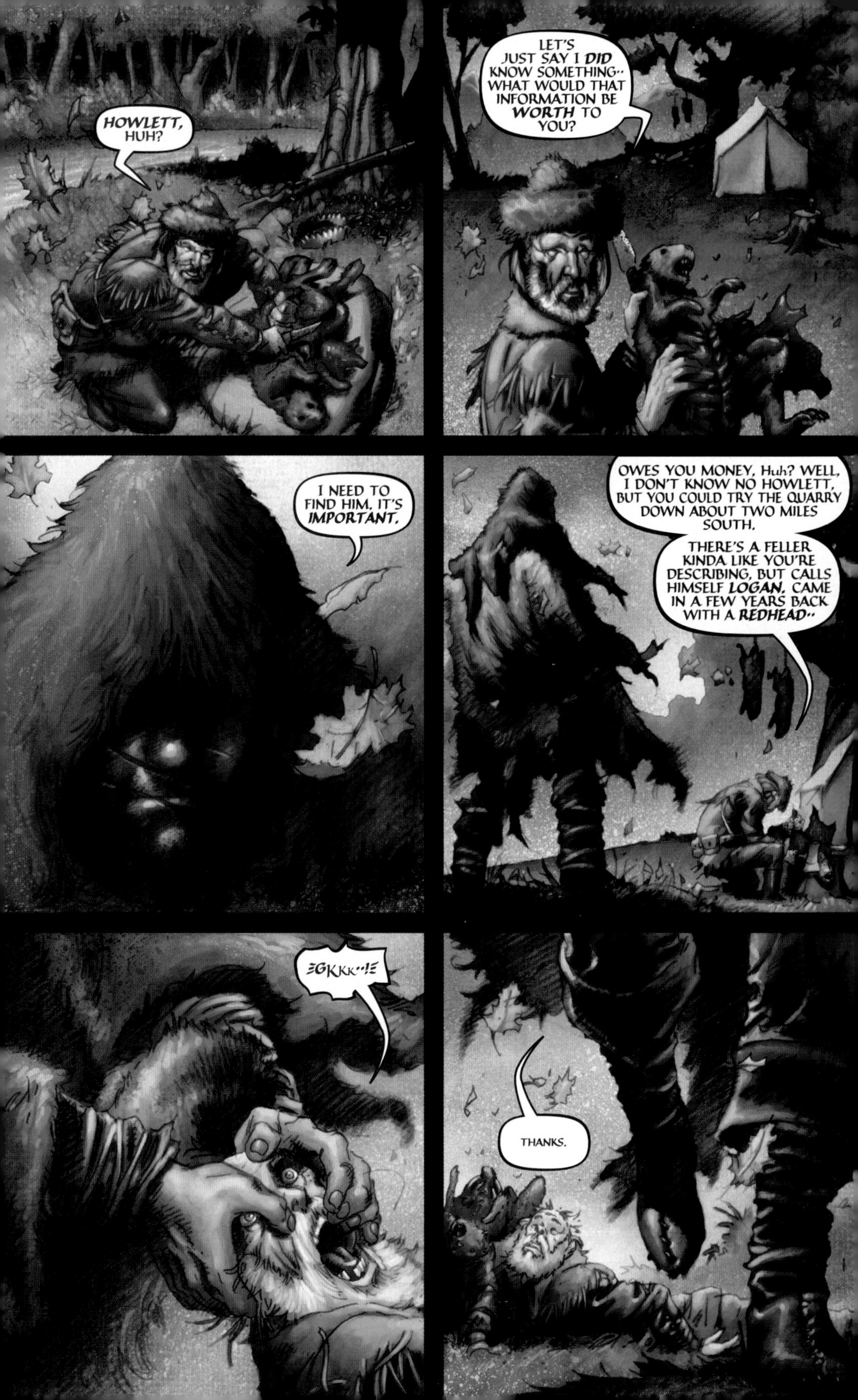
HOWLETT, HUH?
LET'S JUST SAY I DID KNOW SOMETHING.. WHAT WOULD THAT INFORMATION BE WORTH TO YOU?
I NEED TO FIND HIM. IT'S IMPORTANT.
OWES YOU MONEY, Huh? WELL, I DON'T KNOW NO HOWLETT, BUT YOU COULD TRY THE QUARRY DOWN ABOUT TWO MILES SOUTH.
THERE'S A FELLER KINDA LIKE YOU'RE DESCRIBING, BUT CALLS HIMSELF LOGAN. CAME IN A FEW YEARS BACK WITH A REDHEAD..
GKKK..!
THANKS.

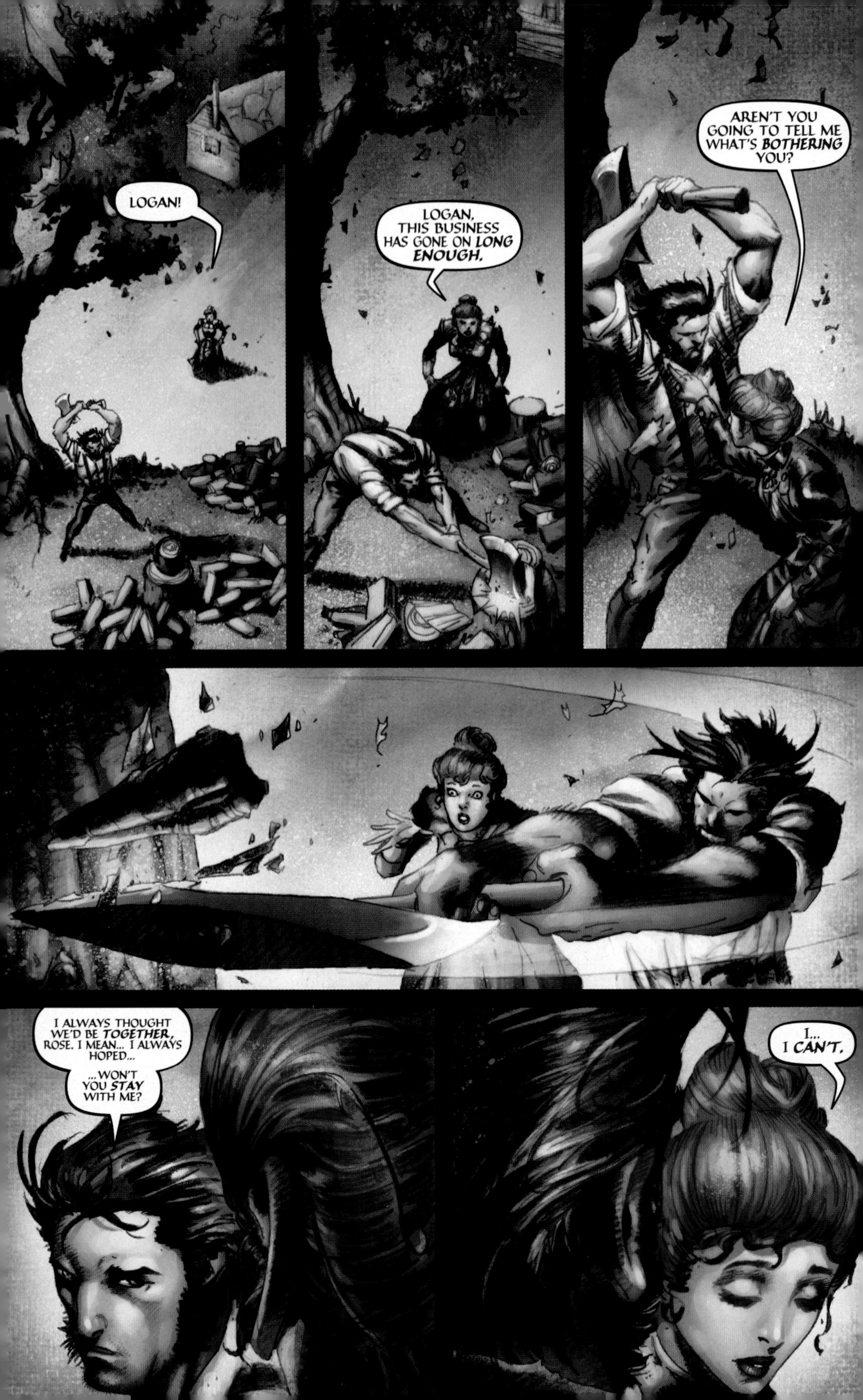
LOGAN!
LOGAN, THIS BUSINESS HAS GONE ON LONG ENOUGH.
AREN'T YOU GOING TO TELL ME WHAT'S BOTHERING YOU?
I ALWAYS THOUGHT WE'D BE TOGETHER, ROSE. I MEAN... I ALWAYS HOPED...
...WON'T YOU STAY WITH ME?
I... I CAN'T.

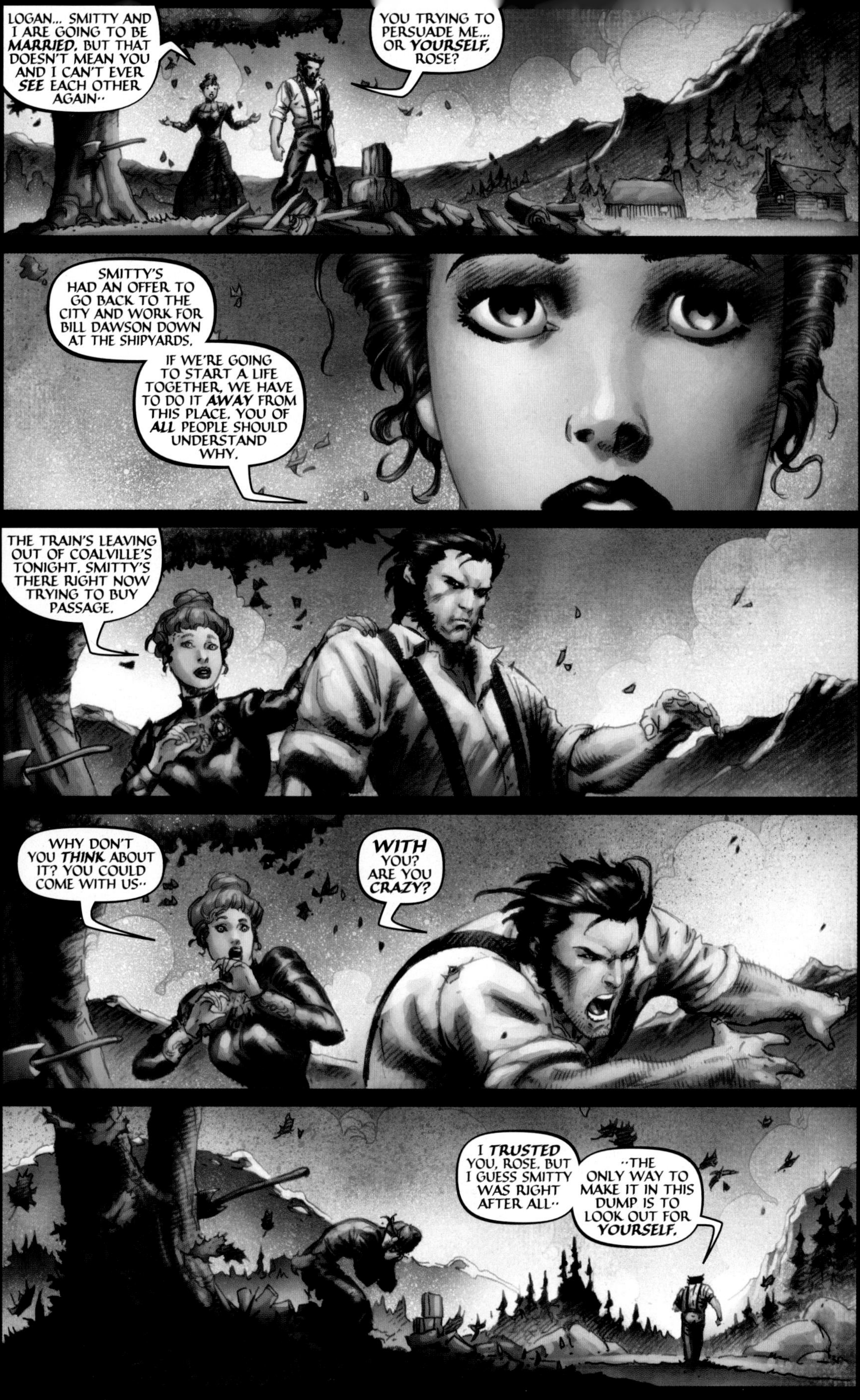
LOGAN... SMITTY AND I ARE GOING TO BE MARRIED, BUT THAT DOESN'T MEAN YOU AND I CAN'T EVER SEE EACH OTHER AGAIN··
YOU TRYING TO PERSUADE ME... OR YOURSELF, ROSE?
SMITTY'S HAD AN OFFER TO GO BACK TO THE CITY AND WORK FOR BILL DAWSON DOWN AT THE SHIPYARDS.
IF WE'RE GOING TO START A LIFE TOGETHER, WE HAVE TO DO IT AWAY FROM THIS PLACE. YOU OF ALL PEOPLE SHOULD UNDERSTAND WHY.
THE TRAIN'S LEAVING OUT OF COALVILLE'S TONIGHT. SMITTY'S THERE RIGHT NOW TRYING TO BUY PASSAGE.
WHY DON'T YOU THINK ABOUT IT? YOU COULD COME WITH US··
WITH YOU? ARE YOU CRAZY?
I TRUSTED YOU, ROSE, BUT I GUESS SMITTY WAS RIGHT AFTER ALL··
··THE ONLY WAY TO MAKE IT IN THIS DUMP IS TO LOOK OUT FOR YOURSELF.

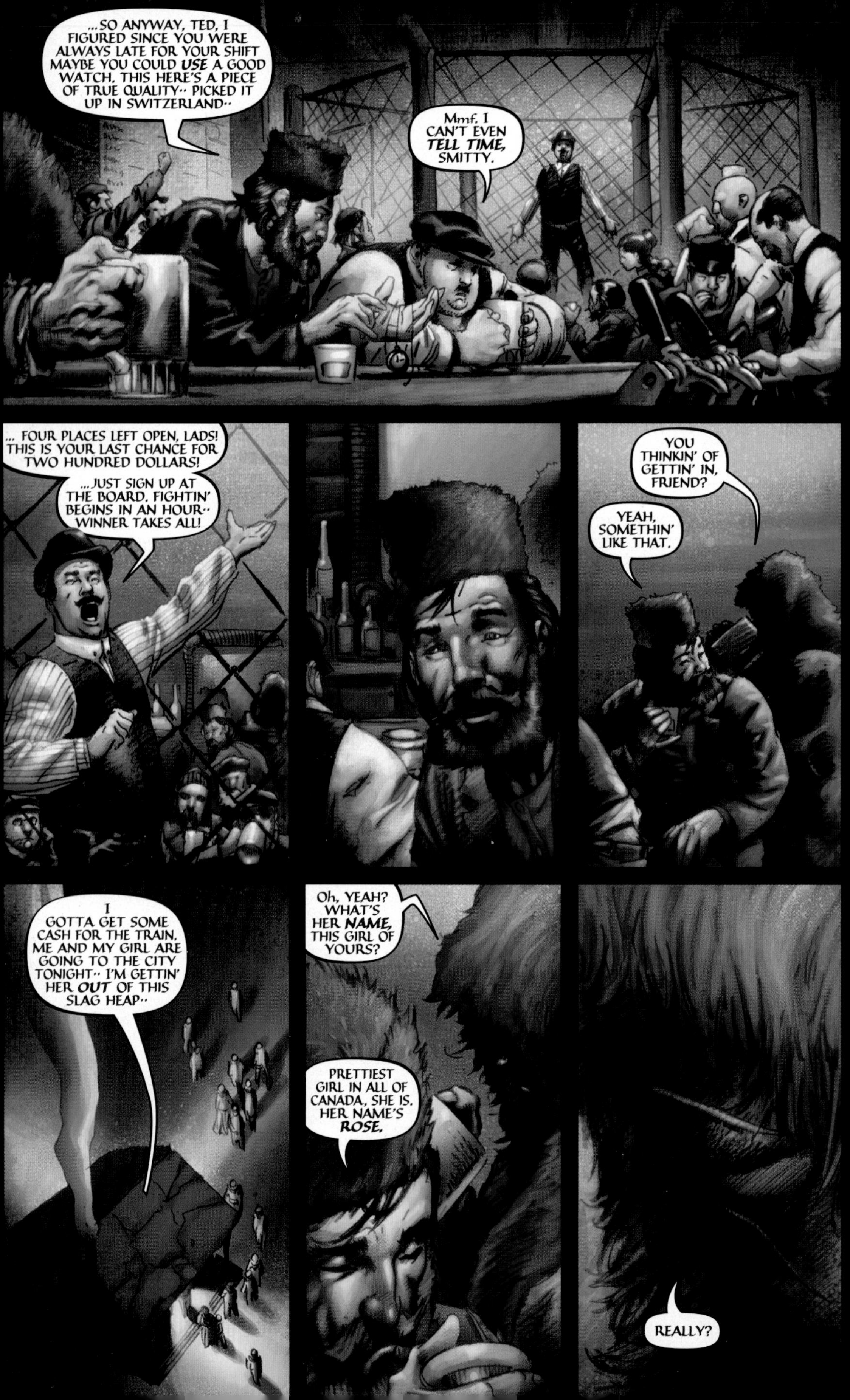
...SO ANYWAY, TED, I FIGURED SINCE YOU WERE ALWAYS LATE FOR YOUR SHIFT MAYBE YOU COULD USE A GOOD WATCH. THIS HERE'S A PIECE OF TRUE QUALITY.. PICKED IT UP IN SWITZERLAND..
Mmf. I CAN'T EVEN TELL TIME, SMITTY.
... FOUR PLACES LEFT OPEN, LADS! THIS IS YOUR LAST CHANCE FOR TWO HUNDRED DOLLARS!
...JUST SIGN UP AT THE BOARD. FIGHTIN' BEGINS IN AN HOUR.. WINNER TAKES ALL!
YOU THINKIN' OF GETTIN' IN, FRIEND?
YEAH, SOMETHIN' LIKE THAT.
I GOTTA GET SOME CASH FOR THE TRAIN. ME AND MY GIRL ARE GOING TO THE CITY TONIGHT.. I'M GETTIN' HER OUT OF THIS SLAG HEAP..
Oh, YEAH? WHAT'S HER NAME, THIS GIRL OF YOURS?
PRETTIEST GIRL IN ALL OF CANADA, SHE IS. HER NAME'S ROSE.
REALLY?

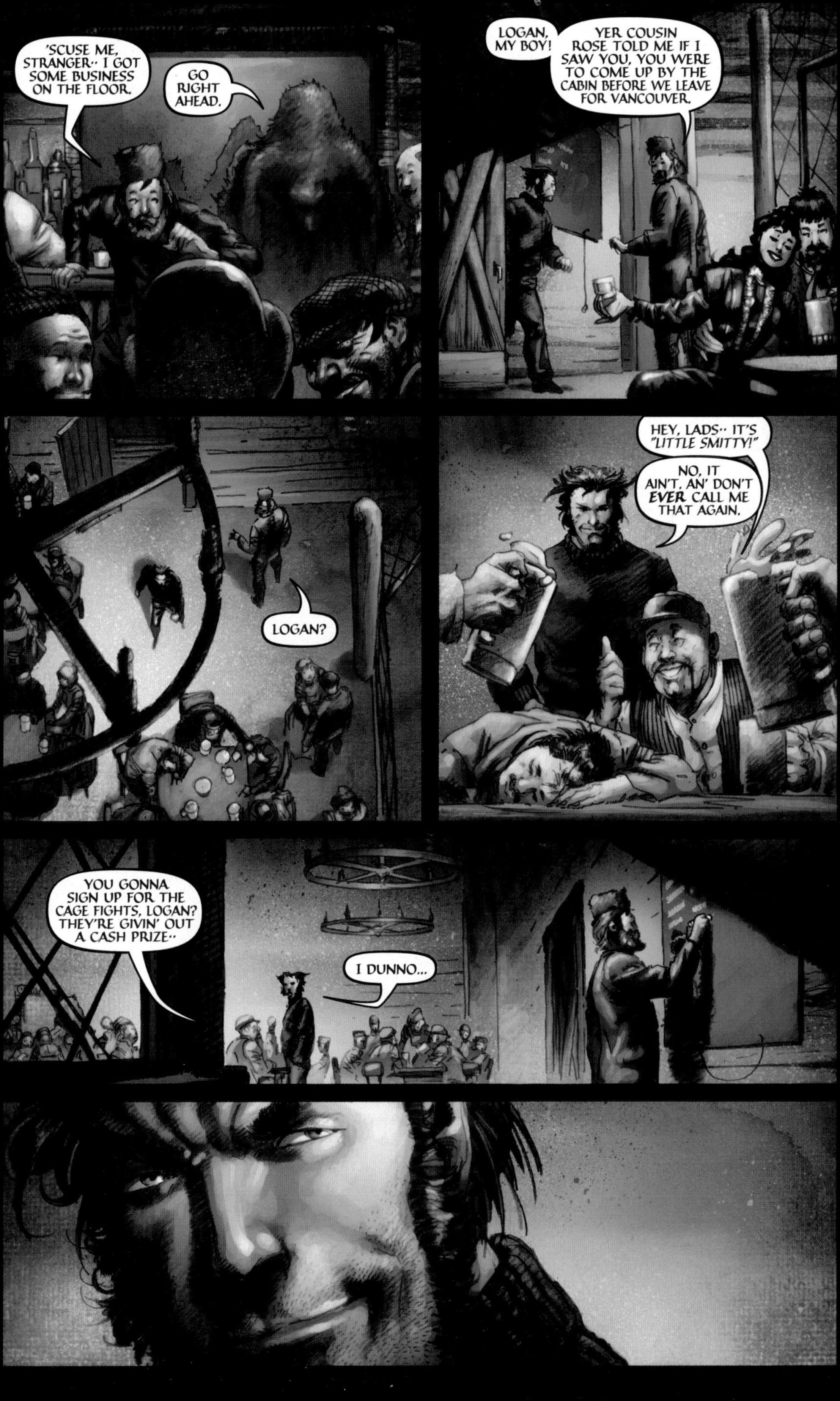
'SCUSE ME, STRANGER·· I GOT SOME BUSINESS ON THE FLOOR.
GO RIGHT AHEAD.
LOGAN, MY BOY!
YER COUSIN ROSE TOLD ME IF I SAW YOU, YOU WERE TO COME UP BY THE CABIN BEFORE WE LEAVE FOR VANCOUVER.
LOGAN?
HEY, LADS·· IT'S "LITTLE SMITTY!"
NO, IT AIN'T. AN' DON'T EVER CALL ME THAT AGAIN.
YOU GONNA SIGN UP FOR THE CAGE FIGHTS, LOGAN? THEY'RE GIVIN' OUT A CASH PRIZE··
I DUNNO...

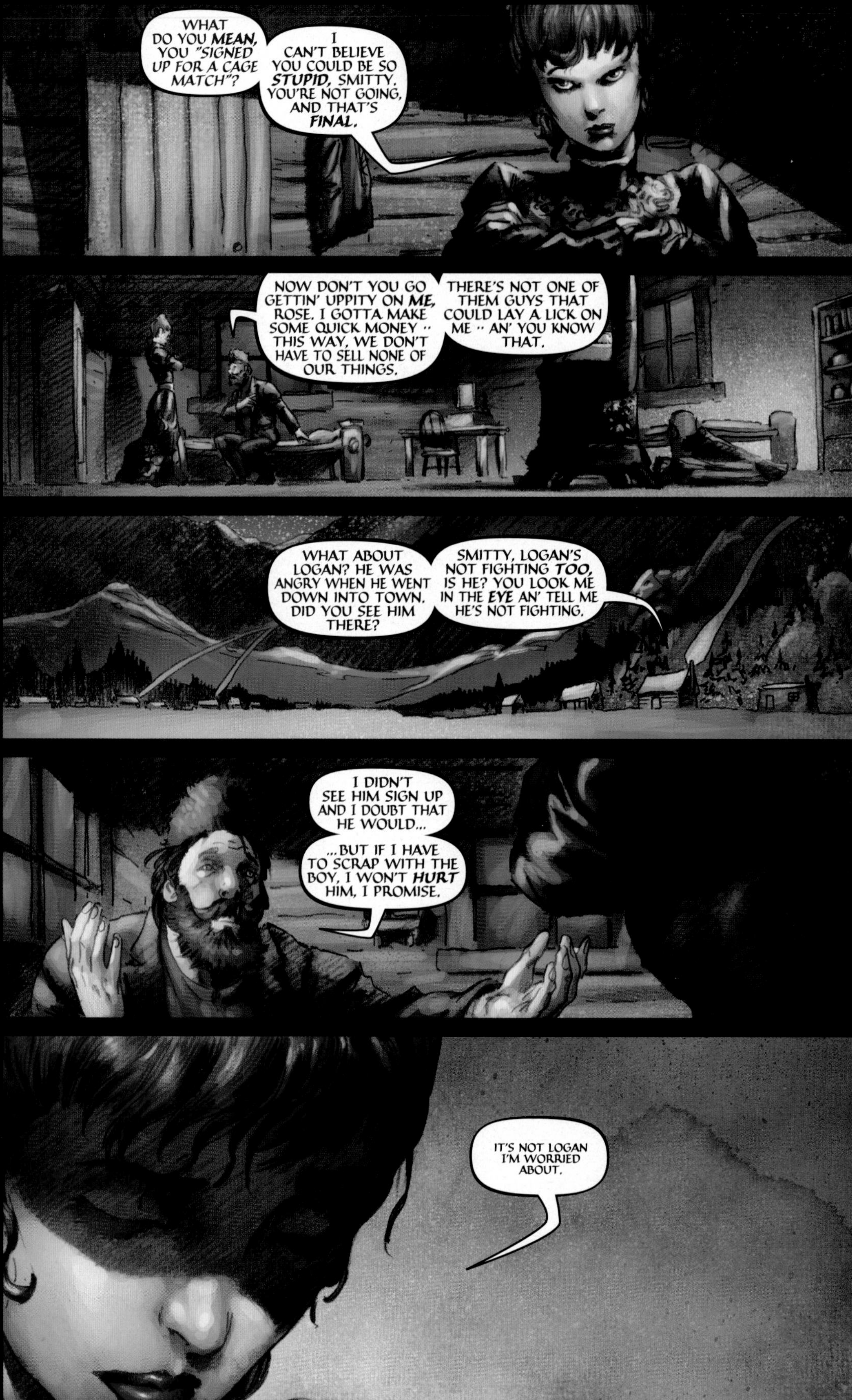
WHAT DO YOU MEAN, YOU "SIGNED UP FOR A CAGE MATCH"?
I CAN'T BELIEVE YOU COULD BE SO STUPID, SMITTY. YOU'RE NOT GOING, AND THAT'S FINAL.
NOW DON'T YOU GO GETTIN' UPPITY ON ME, ROSE. I GOTTA MAKE SOME QUICK MONEY -- THIS WAY, WE DON'T HAVE TO SELL NONE OF OUR THINGS.
THERE'S NOT ONE OF THEM GUYS THAT COULD LAY A LICK ON ME -- AN' YOU KNOW THAT.
WHAT ABOUT LOGAN? HE WAS ANGRY WHEN HE WENT DOWN INTO TOWN. DID YOU SEE HIM THERE?
SMITTY, LOGAN'S NOT FIGHTING TOO, IS HE? YOU LOOK ME IN THE EYE AN' TELL ME HE'S NOT FIGHTING.
I DIDN'T SEE HIM SIGN UP AND I DOUBT THAT HE WOULD...
...BUT IF I HAVE TO SCRAP WITH THE BOY, I WON'T HURT HIM, I PROMISE.
IT'S NOT LOGAN I'M WORRIED ABOUT.

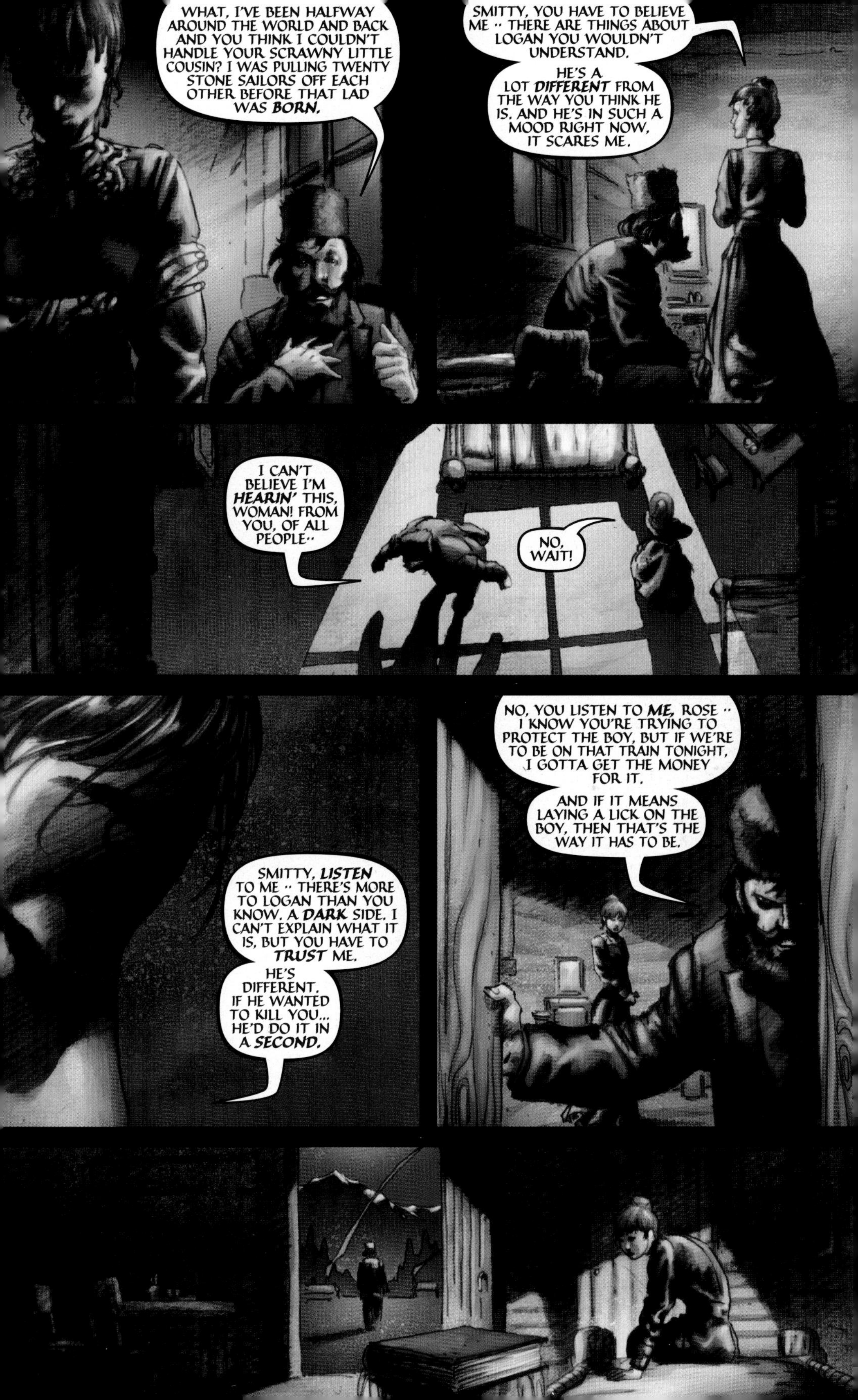
WHAT, I'VE BEEN HALFWAY AROUND THE WORLD AND BACK AND YOU THINK I COULDN'T HANDLE YOUR SCRAWNY LITTLE COUSIN? I WAS PULLING TWENTY STONE SAILORS OFF EACH OTHER BEFORE THAT LAD WAS BORN.
SMITTY, YOU HAVE TO BELIEVE ME -- THERE ARE THINGS ABOUT LOGAN YOU WOULDN'T UNDERSTAND.
HE'S A LOT DIFFERENT FROM THE WAY YOU THINK HE IS, AND HE'S IN SUCH A MOOD RIGHT NOW, IT SCARES ME.
I CAN'T BELIEVE I'M HEARIN' THIS, WOMAN! FROM YOU, OF ALL PEOPLE--
NO, WAIT!
SMITTY, LISTEN TO ME -- THERE'S MORE TO LOGAN THAN YOU KNOW. A DARK SIDE. I CAN'T EXPLAIN WHAT IT IS, BUT YOU HAVE TO TRUST ME.
HE'S DIFFERENT. IF HE WANTED TO KILL YOU... HE'D DO IT IN A SECOND.
NO, YOU LISTEN TO ME, ROSE -- I KNOW YOU'RE TRYING TO PROTECT THE BOY, BUT IF WE'RE TO BE ON THAT TRAIN TONIGHT, I GOTTA GET THE MONEY FOR IT.
AND IF IT MEANS LAYING A LICK ON THE BOY, THEN THAT'S THE WAY IT HAS TO BE.

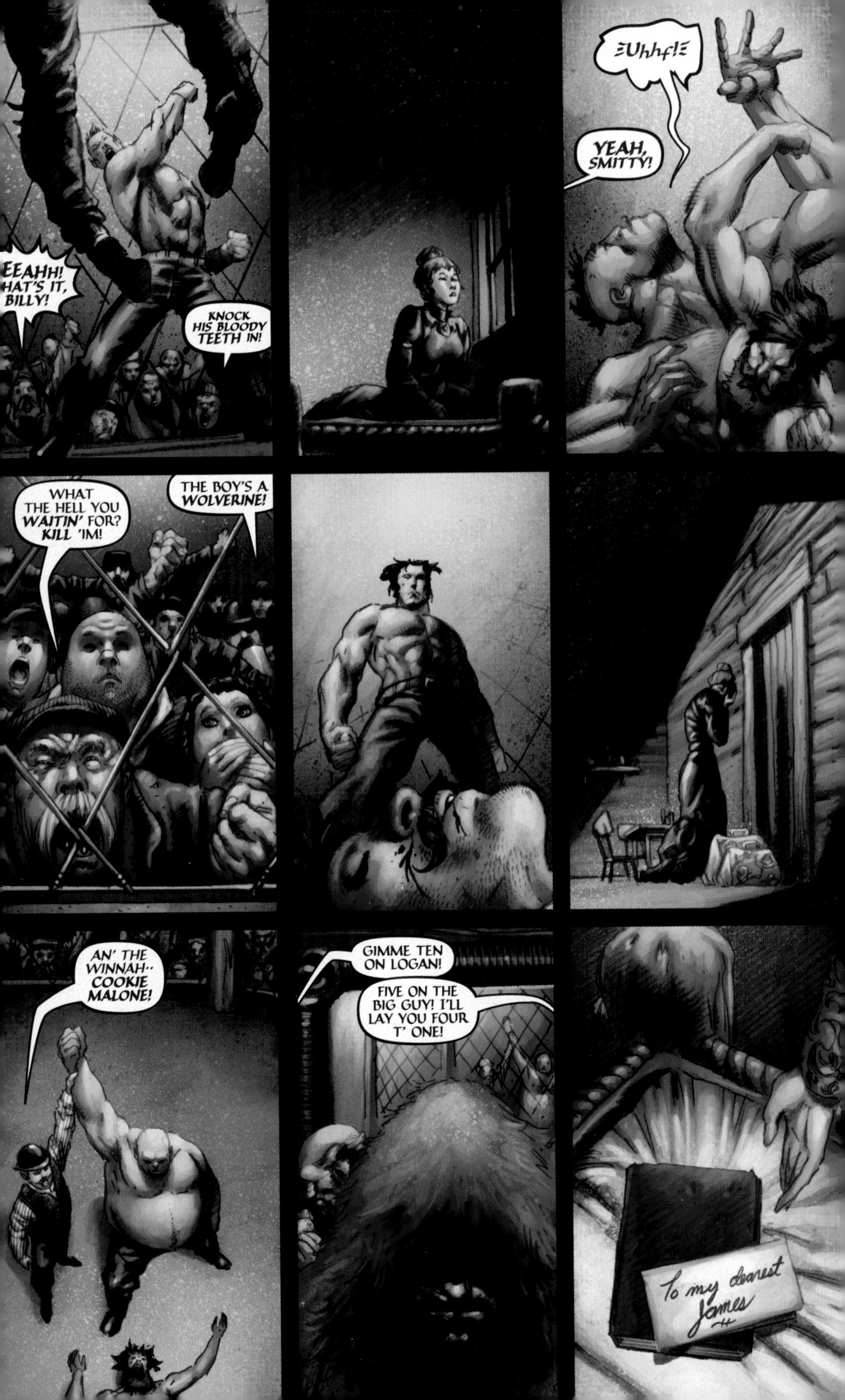
EEAHH! HAT'S IT, BILLY!
KNOCK HIS BLOODY TEETH IN!
Uhhf!
YEAH, SMITTY!
WHAT THE HELL YOU WAITIN' FOR? KILL 'IM!
THE BOY'S A WOLVERINE!
AN' THE WINNAH.. COOKIE MALONE!
GIMME TEN ON LOGAN!
FIVE ON THE BIG GUY! I'LL LAY YOU FOUR T' ONE!
To my dearest James

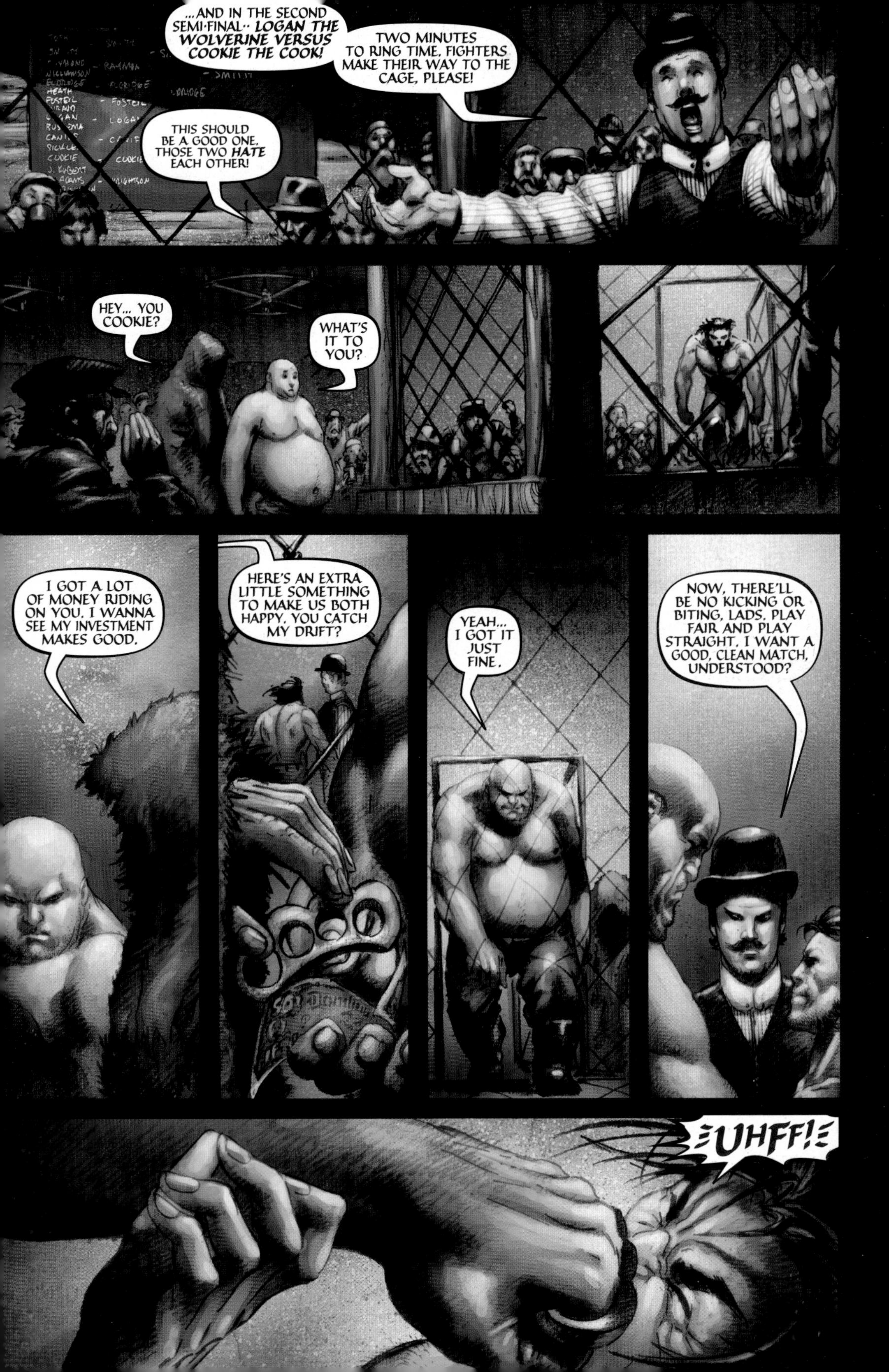
...AND IN THE SECOND SEMI-FINAL.. LOGAN THE WOLVERINE VERSUS COOKIE THE COOK!
TWO MINUTES TO RING TIME. FIGHTERS MAKE THEIR WAY TO THE CAGE, PLEASE!
THIS SHOULD BE A GOOD ONE. THOSE TWO HATE EACH OTHER!
HEY... YOU COOKIE?
WHAT'S IT TO YOU?
I GOT A LOT OF MONEY RIDING ON YOU. I WANNA SEE MY INVESTMENT MAKES GOOD.
HERE'S AN EXTRA LITTLE SOMETHING TO MAKE US BOTH HAPPY, YOU CATCH MY DRIFT?
YEAH... I GOT IT JUST FINE.
NOW, THERE'LL BE NO KICKING OR BITING, LADS. PLAY FAIR AND PLAY STRAIGHT. I WANT A GOOD, CLEAN MATCH. UNDERSTOOD?
UHFF!

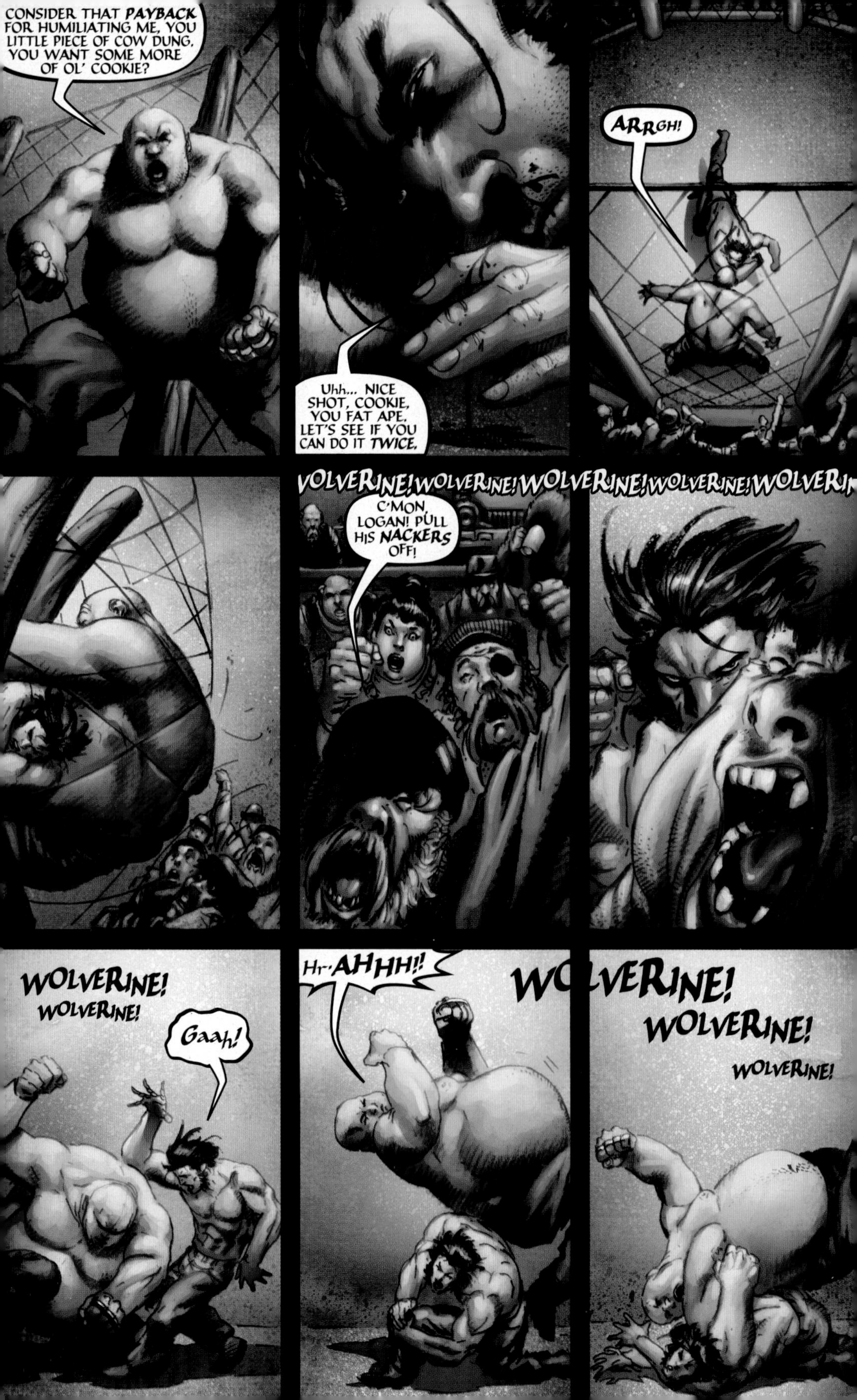
CONSIDER THAT PAYBACK FOR HUMILIATING ME, YOU LITTLE PIECE OF COW DUNG. YOU WANT SOME MORE OF OL' COOKIE?
Uhh... NICE SHOT, COOKIE, YOU FAT APE. LET'S SEE IF YOU CAN DO IT TWICE.
ARRGH!
WOLVERINE! WOLVERINE! WOLVERINE! WOLVERINE!
C'MON, LOGAN! PULL HIS NACKERS OFF!
WOLVERINE!
WOLVERINE!
Gaah!
Hr-AHHH!!
WOLVERINE!
WOLVERINE!
WOLVERINE!

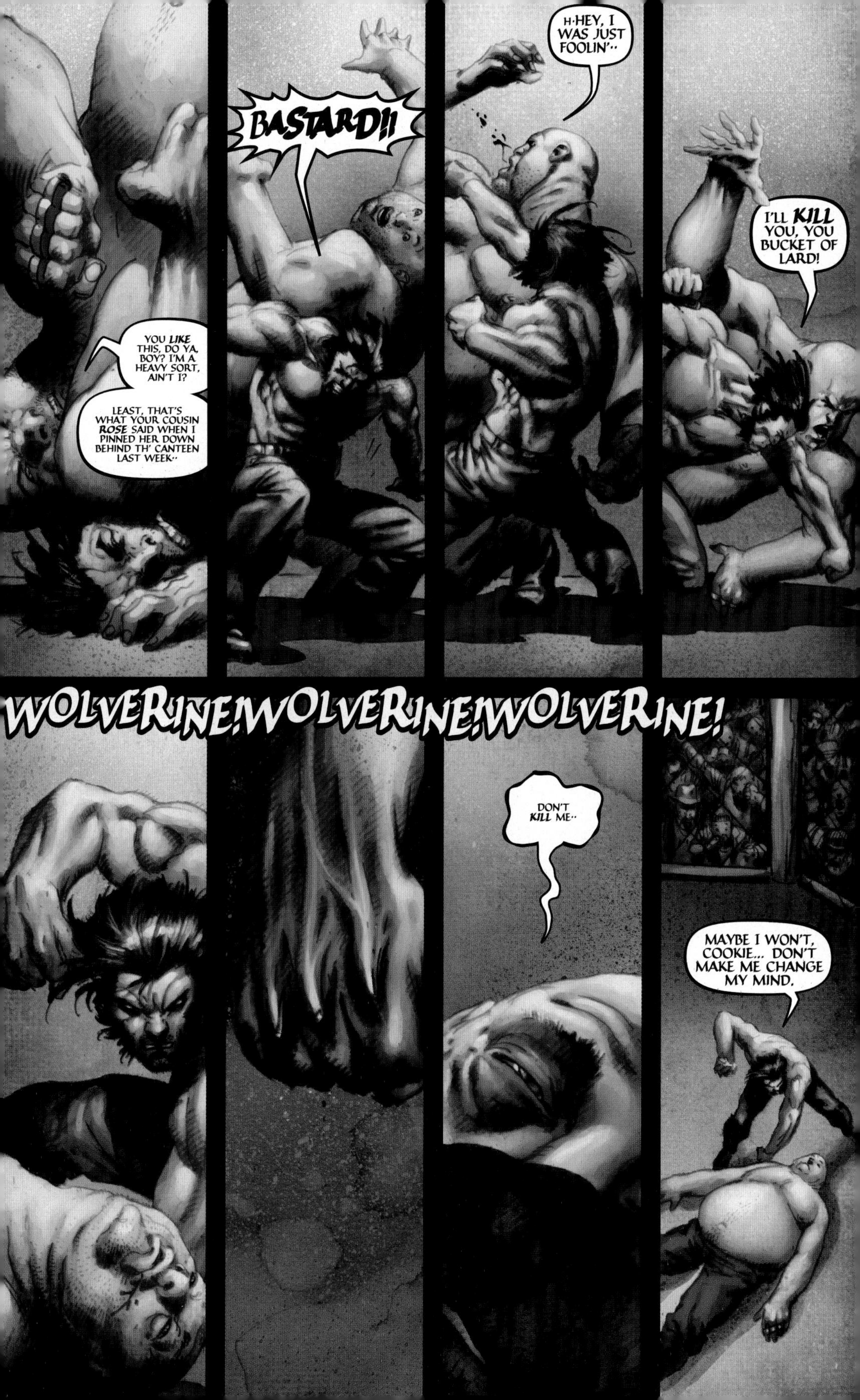
YOU LIKE THIS, DO YA, BOY? I'M A HEAVY SORT, AIN'T I?
LEAST, THAT'S WHAT YOUR COUSIN ROSE SAID WHEN I PINNED HER DOWN BEHIND TH' CANTEEN LAST WEEK..
BASTARD!!
H-HEY, I WAS JUST FOOLIN'..
I'LL KILL YOU, YOU BUCKET OF LARD!
WOLVERINE! WOLVERINE! WOLVERINE!
DON'T KILL ME..
MAYBE I WON'T, COOKIE... DON'T MAKE ME CHANGE MY MIND.

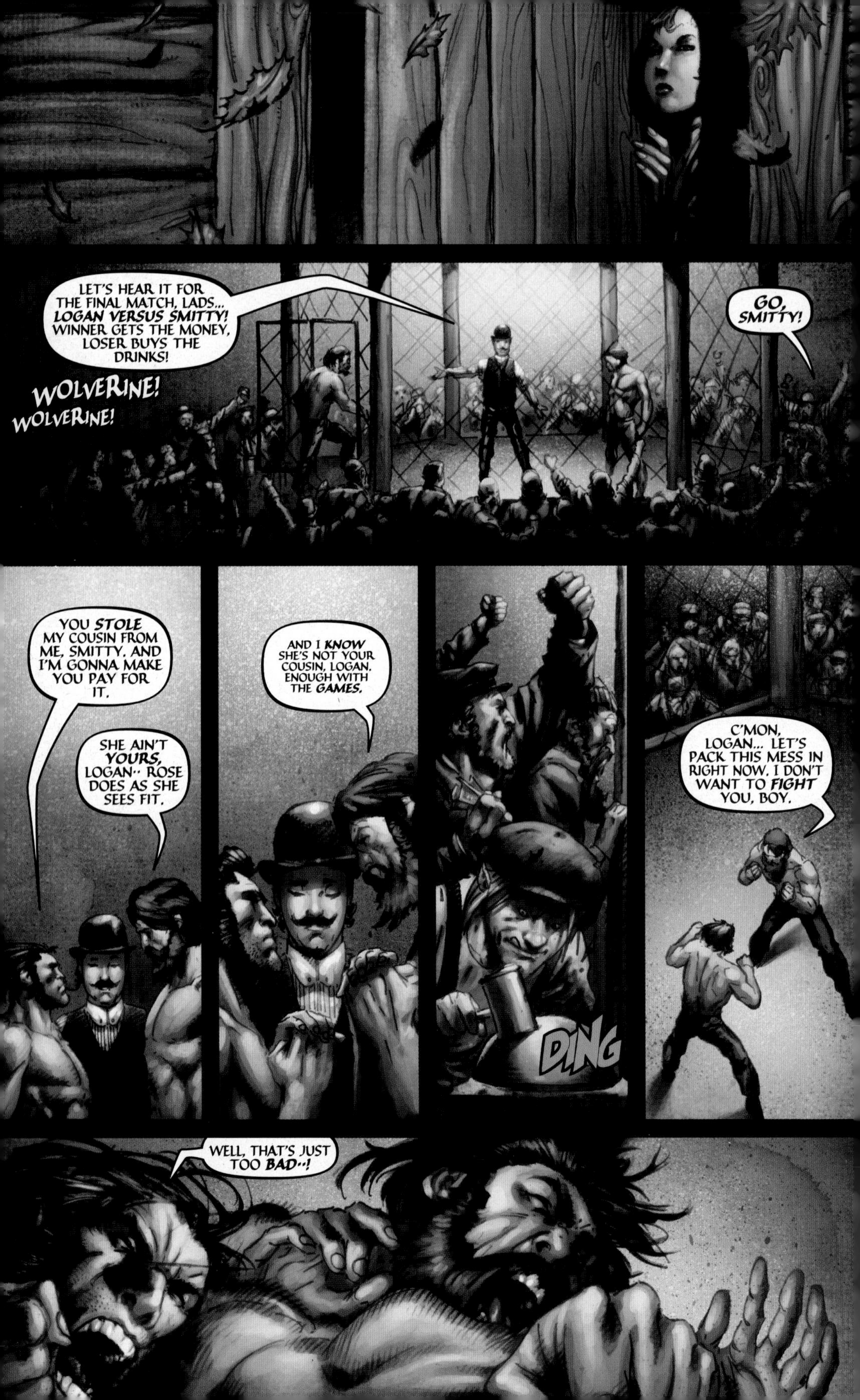

LET'S HEAR IT FOR THE FINAL MATCH, LADS... LOGAN VERSUS SMITTY! WINNER GETS THE MONEY, LOSER BUYS THE DRINKS!
GO, SMITTY!
WOLVERINE! WOLVERINE!
YOU STOLE MY COUSIN FROM ME, SMITTY. AND I'M GONNA MAKE YOU PAY FOR IT.
SHE AIN'T YOURS, LOGAN.. ROSE DOES AS SHE SEES FIT.
AND I KNOW SHE'S NOT YOUR COUSIN, LOGAN. ENOUGH WITH THE GAMES.
DING
C'MON, LOGAN... LET'S PACK THIS MESS IN RIGHT NOW. I DON'T WANT TO FIGHT YOU, BOY.
WELL, THAT'S JUST TOO BAD..!

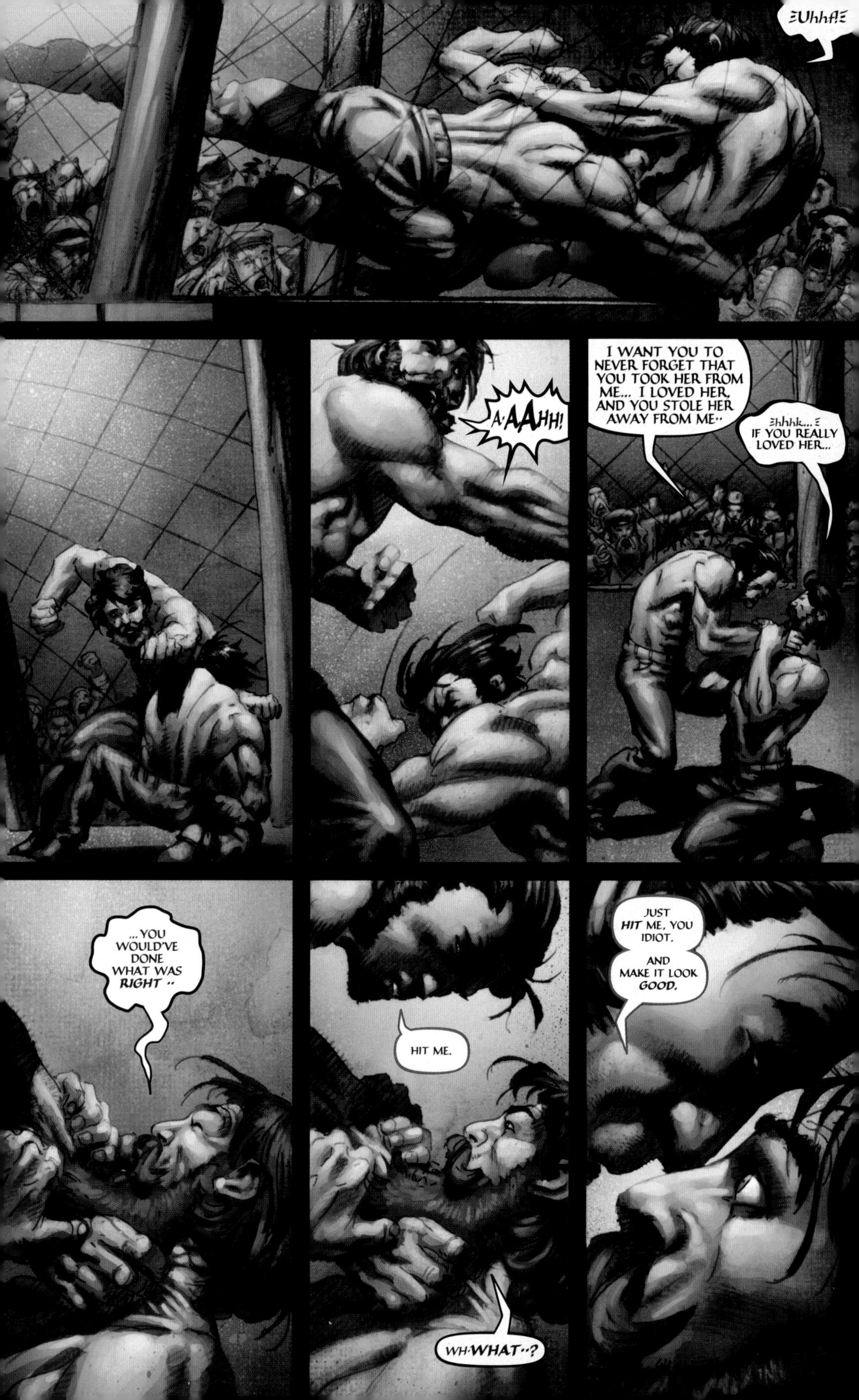

UhhfAE
A-AAHH!
I WANT YOU TO NEVER FORGET THAT YOU TOOK HER FROM ME... I LOVED HER, AND YOU STOLE HER AWAY FROM ME..
hhhk...
IF YOU REALLY LOVED HER...
...YOU WOULD'VE DONE WHAT WAS RIGHT ..
HIT ME.
WH-WHAT..?
JUST HIT ME, YOU IDIOT.
AND MAKE IT LOOK GOOD.

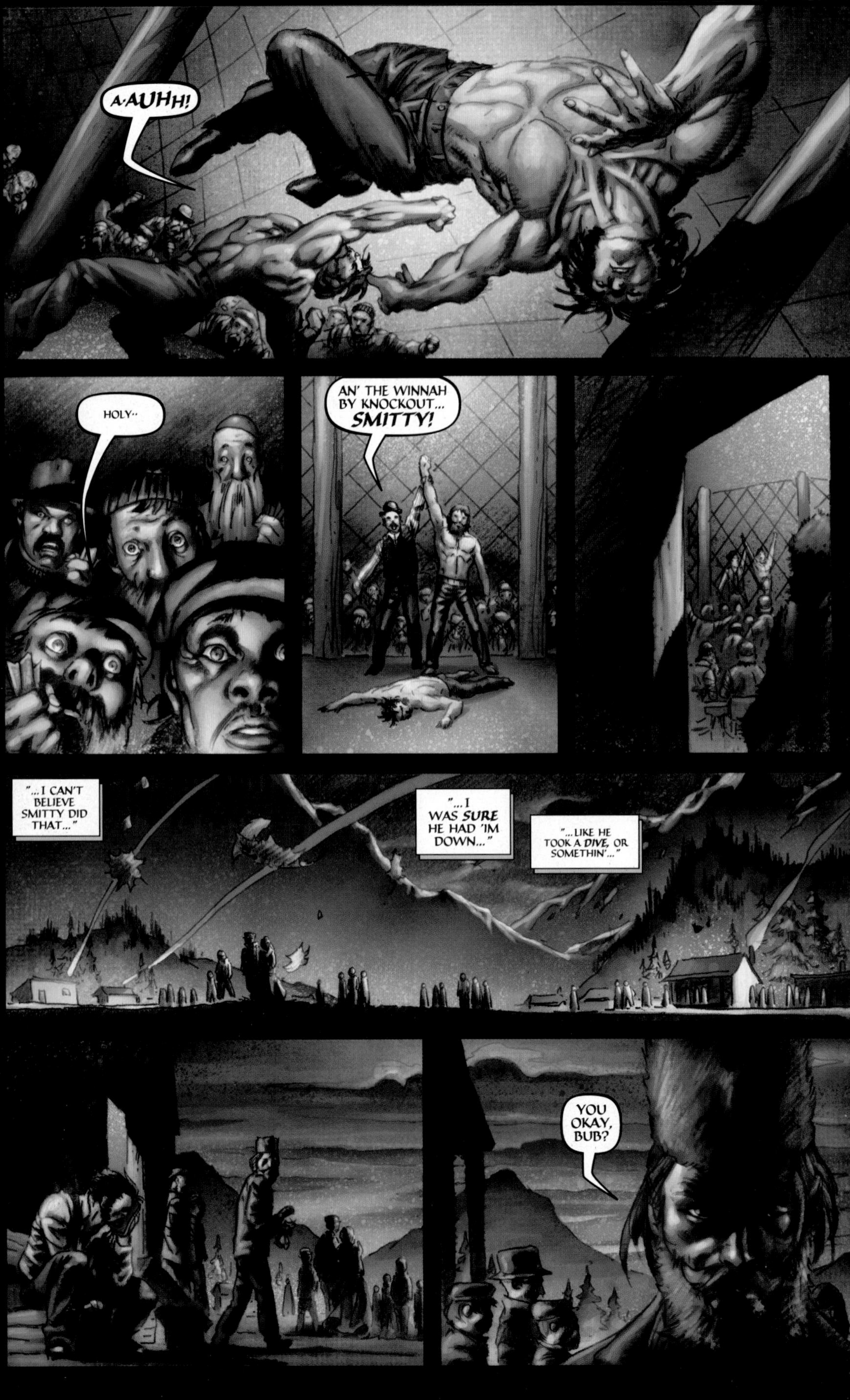
A-AUHH!
HOLY..
AN' THE WINNAH BY KNOCKOUT... SMITTY!
"...I CAN'T BELIEVE SMITTY DID THAT..."
"...I WAS SURE HE HAD 'IM DOWN..."
"...LIKE HE TOOK A DIVE, OR SOMETHIN'..."
YOU OKAY, BUB?

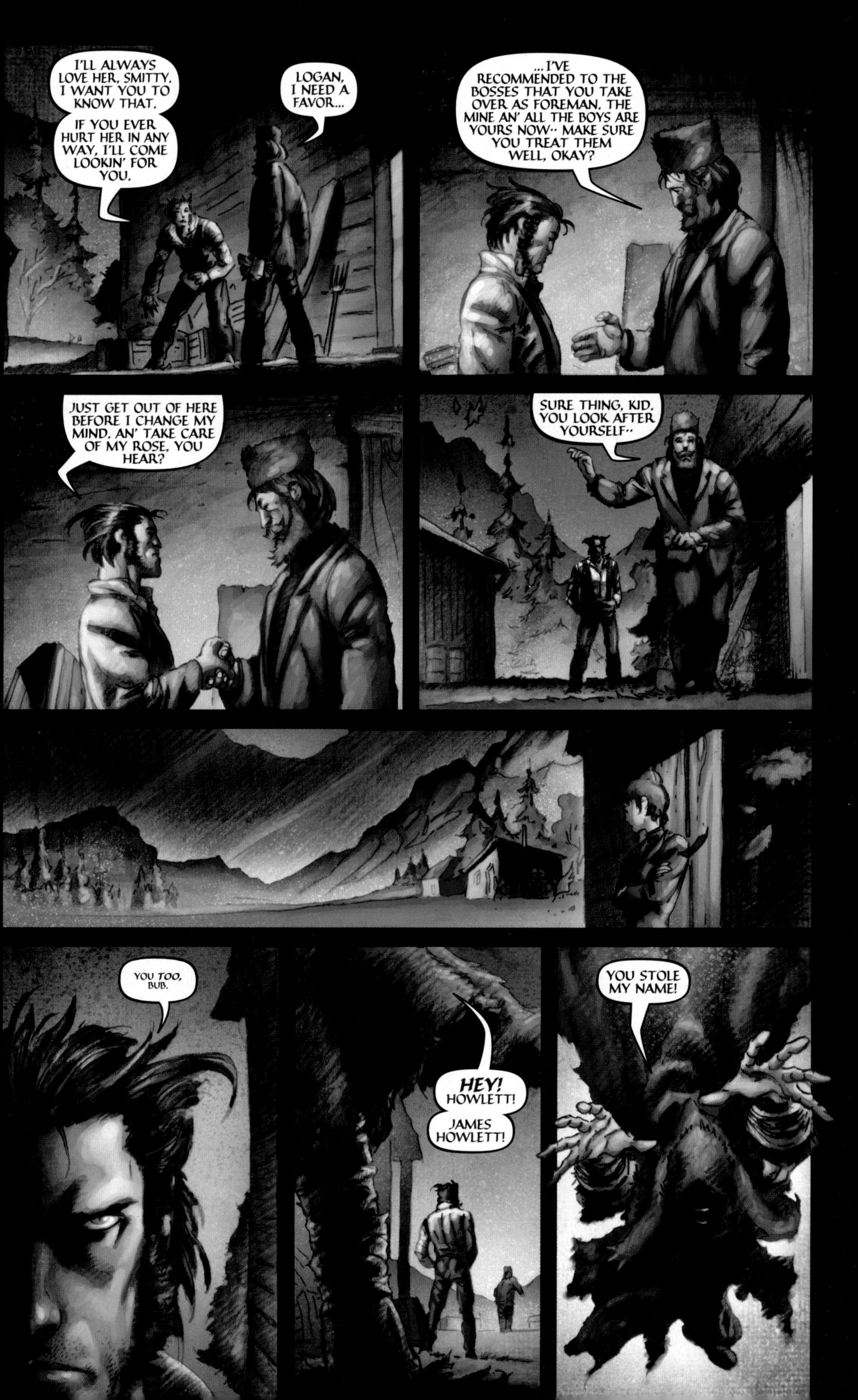
I'LL ALWAYS LOVE HER, SMITTY. I WANT YOU TO KNOW THAT.
IF YOU EVER HURT HER IN ANY WAY, I'LL COME LOOKIN' FOR YOU.
LOGAN, I NEED A FAVOR...
...I'VE RECOMMENDED TO THE BOSSES THAT YOU TAKE OVER AS FOREMAN. THE MINE AN' ALL THE BOYS ARE YOURS NOW.. MAKE SURE YOU TREAT THEM WELL, OKAY?
JUST GET OUT OF HERE BEFORE I CHANGE MY MIND, AN' TAKE CARE OF MY ROSE, YOU HEAR?
SURE THING, KID. YOU LOOK AFTER YOURSELF..
YOU TOO, BUB.
HEY! HOWLETT!
JAMES HOWLETT!
YOU STOLE MY NAME!

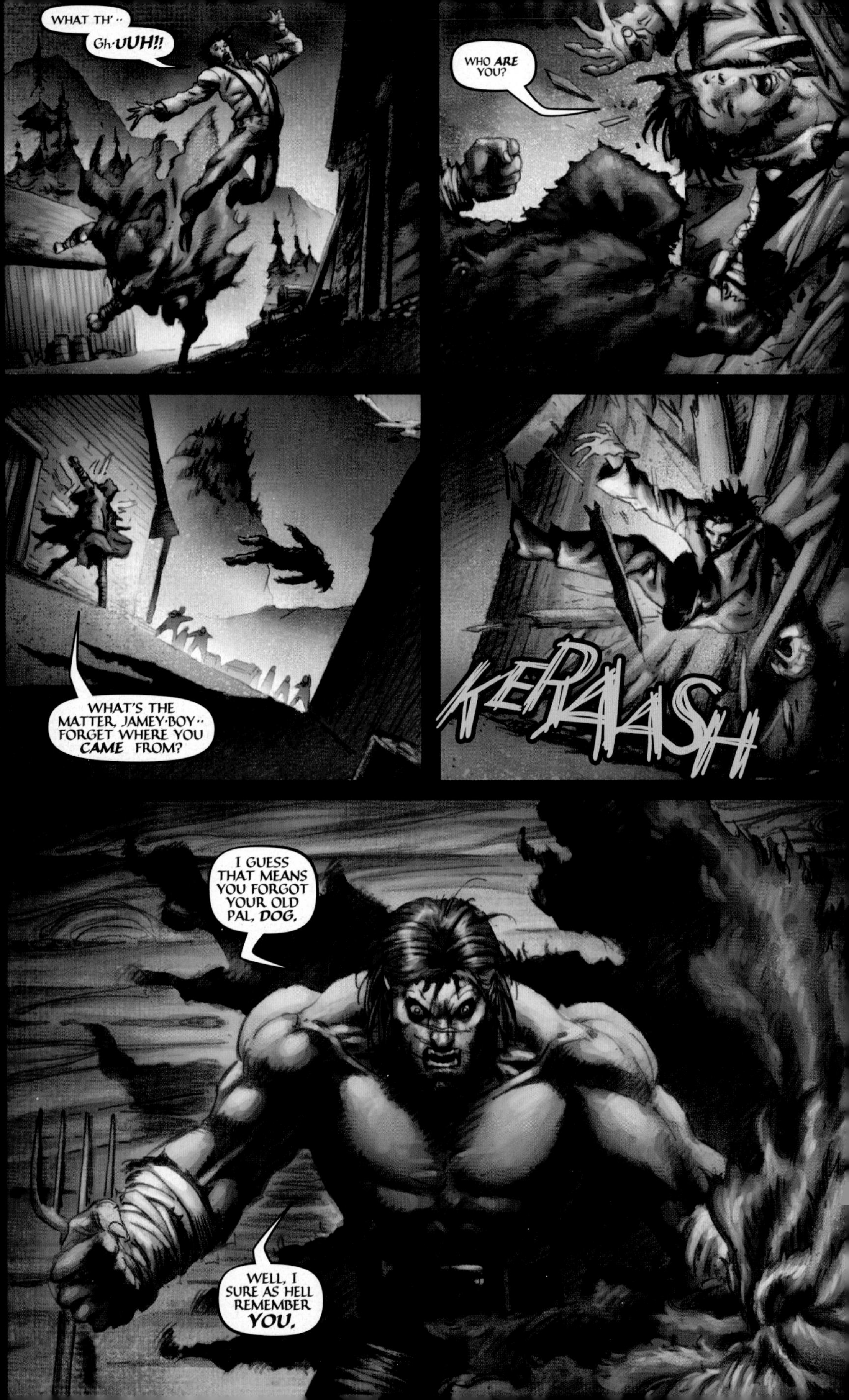
WHAT TH'.. Gh-UUH!!
WHO ARE YOU?
WHAT'S THE MATTER, JAMEY-BOY.. FORGET WHERE YOU CAME FROM?
KERRAASH
I GUESS THAT MEANS YOU FORGOT YOUR OLD PAL, DOG.
WELL, I SURE AS HELL REMEMBER YOU.

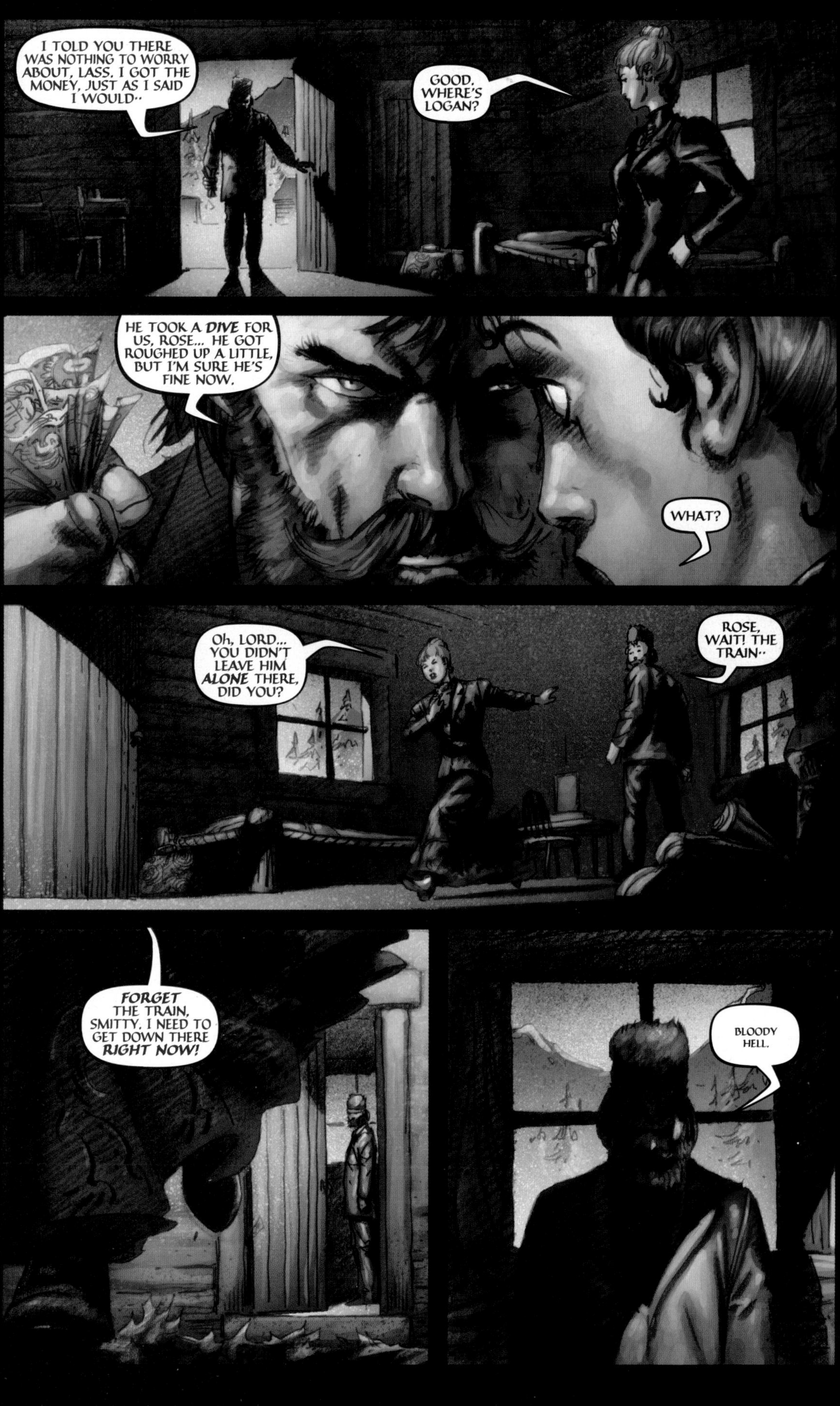
I TOLD YOU THERE WAS NOTHING TO WORRY ABOUT, LASS. I GOT THE MONEY, JUST AS I SAID I WOULD··
GOOD. WHERE'S LOGAN?
HE TOOK A *DIVE* FOR US, ROSE... HE GOT ROUGHED UP A LITTLE, BUT I'M SURE HE'S FINE NOW.
WHAT?
Oh, LORD... YOU DIDN'T LEAVE HIM *ALONE* THERE, DID YOU?
ROSE, WAIT! THE TRAIN··
FORGET THE TRAIN, SMITTY. I NEED TO GET DOWN THERE *RIGHT NOW!*
BLOODY HELL.

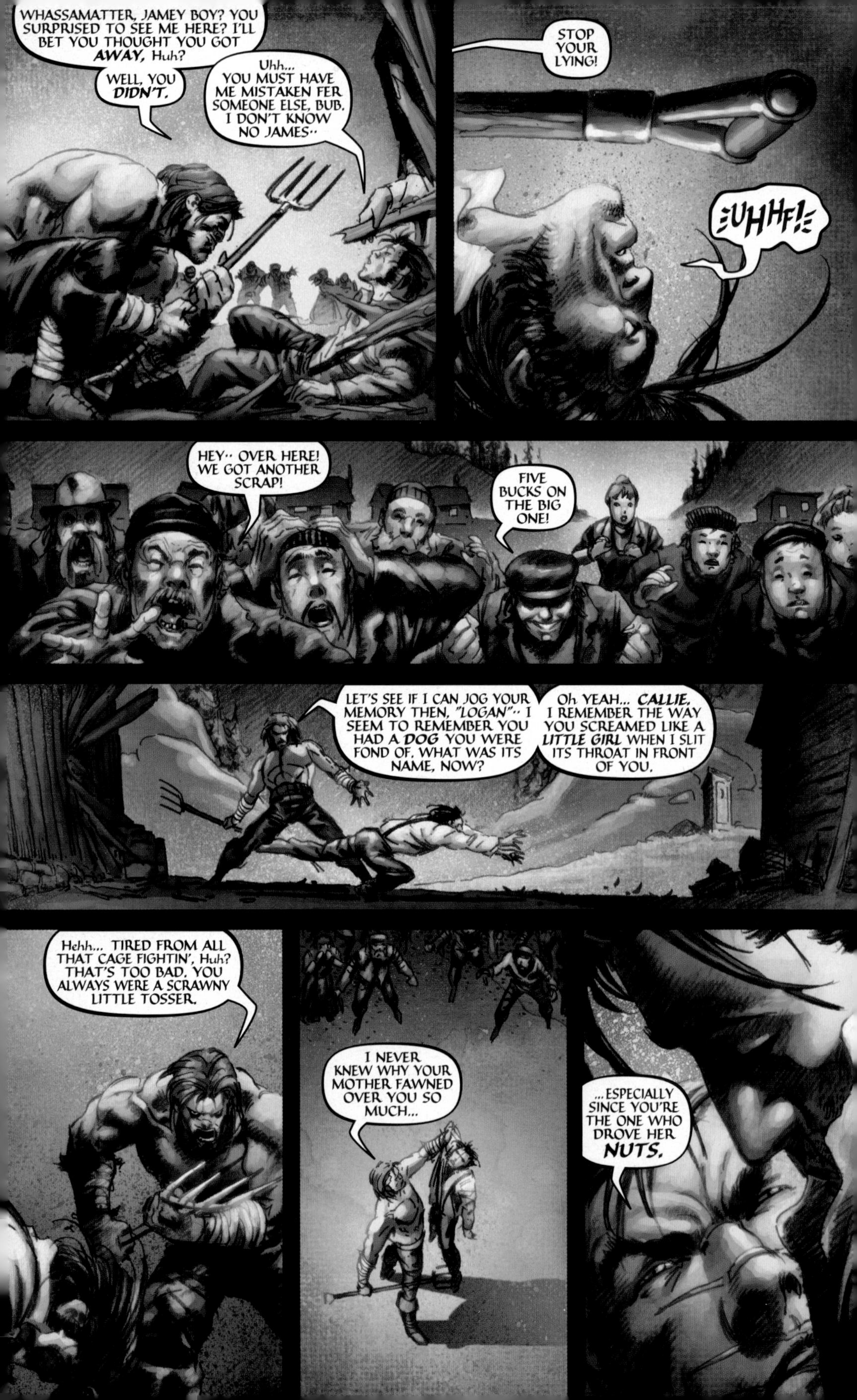

WHASSAMATTER, JAMEY BOY? YOU SURPRISED TO SEE ME HERE? I'LL BET YOU THOUGHT YOU GOT AWAY, Huh?
WELL, YOU DIDN'T.
Uhh... YOU MUST HAVE ME MISTAKEN FER SOMEONE ELSE, BUB. I DON'T KNOW NO JAMES..
STOP YOUR LYING!
UHHF!
HEY.. OVER HERE! WE GOT ANOTHER SCRAP!
FIVE BUCKS ON THE BIG ONE!
LET'S SEE IF I CAN JOG YOUR MEMORY THEN, "LOGAN".. I SEEM TO REMEMBER YOU HAD A DOG YOU WERE FOND OF. WHAT WAS ITS NAME, NOW?
Oh YEAH... CALLIE. I REMEMBER THE WAY YOU SCREAMED LIKE A LITTLE GIRL WHEN I SLIT ITS THROAT IN FRONT OF YOU.
Hehh... TIRED FROM ALL THAT CAGE FIGHTIN', Huh? THAT'S TOO BAD. YOU ALWAYS WERE A SCRAWNY LITTLE TOSSER.
I NEVER KNEW WHY YOUR MOTHER FAWNED OVER YOU SO MUCH...
...ESPECIALLY SINCE YOU'RE THE ONE WHO DROVE HER NUTS.

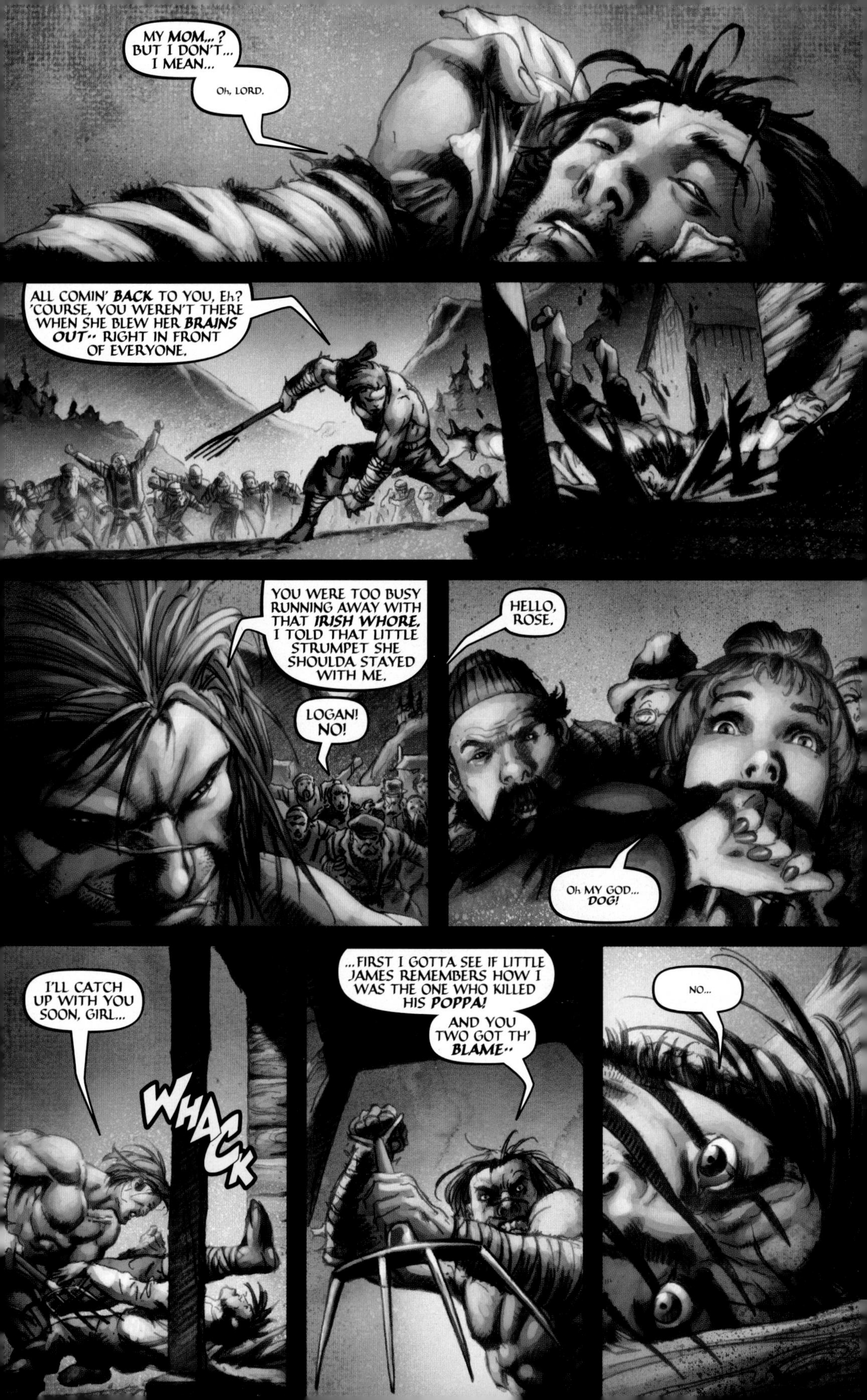

MY MOM...? BUT I DON'T... I MEAN...
Oh, LORD.
ALL COMIN' BACK TO YOU, Eh? 'COURSE, YOU WEREN'T THERE WHEN SHE BLEW HER BRAINS OUT-- RIGHT IN FRONT OF EVERYONE.
YOU WERE TOO BUSY RUNNING AWAY WITH THAT IRISH WHORE. I TOLD THAT LITTLE STRUMPET SHE SHOULDA STAYED WITH ME.
LOGAN! NO!
HELLO, ROSE.
Oh MY GOD... DOG!
I'LL CATCH UP WITH YOU SOON, GIRL...
WHACK
...FIRST I GOTTA SEE IF LITTLE JAMES REMEMBERS HOW I WAS THE ONE WHO KILLED HIS POPPA!
AND YOU TWO GOT TH' BLAME--
NO...

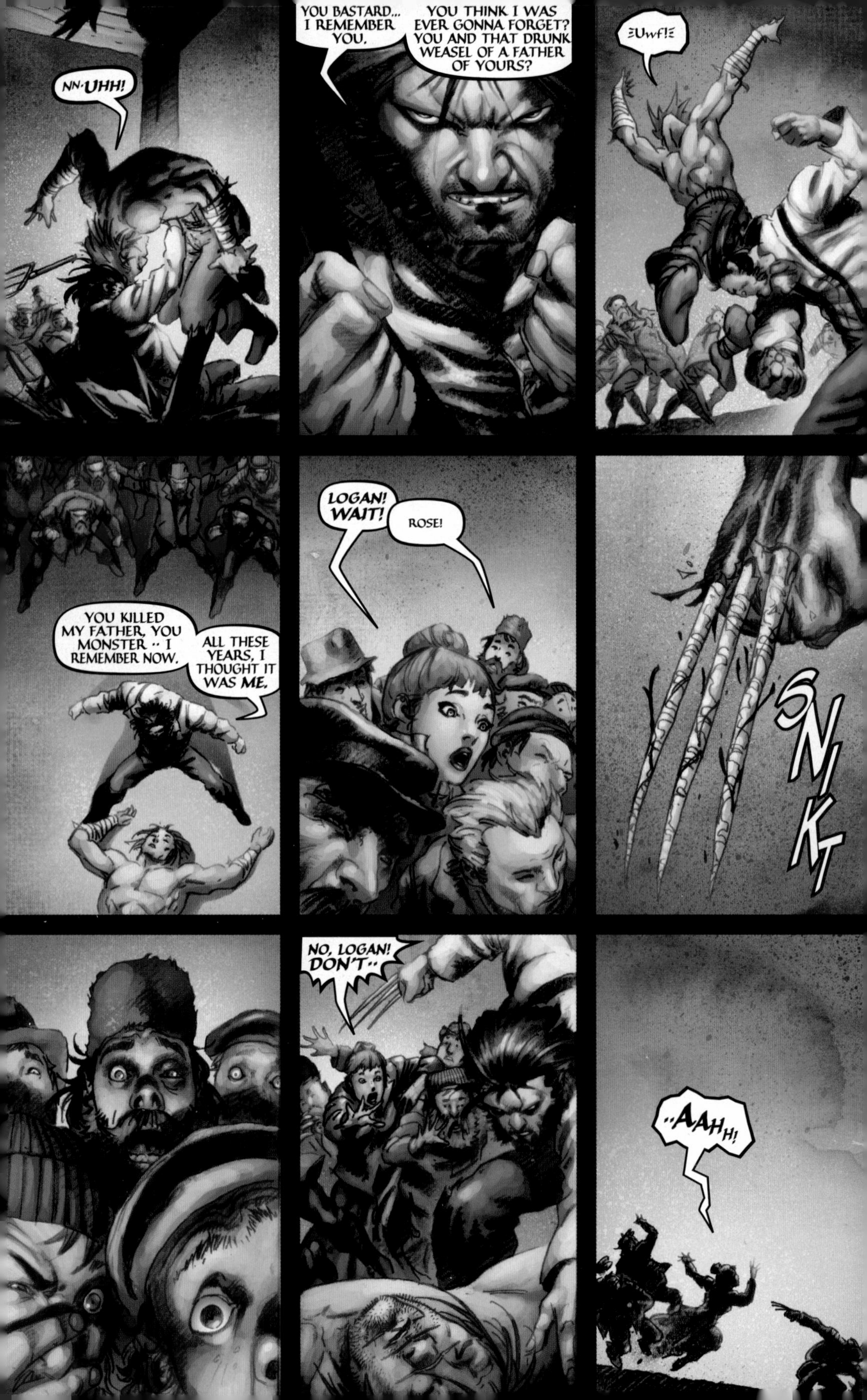
NN·UHH!
YOU BASTARD... I REMEMBER YOU.
YOU THINK I WAS EVER GONNA FORGET? YOU AND THAT DRUNK WEASEL OF A FATHER OF YOURS?
UWF!
YOU KILLED MY FATHER, YOU MONSTER -- I REMEMBER NOW.
ALL THESE YEARS, I THOUGHT IT WAS ME.
LOGAN! WAIT!
ROSE!
SNIKT
NO, LOGAN! DON'T --
--AAHH!

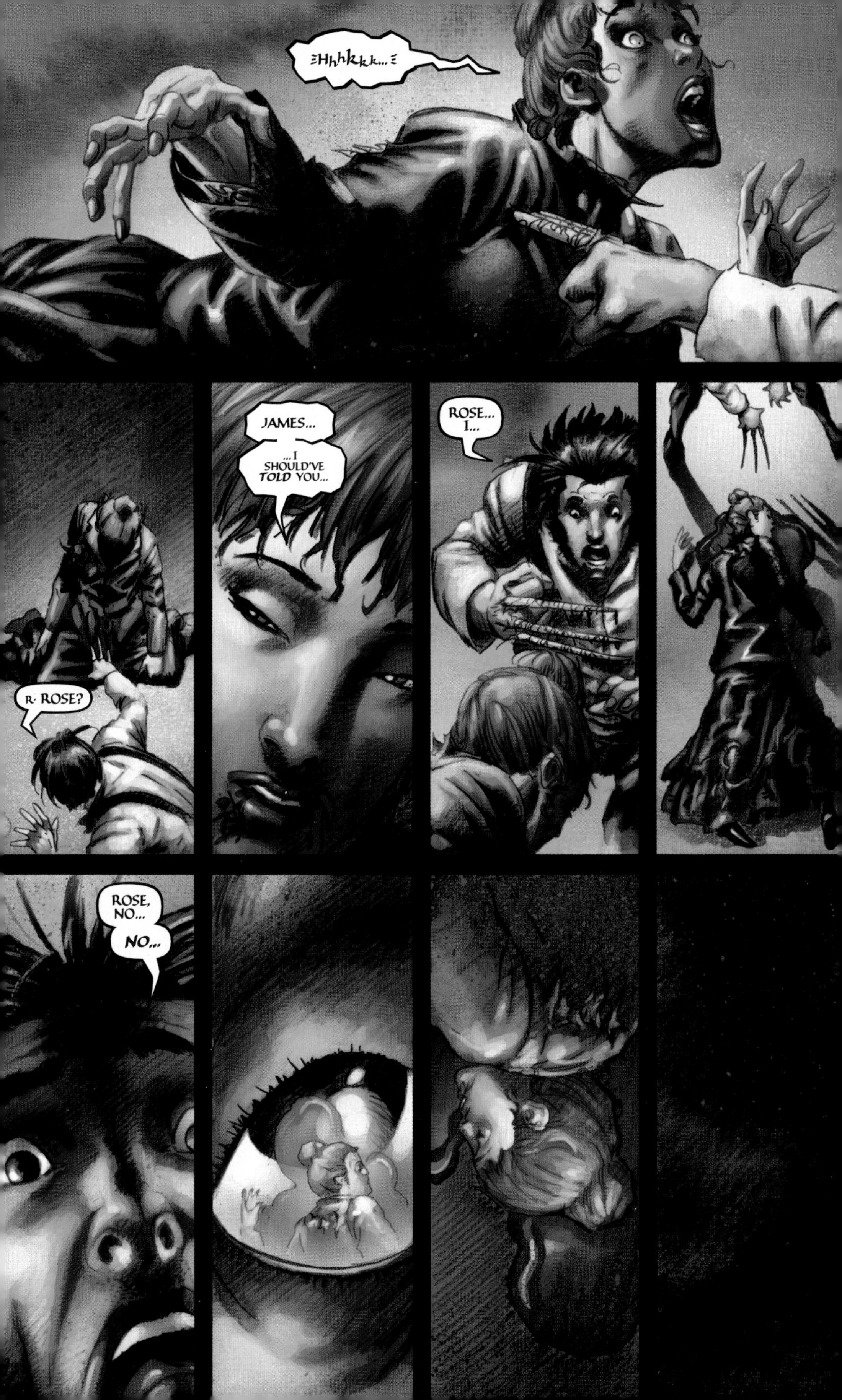
Hhhkkk...
JAMES...
...I SHOULD'VE TOLD YOU...
ROSE... I...
R- ROSE?
ROSE, NO... NO...

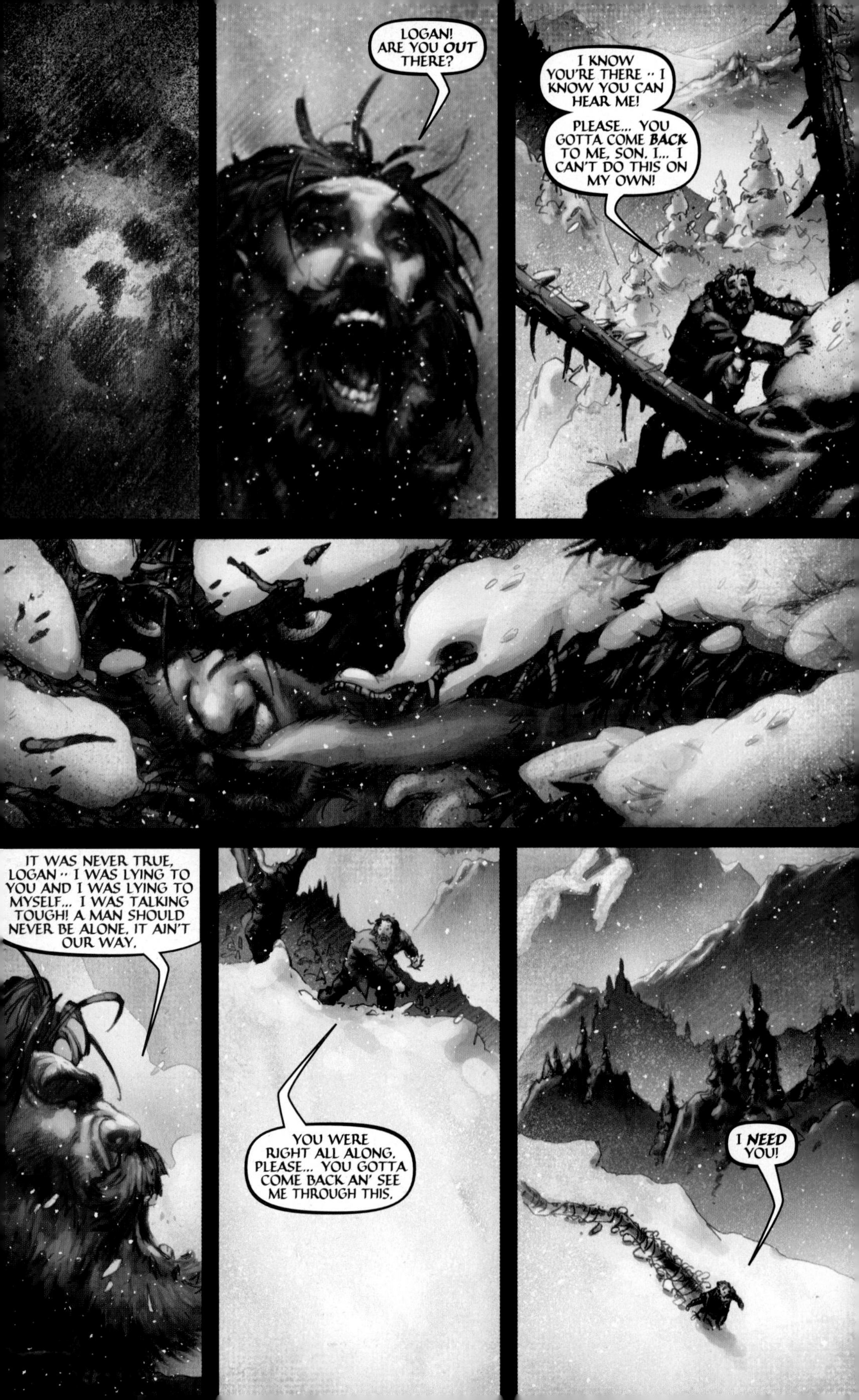
LOGAN! ARE YOU OUT THERE?
I KNOW YOU'RE THERE .. I KNOW YOU CAN HEAR ME!
PLEASE... YOU GOTTA COME BACK TO ME, SON. I... I CAN'T DO THIS ON MY OWN!
IT WAS NEVER TRUE, LOGAN .. I WAS LYING TO YOU AND I WAS LYING TO MYSELF... I WAS TALKING TOUGH! A MAN SHOULD NEVER BE ALONE. IT AIN'T OUR WAY.
YOU WERE RIGHT ALL ALONG. PLEASE... YOU GOTTA COME BACK AN' SEE ME THROUGH THIS.
I NEED YOU!

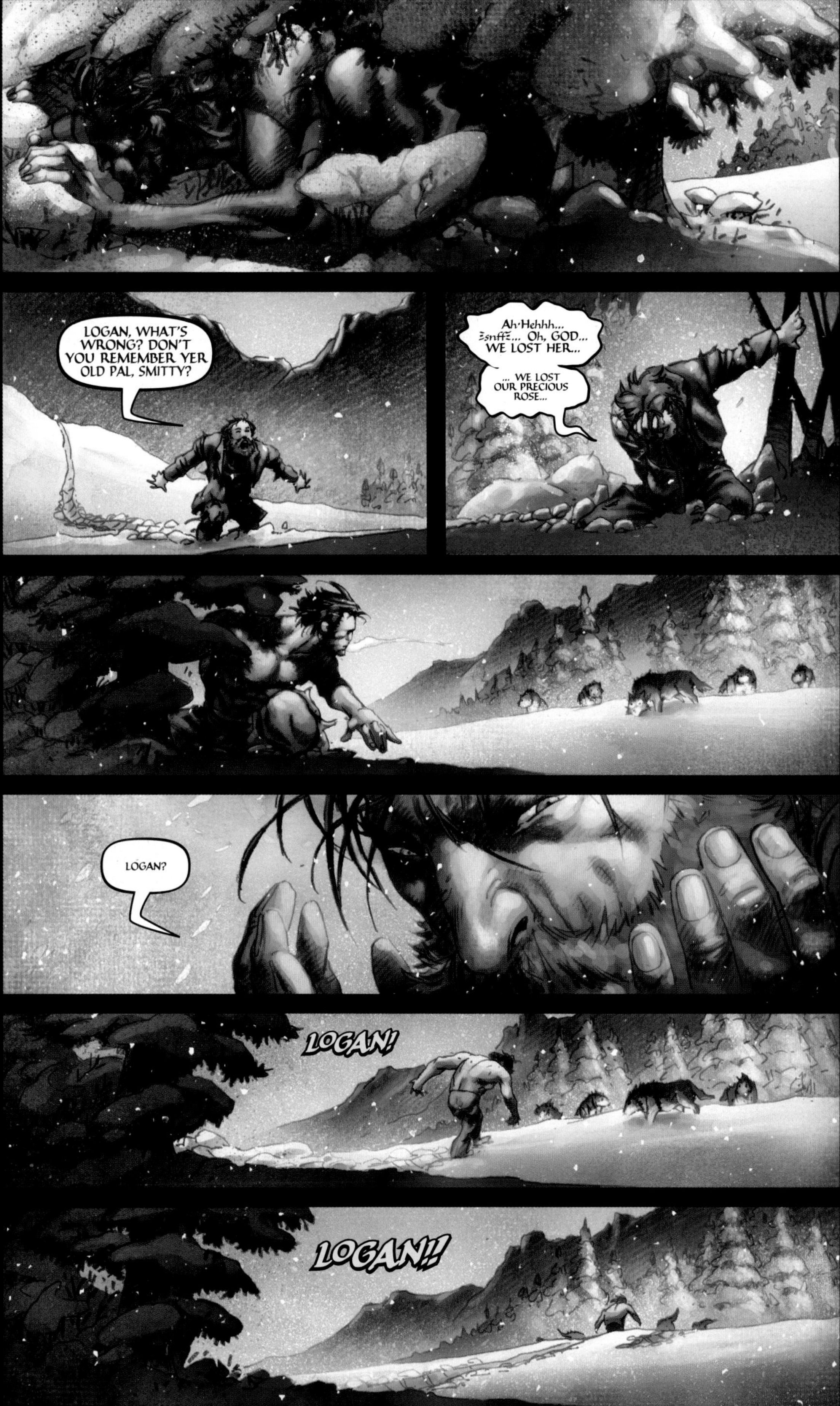
LOGAN, WHAT'S WRONG? DON'T YOU REMEMBER YER OLD PAL, SMITTY?
Ah-Hehhh... snffz... Oh, GOD... WE LOST HER...
... WE LOST OUR PRECIOUS ROSE...
LOGAN?
LOGAN!
LOGAN!!

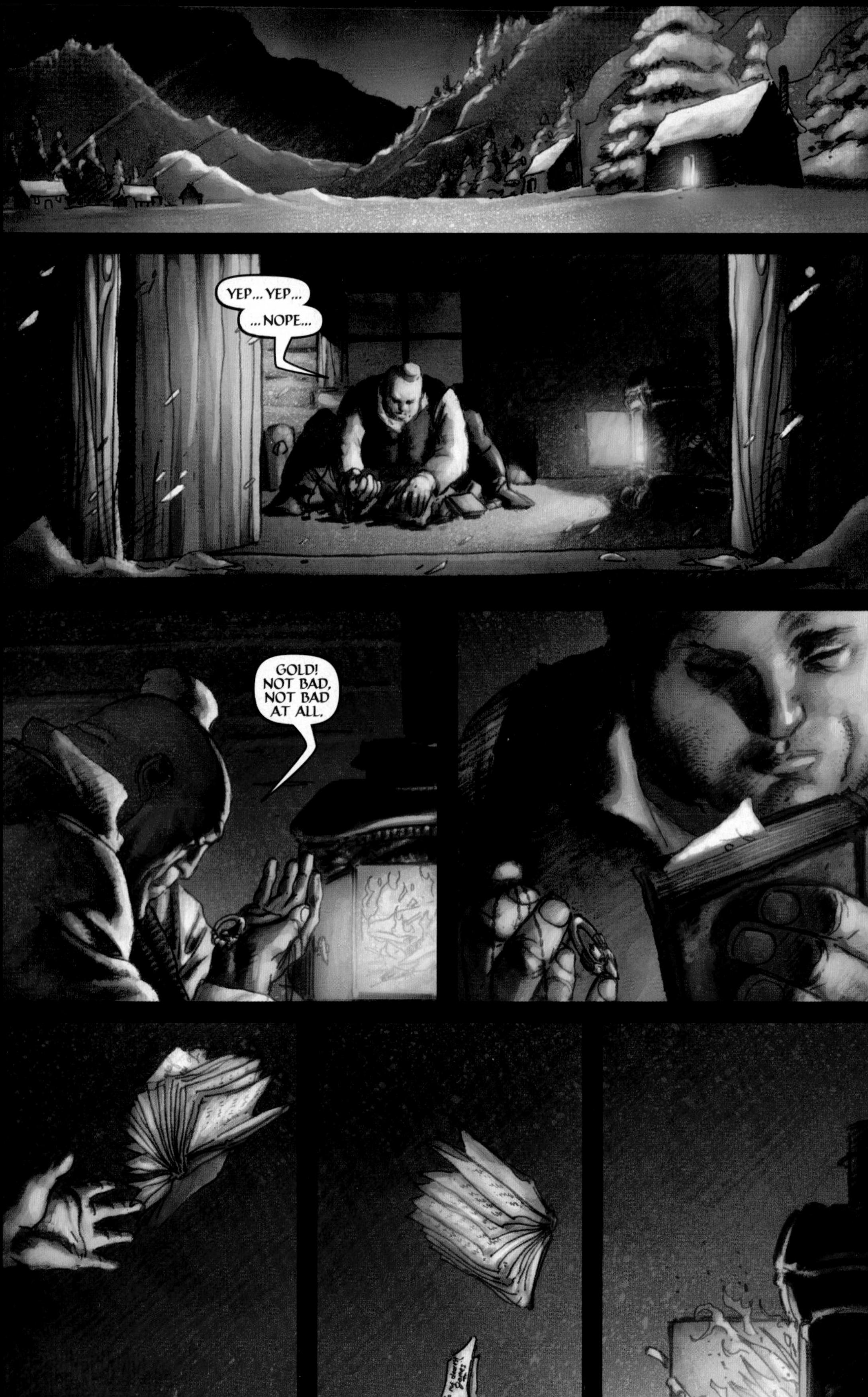
YEP... YEP...
...NOPE...
GOLD! NOT BAD, NOT BAD AT ALL.

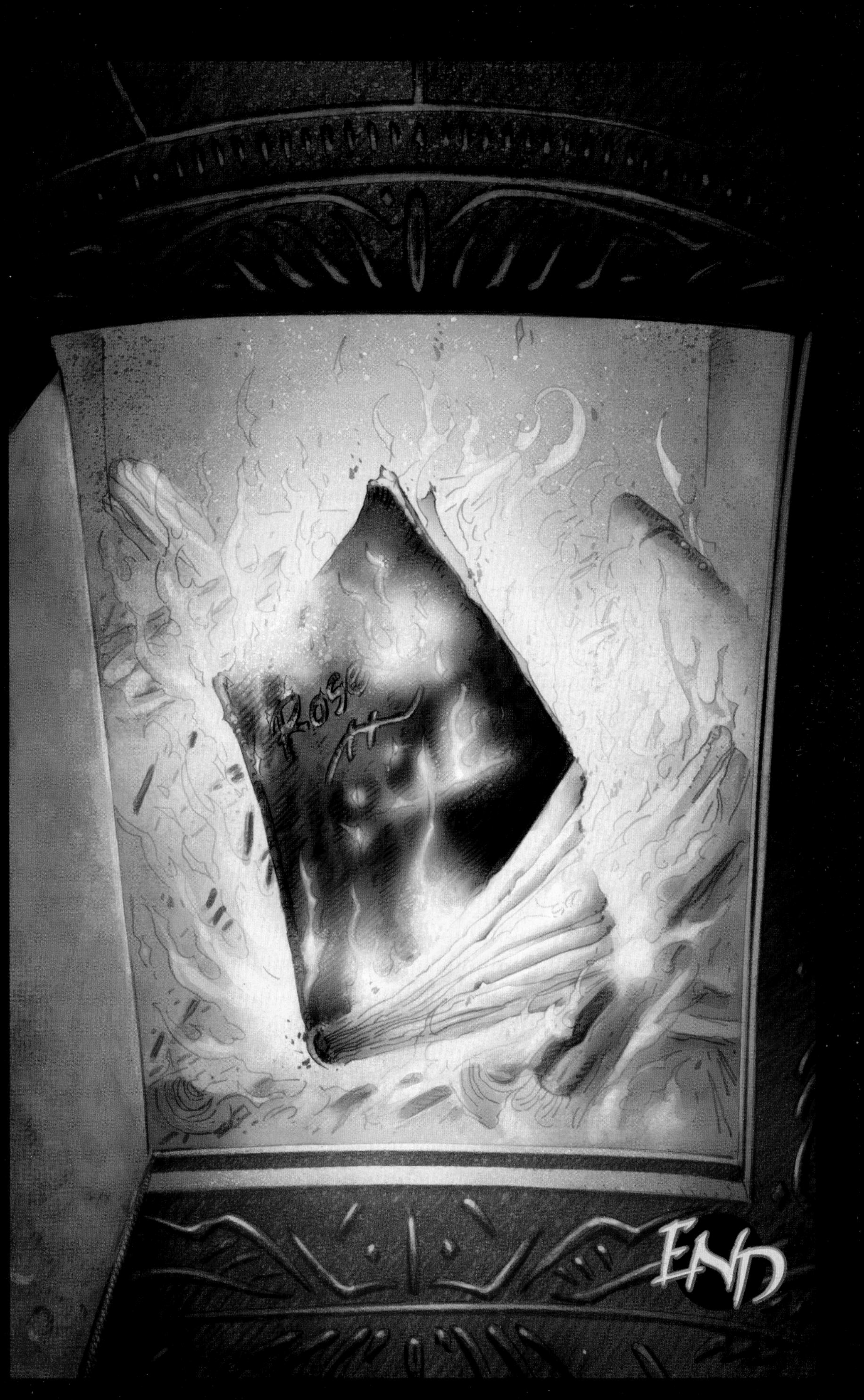
Rose
END

THE BEGINNING

This all started in the basement of Joe Quesada's house in New Jersey.

Joe had just taken on the Chief job and invited his editors to an all-day creative session. Paul Jenkins had flown up from Atlanta to help out. (Paul and Joe had done some great work together in recent years, including THE INHUMANS and THE SENTRY.)

I showed up in the middle of the morning with the meeting already in progress. Joe was standing in front of his new staff with a clipboard and markers, and he was dying up there. Nobody had any ideas for their new boss.

This group of editors was, and is, the best in the business. These were the same men and women who would turn Marvel (and the comics industry) around during the next 18 months. But that morning, they were a quiet bunch. To be fair, and to make a long story short, this team had stuck with Marvel through thick and thin. The thin was the Bankruptcy, when Marvel employees had to survive the deepest depression in the history of the comics market and the tender mercies of Carl Icahn. Conditions like that make you learn to keep your head low, so when Joe asked for hot new ideas, he got a lot of cold blank stares and SECRET WARS III, and INFINITY GAUNTLET IV. This was a very uncomfortable scene and way, way too embarrassing to watch.

So I sat in the corner with Paul, eating donuts, when it hit me . . . I turned to Paul, "What is the greatest story Marvel never told?" He didn't miss a beat: "The Origin of Wolverine." Of course, we're sure we're geniuses, and we're about to spring this on everybody when Joe calls for the lunch break.

Paul and I were so full of sugar and oil that we couldn't eat lunch. We tracked down Joe, who was sitting with an editor munching on a burger. Paul asked Joe, "What is the greatest story Marvel never told?" Joe didn't miss a beat. "The Origin of Wolverine", but then he blurted out "But we could never tell it." The editor patiently explained to Paul and me that our brilliant and original idea had come up (and had been shot down) in every brainstorm session since Wolverine made his spectacular and mysterious first appearance in INCREDIBLE HULK #181. Joe added that revealing the Origin of Wolverine would ruin the character.

Now it's time for fun with Joey. We can't print exactly what I said to Joe, but the gist was "When we named you Editor in Chief, we thought we were passing the torch that lights the House of Ideas. I didn't think I was handing you a big chicken suit." Anyway, Joe got jolted back to being Joe, and got excited enough to blast out forty great marketing ideas in the following four minutes.

Joe started the afternoon session with a challenge to his team, "Bill Jemas wants us to tell the Origin of Wolverine. Bill says this will be the best-selling book in the entire industry in 2001. What should we tell him?"

As a group, the editors politely, but firmly, told me, "no way." Over the next hour, they explained that the essence of Logan is the search for his past; take that away and you destroy the Wolverine character. Destroy Wolverine, the most important X-Men character, and you destroy the X-Men. Destroy the X-Men, the most important Marvel family, and you destroy Marvel.

The bottom line was that Marvel was afraid. We were afraid to tell the story of the most courageous character in our Universe.

Then something interesting happened; the senior editors, Tom Brevoort, Ralph Macchio and Mark Powers started thinking and talking like senior editors. I believe it was Tom who stood up and said, "If we can tell a great story, we should go ahead and tell it. That's what we do."

That whole afternoon, I had the ideas that you are about to read in the following outline swirling around in my brain. I thought that the policy discussion was much more important than a bull session on my little springboard. More importantly, we had to do this right. Some of the best creators in the world work for Marvel and on the X-Men; those people deserved the first shot at writing Origin.

Let's fast-forward over the next several months. Joe kept asking for Origin pitches from the top talent in the industry, and kept getting turned down. He was offering the keys to the Jag, and nobody wanted to drive. Finally, Joe went back to Paul. Paul turned in a pretty fair pitch, but we all (Paul, too) agreed that it wasn't the right way to go.

Now it's March 2001, and we really needed to get this thing started. I went home and sat with my two sons – they were six and nine at the time – and we talked about what Logan would have been like as a kid. What kind of childhood could make a kid grow up as tough as Wolverine on the outside and give him a heart of gold on the inside? This kind...

Bill Jemas
President & COO Publishing,
Consumer Products and New Media

CONFESSIONS OF AN EIC

BY JOE QUESADA

As I'm sure you've noticed by now this compilation of ORIGIN is filled with so much extra stuff that I'm feeling a bit useless at this point. To be quite honest, I'm at a lack for what to write because so much has already been said and said so much better than I could in these few short paragraphs. I mean, I could regale you with funny tales that went even behind-the-scenes of the behind-the-scenes stuff, but then this book would venture off quickly into something more akin to our MAX mature readers imprint than something suitable for the likes of ol' Wolverine.

HURRAYS!

Of course I could use this space to shine a spotlight on the real stars of this book. I mean what can be said about Paul Jenkins, Andy Kubert, Richard Isanove and Comicraft that hasn't already been lavished upon them! Along with Editors Mike Marts and Mike Raicht, they've created not only a new technique in sequential art, but the standard by which all new projects of this era will be measured. What they have created is the first great project of the new comics millennium!

STONES

So, this leads me to a place where I need to either really get to the essence of what this series is all about or stop typing and say, "Thanks, True Believer, for purchasing this book … I hope you enjoyed it!" What did it take to tell this tale! What is really at the core of all this verbiage, ink and paper! It's funny, the one thing that it took for us at Marvel to even consider attempting to write Wolverine's origin is the one ingredient that ol' Wolvie and all our heroes have in spades…

…fearlessness!

It's something that we were really lacking at Marvel at the time, yet it was fearlessness that was the cornerstone upon which Stan Lee, Jack Kirby, Steve Ditko and so many others built the Marvel Universe. As a matter of fact, it had seemed as if every major publisher had become complacent with playing things safe and doing things just because "that's the way they've always been done," even in the face of many a brave creator trying to individually stay the tide of erosion that was eating away at the comics industry. That is until the day Bill Jemas strolled through the door of Marvel.

In my year and a half as Marvel's EIC, I've been continually surprised by Bill's ability to shift gears on the fly, and more importantly, his talent to do so many things. From brilliant business initiatives that have all but saved the comics industry, kept our competition guessing and more importantly, in our rear-view mirror, to being the impetus for stories like the one you've just read.

DISCOVERING THE SECRET

I think the day that everything became perfectly clear to me about Bill was sometime long after the famous meeting in my basement that spawned the idea of Wolverine's origin. I remember Bill walking in with this Marvel strategy card game called "ReCharge." It was just in the process of being designed. All the art looked amazing (as Marvel art always does), so I asked Bill about the game's designers, who they were and how he had found them. Bill's response was as simple as it was shocking, "You're looking at them," he said. That's when the lightbulb went off and all the pieces started

to fall into place. All this time I'd been in awe of this tall, lanky, geeky guy who, if not for the bit of salt and pepper around his temples, could pass for an overzealous, hormone-enraged teenager, anxiously awaiting his dateless prom night. How could he be one of the shrewdest business people I've ever met and one of the brightest creators I've ever been around, and also have a talent for designing strategy games! How can he be so proficient at all these things! That's when I discovered Bill's secret. You see, Bill just doesn't know the meaning of the word can't! It's not in the way his brain is wired. Where most of us would sit there and say, "Well, I've never designed a game before, so I really can't do this," Bill just studies a few games and goes about creating one. So, what is it that keeps him from stopping himself before he starts! What's his X-Factor, his mutant ability! Simple, much like our wonderful, hairy, two-dimensional Canucklehead, Bill is the three-dimensional embodiment of his most vaunted trait. He's fearless!

LIKE A BLUNT HAMMER TO MY HEAD

Now that was one very important lesson for me. You see, it brought back all these memories of being a kid and having that fearless nature, that thing inside you that says, "Hey, I can be an astronaut if I want!" That thing that life tends to beat out of us as we get on with it. It's a lesson that I learned to apply to everything I do now at Marvel because I realized I wasn't learning it for the first time. I was just reminded that, much like Wolverine, we all have this trait deep inside of our forgotten past. We all have a "Rose" in our personal ORIGIN that perhaps we've forgotten with the passage of time. For me, my "Rose" came back to me in a flash by Bill's simple ability to not see defeat as an option or even a roadblock.

DEADLINE

Now, as the caption above looms larger and larger with each passing minute, I realize that I better bring this thing to a close and wrap it up with some snappy encapsulation of my overall point! So what are we really talking about here! After you've read all the inside stuff, the behind-the-scenes history, the sketches and the lost plot points, keep in mind that's not really what this project was all about for us. Sure it makes for interesting reading, but the lesson for me, for all of us at Marvel, was not in the pages, but in the doing. We slowly began believing that this project had to be done and then soon enough we realized that we couldn't not do this project. Why! Because we simply didn't know that we couldn't any longer and that is a belief that we have carried with us ever since. It's the trademark of this new Marvel, which you will see, smell, and taste in every new project and idea we come up with. Will we always succeed! Of course not, but as long as we have the incredible support of the world's greatest fans, it will always be and remain "The Marvel Age" of comics!

"Thanks, True Believer, for purchasing this book … I hope you enjoyed it!"

See ya in the funnybooks,

JQ
EEK!